The
St John Ambulance Brigade
during the
South African War

1899 – 1902

38 Sergeant William Sidney INDER Kendal Division. He served at No 2 and No 13 General Hospitals at Wynberg, Cape Town. He died at Wynberg on 7 January 1902.
(photo *First Aid* October 1902)

The
St John Ambulance Brigade
during the
South African War

1899 – 1902

Simon Jonathan Eyre
MA BM BCh FRCP(Lond) FRCGP

By the same author:

Skippers of the Royal Naval Reserve in the First World War
Surgeons of the Royal Navy in the First World War
The Distinguished Service Medal 1914-1938 The First 25 Years
The Naval Meritorious Service Medal 1919-1928 The First 10 Years
Jubilee and Coronation Medals to the City of London Police 1887-1911
The Service Medal of the Order of St John The Early Years 1899-1925

First Published 2025
© Simon Jonathan Eyre 2025

ISBN 978-1-917426-44-2

Published by TSL Publications (Rickmansworth)

Front cover photo: Ambulance Train Durban   Back cover: R. Scotson medal group

This book is dedicated to

the memory of Professor Peter Beighton who during his lifetime extensively researched the medals awarded to the St John Ambulance Brigade during the South African War 1899-1902.

Contents

List of Illustrations

Abbreviations

Amb	Ambulance
Bde	Brigade
BELF	Belfast
BELM	Belmont
CC	Cape Colony
CM	Master of Surgery
Co	Company
Corpl	Corporal
Coy	Company
DIAM	Diamond Hill
GER	Great Eastern Railway
GWR	Great Western Railway
HRH	Her or His Royal Highness
HS	Hospital Ship
Imp	Imperial
IYH	Imperial Yeomanry Hospital
JOH	Johannesburg
KSA	King's South Africa Medal
KSA01	King's South Africa 1901
KSA02	King's South Africa 1902
MB	Bachelor of Medicine
MD	Doctor of Medicine
NAT	Natal
NFB	National Fire Brigade
NFBUAD	National Fire Brigades Union Ambulance Division
OFS	Orange Free State
Ordly	Orderly
Pte	Private
QSA	Queen's South Africa Medal
RAMC	Royal Army Medical Corps
RHOD	Rhodesia
RoK	Relief of Kimberley
SA01	South Africa 1901
SA02	South Africa 1902
SAC	South African Constabulary
Sgt	Sergeant
SJAB	St John Ambulance Brigade
Sjt	Sergeant
SS	Screw Steamer
Stn	Station
Tpr	Trooper
TVL	Transvaal
WITT	Wittebergen
Yeo	Yeomanry

Acknowledgements

The production of this book would not have been possible without ongoing help from the staff at the Museum of the Order of St John. In particular Sophie Denman has been of huge assistance in arranging visits and access to the necessary documents.

I am particularly grateful for their permission to use images of some of the register entries contained in the O.S.J.J. Register of issue of Special African Bronze Medals 1899-1902.

The images of individual recipients and groups of members who participated during the wars have been largely derived from articles in the *First Aid* Journal and I am deeply indebted to the Order of St John for allowing use of these images. Other images originate from the Wellcome Collection, the Anglo Boer War website and The British Medal Forum and I am extremely grateful to all those who have allowed images to be used in this publication. Images have also been used from William Inder's book *On Active Service with the S.J.A.B. South African War, 1899-1902* and also an image of HS *Simla* from Martin Edward's website Roll of Honour.

I am grateful to Noonan's for once again allowing me to use images of medal groups that have featured in their auctions.

I am also indebted to members of the British Medal Forum for information contained in the major thread regarding the St John Ambulance Brigade Bronze Medals for South Africa which has produced some valuable research paths to follow.

I am particularly grateful to Anne Samson of TSL Publications for her invaluable help and encouragement in setting up and arranging publication of this book. Without her assistance this project would not have come to fruition.

Finally, as always, I am so grateful to my wife Ann for allowing me the time to produce this seventh book.

Introduction

During the latter part of 2024 a large number of Bronze St John Ambulance Brigade medals for the South African War started to appear on the market and it soon became apparent that these were part of a substantial collection of these awards. I already had an interest in awards for the period to medical officers but the large number of these bronze medals appearing sparked my interest in these as well. I soon learnt that these were part of the collection amassed by Professor Peter Beighton, a medical geneticist from Cape Town. He died on 14 June 2023 after a very full and distinguished career particularly looking at inherited disorders of the skeleton and connective tissues.

It also soon came to light that much work had been done by Peter and previously by Ronnie Cole-Mackintosh in the mid 1970s researching the St John Ambulance Brigade medals from the South African War period. Both appeared to have produced a medal roll for the Bronze St John Ambulance Brigade medals but neither had reached the stage of being published although it is my understanding that it had been Peter's intention to produce a definitive work on the subject. He did however write two articles in the *Journal of the Orders and Medals Research Society* which were both published in 2003 which give considerable detail about the origin and award of these medals as well as a book on the early years of the St John Ambulance Brigade Blackpool Division.

In the preparation of this book, I have chosen to once more go back to the original sources, the roll for the Bronze Medals held in the Order of St John archive and the publicly available medal rolls for the Queen's South Africa and King's South Africa medals, to aim to achieve the highest possible degree of accuracy. Much of what had originally emerged from previous research has been confirmed by this process but it is hoped that by adopting this approach a comprehensive medal roll for all the medals will have been generated while highlighting the small number of persistent issues that still have proved impossible to clarify. Any errors arising during the production of this book will be entirely of my own making and I would be pleased to hear from anyone who notes any entries requiring correction. I fully recognise that there are probably many with a deeper understanding of the history of the St John Ambulance Brigade's contribution during the South African War but this volume is an attempt to draw together information that is otherwise scattered in a number of published resources or has not, up until now, been readily available in the public domain.

It is also hoped that this book will provide a fitting memorial to all those men from the St John Ambulance Brigade who volunteered their services during the war and those who supported them in their efforts. If Peter and Ronnie had still been alive to see the publication of this book, I hope that it would have met with their full approval.

Recruitment of the St John Ambulance Brigade

Soon after the start of the commencement of the war in southern Africa on 11 October 1899 it rapidly became apparent to those responsible for organising the medical provision for the armed forces being mobilised for the conflict, that the existing Royal Army Medical Corps would not be able to cope with the demands being place upon it. Medical Officers were not available in sufficient numbers and indeed by the end of the war only just over 600 RAMC Medical Officers had seen service in South Africa. To bolster their numbers a large number of Civil Surgeons were recruited, eventually nearly 1400, to assist in the management of not only the battle casualties but more significantly those who became afflicted by disease, in particular typhoid, during the conflict.

Similarly, it was evident that the numbers of nursing staff and orderlies was going to be insufficient to staff the necessary hospitals and it was for this reason that an appeal for volunteers from the ranks of the St John Ambulance Brigade was made. The subsequent mobilisation of the St John Ambulance Brigade in support of the provision of medical services was remarkably rapid.

The first group of 23 men departed for South Africa on 21 November 1899 just six weeks after the start of the war. These men embarked on the Hospital Ship *Prince of Wales*, but were soon followed four days later by a further group of 55 and thereafter at regular intervals.

A detachment who attended Communion on Easter Sunday 15 April 1900 at the Church of the Order of St John just prior to their departure for South Africa. They are probably part of the 21st contingent of 117 men which embarked five days later.
(Photo *First Aid* October 1900)

2

The table below gives details of the numbers mobilised during the first six months of recruitment up until 19 May 1900. The table indicates the number of each contingent, the date of the contingent's formation, the number of men involved, the destination for the contingent and whether or not they directly embarked for South Africa or not. This gives a very clear indication of the rapid recruitment and deployment of members of the St John Ambulance Brigade during the early part of the war.

1st	21/11/1899	23	HS *Princess of Wales*	Embarked
2nd	25/11/1899	55	War Office	Embarked
3rd	13/12/1899	26	Portland Hospital	Embarked
4th	27/12/1899	22	War Office	To Netley
5th	29/12/1899	50	War Office	Embarked
6th	10/1/1900	100	War Office	To Aldershot Included 12 for Princess Christian Hospital Train
7th	5/2/1900	50	War Office	To Portsmouth
8th	9/2/1900	9	Van Alen's Field Hospital	Embarked
9th	10/2/1900	76	Imperial Yeomanry Hospital	Embarked Includes 25 firemen attached to Brigade
10th	12/2/1900	50	War Office	To Woolwich
11th	21/2/1900	49	War Office	To Aldershot
12th	28/2/1900	14	Langman's Field Hospital	Embarked
13th	28/2/1900	30	Princess Christian Hospital	Embarked
14th	28/2/1900	51	War Office	To Woolwich
15th	7/3/1900	25	War Office	To Aldershot
16th	10/3/1900	12	Imperial Yeomanry Field Hospital	Embarked
17th	14/3/1900	80	War Office	To Aldershot
18th	19/3/1900	44	War Office	To Aldershot
19th	30/3/1900	111	War Office	To Aldershot
20th	9/4/1900	125	War Office	Embarked
21st	20/4/1900	117	War Office	Embarked
22nd	3/5/1900	11	American HS *Maine*	Embarked
23rd	16/5/1900	130	War Office	Embarked
24th	19/5/1900	18	War Office	To Aldershot
25th	19/5/1900	35	War Office	To Aldershot for service with the Rhodesian Field Force

The men proceeded to South Africa on the large fleet of transport ships used to convey the British Forces. The detachments were often of considerable size as can be seen from the photograph of those who formed the staff of 13 General Hospital. They were transported on the SS *Saxon* on its maiden voyage when it left Southampton on 16 June 1900 arriving in Cape Town 15 days later.

Staff of 13 General Hospital in transit to South Africa on SS *Saxon* in June 1900.

One of those who volunteered at a relatively early stage was Superintendent Edward GRAHAM of Haslingden Corps. Initially officers were not permitted to volunteer and although this order was subsequently revoked Edward was accepted by reducing his rank to become 621 1st Class Sergeant. He was part of the 17th contingent initially proceeding to Aldershot on 14 March 1900. Throughout his time in South Africa, he served as a Supply Officer with 21 Field Hospital.

By the end of the war approximately 1770 men were recruited to serve primarily in the various General and Stationary Hospitals that had been established. A further 81 men were directly enrolled into the RAMC for service. In addition to service in the army hospitals a considerable number were detailed to the Imperial Yeomanry Hospitals at Deelfontein and Pretoria as well as a small number serving with the Imperial Yeomanry Field Hospital and Bearer Company responsible for dealing with casualties at the front line. Amongst these men were a number recruited from various Fire Brigades in England. At the time there was a close relationship between those serving in the Fire Brigades and the St John Ambulance Brigade with 28 out of the 48 Fire Brigade volunteers who eventually served in South Africa being members of both organisations. Additionally, in order to help staff the numerous other privately funded hospitals that were established, St John Ambulance Brigade personnel were seconded to The Langman Hospital, The Portland Hospital, The Van Alen American Field Hospital, The Princess Christian Hospital and The Princess Christian Hospital Train.

621 1st Class Sergeant Edward GRAHAM.
(Photo *First Aid* April 1902)

Recruits from Colne Ambulance Division. Eventually 19 men from the Division served in South Africa.

Tibshelf Colliery Ambulance Division.

As the war progressed many men volunteered for further service once their original contract expired often acquiring a new recruitment number in the process. Typical of these were two of the three men in the image below taken from William INDER's book. 1337 Sergeant L.W. FELSTEAD from Leicester Ambulance Division was a new recruit, while 38 Sergeant William Sidney INDER was given a fresh number 1321 and 68 Sergeant H.G. HUNTER became number 1322.

Sergeant L.W. FELSTEAD Leicester Ambulance Division; Sergeant William Sidney INDER
Kendal Ambulance Division and Sergeant H.G. HUNTER Kendal Ambulance Division.

St John Ambulance Brigade Service

The men recruited as Orderlies and Supply Officers were largely employed working on the wards of the various General and Stationary Hospitals which carried the main burden of caring for the sick and wounded during the conflict. Their role was mainly to replace RAMC personnel who could then be released for work at the front and in Field Hospitals.

St John Ambulance Brigade Orderlies serving at No 2 General Hospital at Wynberg
early in 1900.

Tasks would have ranged from personal care for the patients, moving patients when needed, accepting and processing new admissions and supporting the nursing staff in their responsibilities.

An Ambulance Train arriving at Durban.

If the men had been expecting to largely be dealing with battlefield casualties, they would soon realise that a major part of their role involved dealing with a range of infectious diseases. A graphic insight into their work was provided by 137 Staff Sergeant WALKDEN of Bolton Corps who was sent to 3 Stationary Hospital at De Aar. His written account to the Honorary Surgeon at his Corps Headquarters in Bolton, Dr J. Johnston, published in the *First Aid* Journal in May 1900, gives details of the case load they were dealing with:

> Our section for De Aar comprised myself, Sergeant Briggs (Darwen), and thirteen men. Since then, this section has again been split up, eight men having been sent on the ambulance train to take the places of Royal Army Medical Corps men who have come for duty here. The hospital here was formerly a day school, and this part is used for the most serious cases of enteric fever, and is capable of holding about thirty patients. Other wooden erections have been put up and there is now room for some 400 patients. In addition, there is a rest camp where convalescents are kept till fit for duty or transfer. We have seldom more than a dozen beds to spare at a time, fresh patients being brought in as fast as others are moved, sometimes nearly 150 wounded and sick coming in in one batch. You can form some idea of the amount of work for the 50 orderlies and nurses when I tell you that on this week's return, we have 75 cases of enteric fever, about 64 cases of scarlet fever, and many cases of wounded and dysentery, making a rough total of 380. We have had some help this week, the Fifth Stationary Hospital having been waiting orders here as to their destination, and consequently doing duty here till these orders came. To-day these men (including 20 St. John Ambulance men) go to Britstown to form a field hospital for the men engaged in suppressing the rebels at Prieska, thirty miles away. We have received a lot of wounded from Paardeberg and Jacobsdal, and the kit of these men bears evidence of the severe peppering they must have got, coats, mess tins, helmets, and other articles having bullet holes through them in many places. We have had very few deaths in hospital, and nearly all these have been from enteric fever. Those wounded by the Mauser bullets get round very quickly indeed, many going to their duty again in a few days' time. My work here is chiefly clerical, the lot of day and night ward master falling upon me about once each week—a continuous day of 36 hours. We are always supposed to be near at hand if any wounded or sick arrive. We cannot get far away in fact, for martial law is still in evidence here, and strict bounds have to be kept. All the captured army of Cronje, except a few sick, passed through here on their way to the Cape, and it is only such matters that are at all interesting here. I've had a few Boers in hospital here, one or two being rather dangerously ill with enteric fever. Few of the wants of the sick here fail to be supplied, for food and clothing of all kinds are sent in abundance.

Typhoid (enteric fever) was to play a major part in the campaign. Typhoid is a water borne illness due to the bacterium Salmonella Typhi. A person is usually infected through ingesting contaminated water which results in an initial illness with diarrhoea and abdominal cramps. However, in a proportion of patients this is followed by an intense inflammatory reaction in the bowel wall which can lead to bowel perforation, peritonitis and death. During the course of the war an epidemic developed particularly centred on Bloemfontein. Official figures show that in the British Force of 556,653 men, 57,684 (10.4% of the force) became infected and of these 8225 died from the disease (1.47% of the total force and 14.3 % of those infected). By comparison 7582 were killed in action (1.36% of the force) demonstrating the disproportionate effect that the disease had on the force. Additionally, others died from complications of the disease after being repatriated back to England. Understandably the civilian population in South Africa suffered similarly. In total over 22,000 Boers died in the concentration camps set up by the British as well as 15,000 Africans, many of these deaths being attributable to typhoid. The situation gradually improved as the war progressed as sanitation was improved leading to cleaner water supplies. However, towards the end of the war, there was then an outbreak of Bubonic Plague which put further pressure on the overstretched medical resources. The St John

Ambulance Brigade men were to be very much involved in the management of the typhoid epidemic with a considerable number succumbing to the disease themselves.

One of those who died after his return to England was 118 Corporal C.H. POWELL of Crewe Division. His obituary was published in *First Aid* in April 1903 but his death had occurred two years earlier on 4 January 1901. He developed typhoid while serving at No 3 General Hospital at Kroonstad and was sent home but as a result of the debility caused by typhoid, he succumbed to pneumonia in Netley Military Hospital.

118 Corporal C.H. POWELL who died at Netley Hospital on 4 January 1901.
(Photo *First Aid* April 1903)

Hospitals and Bearer Companies

The hospitals which were established were classified depending on their role, overall size and bed number. General Hospitals were intended to be Base Hospitals while Stationary Hospitals were to be sited on the lines of communication to the front. The care of men at the front line was the responsibility of the Field Hospitals and Bearer Companies.

Of necessity the Field Hospitals had to be highly mobile with a nominal allocation of 100 beds but they were equipped to provide immediate care to men before transferring the most seriously wounded or sickest men to the nearest Stationary Hospital or General Hospital. The Stationary Hospitals also retained a degree of mobility so they could be moved as the army advanced. Consequently, they still only had 100 beds, in reality stretchers rather than hospital beds. They provided the first opportunity for surgery when this was required and acted as a holding point either until the men recovered and could be sent back to the front or it became clear they were going to be incapacitated for a more prolonged period requiring their transfer to one of the much larger General Hospitals.

General Hospitals

The General Hospitals were the largest and best equipped hospitals. They were initially based in Cape Town but as the war progressed some were moved up the lines of communication in particular to Pretoria and Bloemfontein. The hospitals had a nominal capacity of 520 beds and could provide the widest possible range of medical and surgical care but needed to expand their capacity as needs demanded.

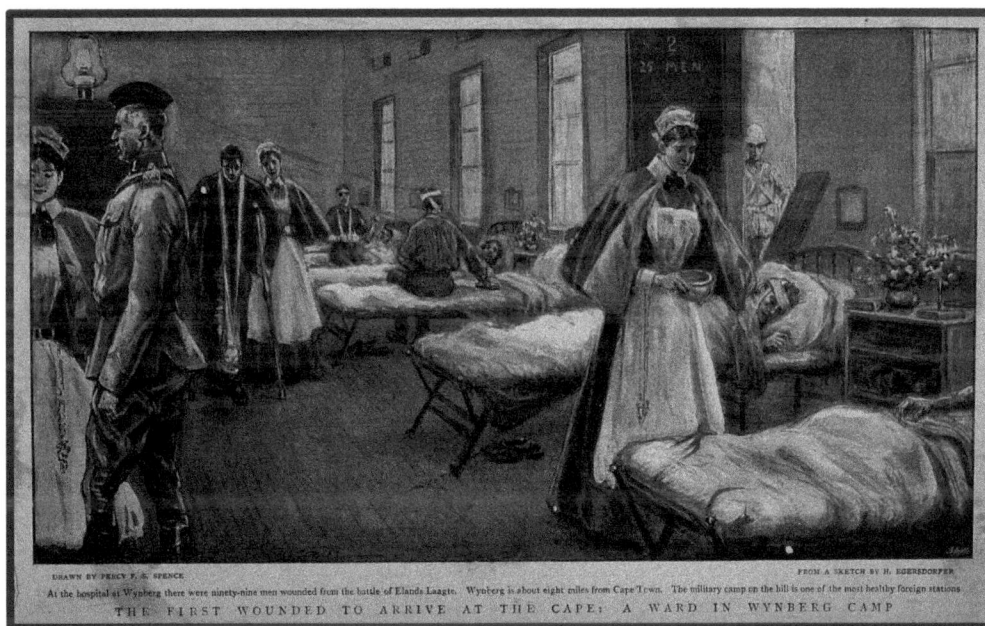

A ward at Wynberg Camp.

The most senior medical and surgical staff were based at these hospitals but also a large number of St John Ambulance Brigade men served at these hospitals for all or part of their time in South Africa, largely acting as ward orderlies alongside Royal Army Medical Corps staff. The General Hospitals normally had a complement of 20 medical officers, a quartermaster, 145 orderlies and eight nursing sisters.

Staff of No 13 General Hospital Wynberg in 1901 including many
St John Ambulance Brigade men.

The hospitals are listed below and it can be seen that as the war progressed No 2 and No 7 General Hospitals moved to Pretoria and No 6 and No 13 to Johannesburg. Also, a number of Stationary Hospitals over time were upgraded to General Hospital status. Additionally, the Imperial Yeomanry Hospitals at Deelfontein and Pretoria were passed over to Government control during 1901 to become part of the General Hospital establishment. It is important to understand that even these most sophisticated of hospitals were often providing their care under canvas rather than in hut accommodation and so subject to all the vagaries of the South African weather during the winter months.

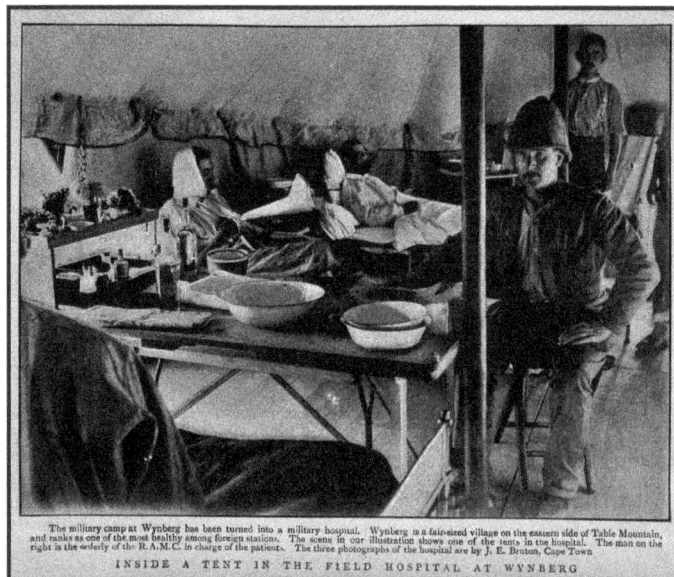

The military camp at Wynberg has been turned into a military hospital. Wynberg is a fair-sized village on the eastern side of Table Mountain, and ranks as one of the most healthy among foreign stations. The scene in our illustration shows one of the tents in the hospital. The man on the right is the orderly of the R.A.M.C. in charge of the patients. The three photographs of the hospital are by J. E. Bruton, Cape Town

INSIDE A TENT IN THE FIELD HOSPITAL AT WYNBERG

Tented accommodation at Wynberg.

Hospital	Site	Beds	Date Opened	Dated Closed
1 General Hospital	Wynberg	520	20 October 1899	31 May 1902
2 General Hospital	Wynberg	54	8 December 1899	1 June 1900
	Pretoria	672	22 July 1900	31 May 1902
3 General Hospital	Rondebosch		22 December 1899	1 June 1900
	Kroonstad	790	1 June 1900	31 May 1902
4 General Hospital	Mooi River	520	12 January 1900	31 May 1902
5 General Hospital (Base Hospital Cape Town)	Cape Town	940	30 March 1900	31 May 1902
6 General Hospital	Naauwpoort		2 March 1900	13 July 1900
	Johannesburg	822	27 July 1900	1 October 1901
7 General Hospital	Estcourt		13 April 1900	26 October 1900
	Pretoria	692	9 November 1900	31 May 1902
8 General Hospital	Bloemfontein	814	27 April 1900	31 May 1902
9 General Hospital	Bloemfontein	553	20 April 1900	31 May 1902
10 General Hospital	Bloemfontein		4 May 1900	7 January 1901
	Norval's Pont	520	18 January 1901	31 May 1902
11 General Hospital (Town Hospital Kimberley)	Kimberley	600	18 May 1900	31 May 1902
12 General Hospital (Section No 3 General Hospital)	Springfontein	500	11 May 1900	31 May 1902
13 General Hospital	Wynberg		20 July 1900	1 February 1901
	Johannesburg	520	3 May 1901	31 May 1902
14 General Hospital (Replaced 4 Stationary Hospital)	Newcastle	520	10 August 1900	31 May 1902
15 General Hospital	Howick	536	20 July 1900	31 May 1902
16 General Hospital (2 Stationary Hospital)	Elandsfontein	536	1 February 1901	31 May 1902
17 General Hospital (4 Stationary Hospital)	Standerton	520	1 February 1901	31 May 1902
18 General Hospital (1 Stationary Hospital)	Charlestown	520	8 February 1901	31 May 1902
19 General Hospital	Pretoria	201	15 June 1900	31 May 1902
20 General Hospital	Elandsfontein	600	1 March 1901	31 May 1902
21 General Hospital (Imperial Yeomanry Hospital)	Deelfontein	800	5 April 1901	31 May 1902
22 General Hospital (Imperial Yeomanry Hospital)	Pretoria	520	20 September 1901	31 May 1902

Stationary Hospitals

The Stationary Hospitals played a pivotal role in the provision of medical services during the war acting as the point of triage to differentiate those who could be returned relatively quickly to the front and those requiring more complex or prolonged care. The St John Ambulance Brigade provided a number of men to act as orderlies in the hospitals.

Hospital	Site	Beds	Date Opened	Dated Closed
1 Stationary Hospital	Frere & Modder Spruit		12 January 1900	13 July 1900
	Charlestown		27 July 1900	1 February 1901
2 Stationary Hospital	East London		22 December 1899	8 June 1900
	Johannesburg		20 July 1900	24 September 1900
	Elandsfontein		28 September 1900	25 January 1901
3 Stationary Hospital	De Aar	370	1 December 1899	31 May 1902
4 Stationary Hospital	Frere & Chieveley		5 December 1899	8 June 1900
	Newcastle		15 June 1900	10 October 1900
	Standerton		31 August 1900	25 January 1901
5 Stationary Hospital	Bloemfontein	219	6 April 1900	31 May 1902
6 Stationary Hospital	Greenpoint	6	10 November 1899	31 May 1902
7 Stationary Hospital	East London	250	1 December 1899	31 May 1902
8 Stationary Hospital	Port Elizabeth	200	1 December 1899	31 May 1902
9 Stationary Hospital	Queenstown	60	23 March 1900	31 May 1902
10 Stationary Hospital	Naauwpoort	377	13 July 1900	31 May 1902
11 Stationary Hospital	Winburg	150	1 June 1900	31 May 1902
12 Stationary Hospital	Wakkerstroom	150	7 September 1900	31 May 1902
13 Stationary Hospital	Pinetown Bridge	250	20 April 1900	31 May 1902
14 Stationary Hospital	Pietermaritzburg	150	13 October 1899	31 May 1902
15 Stationary Hospital	Heidelberg	150	13 July 1900	31 May 1902
16 Stationary Hospital	Mafeking	150	10 August 1900	31 May 1902
17 Stationary Hospital	Middelburg	400	17 August 1900	31 May 1902
18 Stationary Hospital	Krugersdorp	250	27 July 1900	31 May 1902
19 Stationary Hospital	Harrismith	350	24 August 1900	31 May 1902
20 Stationary Hospital	Waterval Onder	120	7 September 1900	31 May 1902
21 Stationary Hospital	Machadodorp	125	12 September 1900	31 May 1902
22 Stationary Hospital	Pietersburg	100	19 April 1901	31 May 1902
23 Stationary Hospital	Warm Bath	75	5 April 1901	31 May 1902
24 Stationary Hospital	Aliwal North	225	30 November 1900	31 May 1902
25 Stationary Hospital	Johannesburg	100	4 October 1901	4 April 1902
26 Stationary Hospital	Beaufort West	100	3 May 1901	31 May 1902
27 Stationary Hospital	Burgersdorp	90	28 December 1900	31 May 1902
28 Stationary Hospital	Worcester	60	31 May 1901	2 May 1902
29 Stationary Hospital	Heilbron	120	15 June 1900	31 May 1902

30 Stationary Hospital	Lindley	180	17 January 1902	31 May 1902
31 Stationary Hospital	Ermelo	86	20 December 1901	31 May 1902
32 Stationary Hospital	Klerksdorp	100	22 June 1900	31 May 1902
33 Stationary Hospital	Zeerust	100	2 November 1900	31 May 1902
34 Stationary Hospital	Ladybrand	40	29 June 1900	31 May 1902
35 Stationary Hospital	Potchefstroom	100	2 November 1900	31 May 1902
36 Stationary Hospital	Barberton	200	5 October 1900	31 May 1902
37 Stationary Hospital	Lydenburg	125	5 October 1900	31 May 1902
38 Stationary Hospital	Rustenburg	100	12 October 1900	31 May 1902
39 Stationary Hospital	Rietfontein	100	19 October 1900	31 May 1902
40 Stationary Hospital	Dundee	100	12 October 1900	31 May 1902
41 Stationary Hospital	Ficksburg	143	8 February 1901	31 May 1902

The photograph below gives a good impression of the staff employed at a Stationary Hospital. Usually there were four medical officers, a quartermaster and 40 men together with nursing staff.

Medical staff at No 12 Stationary Hospital Wakkerstroom.

Temporary Hospitals

Besides the General and Stationary Hospitals, a large number of smaller buildings were converted into medical units when extra provision was required. Particularly when the typhoid epidemic was at its peak during 1900 these facilities provided much needed accommodation for the care of the victims and also providing places where they could be isolated in an attempt to control the spread of the disease.

Hospital Type	Site	Beds	Date Opened	Dated Closed
Temporary Hospital	Aberdeen	17	21 June 1901	7 March 1902
St Andrew's College Hosp	Bloemfontein	61	15 June 1900	4 January 1901
Temporary Hospital	Boshof	40	18 May 1900	31 May 1902
Temporary Hospital	Brynvilla Camp	5	15 December 1899	29 December 1899
Temporary Hospital	Bulawayo	45	18 January 1901	31 May 1902
Temporary Hospital	Calvinia	37	21 June 1901	31 May 1902
Temporary Hospital	Carnarvon	32	4 January 1901	31 May 1902
Temporary Hospital	Christiana	18	22 November 1901	31 May 1902
Sanatorium	Claremont	50	30 March 1900	7 June 1901
Temporary Hospital	Cradock	50	12 July 1901	31 May 1902
Temporary Hospital	Danielskuil	11	26 April 1901	31 May 1902
Temporary Hospital	Dewetsdorp	60	29 June 1900	29 November 1900
Temporary Hospital	Douglas	5	13 September 1901	31 May 1902
Temporary Hospital	Edenburg	25	24 August 1900	31 May 1902
Temporary Hospital	Eerstefabrieken	10	17 August 1900	3 May 1901
Field Hospital	Eshowe	16	13 October 1899	31 May 1902
Convent Hospital	Estcourt	100	10 November 1899	15 June 1900
Temporary Hospital	Frankfort	100	12 October 1900	1 February 1901
Temporary Hospital	Graaff Reinet	61	4 January 1901	31 May 1902
Temporary Hospital	Greytown	24	4 October 1901	1 November 1901
Temporary Hospital	Griquatown	5	4 January 1901	31 May 1902
Temporary Hospital	Klip Drift	16	23 February 1900	16 March 1900
Temporary Hospital	Koffiefontein	18	2 August 1901	31 May 1902
Temporary Hospital	Komati Poort	60	22 February 1901	31 May 1902
Temporary Hospital	Krantz Kop	18	8 November 1901	3 January 1902
Temporary Hospital	Kroonstad Hotel	14	29 June 1900	13 July 1900
Temporary Hospital	Kuruman	14	7 June 1901	31 May 1902
Temporary Hospital	Ladysmith	16	4 October 1901	14 March 1902
Temporary Hospital	Ladysmith	30	13 October 1899	31 May 1902
Temporary Hospital	Lichtenburg	50	7 December 1900	31 May 1902
Temporary Hospital	Lindley	120	6 July 1900	27 July 1900
Temporary Hospital	Matjiesfontein	25	17 January 1902	31 May 1902
Temporary Hospital	Modder River	50	23 March 1900	1 June 1900
Temporary Hospital	Naauwpoort	20	20 October 1899	3 November 1899

Temporary Hospital	Norval's Pont	75	25 May 1900	15 October 1900
Temporary Hospital	Nottingham Rd	12	1 December 1899	8 December 1899
Temporary Hospital	Orange River	40	23 March 1900	31 May 1902
Temporary Hospital	Otto's Hoop	4	26 October 1900	28 December 1900
Temporary Hospital	Pienaar's Poort	16	24 August 1900	13 August 1901
Temporary Hospital	Pienaars River	81	20 September 1901	24 January 1902
Temporary Hospital	Port Nolloth	50	18 April 1902	31 May 1902
Race Course Hospital	Pretoria	60	15 June 1900	31 May 1902
Railway Rest Hospital	Pretoria		3 August 1900	17 January 1902
Temporary Hospital	Prieska	22	30 March 1900	31 May 1902
Temporary Hospital	Putters Kraal	30	1 December 1899	8 December 1899
Temporary Hospital	Rouxville	5	15 June 1900	14 September 1900
Temporary Hospital	Rouxville	5	21 December 1900	4 January 1901
Temporary Hospital	Schmidt's Drift	5	23 August 1901	31 May 1902
Temporary Hospital	Senekal	80	20 July 1900	28 August 1900
Palace Hospital	Simon's Town	67	20 October 1899	31 May 1902
Temporary Hospital	Smithfield	25	1 June 1900	3 August 1900
Temporary Hospital	Stellenbosch	9	19 January 1900	31 May 1902
Temporary Hospital	Sterkstroom	17	16 February 1900	6 April 1900
Temporary Hospital	Tarkastad	25	31 May 1901	10 January 1902
Temporary Hospital	Thabanchu	20	11 May 1900	31 May 1902
Temporary Hospital	Tiger Kloof	40	24 January 1902	31 May 1902
Temporary Hospital	Ventersdorp	50	4 January 1901	31 May 1902
Temporary Hospital	Verde	100	19 October 1900	15 March 1901
Temporary Hospital	Vereeniging	40	20 July 1900	12 October 1900
Temporary Hospital	Viljoen's Drift	20	20 July 1900	14 October 1900
Temporary Hospital	Vryburg	27	11 January 1901	31 May 1902
Temporary Hospital	Vryheid	50	25 October 1901	31 May 1902
Temporary Hospital	Wepener	26	29 June 1900	25 January 1901

Field Hospitals and Bearer Companies

Field Hospitals bearing numbers between 1 and 26 operated throughout the field of conflict during the war together with a particular Field Hospital operating for native or 'non-white' troops and the Field Hospital provided by the Imperial Yeomanry. Linked to these there were a total of 18 Bearer Companies numbered between 1 and 22 together with an additional Bearer Company provided linked to the Imperial Yeomanry Field Hospital. A number of St John Ambulance Brigade personnel served with these units during the course of the war.

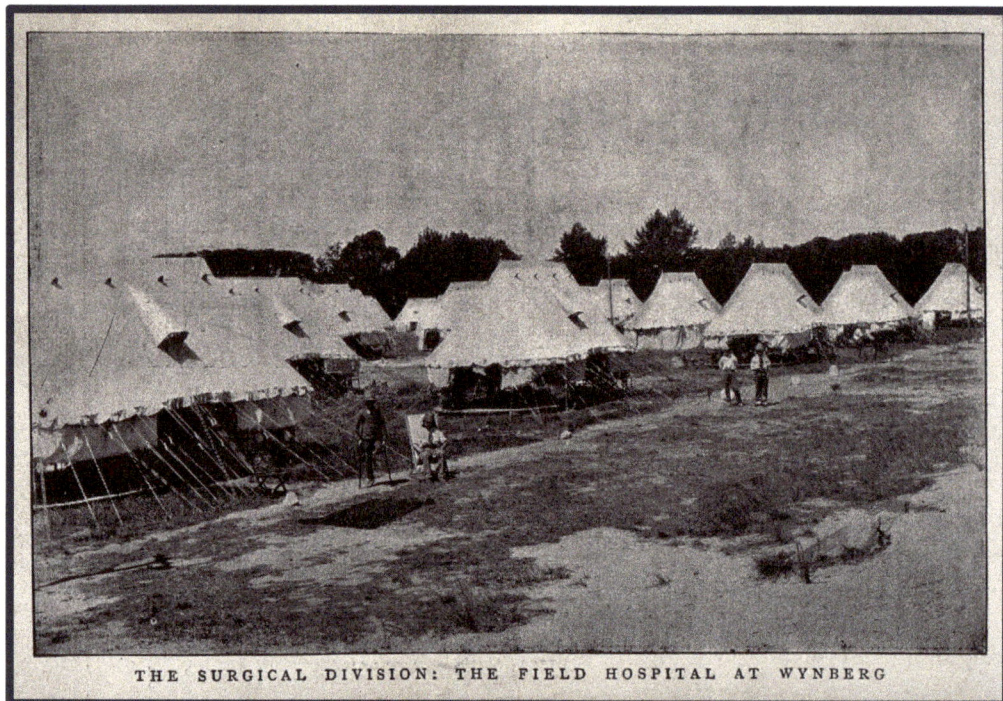

THE SURGICAL DIVISION: THE FIELD HOSPITAL AT WYNBERG

The Field Hospital at Wynberg. Although sited at the major base at Wynberg this shows the typical kind of accommodation provided at Field Hospitals.

Private Hospitals

Finally, there were also a number of privately funded hospitals established during the course of the war and these are summarised below. Further details of the St John Ambulance men who served in some of them are given in more detail in the subsequent pages.

Hospital	Site	Beds	Date Opened	Dated Closed
Edinburgh Hospital	Norval's Pont	150	18 May 1900	18 January 1901
Imperial Yeomanry Hospital	Deelfontein	1000	23 March 1900	29 March 1901
Imperial Yeomanry Hospital	Pretoria	530	24 August 1900	13 September 1901
Imperial Yeomanry Hospital	McKenzie's Farm		24 August 1900	29 March 1901
Imperial Yeomanry Hospital	Elandsfontein	138	19 July 1901	20 December 1901
Irish Hospital	Bloemfontein	100	20 April 1900	29 June 1900
Irish Hospital	Pretoria		15 June 1900	9 November 1900
Langman Hospital	Bloemfontein	180	13 April 1900	20 July 1900
Langman Hospital	Pretoria		3 August 1900	26 October 1900
Portland Hospital	Rondebosch	160		
Portland Hospital	Bloemfontein		27 April 1900	21 July 1900
Princess Christian Hospital	Pinetown Bridge	200	20 April 1900	
Scottish National Hospital	Kroonstad	300	8 June 1900	12 October 1900
Van Alen American Field Hospital	Kimberley	100	13 March 1900	6 July 1900
Welsh Hospital	Springfontein	200	8 June 1900	3 August 1900
Welsh Hospital	Pretoria		17 August 1900	24 September 1900

Imperial Yeomanry Hospitals

The Imperial Yeomanry Hospitals were set up to specifically serve the needs of the large force of Imperial Yeomanry that were deployed in South Africa.

A base hospital of 500 beds was initially envisaged and the personnel, including 111 Orderlies, and equipment needed were transported between mid-February and early March 1900. It had been anticipated the hospital would be based in Cape Town but because of the army's advance towards Pretoria at that stage, the decision was made to establish the hospital at Deelfontein on the Cape Town to Kimberley railway line. Accommodation was largely in huts and the staffing levels in the hospital higher than in other hospitals allowing a high standard of care to be provided.

The Base Hospital of the Imperial Yeomanry is at Deelfontein, where it has 625 beds. Deelfontein, which is situated twenty-nine miles south of De Aar, is a small place, with no station proper, but consists of a siding and pumping station. Our photographs are by J. Hall Edwards

NO. 7 TENT OF THE IMPERIAL YEOMANRY HOSPITAL AT DEELFONTEIN

Tented accommodation at Deelfontein with prefabricated huts in the back ground.

In addition to the 111 orderlies the staff at Deelfontein included 19 medical officers, a chaplain, 40 nurses, 10 dressers who were mainly medical students from the Westminster Hospital in London, and 10 ward maids.

Alongside the establishment of the Base Hospital, a Field Hospital and Bearer Company were also set up including 12 members of the St John Ambulance Brigade. Their role was to transport casualties from the front line to the Field Hospital. As a result the St John Ambulance Brigade men would have been very much in the thick of the fighting in the areas where they were serving.

As the war moved more into the Transvaal, Deelfontein became a less central location and a second Imperial Yeomanry Hospital was established at Pretoria initially with 400 beds. It opened on 24 August 1900 and its bed capacity was soon increased to 530. It was eventually staffed by 15 medical officers, 10 nursing sisters, eight ward maids and 136 orderlies and other subordinate staff.

In addition to the two Base Hospitals and the Field Hospital, three more minor units were set up. At Mackenzie's Farm at Maitland a branch hospital of 100 beds was organised mainly catering for wounded Yeomanry men awaiting repatriation. A further 140 bed facility was set up at Elandsfontein to cater for the Yeomanry in the area and functioned from 29 June to 28 December 1901 at which point it was no longer required. Finally, a small Officer's convalescent home was set up at Chesham House in Johannesburg. This was mainly manned by staff from the Field Hospital and Bearer Company that were disbanded at the end of February 1901 because they were no longer required.

The St John Ambulance contribution to the staffing of the Imperial Yeomanry Hospitals was considerable. Those serving with the Imperial Yeomanry Hospital Staff were not allocated service numbers and unfortunately nothing indicating who the St John Ambulance Brigade men were is noted on the Queen's South Africa Medal roll. As a result reconciling the names on the Imperial Yeomanry Hospital Roll with known recipients of the St John Ambulance Medal is not straightforward. How-

The four-wheeled heavy army regulation ambulances, which, designed for use with infantry, prove to be quite unsuited for the work required by rapidly moving mounted troops in South Africa. It has been found that one of the best ways of carrying the wounded, provided that they can sit up, is in panniers on mules. Mr. Manders, the medical officer of the 11th Battalion Imperial Yeomanry, has invented a two-wheeled car constructed like a Cape cart, so that it can move as quickly as cavalry and can travel wherever artillery can go. With mules to bring them down the rocky heights, and a car to receive them, no time is lost in rendering the necessary assistance to the wounded

THE TRANSPORT OF WOUNDED FROM THE FIELD OF BATTLE: THE WORK OF THE AMBULANCE MEN

The Imperial Yeomanry Bearer Company in action.

ever, it has proved possible to confidently identify 83 men of the St John Ambulance Brigade who served with the Imperial Yeomanry including 28 men who were recruited from fire brigades but were also members of the St John Ambulance Brigade. Of these 83 men, 12 served in the Imperial Yeomanry Bearer Company. In addition to these 83, a further 17 are definitely known to have been directly recruited from Fire Brigades but without affiliation to the St John Ambulance Brigade. Almost all, apart from those who were members of the Bearer Company, served at Deelfontein. The men recruited later, forming the 3rd and 4th contingents of the Fire Brigade recruits, were sent to the Imperial Yeomanry Hospital at Pretoria with the exception of George EDGES who served at the

Field Hospital. When the Imperial Yeomanry Bearer Company was disbanded in September 1900, of the 12 St John Ambulance Brigade men who were serving, two transferred to Maitland Imperial Yeomanry Hospital, one joined the Duke of Edinburgh's Volunteer Rifles and one returned to England but subsequently came back to South Africa. The details of these 12 men are given below.

Name	SJAB No	Ambulance Division or Corps	Rank	Notes
COX, A	619	Oxford Division	Private	A J COX on QSA medal roll
COX, W	732	Leicester Corps	Private	Joined Duke of Edinburgh's Volunteer Rifles Cape Town September 1900 F W COX on QSA medal roll
ELLIS, A E R	640 (1844)	Leicester Corps	Supply Officer	Sent home 3 September 1900 but returned to South Africa (Formerly at Portland Hospital)
HOOK, G	643	Leicester Corps	Private	
LIVERMORE, A J	724	Great Eastern Railway Corps	Corporal	Transferred to Maitland Imperial Yeomanry Hospital September 1900
PHILLIPS, J H	734	Leicester Corps	Private	J PHILLIPS on QSA medal roll
SCOTSON, R	668	Manchester Post Office Division	Corporal	
SHAW, H	658	Northampton Corps	Orderly	Also served at Imperial Yeomanry Hospital Pretoria
SWETTENHAM, J A	671	Manchester Post Office Division	Corporal	
TAYLOR, S	654	Derby Division	Private	Transferred to Maitland Imperial Yeomanry Hospital 3 September 1900
VICKERY, J A	736	Redruth Division	Private	
WESLEY, W	722	Great Eastern Railway Corps	Sergeant	

The details of the 71 St John Ambulance Brigade men known to have served at Deelfontein Imperial Yeomanry Hospital are detailed below. Where a man also received the National Fire Brigade Union Ambulance Division Medal this is shown in the notes column. Also, where a man died during the war or in the following few years this is also noted. The report published after the war states a total of 76 St John Ambulance Brigade men served at Deelfontein so clearly it has not proved possible to identify all of them.

Name	SJAB No	Ambulance Division or Corps	Rank	Notes
AINGE, A	379	Birmingham Corps	Sergeant	
ALEXANDER, Samuel A	313	NFB Ilford	Sergeant	NFBUAD Medal Died 1902 Essex
BAKER, J L	388	Birmingham Corps	Private	
BALDWIN, J W	332	Barnoldswick Division	Private	
BARRETT, J W L	288	Metropolitan Corps	Private	Died Deelfontein 6 September 1900
BOOKER, Leonard A G	308	NFB Bognor	Private	NFBUAD Medal
BROWN, E T	386	Birmingham Corps	Private	
BROWN, Wilfred H	327	NFB Sandown	Private	NFBUAD Medal
BURGESS, A	286	Metropolitan Corps	Private	
BUTTON, L	319	NFB Haywards Heath	Acting Sergeant Major	Remained in South Africa NFBUAD Medal
BYETT, H E	291	Metropolitan Corps	Sergeant	
COOKE, H H	337	NFB Bedford	Sergeant	NFBUAD Medal
COX, G W	328	Reading Division	Staff Sergeant	
DAVIS, J C	465	Metropolitan Corps	Sergeant	DAVIES on QSA Medal roll
DOWN, J F	316	NFB Exeter	Private	NFBUAD Medal
DUXBURY, A E	312	NFB Darwen	Private	NFBUAD Medal DUXBURY, W T on QSA medal roll
EDWARDS, Charlie J	317	NFB Haywards Heath	Private	NFBUAD Medal
ELWELL, R W	287	Metropolitan Corps	Sergeant	
FERGUSON, Alfred	309	NFB Haywards Heath	Private	NFBUAD Medal
FIELD, J W	297	Metropolitan Corps	Private	
GROVES, S F	353	Dowlais Division	Lance Corporal	
HANBURY, A E	321	NFB Woodstock	Private	Possibly Pte 31647 62nd Company Imperial Yeomanry NFBUAD Medal
HERN, Harold Edmund	326	NFB Exeter	Lance Corporal	NFBUAD Medal Died Exeter age 29 1907
HOLMES, R	437	Keswick Division	Private	
HORNBROOK, J	456	NFB Cockington	Sergeant	NFBUAD Medal
HOWELL, J	394	Sheffield Corps	Sergeant	
KNIGHT, F B	468	Metropolitan Corps	Private	
LANCASTER, E	380	Birmingham Corps	Corporal	
LAWRENCE, W L	292	Swindon Division	Lance Corporal	
LEWIS, E K	293	Swindon Division	Private	
LYONS, T H	322	NFB Croxley Mills Dickinson's Fire Brigade	Lance Corporal	NFBUAD Medal

MEAKINS, C T	325	NFB Stony Stratford	Private	NFBUAD Medal
MORRIS, A	352	Dowlais Division	Lance Corporal	
MOULDS, W E	393	Sheffield Corps	Private	
MURRAY, N R	290	Metropolitan Corps	Sergeant	
NEVE, B	296	Metropolitan Corps	Private	
NEWMAN, Frank B	338	NFB Bedford	Lance Corporal	NFBUAD Medal
NEWPORT, Herbert H	311	NFB Frome	Private	NFBUAD Medal
OLIVER, W C	285	Metropolitan Corps	Sergeant	
ORCHARD, C	438	Metropolitan Corps	Acting Sergeant Major	
PAINE, G	323	NFB Newhaven	Private	NFBUAD Medal
PALLETT, W	384	Birmingham Corps	Private	
PALMER, C	461	Metropolitan Corps	QM Sergeant	
PARNALL, J	299	Metropolitan Corps	Civilian Compounder	
PETT, Monty W	314	NFB Exeter	Private	NFBUAD Medal
PRICE, J	298	Metropolitan Corps	Corporal	
SANTEN, B	329	Metropolitan Corps	Sergeant	
SAWFORD, James S	320	NFB Aylesbury	Private	NFBUAD Medal
SHIPLEY, G W	289	Metropolitan Corps	Private	
SLATER, A W	318	NFB Barnes/Mortlake	Sergeant	NFBUAD Medal
SMITH, H	382	Birmingham Corps	Private	
SMITH, H J	305	NFB Marlow	Corporal	NFBUAD Medal
SMITH, J W	306	NFB Barnes/Mortlake	Sergeant	NFBUAD Medal
SONNENFIELD, M W	310	NFB	Corporal	NFBUAD Medal
SOUTHWOOD, C	284	Metropolitan Corps	Sergeant	
SPENDLOVE, H C	387	Birmingham Corps	Private	
STANLEY, P	342	Ilkeston Corps	Private	
STEVENS, Thomas	304	NFB Cockington	Private	NFBUAD Medal
STEVENSON, John W	373	Ironbridge Corps	Private	
THOMAS, G	331	Ebbw Vale Division	Private	
TRIMMER, Alfred J	302	NFB Bedford	Acting Sergeant Major	NFBUAD Medal
TYMMS, P	418	Handsworth & Smethwick Corps	Sergeant	
UZZELL, William John	295	Great Western Railway	Private	
WALKER, F J	294	Swindon Division	Private	
WALTERS, T	381	Birmingham Corps	Private	
WANT, W H	383	Birmingham Corps	Private	
WARN, A E	307	NFB Croxley Mills Dickinson's Fire Brigade	Private	NFBUAD Medal

WEBBER, R	324	NFB Exeter	Private	NFBUAD Medal
WESTON, S B	301	Metropolitan Corps	Private	
WILLMORE, Charles E	303	NFB Hythe	Sergeant	NFBUAD Medal Died Deelfontein 2 January 1901
WOOD, F H	385	Birmingham Corps	Private	

The main group of men who were recruited were allocated numbers between 284 and 332. One gap in the sequence on the St John Ambulance Bronze Medal roll is detailed as 330 Private J. GRADNER from Ebbw Vale Division. It seems highly likely that this man also served at Deelfontein as the next man entered in the register, who is known to have been at Deelfontein, 331 Private G. THOMAS, was clearly one of his colleagues also from Ebbw Vale Division. However, Private GRADNER's Bronze Medal roll entry poses some problems. It seems highly likely that the surname in the Bronze Medal roll is incorrect and should be GARDENER. From the census returns relating to that period there are no men with the surname GRADNER from Ebbw Vale while there are a number of families with the surname GARDENER. If that is the case the closest match on the Imperial Yeomanry Hospital Staff Queen's South Africa Medal roll is Corporal G. GARDENER and it does seem most probable, but not certain, that this is the same man.

One of the men at Deelfontein featured in Our Portrait Gallery in the *First Aid* Journal in September 1901. Superintendent C. ORCHARD of Merton and Wimbledon Ambulance Division, Metropolitan Corps, was another of the men who reverted to the ranks in order to volunteer to serve in South Africa. He was given the post of Chief Orderly-Room Clerk at Deelfontein on his arrival there. During the latter part of his service, he was one of the men moved to Pretoria when the Imperial Yeomanry Hospital was opened there.

438 Superintendent C. ORCHARD Merton and Wimbledon Ambulance Division.
(Photo *First Aid* september 1901)

The Portland Hospital

This was one of the first initiatives to organize a privately funded hospital. The project commenced in November 1899 and included a donation of £5000 from the Duke of Portland which gave rise to the naming of the hospital. Initially projected to have 104 beds this was expanded to 160 beds. The hospital and staff left for South Africa during early December 1899 and the hospital opened in Cape Town on 8 January 1900 being attached to No 3 General Hospital at Rondebosch. On 19 April 1901 it was moved to Bloemfontein attached to No 8 General Hospital at the height of the typhoid epidemic occurring there. The hospital remained at Bloemfontein until it was closed in July 1900. The hospital was to prove a model demonstrating how such a hospital should be run particularly in regard to the identification of the causes of the typhoid outbreak and the way in which the patients were managed.

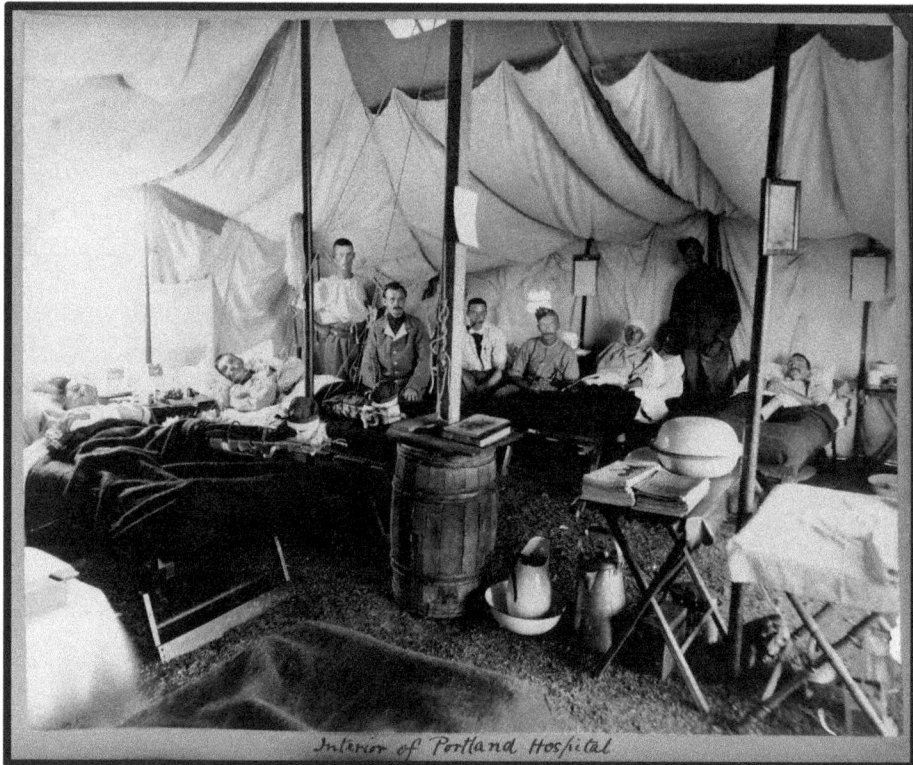

Interior of the tented Portland Hospital.

De Villiers records that 33 members of the St John Ambulance Brigade were initially sent to help staff the hospital. The Queen's South Africa Medal Roll for these men is found in WO 100/225/235-236 but in fact 35 men's names appear on this medal roll for the Portland Hospital so reconciling the list of men on the Queen's South Africa Medal roll with the known recipients of the Bronze St John Ambulance Brigade poses some challenges. 26 of the men are readily identified as their recruitment numbers fall within the range 81 to 106. However, there are gaps in the Bronze St John Ambulance Brigade Medal roll for numbers 83 and 84 and numbers 107 to 110. There are six men, M.M. BOYD,

BUSHELL, G.T. EVANS, W.M. MARKER, RYAN and P.S. SCETTRINO on the Portland Hospital Queen's South Africa Medal roll list whose numbers can't be found so it seems extremely likely that these missing six numbers belong to these men. Unfortunately, no Bronze medals with these numbers have yet appeared on the market to confirm this suspicion. There is one other man Private A. HEATON whose Queen's South Africa Medal roll entry is marked "not recommended" so for whatever reason he did not receive his medal and presumably also would not have received a Bronze St John Ambulance Brigade medal. That would thus tally with the 33 men initially recruited.

There are then two men who are likely to have worked at the Portland Hospital as later recruits, 640 A.E.R. ELLIS from Leicester Corps and 185 G.R.N. COLLINS from Metropolitan Corps. There is an F. COLLINS on the Queen's South Africa Medal roll for the Portland Hospital but no G.R.N. COLLINS. There are only two men with the surname Collins on the Bronze St John Ambulance Brigade Medal roll and Henry Thomas COLLINS is already present on the Portland Hospital Queen's South Africa Medal roll. It therefore seems likely that F. COLLINS and G.R.N. COLLINS are the same man. He is noted as having acted as personal servant to Lord William Bentinck.

One man is known to have died during his period of service at the Hospital. Private Henry James BORER who was from Caterham Ambulance Division died at Bloemfontein on 12 June 1900 at a time when the hospital was combating both the typhoid epidemic and the outbreak of the streptococcal skin illness, erysipelas, which in the pre-antibiotic era could prove rapidly fatal. It may well be that Sergeant A.E.R. ELLIS acted as his replacement.

The staff of the Portland Hospital.

The full list of the 35 men allocated to the Portland Hospital is provided below.

Name	SJAB No	Ambulance Division or Corps	Rank	Duties at Hospital
BLEASDALE, Robert	101	Bolton Corps	Private	Ward 1 Orderly
BORER, Henry J	97	Caterham Division	Private	Enteric Ward 18 Orderly
BOTTERILL, Thomas	99	Kettering Corps	Private	Assistant Pack Store
BOYD, M M	NONE		Private	Provision/Linen Store
BUSHELL,	NONE		Private	Assistant Cook
COLLINS, G R N	185	Metropolitan Corps	Private	Office Orderly
COLLINS, Henry T	93	Metropolitan Corps	Private	Officers Servant
COMPSTON, Frederick	100	Crawshawbooth Division	Private	Ward 6 Orderly
ELLIS, A E R	640	Leicester Corps	Supply Officer	
ELLIS, Francis J	91	Metropolitan Corps	Private	Ward 11 Orderly
EVANS, Fredrick R	79	Herne Bay Division	Staff Sergeant	Pack Store/Sanitary Duties
EVANS, G T	NONE		Chef	Chef Sick Officers
FREEMAN, Henry F	92	Northampton Corps	Private	Operating Theatre Orderly
HARNESS, John W	87	Hull Corps	Private	Ward 7 Orderly
HARPER, William J	88	North Staffs Corps	Private	Ward 10 Orderly
HARRIS, Edgar J F	98	Redruth Division	Private	Enteric Ward 16 Orderly
HEATON, Alfred	NO MEDAL		Private	
HOLLOWAY, Harry	86	Warrington Corps	Private	Ward 3 Orderly
JOHNSON, William T	94	Northampton Corps	Supply Officer	In Charge Enteric Linen
MARCHANT, Thomas	106	Caterham Division	Private	Enteric Ward 16 Orderly
MARKER, W M	NONE		Private	Officers Servant
MATTHEWS, Herbert	89	Hull Corps	Private	Enteric Ward 18 Orderly
McNAMARA, William J	81	Leicester Corps	Staff Sergeant	Assistant Compounder
MITCHELL, William	105	Metropolitan Corps	Private	In Charge Transport
MOORE, John	102	Welbeck Division	Private	Enteric Ward 16 Orderly
NEWNES, John E	85	Warrington Corps	Private	Ward 5 Orderly
PALLETT, Arthur P	90	Metropolitan Corps	Private	Ward 12 Orderly
PEAT, George	80	Welbeck Division	Staff Sergeant	Assistant Steward/Compounder
POTTINGER, James A	103	Welbeck Division	Sergeant	Ward 9 Orderly
RYAN,	NONE		Private	Ward 4 Orderly
SAYER, James H	82	Metropolitan Corps	Staff Sergeant	Hospital Master Cook
SCETTRINO, P	NONE		Private	Chef Officers Mess
SQUIRES, David	95	Christchurch Division	Private	Ward 8 Orderly
STRATFORD, Samuel	96	Withernsea Division	Private	Ward 2 Orderly
WILSON, Ernest L	104	Gateshead Fell Division	Private	Convalescent Ward 13 Orderly

The Langman Hospital

The Langman Hospital was established as a result of witnessing the success of the Portland Hospital. It was financed through the philanthropic generosity of Mr John L. Langman. Planning for the hospital which was to have 100 beds commenced in January 1900. All the necessary equipment and staff were rapidly gathered together and the unit left Tilbury on 28 February 1900 arriving 28 days later at Cape Town. From there the equipment and personnel were transported to Bloemfontein which at the time was in the grip of a typhoid epidemic. They accepted their first patients on 8 April but unfortunately an outbreak of the skin infection erysipelas severely curtailed its activities during June and July. The hospital moved in the latter part of July to Pretoria where it was attached to No 2 General Hospital opening on 2 August. Eventually the hospital was transferred to Government control on 4 November. During its relatively brief period of operation the hospital treated 1211 patients.

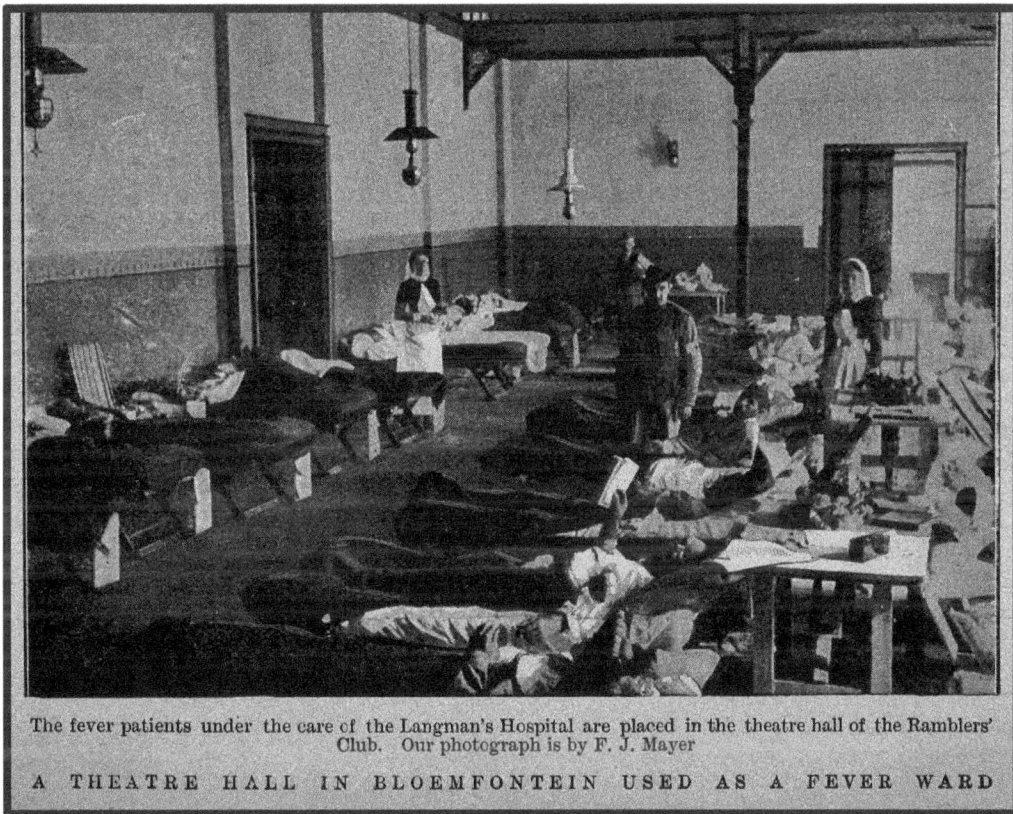

The fever patients under the care of the Langman's Hospital are placed in the theatre hall of the Ramblers' Club. Our photograph is by F. J. Mayer

A THEATRE HALL IN BLOEMFONTEIN USED AS A FEVER WARD

A fever ward at Langman's Hospital.

The St John Ambulance Brigade provided 14 men to help staff the hospital with 13 serving as Privates and one as a Sergeant Major. Their details are as follows:

Name	SJAB No	Ambulance Division or Corps	Rank
BAKER, Cecil W	555	Sheffield Corps	Sergeant Major
BARRINGER, G	535	Preston Corps	Private
DAYKIN, T H	505	Sheffield Corps	Private
FOSTER, A	531	Oldham Corps	Private
FOSTER, Walter James	529	Preston Corps	Private
HALES, A	502	Sheffield Corps	Private
MARRISON, H	497	Preston Corps	Private
MARTIN, A H	422	Preston Corps	Private
MULLOWNEY, J	536	Keswick Division	Private
PICKUP, Thomas	512	Haslingden Corps	Private
RICE, A H	508	Preston Corps	Private
SWARBRICK, R	532	Northampton Corps	Private
WETHERALL, D H	345	Reading Division	Private
WINYARD, E H G	498	Sheffield Corps	Private

Of these 14 men two were awarded the Distinguished Conduct Medal. 498 Private E.H.G. WINYARD was Mentioned in Dispatches announced in the *London Gazette* on 10 September 1901 followed soon afterwards by his award of the Distinguished Conduct Medal. 555 Sergeant Major C.W. BAKER was first Mentioned in Dispatches in the *London Gazette* on 29 July 1902 with the announcement of his Distinguished Conduct Medal award on 31 October 1902. These two men were the only members of the St John Ambulance Brigade to be awarded the Distinguished Conduct Medal during the war.

555 Sergeant Major Cecil W. BAKER Metropolitan Corps.

Medals to 1st Class Superintendent Officer Cecil BAKER
including the Distinguished Conduct Medal.

Van Alen American Field Hospital

Mr J. van Alen was an American citizen living in London during the early part of the South African War. He obtained permission to go to South Africa with a small section of a Field Hospital equipped and staffed at his own expense. The organisation of the hospital commenced on 26 January 1900 and as part of the staffing requirement nine St John Ambulance Brigade men were recruited to act as Orderlies, the Wardmaster and Compounder. The Hospital arrived in Cape Town between 6 and 10 March. It commenced activities at Newton Camp near Kimberley on 13 March and subsequently with Lord Methuen's column in areas to west and north of Kimberley. It also served at Boshoff and near Heilbron. On 4 July it was noted that the contracts of the St John Ambulance Brigade staff members had expired and the hospital was therefore transferred two days later to the Government at Paaderkraal.

Of the nine St John Ambulance Brigade men, one 367 Private Thomas STONIER, died from enteric fever on 14 July at Johannesburg. One of the other men, 446 John E. HANCOCK, went on to serve with the South African Constabulary and his profile, which was published in the *First Aid* Journal in April 1901, is included in this book under the section covering the Constabulary. All nine men received the Queen's South Africa medal and are included on the medal roll in WO100/225/238.

Name	SJAB No	Ambulance Division or Corps	Rank
BLACKBAND, J			1st Grade Orderly
GRAHAM, W	417	Padiham Division	1st Grade Orderly
GUY, F J V	466	Metropolitan Corps	Compounder
HANCOCK, John E	446	North Staffs Corps	Wardmaster
KENYON, J W	421	Oldham Corps	2nd Grade Orderly
LANE, Charles William	333	Isle of Wight Corps	2nd Grade Orderly
LINGARD, James	405	Accrington Corps	1st Grade Orderly
MORRIS, A J	334	Isle of Wight Corps	2nd Grade Orderly
STONIER, Thomas	367	North Staffs Corps	1st Grade Orderly

Eight of the men are readily identifiable on the St John Ambulance Brigade Bronze Medal roll but there is no entry in the Bronze Medal register to J. BLACKBAND. He should have been eligible as the other eight men were for the medal so it may be that his award was one related to one of the missing numbers in the St John Ambulance Brigade Bronze Medal register.

QSA awarded to 1st Grade Orderly J. BLACKBAND Van Alen
American Field Hospital.

The Princess Christian Hospital

Mr Alfred Moseley, a businessman from South Africa, expressed a desire to donate a mobile hospital based at Kimberley but he was convinced by those managing the provision of medical care that this location would be impracticable. He therefore opted to provide a hospital similar to the Portland and Langman Hospitals and this was approved on condition that the accommodation provided was in huts rather than tents for the 100 proposed beds. HRH Princess Christian consented to her name being used for the hospital at Mr Moseley's request.

The equipment and personnel embarked from Southampton on the SS *Assaye* in late February with others following on 3 March 1900. On arrival in Cape Town on 10 March the hospital was transferred to Durban where it was erected at Pinetown. During the transit the staff were inoculated with the innovative Wright typhoid vaccine which meant that subsequently none of those vaccinated contracted the disease. With the spread of the typhoid epidemic in Natal the capacity of the hospital was soon extended to 200 beds. By the end of April, the hospital was receiving patients and continued to operate in a private capacity until 20 July when Mr Mosely passed ownership to HRH Princess Christian and thence to the Government to become No 13 Stationary Hospital. During the three months of private operation 327 men were treated of whom 165, just over half, were typhoid victims.

Among the staff members initially sent to man the hospital were six Supernumerary Officers, 12 First Grade Orderlies and 12 Second Grade Orderlies from the St John Ambulance Brigade. None of these men appear to have had medals named to the Princess Christian Hospital, presumably because the hospital passed out of private ownership during their tour of duty. But the Queen's South Africa Medal roll for No 13 Stationary Hospital WO100/225/65-66 contains the names of 40 St John Ambulance Brigade men so presumably this list includes the 30 men initially assigned to the Princess Christian Hospital together with an additional 10 men posted there as the capacity of the hospital was increased. The details of the 40 men are given below.

Name	SJAB No	Ambulance Division or Corps	Rank
ABLEWHITE, H	509	Shipley Corps	Supply Officer
ADAMS, J T	1026	Oldham Corps	Orderly
BARNES, T	510	Shipley Corps	Orderly
BARON, J	1054	Bolton Corps	Orderly
BREAKELL, J	1076	Preston Corps	Orderly
BRIERLY, L	1029	Oldham Corps	Orderly
BUTCHER, H W	530	Blackpool Division	Supply Officer
COX, W	1103	Birmingham Corps	Orderly
CROSS, J	1056	Bolton Corps	Orderly
DUNN, C	1022	Oldham Corps	Orderly
ENGLAND, A	484	Tibshelf Corps	Orderly
FOX, C H	519	Blackpool Division	Orderly
GARDNER, F W	1102	Birmingham Corps	Supply Officer
GEE, Ernest	501	Sheffield Corps	Orderly
HOGG, R	534	Preston Corps	Orderly
HOLDEN, J	1077	Preston Corps	Orderly
HOLMSHAW, W H	1119	Sheffield Corps	Orderly
HOYLE, A	1020	Rochdale Corps	Orderly
HULME, P	491	North Staffs Corps	Orderly
JOLLY, John	524	Blackpool Division	Orderly
JONES, S H	494	North Staffs Corps	Orderly
JOULE, H	474	Bolton Corps	Orderly
KAY, J	1065	Bolton Corps	Orderly
LIDDELL, T	500	Sheffield Corps	Orderly
MEADOWS, J	1042	Abram Colliery Division	Orderly
MILLICHAMP, E A	1027	Oldham Corps	Orderly
PICKARD, W	1049	Dalton-in-Furness Division	Orderly
PRICE, John	499	Sheffield Corps	Orderly
ROGERSON, W	533	Preston Corps	Supply Officer
SHARPLES, W	538	Walton-le-Dale Division	Orderly

SIMS, J A	1097	Derby Division	Orderly
TAYLOR, S	1087	Haverhill Division	Orderly
TILDESLEY, W	493	North Staffs Corps	Supply Officer
TURNER, J H	504	Kendal Division	Supply Officer
VENN, Charles H	473	Bolton Corps	Orderly
WAINSCOTT, H	1120	Sheffield Corps	Orderly
WALKER, J	943	Clitheroe Division	Orderly
WALLBANK, T	537	Preston Corps	Orderly
WARD, Ernest	1092	Tibshelf Corps	Orderly
WILLIS, W	495	North Staffs Corps	Orderly

The Princess Christian Hospital Train

Early during the war Sir John Furley was tasked with supervising the construction of a hospital train for service in South Africa. The Borough of Windsor donated just over £6000 towards the project and in view of Princess Christian's interest in hospital work the proposed train was named after her. After several failed attempts to convert existing carriages the train was eventually specially built by the Birmingham Railway and Carriage Company. Work commenced in October 1899 and was completed just 10 weeks later. The disassembled train was transported during December to South Africa and reassembled ready for use by 17 March 1900. The train served in a private capacity, transporting both sick and battle casualties, until handed to the Secretary of State for War in June 1901 on the condition that it continued only to be used as hospital train.

The Princess Christian Hospital Train.

Among those who staffed the train were 12 St John Ambulance Brigade personnel. They are listed in the Queen's South Africa Medal roll in WO100/225/75 and their details are given below. One of the men, Supply Officer Percy W. PLUMB died at Kimberley while undertaking a second tour of duty at No 11 General Hospital on 13 January 1901.

Name	SJAB No	Ambulance Division or Corps	Rank
ABBOTT, J	205	Wellingborough Corps	Orderly
BLACK, J J	271	Metropolitan Corps	Orderly
ELLIS, C W P	111	Faversham Division	Supply Officer
ELLIS, W J	283	Herne Bay Division	Orderly
GORHAM, A S	226	Ramsgate Corps	Orderly
HARRIS, J	272	Metropolitan Corps	Orderly
HINKS, H J E	112	Faversham Division	Supply Officer
JACKSON, J T	246	Hazelgrove Division	Orderly
JOHNSON, J	204	Nuneaton Division	Orderly
PLUMB, Percy W	214	Metropolitan Corps	Supply Officer
RIDOUT, W W	238	Herne Bay Division	Orderly
TWEEDALE, W	253	Rochdale Corps	Orderly

Hospital Ships

Just before the start of the war it was clear that the provision of hospital beds on ships to repatriate casualties would be inadequate. Two hospital ships were specially commissioned and equipped in England prior to sailing to South Africa. The *Princess of Wales* was refurbished just as the war commenced eventually arriving in Cape Town in early January 1900. The other ship was largely financed with support raised by a committee comprised of American women based in London. The Hospital Ship *Maine*, after being fitted out, arrived in Cape Town on 21 January 1900. Eight other transport ships were converted soon after at Durban to initially mainly act as stationary hospitals. These were required to alleviate the severe shortage of hospital beds in Durban available to deal with the sick and wounded from the Natal campaign. Many of these ships were converted over a very short time scale, as short as 15 days in some cases. By 9 March 1900 eight Hospital Ships were anchored in Durban Harbour providing a combined capacity of 1100 beds. Over the following months these ships would gradually become more involved in transporting sick and wounded back to England.

On at least six of these ships it is clear from the Queen's South Africa Medal roll that St John Ambulance Brigade men were deployed to serve mainly on the ships on their return back to England at the end of their contracts. In addition, it also seems very likely that others would have been similarly employed as Orderlies and Supply Officers caring for the sick and wounded on their journey home but the details haven't been recorded.

No	Ship	Tons	Date Built	Owners	Beds	SJAB men
6	HS *Avoca*	5183	1891	British India Associated Steamers		0
1	HS *Dunera*	5413	1891	British India Associated Steamers		21
28	HS *Lismore Castle*	2606	1891	Union Castle Line	120	0
	HS *Maine*	2809	1887	Atlantic Transport Line	218	17
4	HS *Nubia*	5914	1894	P&O Steam Navigation Co.	300	23
40	HS *Orcana*	4803	1893	Pacific Steam Nav Co.	166	1
	HS *Princess of Wales*	3020	1874	Ex Yachting cruiser *Midnight Sun*	178	23
2	HS *Simla*	5884	1895	P&O Steam Navigation Co.		38
11	HS *Spartan*	3491	1881	Union Castle Line	120	0
10	HS *Trojan*	3555	1880	Union Castle Line	160	0

HS *Dunera*

HS *Dunera* was among the ships initially used to supplement the bed capacity at Durban. However later in the year 21 men from the St John Ambulance Brigade were assigned to serve in the ship as Orderlies and Supply Officers being transferred to the vessel on 18 December 1900. The ship sailed for England on 25 December carrying 263 invalids, 223 sick and 40 wounded.

In addition, two men 936 Orderly C. H. JERVIS from Kettering Corps and 1121 Orderly C. JONES from Sheffield Corps were invalided to HS *Dunera* from No 15 General Hospital at Howick on 17 September 1900. The ship sailed for England on 26 September arriving at Plymouth on 18 October.

The men are mainly listed on the Queen's South Africa Medal roll WO100/225/65-66.

Hospital Ship *Dunera* Transport No 1

Name	SJAB No	Ambulance Division or Corps	Rank
ABLEWHITE, H	509	Shipley Corps	Supply Officer
ADAMS, J T	1026	Oldham Corps	Orderly
BREAKELL, J	1076	Preston Corps	Orderly
BRIERLY, L	1029	Oldham Corps	Orderly
COX, W	1103	Birmingham Corps	Orderly
CROSS, J	1056	Bolton Corps	Orderly
GARDNER, F W	1102	Birmingham Corps	Supply Officer
HOYLE, A	1020	Rochdale Corps	Orderly
KAY, J	1065	Bolton Corps	Orderly
KENWORTHY, B	1723	Oldham Corps	Orderly
LIDDELL, T	500	Sheffield Corps	Orderly
MAYOR, W	1721	Oldham Corps	Orderly
MEADOWS, J	1042	Abram Colliery Division	Orderly
MILLICHAMP, E A	1027	Oldham Corps	Orderly
NORTON, J A	1730	Oldham Corps	Orderly
PICKARD, W	1049	Dalton-in-Furness Division	Orderly
SIMS, J A	1097	Derby Division	Orderly
TAYLOR, S	1087	Haverhill Division	Orderly
TILDESLEY, W	493	North Staffs Corps	Supply Officer
TURNER, J H	504	Kendal Division	Supply Officer
WAINSCOTT, H	1120	Sheffield Corps	Orderly

HS *Maine*

A committee of American women came together to raise funds in London for a hospital ship. With a target budget of £30,000 after 2 months £40,000 had been raised. The ship chosen was a cattle transport which was converted at an eventual cost of £28,000.

While the senior medical staff were all American, a considerable number of St John Ambulance Brigade men were allocated to serve on the ship as Orderlies. The ship had 137 beds. It was destined to make two voyages to South Africa but also spent a period as a Stationary Hospital anchored off Durban from 2 February to 17 March 1900. The ship left for the return journey to England on its first voyage on 17 March. After the vessels' return to South Africa, the second voyage back to England commenced on 9 June with 159 invalided men, 91 sick and 58 wounded arriving on 3 July. A third voyage to South Africa was envisaged but instead the ship was sent to China where it was felt the need was greater leaving on 12 July 1900.

Hospital Ship *Maine*.

In total 17 men qualified for the Queen's South Africa Medal with at least some of their service on HS *Maine*. Many of the St John Ambulance Brigade men remained with the ship for the duration of its subsequent service in China during the remainder of 1900. As a consequence of their service, 14 of the 17 men who served on the ship in South Africa also received the China War Medal without clasps. The main Queen's South Africa Medal roll for those serving on HS *Maine* contains 11 names, but without their St John Ambulance Brigade numbers being noted. This is to be found in WO100/225/53 and WO100/225/248. They represent a contingent of men with St John Ambulance Brigade recruitment numbers in the block 1127 to 1137. There are also six additional men who are mentioned elsewhere in the Queen's South Africa Medal rolls. Although not specifically mentioned as having served on HS *Maine* in the Queen's South Africa Medal rolls, they do appear on the China Medal roll in WO100/96/38+39 for their service on the ship. It is not entirely clear how many of these six men served on the first two voyages that HS *Maine* made to South Africa. The 14 men who are present on the China Medal roll for HS *Maine* are marked with an * in the following table which details the men from the St John Ambulance Brigade who served on the ship.

Name	China Medal	SJAB No	Ambulance Division or Corps	Rank
BEEBY, Samuel	*	130	Kettering Corps	Orderly
BOWCOCK, William H	*	1130	Bolton Corps	Orderly
CLARK, Thomas Bryan	*	1136	Nelson Corps	Orderly
GREEN, Frederick W	*	132	Wellingborough Corps	Orderly
HOWARD, Edwin M	*	1128	Oldham Corps	Orderly
JOHNSON, Thomas H	*	121	Hull Corps	Orderly
KINGSTON, Samuel	*	117	Northampton Corps	Orderly
NUTTER, James	*	1135	Blackpool Division	Orderly
RHODES, H		1127	Oldham Corps	Orderly
ROBINSON, John		1132	Bolton Corps	Orderly
ROBINSON, John W	*	850	Northampton Corps	Orderly
STONE, William H	*	127	Metropolitan Corps	Orderly
SUTTON, George T	*	1131	Bolton Corps	Orderly
TRESCOWTHICK, John C	*	1134	Blackpool Division	Orderly
WALLBANK, W H		1133	Bolton Corps	Supply Officer
WILSON, John H	*	1129	Oldham Corps	Orderly
WOOD, John	*	1137	Nelson Corps	Orderly

One surname which could give rise to confusion is ROBINSON. John W. ROBINSON 850 of Northampton Corps received his Queen's South Africa Medal for service at No 8 General Hospital but was one the six additional men not specifically mentioned on the Queen's South Africa Medal roll for HS *Maine*. J. ROBINSON 1132 of Bolton Corps is one of the 11 men on the Queen's South Africa Medal roll for HS *Maine*. He along with two others did not go on to serve with the ship in China. He subsequently saw further service with a new recruitment number 1899 transferring to the South African Constabulary A Division as a Medical Corporal A1867. Although having the same surname and first initial it does seem that these are two distinct individuals from different St John Ambulance Divisions.

The ship was to survive to see service in the lead up to the start of World War One but it ran aground off the Isle of Mull on 18 June 1914 and was finally abandoned there because it was felt uneconomic to salvage.

HS *Nubia*

On 29 December 1900 23 men of the St John Ambulance Brigade were transferred from No 15 General Hospital to serve on the converted Hospital Ship *Nubia*. They are listed on the Queen's South Africa Medal roll WO100/225/161-165. HS *Nubia* sailed for England on 7 January 1901 with 270 invalided men aboard, 253 sick and 17 wounded.

Hospital Ship *Nubia* Transport No 4.

Name	SJAB No	Ambulance Division or Corps	Rank
ALLEN, H W	983	Crewe Division	Orderly
BAGLEY, W	908	Derby Division	Orderly
BILLINGSLEY, E	964	Dudley Corps	Orderly
BOWDEN, H	1094	Metropolitan Corps	Orderly
BURNMAN, G W	949	Metropolitan Corps	Orderly
CHALLINOR, L	934	Oldham Corps	Orderly
COGGS, J H	974	Metropolitan Corps (Wembley)	Orderly
CROSSLEY, J	898	Bolton Corps	Orderly
ENTWISTLE, J	1033	Tottington Division	Orderly
FELLOWS, E E	967	Dudley Corps	Orderly
FREEMAN, T	907	Derby Division	Orderly
GREENFIELD, A	1015	Sheffield Corps	Orderly
GRIFFITHS, W E	966	Dudley Corps	Orderly
HADFIELD, F W	1055	Bolton Corps	Orderly
HAMMON, C A	946	Padiham Division	Orderly
HANKINSON, G W	963	Preston Corps	Supply Officer

HOBART, J C	1012	Sheffield Corps	Orderly
HOLT, R	902	Bolton Corps	Orderly
HOYLE, F	1019	Rochdale Corps	Orderly
HULSE, W J	1014	Sheffield Corps	Orderly
LEE, T	895	Bolton Corps	Orderly
LEECE, T	896	Bolton Corps	Orderly
PITCHFORD, John H	1069	Welbeck Division	Orderly

HS *Orcana*

Just one man from the St John Ambulance Brigade appears to have been employed on the Hospital Ship *Orcana*, 530 Supply Officer H.W. BUTCHER from Blackpool Division being transferred to HS *Orcana* from No 13 Stationary Hospital at Pinetown Bridge on 17 July 1900. The ship left for England on 20 July carrying 181 invalided men, 172 sick and nine wounded and arrived at Plymouth on 8 August 1900.

Hospital Ship *Orcana* Transport No 40.

HS *Princess of Wales*

In September 1899 a decision was made to purchase a suitable vessel to prepare for service as a hospital ship to be available in the event of war. A yachting cruiser *Midnight Sun* was considered suitable and refurbished by Whitworth and Co on the River Tyne. The converted ship sailed to the Thames on 18 November 1899.

Hospital Ship *Princess of Wales*.

The vessel was refitted to a very high standard with 178 beds, a full operating theatre and X ray apparatus. All the cost was covered by HRH the Princess of Wales and the ship was renamed after her in recognition of this.

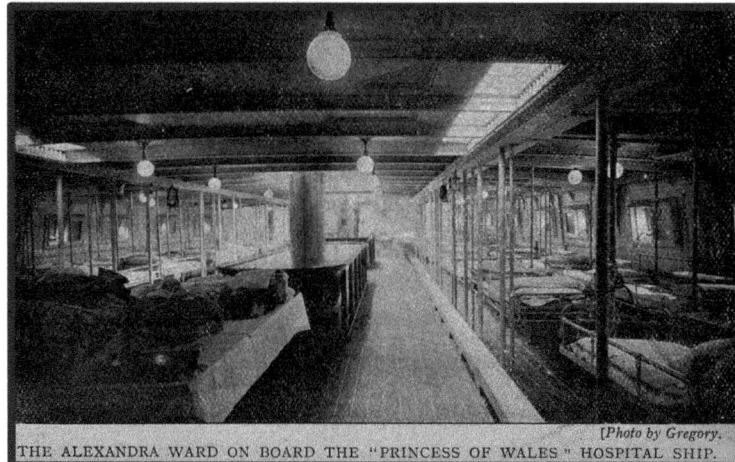

Alexandra ward on board the Hospital Ship *Princess of Wales*.

The ship sailed for South Africa on 8 December 1899. In total the ship made three voyages from South Africa back to England including a period between 27 September and 5 November 1900 anchored at Durban acting as a Stationary Hospital. In total 728 patients were treated on the ship.

Unfortunately, the vessel was plagued with mechanical difficulties and was relatively slow taking three to four weeks to travel from South Africa to England rather than the two weeks taken by most of the Transport ships being used so was regarded by the authorities as a questionable and expensive enterprise. Perhaps none of this was particularly surprising as the ship was built in 1874 so was over 25 years old before it was refurbished.

As part of the staffing requirement, 23 members of the St John Ambulance Brigade were recruited, these being the first St John Ambulance Brigade volunteers to travel to South Africa and their details are given below. The men are listed on the Queen's South Africa Medal roll WO100/225/241-242.

Name	SJAB No	Ambulance Division or Corps	Rank
BLACKBURN, J W	22	Dewsbury Corps	Private
BOSWORTH, E	9	Wellingborough Corps	Private
BROOKBANK, G W	15	Metropolitan Corps	Private
COWIN, L B	2	Metropolitan Corps	1st Class Supernumerary Officer
COX, H F	1	Metropolitan Corps	1st Class Supernumerary Officer
EKINS, F	4	Northampton Corps	Private
FIELD, F	17	Dewsbury Corp	Private
HOLMES, W	10	Wellingborough Corps	Private
HOYLE, J H	19	Haslingden Division	Private
HUNT, G L	16	Hull Corps	Private
LAMB, T	6	Hull Corps	Private
LANCHBERRY, W E	20	Westgate-on-Sea Division	Private
LEGGE, H G B	3	Metropolitan Corps	1st Class Supernumerary Officer
LISTER, C	21	Leeds Corps	Private
MADEN, E	14	Nelson Corps	Private
PANTER, A N	7	Keswick Division	Private
PATERSON, A W	23	Ramsgate Corps	Private
RYALL, H B	5	Metropolitan Corps	Private
SAUNDERS, A E	11	Metropolitan Corps	Private
SLATER, W	8	Nelson Corps	Private
WATKINS, F H	12	Metropolitan Corps	Private
WELLARD, R E	13	Reading Division	Private
WILLIMGHAM, E	18	Hull Corps	Private

HS *Simla*

A total of 38 men from the St John Ambulance Brigade were assigned to the Hospital Ship *Simla*. Two of them were transferred from No 13 Stationary Hospital at Pinetown Bridge on 16 August 1900 with the ship sailing for England on 27 August with 274 invalided men 258 sick and 16 wounded. The ship arrived at Southampton on 18 September 1900. A further 36 men transferred to HS *Simla* on 14 November 1900 from No 14 General Hospital at Newcastle. Also two men, 1414 Orderly W. HARWOOD and 1428 Orderly W. WALKER were invalided from No 14 General Hospital on 14 November 1900 to return to England. HS *Simla* sailed back to England carrying approximately 274 invalids, 235 sick and 39 wounded, on 26 November 1900. The ship arrived at Southampton on the morning of 18 December. The men who served on HS *Simla* are listed in the Queen's South Africa Medal roll WO100/225/58-59.

Hospital Ship *Simla* Transport No 2.

Among those sent to HS *Simla* was William Carey from Hebden Bridge Corps, a Corps which provided a number of men who served on the ship.

1418 Private William CAREY Hebden Bridge Ambulance Division.

44

Name	SJAB No	Ambulance Division or Corps	Rank
ACKERLEY, A W	1412	Hebden Bridge Corps	Orderly
ASHWORTH, W	1419	Hebden Bridge Corps	Orderly
BLAKE, A J W	1391	Leicester Corps	Orderly
BLANSHARD, G	1410	Dewsbury Corps	Orderly
BOLSTER (JUNIOR), G	1400	St John Ambulance Brigade	Orderly
BONYNGE, C A	1399	St John Ambulance Brigade	Orderly
BOWEN, C T M	1377	Mill Bay Division	Orderly
BURNE, F R	1395	St John Ambulance Brigade	Orderly
CAREY, William	1418	Hebden Bridge Corps	Orderly
CLAY, W	1411	Hebden Bridge Corps	Orderly
COWLEY, T E	1382	Wellingborough Corps	Orderly
CRAIG, R J C K	1392	St John Ambulance Brigade	Orderly
CROFT, C	1388	Weston-Super-Mare Division	Orderly
ELLIS, J E	1407	Bradford Corps	Orderly
FAULKNER, J E P	1383	Wellingborough Corps	Orderly
FAULKNER, J W	1384	Wellingborough Corps	Orderly
FIELDING, R H	1416	Hebden Bridge Corps	Orderly
FOX, C H	519	Blackpool Division	Orderly
FRANKLIN, H T	1401	St John Ambulance Brigade	Orderly
GREENWOOD, W	1417	Hebden Bridge Corps	Orderly
HARNESS, C H	1379	Hull Corps	Orderly
HELLIWELL, J H	1415	Hebden Bridge Corps	Orderly
HOBSON, C	1402	Doncaster Division	Orderly
HODGSON, J H H	1422	Hebden Bridge Corps	Orderly
INSKIP, T	1425	Birchwood Corps	Orderly
JOHNSON, H	1403	Doncaster Division	Orderly
KITCHEN, A	1421	Hebden Bridge Corps	Orderly
NEEDHAM, W J	1405	Welbeck Division	Orderly
NUNN, R	1385	Haverhill Division	Orderly
PAKES, F	1380	Northampton Corps	Orderly
QUINCEY, Albert S	1381	Wellingborough Corps	Orderly
RICHARDS, J	1397	St John Ambulance Brigade	Orderly
SELLARS, H R	1406	Bradford Corps	Orderly
SMITH, R J	1393	St John Ambulance Brigade	Orderly
STANSFIELD, J W	1409	Dewsbury Corps	Orderly
TAYLOR, R W	1426	Birchwood Corps	Orderly
WALLBANK, T	537	Preston Corps	Orderly
WARREN, W S	1389	Weston-Super-Mare Division	Orderly

As the war progressed other Transport ships were used to carry casualties and those invalided back to England but to what extent these ships were formally converted to undertake this role isn't clear. Some St John Ambulance Brigade men are noted on the medal rolls as being allocated to three of these ships presumably for duties to care for the sick and wounded being repatriated to England.

No	Ship	Tons	Date Built	Owners	SJAB men
42	SS *Formosa*	4045	1892	P&O Steam Navigation Co	9
81	SS *Manhattan*	1892	1891	Liverpool & Great Western Steamship Co	7
93	SS *Montrose*	7094	1897	Elder Dempster & Co	5

SS *Formosa*

On 6 December 1900 eight men were transferred from No 13 Stationary Hospital at Pinetown Bridge for duties aboard SS *Formosa* with one further man following two days later. The men are listed on the Queen's South Africa Medal roll WO100/225/65-66.

Name	SJAB No	Ambulance Division or Corps	Rank
ENGLAND, A	484	Tibshelf Corps	Orderly
HOGG, R	534	Preston Corps	Orderly
HULME, P	491	North Staffs Corps	Orderly
JONES, S H	494	North Staffs Corps	Orderly
JOULE, H	474	Bolton Corps	Orderly
PRICE, John	499	Sheffield Corps	Orderly
ROGERSON, W	533	Preston Corps	Supply Officer
SHARPLES, W	538	Walton-le-Dale Division	Orderly
VENN, Charles H	473	Bolton Corps	Orderly

SS *Manhattan*

On 28 November 1900 seven St John Ambulance Brigade men were transferred from No 14 General Hospital at Newcastle for duties aboard SS *Manhattan*. The men are listed on the Queen's South Africa Medal roll WO100/225/58-60. The ship sailed for England on 6 December 1900 with 240 invalided men aboard, 208 sick and 32 wounded and arrived at Southampton on 4 January 1901. She was later wrecked in Table Bay Cape Town on 15 August 1902.

Name	SJAB No	Ambulance Division or Corps	Rank
ALLETSON, J W	1404	Welbeck Division	Orderly
AUSTIN, E	1398	St John Ambulance Brigade	Orderly
BOWRON, G	1386	Mill Bay Division	Orderly
HUBY, C G	1378	Hull Corps	Orderly
JONES, C W	1387	Mill Bay Division	Orderly
WADSWORTH, J W	1413	Hebden Bridge Corps	Orderly
WHEELHOUSE, G	1420	Hebden Bridge Corps	Orderly

SS *Montrose*

On 8 September five St John Ambulance Brigade men were transferred from No 13 Stationary Hospital at Pinetown Bridge for duties aboard SS *Montrose*. The ship sailed for England on 21 September carrying 500 sick and 124 wounded men and arrived at Southampton on 18 October. The men are listed on the Queen's South Africa Medal roll WO100/225/65-66.

Name	SJAB No	Ambulance Division or Corps	Rank
BARON, J	1054	Bolton Corps	Orderly
HOLDEN, J	1077	Preston Corps	Orderly
HOLMSHAW, W H	1119	Sheffield Corps	Orderly
WALKER, J	943	Clitheroe Division	Orderly
WARD, Ernest	1092	Tibshelf Corps	Orderly

St John Ambulance Brigade Casualties

In total 66 men from the St John Ambulance Brigade died during the conflict, 3.3% of those who volunteered, almost all due to the effects of typhoid which claimed over 8000 lives of military personnel during the course of the war. In most cases the ambulance brigade men would have contracted disease from either contaminated water in the hospital they were working in or through contact with patients suffering from typhoid. There was a particularly severe outbreak at the General Hospitals in Bloemfontein. Between 24 May and 12 June 1900 eight St John Ambulance Brigade men died at No 8 and No 9 General Hospitals and a further six died in the subsequent six weeks. This amounted to over 20% of all the casualties that were to occur amongst the men of the St John Ambulance Brigade during the course of the war.

One of those who succumbed to typhoid was 214 Sergeant Percy PLUMB from No 1 St John Gate Division Metropolitan Corps. He had originally gone to South Africa in January 1900 as part of the 6th contingent to serve on the Princess Christian Hospital Train. Despite developing rheumatic fever during that time, he returned to South Africa to undertake a second tour of duty at No 11 General Hospital Kimberley. Unfortunately, he contracted typhoid and died from this at the hospital on 13 January 1901. His obituary appeared in the *First Aid* Journal in February 1902.

214 Sergeant Percy W. PLUMB Metropolitan Corps who died 13 January 1901
at Kimberley from the effects of typhoid.
(Photo *First Aid* February 1902)

Another very notable casualty was 38 Sergeant William Sidney INDER. A huge debt of gratitude is due to him for meticulously documenting his experiences in both his tours of duty first at No 2 General Hospital Wynberg and subsequently at No 13 General Hospital also based at Wynberg. His account was published posthumously in 1903 in a book entitled *On Active Service with the St John Ambulance Brigade South African War 1899-1902* and gives a great deal of detail not only about his own experiences but those of other members of the St John Ambulance Brigade serving alongside him. At the end of his second tour of duty, by which time he had been appointed a Wardmaster, he joined the Imperial Military Railway in Johannesburg and was sent from there to Bloemfontein. After spending time at Viljoen's Drift he contracted pneumonia from which he died at Bloemfontein on 7 January 1902. His lengthy obituary was published in the *First Aid* Journal in October 1902.

Sergeant William Sidney INDER Kendal Ambulance Division Obituary.
(Photo *First Aid* October 1902)

The table below summarises the details of those known to have died. Many of those who are simply described as having died from disease almost certainly died as a consequence of contracting typhoid.

Name	SJAB No	Ambulance Division or Corps	Place death	Date	Cause
ALDER, George W	814	Clitheroe	Bloemfontein	7/6/1900	Disease
ALEXANDER, Samuel A	313	NFB Ilford	Woodford Essex	1/12/1901	Typhoid
APPLEGATE, David J	791	Rochdale	Bloemfontein	21/6/1900	Disease
BARRETT, J W L	288	GWR	Deelfontein	6/9/1900	Typhoid
BETTLES, Charles R	454	Wellingborough	Bloemfontein	29/6/1900	Disease
BIRTWISTLE, Samuel H	584	Bolton	Cape Town	09/7/1900	Disease
BORER, Henry J	97	Caterham	Bloemfontein	12/6/1900	Typhoid
BROCK, John T	1290	GWR	Johannesburg	3/8/1900	Disease
BROWN, Joseph T	607	Belper	Bloemfontein	6/6/1900	Disease
BUCK, Percy	602	Sheffield	Bloemfontein	4/6/1900	Disease
CLARKSON, S H T	119	Dudley	Orange River Stn	14/5/1900	Disease
CLEMENTS, William	457	Metropolitan	Bloemfontein	24/5/1900	Disease
COOPER, Francis H	348	Leicester	Bloemfontein	3/7/1900	Disease
COX, William	1883	Oldham	Standerton	23/5/1901	Disease
DIXON, William		Bolton	UK	Unknown	Rheumatic Fever
DOE, Bertie	973	Metropolitan	Ladysmith	22/6/1900	Dysentery
ELLIS, Arthur	863	Wellingborough	Johannesburg	22/8/1900	Disease
ERRINGTON, John	1504	Morecombe	Pietermaritzburg	19/12/1900	Typhoid
FARROW, Albert	1762	Northampton	HMT *Pinemore*	17/7/1901	Pneumonia
GIDDENS, Charles	41 (1794)	Metropolitan	Kroonstad	5/5/1901	Disease
GOODWIN, John H	639	Ipswich	Bloemfontein	17/6/1900	Disease
GRACE, Richard	1408	Dewsbury	Newcastle	19/1/1901	Disease
GREEN, George	764	Barnoldswick	Dewetsdorp	1/5/1900	Disease
HARRIS, Thomas	1095	GWR	At Sea	19/7/1900	Heatstroke
HAWKINS, Ernest A	430	Metropolitan	Pretoria	8/1/1901	Disease
HAWORTH, Thomas H	979	Edenfield	Pietermaritzburg	31/7/1900	Typhoid
HEYWOOD, Joseph	340	Oxford	Estcourt	25/8/1900	Brain Abscess
HOLDEN, George E	839	Preston	Bloemfontein	12/6/1900	Disease
HOUGHTON, Edward	195	Walton le Dale	Bloemfontein	17/6/1900	Disease
HUGILL, John W	1043	Nelson	Howick	1/10/1900	Typhoid
INDER, William S	38 (1321)	Kendal	Bloemfontein	7/1/1902	Pneumonia
ION, William W	786	Kendal	Springfontein	13/7/1900	Typhoid
KING, John	1423	Hebden Bridge	Newcastle	30/10/1900	Disease
KNIGHT, William	1201	Leeds	Bloemfontein	27/7/1900	Disease

LANCHBERRY, William E	20	Westgate-on-Sea	Netley UK	15/7/1900	Typhoid
LEADER, Frederick G	721	GER	Wynberg	5/7/1900	Disease
LISTER, Higston	511	Shipley	Pinetown	12/6/1900	Typhoid
MADDOCK, Joseph	544	Warrington	Mafeking	18/1/1901	Disease
MALKIN, John W	148	Warrington	Woodstock	19/3/1900	Disease
MANSHIP, Ernest	1122	Sheffield	Howick	16/9/1900	Typhoid
MARSDEN, Arthur	250	Southport	Bloemfontein	18/4/1900	Disease
MASSEY, Richard	1470	Oldham	Pretoria	2/12/1900	Disease
PEARCE, Charles	563	Birmingham	Bloemfontein	29/5/1900	Disease
PEGLEY, William	114	Metropolitan	London Hospital	25/7/1900	Unknown
PEGRAM, William C	818	GER	Mooi River	11/8/1900	Typhoid
PICKLES, George H	756	Hebden Bridge	Naauwpoort	8/5/1900	Disease
PICKLES, John	758	Hebden Bridge	Senekal	2/7/1900	Typhoid
PLUMB, Percy W	214 (1526)	Metropolitan	Kimberley	13/1/1901	Typhoid
REDHEAD, Edward D	1441	Kendal	Potchefstroom	26/2/1902	Typhoid
RICHARDSON, Wallace R	51	Metropolitan	Wynberg	30/3/1900	Disease
ROBERTSON, Francis	717	GWR	Senekal	17/7/1900	Disease
SAWFORD, John W	133	Wellingborough	Orange River Stn	30/4/1900	Disease
SIDDLE, Fred	1505	Morecombe	Standerton	21/11/1900	Disease
SMITH, F	1461	Oldham	Vet River	5/3/1902	Disease
SMITH, Stanley	761	GWR	Kimberley	13/7/1900	Typhoid
STONIER, Thomas	367	Tunstall	Johannesburg	14/7/1900	Typhoid
TAYLOR, William	1538	Oldham	Standerton	15/5/1901	Disease
THORNBER, William	450	Burnley	Bloemfontein	3/6/1900	Disease
THORNLEY, Oliver	1334	Royston	Wynberg	8/9/1900	Disease
THORNTON, William	1702	Crewe	Elandsfontein	1/3/1901	Disease
WEST-SYMES, Edward B	885 (1582)	Leeds	Wynberg	28/4/1901	Disease
WILLMORE, Charles	303	NFB Hythe	Deelfontein	2/1/1901	Pneumonia
WINDLE, Thomas	693	Clitheroe	Bloemfontein	15/7/1900	Disease
WOODHAM, Albert	131	Wellingborough	Orange River Stn	24/3/1900	Disease

Additionally, two of the men directly recruited to the RAMC in 1901 died during the course of their service.

HESELDEN, William Henry	15890	Heckmondwike & Liversedge	Norval's Pont	6/3/1902	Disease
TURNER, Arthur	16599	Preston	Pretoria	9/5/1902	Disease

There were also two other Fire Brigade men, who were not seconded to the St John Ambulance Brigade, who died during the War.

EDGES, George	NFB Stamford		1902	
SANDERS, George S	NFB Cockington	Cape Town	27/11/1901	Heart Failure

Medals awarded to the St John Ambulance Brigade for service during the South African War

Men from the St John Ambulance Brigade were eligible for up to four medals as a result of their service in South Africa but only a relatively small number received the King's South Africa Medal and even fewer the National Fire Brigade Union Ambulance Division Medal for South Africa. In practice most men received a pair of medals, the Bronze St John Ambulance Brigade Medal for South Africa and the Queen's South Africa Medal.

Bronze St John Ambulance Brigade Medal

A decision to award a specific medal to the men of the St John Ambulance Brigade was made during 1901. An announcement of the decision was published in the *First Aid* Journal in October of that year.

It is announced that the Order of the Hospital of St. John of Jerusalem in England have decided to present a special medal to all the St. John Ambulance Brigade men who have been on active service in South Africa. The medal is to be specially struck, and will be worn with the South African War Medal on the brigade regulation uniform. It will shortly be issued for all who are entitled to receive it. The decision of the Order to recognise the men's services has caused much gratification.

Announcement of the decision to award a special medal to St John Ambulance Brigade men for active service in South Africa. (Photo *First Aid* October 1901)

The number of men who were eligible at the time of the announcement was already substantial and by the end of the War the total reached over 1900.

The medal was 37mm diameter and made only in Bronze. No clasps were awarded with the medal.

Obverse: Uncrowned effigy of King Edward VII.

Reverse: Order of St John arms with South Africa 1899 and 1902. Around the outside is the Latin inscription MAGNU PRIORATUS ORDINIS HOSPITALIS SANCTI JOHANNIS JERUSALEM IN ANGLIA.

This translates as "Grand Priory of the Order of the Hospital of St John of Jerusalem in England".

Suspension: Swivelling straight suspender.

Ribbon: Black with narrow white edge bands.

Naming: Engraved with some variation in the engraving style between different Divisions and Corps. Naming includes the man's number, initials, surname and Division or Corps to which they belonged.

SJAB Bronze Medal Obverse.

SJAB Bronze Medal Reverse.

The medals issued to members of the St John Ambulance Brigade who were also members of Fire Brigades were simply engraved SJAB rather than with the name of the Division or Fire Brigade from which they originated. A smaller batch of 10 medals numbered 1392 to 1401 were also named to St John Ambulance Brigade but the reason for this isn't known.

Queen's South Africa Medal and King's South Africa Medal

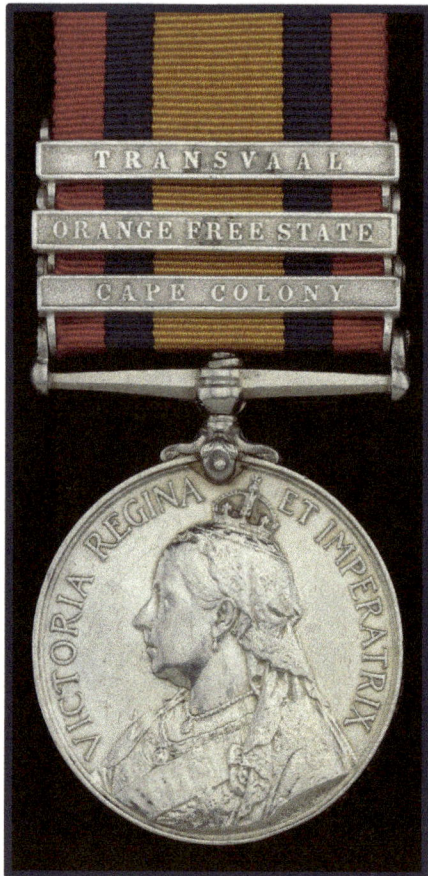

Queen's South Africa Medal Obverse.

King's South Africa Medal Obverse.

Both medals were 36mm in diameter and both produced in silver with no bronze medals being awarded to men from the St John Ambulance Brigade.

Obverse: Jubilee bust of Queen Victoria on the Queen's South Africa Medal and the uncrowned effigy of King Edward VII on the King's South Africa Medal.

Reverse: Britannia holding the flag and a laurel wreath with soldiers and warships in the background with South Africa around the upper part.

Suspension: Swivelling straight suspender.

Ribbon: The Queen's South Africa Medal has a central orange stripe flanked by a narrow blue stripe and red stripe either side. The King's South Africa Medal has three equal stripes of green, white and orange.

Naming: Both medals have impressed naming to the St John Ambulance Brigade or the other units the men were assigned to.

Clasps: Most men received the Cape Colony, Orange Free State, Transvaal or Natal claps with those returning for a second tour of duty often being eligible for one or both of the clasps South Africa 1901 and South Africa 1902. The men's clasp entitlement is included in the medal roll in Appendix I.

National Fire Brigade Union Ambulance Division Medal for South Africa

NFBUAD Medal Obverse.

NFBUAD Medal Reverse.

This special medal was issued by the National Fire Brigade Union to recognise the contribution of their members to the war effort. The medal was 36mm in diameter and produced only in silver.

Obverse: Bust of a helmeted fireman with a Geneva Cross and South Africa 1899 1902 around the edge.

Reverse: Laurel wreath surrounded by the inscription NATIONAL FIRE BRIGADES' UNION AMBULANCE DIVISION.

Suspension: Swivelling straight suspender.

Ribbon: Narrow central red stripe flanked by a white stripe, broader blue stripe and white edges on both sides.

Naming: The recipient's name is engraved in the centre of the wreath on the reverse of the medal.

The image of 771 Joseph WRIGHT clearly shows his group of medals including both the Bronze St John Ambulance Brigade and Queen's South Africa medals awarded to him for his service in South Africa. His other awards are the Territorial Force Efficiency Medal, his Serving Brother badge and the Order of St John Service Medal awarded to him in 1914.

771 Superintendent Joseph WRIGHT Kendal Division.

Naming of Medals to the St John Ambulance Brigade

Bronze Medals

The numbering, rank and naming on the bronze medals issued to the St John Ambulance Brigade men does show a degree of variability in style. This is probably best demonstrated by illustrating a variety of numbers and ranks, names and divisions.

Numbers and ranks

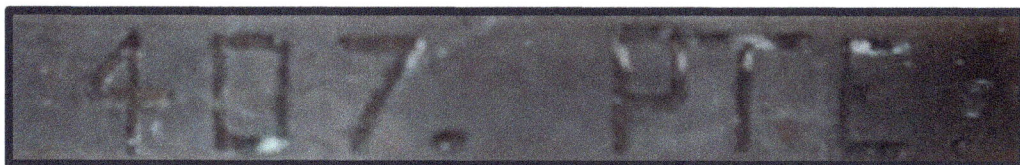

407 Private G. PARKINSON.

430 Private E.A. HAWKINS.

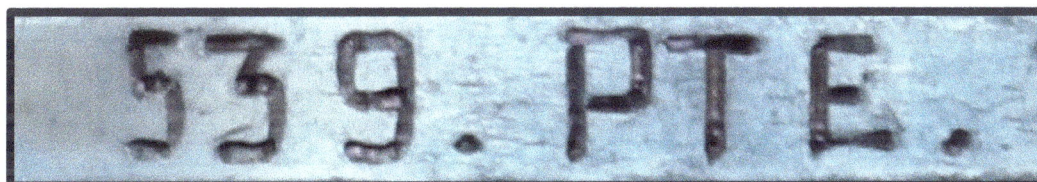

539 Private T. PARKER.

668 Private R. SCOTSON.

999 Private H. RAWSTRON.

1069 Private J.H. PITCHFORD.

1342 Private W. CLARK.

1364 Sergeant F.R. COOPER.

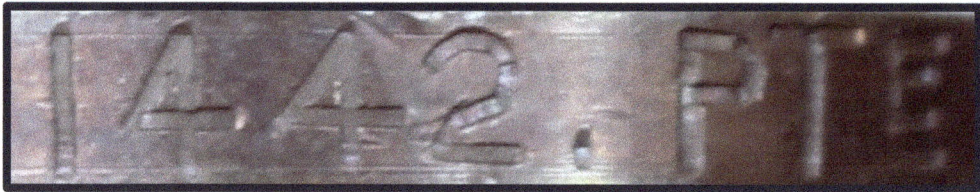

1442 Private H.E. INDER.

1676 Private C.J. RAINBOW.

16546 Private R. ROBERST RAMC.

Chief Surgeon J. B. WILKINSON.

Names

W. CLARK.

F.R. COOPER.

E.A. HAWKINS.

H.E. INDER.

G. PARKINSON.

W. RAWSTRON.

J.B. WILKINSON.

1

Divisions and Corps

Accrington Corps (42 medals to the Corps).

Gateshead Fell Division (4 medals to the Division).

Handsworth & Smethwick Corps (17 medals to the Corps).

Kendal Division (16 medals to the Division).

Kettering Corps (12 medals to the Corps).

Manchester Post Office Division (12 medals to the Division).

Metropolitan Corps (196 medals to the Corps).

Newchurch Division (5 medals to the Division).

Oldham Corps (130 medals to the Corps).

Preston Corps (103 medals to the Corps).

Walton-le-Dale Division (17 medals to the Division).

Welbeck Division (31 medals to the Division).

QSA Medals

The QSA and KSA medals show a much higher degree of consistency in their naming. All the medals appear to be impressed with no engraved medals having been seen. The naming follows the basic principle of the number followed by the rank, the man's initials and name and finally the unit name. Almost all the medals are named to the St John Ambulance Brigade although some men have medals named to other units that they served with in a second or subsequent term of service. The naming St John Ambulance Brigade does vary slightly with the final colon being absent on some medals.

Numbers and Rank

430 Orderly E.A. HAWKINS.

1069 Orderly J.H. PITCHFORD.

1364 Supply Officer F.R. COOPER.

16546 Pte J. ROBERTS RAMC.

Name

H.E. INDER.

J.H. PITCHFORD (W H PITCHFORD on bronze medal).

C.J. RAINBOW.

R. SCOTSON.

Unit

St John Ambulance Brigade (no colon at end of unit name).

St John Ambulance Brigade.

Imperial Yeomanry Bearer Company (12 medals to this unit from the St John Ambulance Brigade).

Medals to the Royal Army Medical Corps

On 11 March 1901 a special army order was made by which members of the St John Ambulance Brigade were invited to volunteer for service under favourable terms, but in their own capacity, as members of the Royal Army Medical Corps. This was made clear in Brigade Order 40 of 10 April 1901. Consequently, the men were directly recruited into the Royal Army Medical Corps and provided with Royal Army Medical Corps service numbers rather than St John Ambulance Brigade recruitment numbers. All the men were enlisted with the rank of private.

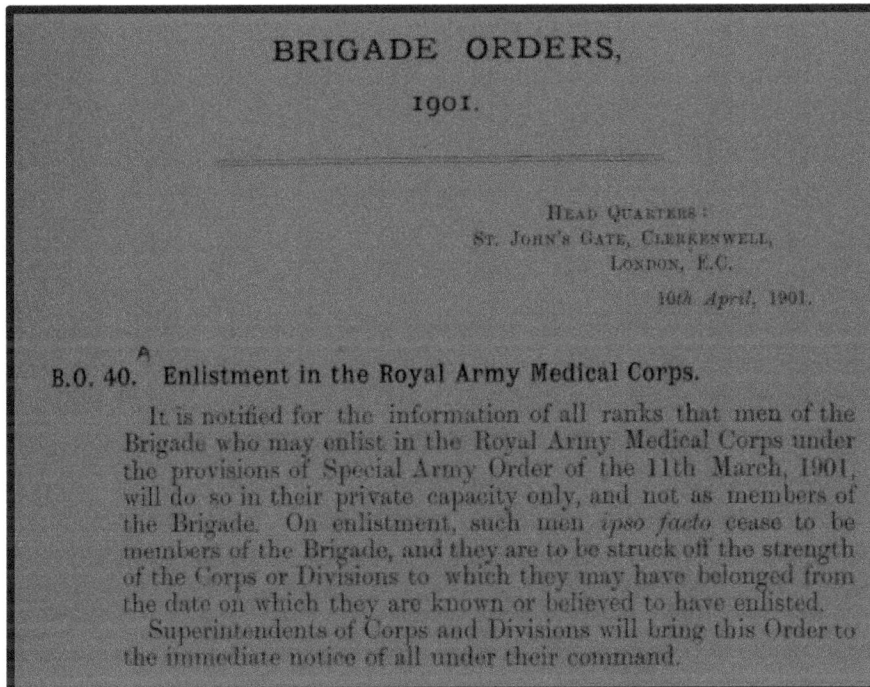

Brigade Order 40 announcing the enlistment of men to the RAMC in a private capacity.

As a result of this recruitment drive the St John Ambulance Brigade Commissioner's annual report for 1901 stated that 112 volunteers had offered their services. In the Bronze medal register of those who were specially recruited, 83 men are listed with service numbers ranging from 15822 to 17677 the vast majority of whom were volunteering for the first time. As is mentioned in the section dealing with the St John Ambulance Brigade Bronze medal register, two recruits appear to have duplicated entries. Private G. EDWARDS, appears on this roll as 16632 but is also present on the main volunteer roll with St John Ambulance Brigade number 1832. Similarly, Private J. JAMES 16603 is present on the main medal roll as St John Ambulance Brigade number 1159 (and subsequently 1869). So, in fact there are 81 unique men recruited for the first time to the RAMC rather than the 83 suggested by the register. The full list of these men is given in Appendix II.

It was Peter Beighton's contention that the difference between the 83 men on the Royal Army Medical Corps register and the 112 recruits recorded in the Brigade Commissioner's report was due to 29 men who were recruited but who had previously completed a tour of duty. However, it appears that the 112 recruits probably are comprised of 81 new recruits and 31 men, including the two men mentioned above, with previous St John Ambulance Service in South Africa re-enlisting. From this group of 31 men, as well as the two men previously mentioned, 11 others have been identified from cross references in the Queen's South Africa Medal roll and they are listed below. Those names marked with an * were also entitled to the King's South Africa Medal because of the duration of their accumulated service in South Africa.

Name	KSA	SJAB Number	RAMC Number
DIXON, Robinson		1040	16704
EDWARDS, George		1832	16632
EVANS, Timothy		605	15974
GREENFIELD, A. H.	*	1138	15792
HAGGAR, William Thomas	*	436	16368
HULSE, W. John	*	1014	15705
JACKSON, George		1163	15869
JOLLY, John	*	524	15653
KENDALL, Joseph		1006	16545
MIDDLETON, Fred		54	16239
WILKINS, A. G.		1503	16487

Pte. T. Evans.

605 Private T. EVANS Sheffield Corps. Later transferred to
RAMC as 15974.

All the men serving directly with the RAMC were entitled to the Queen South Africa Medal. Those men recruited for the first time qualified for the South Africa 1902 clasp but were not entitled to the King's South Africa medal. However, five of the men who were recruited for their second term of duty were eligible for the King's South Africa Medal because of their accumulated service. The medal group to 15792 Private A.H. GREENFIELD RAMC who was one of these five men is illustrated below. His Queen's South Africa Medal is named to the St John Ambulance Brigade and bears his St John Ambulance Brigade number 1138 while his King's South Africa Medal is numbered 15792 RAMC.

Medal trio to Private A.H. GREENFIELD RAMC 15792 and SJAB 1138.

Two of the Royal Army Medical Corps recruits died during the course of their service. 15890 William Henry HESELDEN of Heckmondwike & Liversedge Ambulance Division died of disease at Norval's Point on 6 March 1902 and 16599 Arthur TURNER of Preston Corps died at Pretoria on 9 May 1902.

Medals to the South African Constabulary

Another major unit which actively recruited from the ranks of the St John Ambulance Brigade returning to South Africa for further duty was the South African Constabulary. This was a paramilitary force set up in 1900 to police the two Boer republics of Transvaal and Orange Free State and quickly grew into a large force of well over 10,000 men. Peter Beighton felt that over 50 men joined and of these 21 were eligible because of their accumulated service for the King's South Africa Medal. It has proved possible to definitely identify 58 men who were recruited into the South African Constabulary including the 21 men confirmed as King's South Africa Medal recipients, together with a further two men who possibly served with the Constabulary.

Three of these men were profiled in the *First Aid* Journal at some stage. The first of these was published in April 1901 featuring First Officer John E. HANCOCK of Tunstall Ambulance Division, North Staffordshire Corps. After tragically losing both his wife and only child, he volunteered for service in South Africa as recruit number 446. From January 1900 he served as Wardmaster at the Van Alen American Field Hospital for six months. After his return to England, he joined the South African Constabulary C Division as 1st Class Sergeant C2110 being finally discharged on 5 April 1902. He did not have sufficient accumulated service to qualify for the King's South Africa medal.

446 First Officer John E. HANCOCK Tunstall Ambulance Division North Staffordshire Corps.
(Photo *First Aid* April 1901)

The second profile was of Sergeant Leonard COWIN of No 1 St Johns Gate Division. As recruit number 2, he was a member of the first contingent to travel to South Africa on HS *Princess of Wales*. He completed two terms of service with this ship before re-enlisting with the South African Constabulary E Division as 1st Sergeant E3034. His entry in "Our Portrait Gallery" was published in *First Aid* in October 1901.

Our Portrait Gallery.

SERGT. LEONARD B. COWIN, No. 1 ST. JOHN'S GATE DIVISION, ST. JOHN AMBULANCE BRIGADE, ATTACHED SOUTH AFRICAN CONSTABULARY.

SERGT. LEONARD B. COWIN, whose portrait we present to our readers this month is well known in Metropolitan ambulance circles, where he is a general favourite.

Sergt. Cowin took his first certificate in December of the year 1898, joining the St. John's Gate No. 1 Division in the February of the following year.

When the call for volunteers for service on board the Hospital Ship *Princess of Wales* was made Sergt. Cowin was one of the first to volunteer, and he completed two terms of six months each on board that vessel. On returning to England, the Insurance Company in whose employment he was engaged, promoted him to a higher post in recognition of the service he had rendered to his country. Unfortunately however for our friend, the company shortly afterwards amalgamated with another and larger concern, and Sergt. Cowin assuming that the combination would not materially advance his future prospects, elected to once more volunteer for service in South Africa, and accordingly on the formation of an ambulance contingent for Baden Powell's South African Constabulary, volunteered for the service, and once more proceeded to the front. That he will worthily maintain the reputation of his Corps his friends are thoroughly assured, for he has already been recommended for promotion, and we are sure that his old comrades in this country will wish him the best of health and a prosperous future in the prosecution of the work in which he takes so great an interest.

2 Sergeant Leonard B. COWIN No 1 St Johns Gate Division Metropolitan Corps.
(Photo *First Aid* October 1901)

The profile for Harry GREENWOOD was published in January 1903. A Superintendent in the Dewsbury Corps, he took a drop in rank to First Class Sergeant in order to be able to enlist at a time when more senior officers were prohibited from doing so. He enrolled as number 188 and served as a Supply Officer with 20 Bearer Company serving with Lord Roberts' Column. During that first tour of duty, he was present at the actions at Johannesburg, Diamond Hill and Wittebergen with the company. On completion of his first tour of duty he transferred to the South African Constabulary on 9 February 1901 serving as 1st Sergeant E646 with E Division. He was discharged at the end of his contract on 21 February 1902 with sufficient accumulated service to qualify for the King's South Africa medal.

188 Sergeant Harry GREENWOOD Superintendent in the Dewsbury Corps.
(Photo *First Aid* January 1903)

Medals to members of the Fire Brigades

Over the years there has been considerable uncertainty over the number of men from the fire brigades who served in South Africa but it seems most probable that 48 served and received the National Fire Brigade Union Ambulance Division Medal. Twenty-eight of these men were definitely also awarded the Bronze St John Ambulance Brigade medal as they were also members of the St John Ambulance Brigade. The other 20 men were directly recruited from the fire brigades but did not have any St John affiliation. Therefore, 20 of the men would have been in receipt of the National Fire Brigade Ambulance Division Medal and the Queen's South Africa Medal while the other 28 would additionally have received the Bronze St John Ambulance Brigade Medal.

Medal pair to 320 Private James SAWFORD.

In 46 instances it has been possible to verify the men's Queen's South Africa Medal entitlement but Walter STONE and H.J. GREENFIELD remain unidentified on the Queen's South Africa Medal roll.

The other name causing difficulty is T.W. DOWNING as he is not mentioned by either Peter Jordi or Peter Beighton in their articles about the medal but it does seem probable that he was a member of the 3rd or 4th contingent of recruits.

The National Fire Brigade Union Ambulance Division Medals were presented by the Duchess of Marlborough on 16 July 1903 in the Western Gardens at Earls Court. The event was widely reported including the account of the event in the *London Daily News*:

A very pretty scene was enacted yesterday afternoon in the Western Gardens of the Earl's Court Exhibition, when the Duchess of Marlborough presented the NFBs' Union silver medals to thirty-three ambulance firemen who had served at the IYH, Deelfontein, during the recent South African War. Forty-seven ambulance firemen were entitled to the medal, but fourteen were unable to be present, and their medals were received on their behalf by representatives of their brigades. From inquiries made by our representative it would appear that many of the firemen are really excellent male nurses.

As can be seen the number of 47 medals is mentioned in the account with 33 being personally presented on the day. In fact, by the date of presentation, four men had died Samuel ALEXANDER, George EDGES, George SAUNDERS and Charles WILLMORE. However overall, it seems likely that 44 medals were issued directly to the recipients either in person or sent to them and the four medals to those deceased were sent to their relatives. However, a degree of uncertainty still remains over the exact number of medals issued. The details of all those believed to have received the NFB Ambulance Division Medal are listed in Appendix VII.

In addition to the four men noted above who died during the war, one of the other recipients Harold HERN died on 28 September 1907 at the relatively young age of 29 but it is not believed his death was related to his previous service in South Africa.

The Firemen's Queen's South Africa Medals had been presented earlier to around half of the men at a ceremony the previous year by HM Queen Alexandra at Devonshire House on 11 August 1902.

AMBULANCE-FIREMEN WHO RECEIVED THEIR WAR MEDALS FROM THE HANDS OF HER MAJESTY THE QUEEN, AUGUST 11th, 1902.

Firemen awarded the Queen's South Africa Medal 11 August 1902.
(Photo *First Aid* August 1902)

The Register Book for the Bronze St John Ambulance Brigade Medal for South Africa

The record of the Bronze St John Ambulance Brigade medals issued for service in South Africa is contained in a register held by the archive of the Order of St John in Clerkenwell London.

The register is in four sections. The most significant part of the register records the medals issued to the main body of volunteers. There is a smaller subsection for those who were recruited on favourable terms into the Royal Army Medical Corps in 1901. In addition, there are is a separate list of those who had a particular role in recruiting and training members for service in South Africa and finally a record of the 15 senior members of the Order of St John at the time of the war.

All the entries are made in a very neat and readable cursive style. The degree of accuracy in the register overall appears good but where there are minor errors which have been detected these are noted in the detailed medal rolls in Appendices I to IV. Each of the four sections of the register have been kept separate for clarity rather than incorporating them into one overall list.

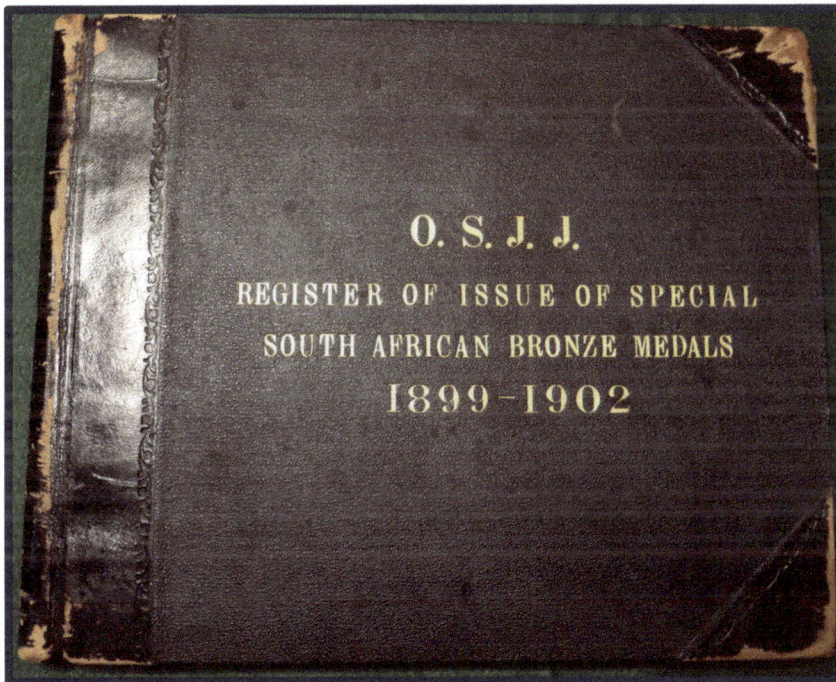

Register of the Bronze St John Ambulance Brigade Medals.

Page number 11 in the register is a typical page in the register demonstrating the style of the entries and the information recorded.

Register page number 11 containing recruit numbers 188 to 207.

The first column provides the recruit number which is the number to be found engraved on the individual medals and is the number the men were allocated when they first reported for duty. These numbers generally run sequentially over the first few hundred entries with a few notable gaps but as the numbers reach above 1500 the apparent gaps in the number sequence increase. In many cases the numbers were allocated to men reporting for their second tour of duty so they were already included in the Bronze medal register and not included a second time. In other cases, there may have been men who did not eventually see service in South Africa because of the cessation of hostilities. The highest number recorded is 1942 Private S. NEWELL of Wellingborough Corps.

Register page for the last recipients of the Bronze St John Ambulance Brigade Medal.

The second column gives the rank the man held when recruited for service in South Africa. In a small number of instances this was a rank considerably lower than the rank they held in their Division. The reason for this is, that at the time they volunteered, more senior members of the organisation were barred from going to South Africa, so they accepted a reduction in rank in order to be eligible to serve.

The third column lists the surname and initials of the men. The recorded names appear to be extremely accurate with only the occasional inconsistencies in the initials recorded or minor spelling variations in the surname when compared to the Queen's and King's South Africa Medal rolls.

The fourth column provides the name of the Division or Corps the man originated from. This can prove useful when trying to identify the person when only the surname and initials are available. In the case of 28 fire brigade members who were also St John Ambulance Brigade members, only SJAB is engraved on their medals with no reference to the fire brigade they were recruited from. In the medal register their entries are simply annotated St John Ambulance Brigade. The other 20 men who were fire brigade members, but not St John Ambulance Brigade members, who served during the war were ineligible for the Bronze St John Ambulance Brigade Medal. The numbers on these medals are 302-327, 337, 338 and 456.

Register page for numbers 289 to 310 including several named to St John Ambulance Brigade.

There is a further batch of medals similarly named SJAB numbered 1392 to 1401 and 1558. Some of these men were assigned to the Hospital Ship *Simla* but the reason why these medals do not include the Ambulance Division the men were from is not known.

There is a final column headed date of issue but there are no dates indicated for any of the medals. In total 1768 entries are present in the register in this main listing of recipients.

There is a particular problem over two entries to men named COOPER from Preston Corps with numbers 35 and 1364. The entry for the man numbered 35 has the initials F.R. as do all the Queen's South Africa Medal roll entries relating to both service numbers. The Bronze Medal Register entry for 1364 is T.R. COOPER which is likely to be a clerical error with his first initial in fact being F. rather than T. It is possible that there are two men with exactly the same surname and initials from the same Corps but it is also possible that these are one and the same man who was initially allocated number 35 but then re-joined with the service number 1364 for a second tour of duty. Unfortunately, it hasn't been possible to ascertain with certainty whether both numbers were allocated to the same man as none of the Queen's South Africa Medal roll entries have both numbers associated with the entry, but it is known that there are two Queen's South Africa Medals to F.R. Cooper one with number 35 and the other 1364. In view of the uncertainty the entries under the two numbers have been kept separate.

The following section is headed:

The following members of the St John Ambulance Brigade specially enlisted in the Royal Army Medical Corps were also the Order of St John Special South African Bronze Medal and passed by the Finance General Services Committee.

The entries that follow all contain similar details to those in the previous list except the numbers are their RAMC numbers and it is this number that appears on their medals. The numbers run irregularly from 15822 to 17617. All the men recruited held the rank of Private.

Register page for RAMC men who were recipients of the
Bronze St John Ambulance Brigade Medal.

There is a particular issue with the entries for J.D. BROUGHTON and A. BRIERLEY on page 91 of the register. The number issued to Private BROUGHTON, as derived from his Queen's South Africa Medal roll entry, is in fact 15893 rather than 15875 as indicated in the Bronze Medal register. The entry for Private BRIERLEY has no number whereas in fact his number in the Queen's South Africa Medal roll is 15875. Also, the entries for A. MELLOR and G. MELLOR appear to be transposed with their correct numbers being 15833 and 15832 respectively. Otherwise, the register entries appear to be accurate although in a number of instances it hasn't proved possible to identify the men's Queen's South Africa Medal entitlement.

Register page for RAMC men numbered 15866 to 15972 including numbering anomalies.

The last two entries on the list have a cross beside them. One of the two men, Private G EDWARDS 16632 from Ironbridge Corps also appears on the main volunteer list with number 1832. Whether this actually resulted in a double issue of the bronze medal is unknown but it certainly represents at least a clerical error. The other name, Private J. JAMES 16603 from Hull Corps is more problematical. There is a Private J. JAMES in the main volunteer list with SJAB numbers 1159 and 1869 and he is confirmed as being the same man as has the RAMC number 16603 in WO100/225/27. However, his main listing in the volunteer part of the register has his unit as Leeds Corps while the RAMC register has his unit as Hull Corps. Therefore, either this is a simple clerical error or the man moved from Leeds to Hull before his RAMC service commenced in 1901. Thus, the number of unique men on the RAMC register appears in fact to be 81 rather than the 83 names listed.

Register entries to men duplicated on the RAMC list of recipients.

The third section of the register lists the 39 men and one woman who were awarded the medal in recognition of their role in preparing the men for their service in South Africa prior to their embarcation. Many of the men were medially qualified holding the rank of Honorary Surgeon while others were Chief Superintendents within their Corps or held a senior position in their district. Six of the recipients were men of lower rank but the particular reason for their awards is not known. Because these 39 men and one woman did not themselves proceed to South Africa, they were not entitled to the Queen's South Africa Medal.

Register page giving details of Senior Trainers.

The fourth and shortest section in the register actually appears at the start of the register. It details the 15 leading members of the Order of St John at the time of the war who were awarded the medal. Again, they did not themselves travel to South Africa and were not entitled to the Queen's South Africa Medal. The list includes the only other female recipient of the medal, The Viscountess Knutsford, the wife of The Viscount Knutsford, the Director and Chairman of the Ambulance Department.

Register page containing details of the 15 notable recipients of the
St John Ambulance Brigade Bronze Medal.

Analysis of the Medal awards to the St John Ambulance

From the full roll of the various medals awarded to the St John Ambulance it is possible to analyse the awards that were made in various ways.

Bronze St John Ambulance Brigade Medal

The Bronze awards were made to three main groups, the main body of volunteers totalling 1768, the 83 men on the list of those directly recruited to the Royal Army Medical Corps who were believed hadn't seen prior service (although two of the men listed may in fact be duplicated in the main volunteer roll) and the 40 men who helped to prepare the volunteers for their overseas service. In addition, were the 15 awards made to the leadership of the St John Ambulance Brigade at the time of the war. This gives an overall total of 1906 including the possibly duplicated awards on the RAMC register. In addition, there are seven men, six who served at the Portland Hospital and one at The Langman Hospital, who should have been eligible for the Bronze award and for whom there would be corresponding number gaps in the Bronze Medal Register sequence but whose names are not included in the register. Also, there are two men, 212 (1704) L. WOOD and 1694 J. JACKSON, who have QSA Medal roll entries but are not present on the St John Ambulance Brigade Bronze Medal roll. The breakdown of these awards by Ambulance Divisions and Corps is given below

Ambulance Division Corp or District	Main Roll	RAMC	Seniors	Total
Abram Colliery Division	4			4
Accrington Corps	39	2	1	42
Adlington & Heath Charnock Division	1			1
Adlington Division	1			1
Babbington Corps	2			2
Bacup Division	7			7
Barnoldswick Division	22	5		27
Barrowford Division	11			11
Bath City Division	1			1
Bedford Division	2	2		4
Belfast Division	1			1
Belper Division	5			5
Birchwood Corps	8			8
Birmingham Corps	40		1	41
Blackpool Division	30	2	2	34
Bolton Corps	106	2	3	111
Boughton Division		1		1
Bradford Corps	26			26
Brierfield Division	6			6
Bristol Corps	2			2
Brynmawr Division	4			4
Burnley Division	10	1		11
Bury Division	21			21

Caterham Division	2			2
Christchurch Division	1			1
Clitheroe Division	13	1		14
Colne Division	19	1		20
Crawshawbooth Division	1			1
Crewe Division	6	1		7
Dalton-in-Furness Division	6			6
Denaby Cadeby Main Division	4			4
Denaby Main Division	1			1
Derby Corps	6		1	7
Derby Division	29	1		30
Desborough Division	3			3
Dewsbury Corps	28			28
Doncaster Division	2			2
Dover Division	2			2
Dowlais Division	5			5
Dudley Corps	9			9
Ebbw Vale Division	3			3
Edenfield Division	12			12
Faversham Division	2			2
Foulridge Division	3			3
Gainsborough Division	1			1
Gateshead Fell Division	3	1		4
Great Eastern Railway Corps	15			15
Great Western Railway	1			1
Halifax Division	1			1
Hallaton Division	2			2
Handsworth & Smethwick Corps	16		1	17
Hapton Division	3			3
Haslingden Corps	23		1	24
Haverhill Division	3			3
Hazelgrove Division	5			5
Heanor Division	9			9
Hebden Bridge Corps	34			34
Heckmondwike & Liversedge Division		2		2
Herne Bay Division	5			5
Heywood Division	5			5
Hull Corps	29	2		31
Ilkeston Corps	11			11
Ipswich Corps	4			4
Ironbridge Corps	10	5	1	16

Isle of Wight Corps	13			13
Keighley Corps	6	1		7
Kendal Division	16			16
Keswick Division	3			3
Kettering Corps	10	1	1	12
Leeds Corps	62	9	1	72
Leicester Corps	50	1	2	53
Lincoln Adult School Division	4			4
Madeley Division	2			2
Manchester Post Office Division	12			12
Market Harborough Division	4			4
Medbourne Division	3			3
Metropolitan Corps	191	5		196
Mill Bay Division	8			8
Millom Iron Works Division		4		4
Morecombe Division	12			12
Nelson Corps	30			30
New Farnley Division	4			4
Newchurch Division	5			5
Newton Abbott Division	2	1		3
Newtown Division	1			1
No I District			12	12
No II District Staff	1		1	2
No III District			2	2
No IV District			1	1
No V District			1	1
North Staffs Corps	23			23
Northampton Corps	34			34
Nuneaton Division	11		1	12
Oldham Corps	128		2	130
Olney Division	1			1
Oundle Division	1			1
Oxford Division	5			5
Oystermouth Division	3			3
Padiham Division	15			15
Penrith Division	4			4
Portsmouth Division	3			3
Preston Corps	85	16	2	103
Radcliffe Division	13			13
Ramsgate Corps	5			5
Rawtenstall Corps	2			2
Reading Division	9	1		10

Redruth Division	5			5
Rishton Division	12			12
Rochdale Corps	19			19
Royton Division	6			6
Rushton Division	1			1
Sheffield Corps	43		1	44
Shipley Corps	5			5
Southport Division	4			4
St John Ambulance Brigade	36			36
Swindon Division	3	1		4
Tibshelf Corps	14			14
Tottington Division	5			5
Walton-le-Dale Division	16	1		17
Walton-le-Dale Nursing Division			1	1
Warrington Corps	13	6		19
Welbeck Division	31			31
Wellingborough Corps	47		1	48
Westgate-on-Sea Division	2			2
Weston-Super-Mare Division	4			4
Whaley Bridge Division	10	4		14
Whalley Division	6			6
Winsford Division	2			2
Withernsea Division	6	1		7
Woking Division		1		1
Worksop Division	11	1		12
Totals	1768	83	40	1891

There is no evidence that the Bronze St John Ambulance Medal was awarded to the eight Local South African members of the St John Ambulance Brigade who are present on the Queen's South Africa Medal roll.

Queen's South Africa Medal

All the men who served in South Africa should have been eligible for the Queen's South Africa medal. The number of medals definitely identified together with the different numbers of clasps are summarised for both the main volunteer body and the RAMC recruits.

Clasp Number	Main Roll	RAMC	Total
None	151	0	151
1	653	7	660
2	551	31	582
3	301	25	326
4	80	9	89
5	27	6	33
6	3	0	3
7	0	0	0
8	0	0	0
QSA Total	1766	78	1844

Similarly, it is possible to record the numbers of each clasp type awarded to these men

Clasp	Main Roll	RAMC	Total
CC	1245	48	1293
OFS	764	21	785
TVL	414	27	441
NAT	349	0	349
SA01	217	39	254
SA02	51	77	128
KSA01	42	0	42
KSA02	43	0	43
JOH	16	0	16
DIAM	13	0	13
BELF	3	0	3
WITT	58	0	58
RoK	1	0	1
RHOD	1	0	1
TOTAL	3217	210	3427

Approximately 660 awards were made with a single clasp and these are summarised below.

Clasp	Main Roll	RAMC	Total
CC	367	0	367
OFS	2	0	2
TVL	48	0	48
NAT	260	0	260
SA01	9	0	9
SA02	0	6	6
TOTAL	653	7	660

In addition, eight local South African men were awarded the Queen's South Africa Medal. Six of the men received the Belmont clasp, six (but not the same six) the clasps for Orange Free State and Transvaal and one the clasp for Cape Colony. One also received the King's South Africa Medal.

Name	Rank	Clasps	QSA Reference	Service
ABBOTT, A E	Private	BELM	WO100/225/78	Base Hospital Wynberg
BARTON, J G	Orderly	OFS TVL BELM	WO100/225/61	Base Hospital Wynberg
BECKLEY, E	Private	BELM	WO100/225/78	Base Hospital Wynberg
GAUNT, J F	Orderly	OFS TVL KSA01 KSA02	WO100/225/62 WO100/352/18	Base Hospital Wynberg KSA roll J.A. GAUNT
KING, R	Orderly	OFS TVL BELM	WO100/225/63	Base Hospital Wynberg No 2 Ambulance Train
LEITH, G	Orderly	CC OFS TVL	WO100/225/63	Base Hospital Wynberg
LENNIE, G	Orderly	OFS TVL BELM	WO100/225/63	Base Hospital Wynberg
SYMINGTON, P	Orderly	OFS TVL BELM	WO100/225/64	Base Hospital Wynberg

There are a few instances in which a double issue of the Queen's South Africa Medal is known to have occurred. Four of these are listed below but it seems likely that other second issues of the Queen's South Africa Medal may have been made when men re-enlisted having completed their first period of service. The clasps seen with the medal are listed with the men's actual entitlement where known noted in brackets.

Name	1st Issue	Unit and No	2nd Issue	Unit and No
INDER, Henry E	OFS TVL NTL	SJAB 1442	CC OFS TVL SA01	Scottish Horse 25839
JACKSON, George	NO CLASP (CC OFS)	SJAB 1163	CC OFS TVL SA01 SA02 (CC SA02)	RAMC 15869
KENDALL, Joseph	NAT	SJAB 1006	SA01 SA02	RAMC 16545
MURRAY, G	OFS TVL (OFS TVL)	SJAB 1677	OFS TVL SA01	SJAB 1677

King's South Africa Medal

Forty-five men from the St John Ambulance Brigade have been identified as being eligible for the award of the King's South Africa Medal, most involving their further service with other units in the latter part of the war. This includes one local South African member of the St John Ambulance Brigade. Their awards were with the following units.

Unit when KSA awarded	Number of KSA medals awarded
Cape Medical Staff Corps	1
Imperial Hospital Corps	1
Imperial Yeomanry	1
Imperial Yeomanry Hospital	4
Natal Volunteer Composite Regiment	1
Royal Army Medical Corps	5
1st Scottish Horse	1
St John Ambulance Brigade	9
St John Ambulance Brigade (Local)	1
South African Constabulary	21
Total	45

The King's South Africa medals were awarded to men from the following Divisions and Corps.

Division or Corp	Number awarded
Barnoldswick Division	1
Barrowford Division	1
Birmingham Corps	2
Blackpool Division	1
Bolton Corps	1
Bradford Corps	1
Burnley Division	1
Derby Corps	2
Dewsbury Corps	1
Handsworth & Smethwick Corps	1
Isle of Wight Corps	1
Kendal Division	3
Kettering Corps	1
Leicester Corps	1
Metropolitan Corps	9
North Staffs Corps	1
Oldham Corps	3
Preston Corps	3
Sheffield Corps	1

St John Ambulance Brigade	1
St John Ambulance Brigade (Local)	1
St John Ambulance Brigade (NFB Haywards Heath)	1
Tottington Division	1
Warrington Corps	1
Welbeck Division	1
Wellingborough Corps	2
Weston-Super-Mare Division	1
Worksop Division	1
Total	45

Details of all the St John Ambulance Brigade men who were awarded the King's South Africa Medal are listed in Appendix V.

Appendix I

Main Volunteer Medal Roll

The main body of volunteers on the Bronze St John Ambulance Brigade Medal roll total 1768 and they are listed below. All the recipients were male all coming from Ambulance Divisions and Corps. Where it has been possible to elucidate the men's forenames these are included rather than just the initials that appear in the medal register. As mentioned before there are seven men, six who served at the Portland Hospital and one at The Langman Hospital, who should have been eligible for the Bronze award and for whom there would be corresponding number gaps in the Bronze Medal Register sequence but whose names are not present in the register. Also, there are two men, 212 (1704) L. WOOD and 1694 J. JACKSON, who have Queen's South Africa Medal roll entries but are not present on the St John Ambulance Brigade Bronze Medal roll.

There are instances of two entries to men of the same surname, initials and Ambulance Division or Corps but with differing numbers. It is possible that in some instances these entries relate to the same man but where confirmation of this has not proved possible both entries have been retained.

A number of men were entitled to both the Cape Colony and Natal clasps and in this situation normally only the Cape Colony clasp would have been issued. However, where both clasps are mentioned in the rolls, both have been noted against the man's entry as it is clear that in a small number of cases a double issue of the Queen's South Africa Medal resulted from men's multiple periods of service with both clasps being issued.

The Queen's South Africa Medal rolls give an indication of where men served. Where there are entries on a number of different Queen's South Africa Medal rolls for an individual, it can on occasions be difficult to ascertain the correct order in which men's placements occurred. However, every attempt has been made to ensure the placements are listed in chronological order. Not all the medal roll entries in 68/AMC/301, which are part of WO100/225, have been included, but only those giving unique or additional information. This was to avoid including a considerable number of medal roll references giving only duplicated information.

ABBOTT, J. Private 205 Wellingborough Corps Medal Clasps: NAT.
Medal Roll Reference: WO100/225/75 Orderly Princess Christian Hospital Train.
ABBOTT, L. Private 578 Oldham Corps Medal Clasps: CC OFS TVL.
Medal Roll Reference: WO100/225/196 Orderly 24 Field Hospital. To Base invalided 8 September 1900.
ABLEWHITE, H. 1st Class Sergeant 509 Shipley Corps Medal Clasps: NAT.
Medal Roll Reference: WO100/225/65 Supply Officer 13 Stationary Hospital. To HS *Dunera* 18 December 1900.
ACKERLEY, A. W. Private 1412 Hebden Bridge Corps Medal Clasps: No Clasps.
Medal Roll Reference: WO100/225/58 Orderly 14 General Hospital. To HS *Simla* for duty 14 November 1900.
ADAMS, C. W. Private 460 Metropolitan Corps Medal Clasps: CC OFS.
Medal Roll Reference: WO100/225/133 Orderly 8 General Hospital. To England 20 July 1900.
ADAMS, G. D. Private 369 Kettering Corps Medal Clasps: NAT.
Medal Roll Reference: WO100/225/128 Orderly 7 General Hospital. To England time expired.
ADAMS, J. T. Private 1026 Oldham Corps Medal Clasps: NAT.
Medal Roll Reference: WO100/225/65 Orderly 13 Stationary Hospital. To HS *Dunera* 18 December 1900.

ADCROFT, A. Private 1374 Preston Corps Medal Clasps: CC.
Medal Roll Reference: WO100/225/157 Orderly 13 General Hospital. To England expired contract 27 January 1901.
AFFLECK, F. H. Private 1327 Metropolitan Corps Medal Clasps: CC OFS TVL KSA01 KSA02.
Medal Roll Reference: WO100/225/157+200+WO100/352/15 Orderly 13 General Hospital. To Pretoria 18 December 1900 7 Bearer Company 14 Brigade 7th Division.
AINGE, A. Private 379 Birmingham Corps Medal Clasps: CC.
Medal Roll Reference: WO100/130/217 Sergeant Imperial Yeomanry Hospital Deelfontein.
AINSWORTH, G. Private 1302 Preston Corps Medal Clasps: CC TVL.
Medal Roll Reference: WO100/224/172 Private Rhodesian Field Force Hospital.
AINSWORTH, W. Sergeant 1258 Rishton Division Medal Clasps: CC OFS.
Medal Roll Reference: WO100/225/138 Supply Officer 9 General Hospital. To Base Detail 12 October 1900.
ALDER, George W. Private 814 Clitheroe Division Medal Clasps: CC OFS.
Medal Roll Reference: WO100/225/138 Orderly 9 General Hospital. Died of disease Bloemfontein 7 June 1900.
ALEXANDER, Samuel Alfred Private 313 St John Ambulance Brigade (NFB Ilford) Medal Clasps: CC SA01. NFBUAD Medal.
Medal Roll Reference: WO100/130/217+252 Sergeant Imperial Yeomanry Hospital Deelfontein. Died 1 December 1901 at Woodford, Essex due to complications from typhoid.
ALLEN, H. W. Private 983 Crewe Division Medal Clasps: NAT.
Medal Roll Reference: WO100/225/161 Orderly 15 General Hospital. Transferred to HS *Nubia* 29 December 1900.
ALLEN, J. E. Private 1886 Blackpool Division Medal Clasps: CC.
Medal Roll Reference: WO100/225/54+107 Orderly 11 General Hospital. 1 General Hospital. To England on termination of engagement.
ALLERTSON, H. Private 1603 Welbeck Division Medal Clasps: CC OFS TVL.
Medal Roll Reference: WO100/225/157 Orderly 13 General Hospital. To England expired contract 10 April 1901.
ALLETSON, J. W. Private 1404 Welbeck Division Medal Clasps: No Clasps.
Medal Roll Reference: WO100/225/58 Orderly 14 General Hospital. To SS *Manhattan* for duty 28 November 1900.
ANDERSON, W. Private 489 Leicester Corps Medal Clasps: CC OFS.
Medal Roll Reference: WO100/225/61+138 Orderly Base Hospital Wynberg 9 General Hospital. To Base Detail 5 February 1901.
ANDREWS, W. Private 1853 Leicester Corps Medal Clasps: CC OFS SA01.
Medal Roll Reference: WO100/225/86+114 Orderly 3 General Hospital. Transferred to Base Detail RAMC. Home 9 July 1901.
ANNABLE, W. Private 741 Heanor Division Medal Clasps: CC WITT.
Medal Roll Reference: WO100/225/192 Orderly Attached 21 Field Hospital. Discharged.
ANTHONY, R. E. Private 72 Derby Corps Medal Clasps: CC OFS.
Medal Roll Reference: WO100/225/114 Orderly 3 General Hospital. Transferred to Base Detail RAMC.
APPLEGATE, David J. Private 791 Rochdale Corps Medal Clasps: CC OFS.
Medal Roll Reference: WO100/225/133 Orderly 8 General Hospital. Died of disease Bloemfontein 21 June 1900.
APPLETON, J. G. Private 459 Metropolitan Corps Medal Clasps: CC OFS.
Medal Roll Reference: WO100/225/61+133 Orderly Base Hospital Wynberg. 8 General Hospital. To England 23 January 1901.

ARCHER, G. E. W. Private 1116 Sheffield Corps Medal Clasps: NAT.
Medal Roll Reference: WO100/225/118 Orderly 4 General Hospital. Sent to England time expired 9 September 1900.
ARCHER, H. Private 663 Medbourne Division Medal Clasps: CC WITT.
Medal Roll Reference: WO100/225/203 Orderly 21 Bearer Company. Sent home for discharge August 1900.
ARSCOTT, F. Private 1001 Mill Bay Division Medal Clasps: NAT.
Medal Roll Reference: WO100/225/161 Orderly 15 General Hospital. Transferred to England 26 August 1900. E Division South African Constabulary
ASH, J. Private 420 Metropolitan Corps Medal Clasps: CC OFS.
Medal Roll Reference: WO100/225/133 Orderly 8 General Hospital. To England 23 January 1901.
ASHBY, J. Private 719 Great Eastern Railway Corps Medal Clasps: CC SA01.
Medal Roll Reference: WO100/225/54+83 Orderly 11 General Hospital. To England on termination of engagement.
ASHCROFT, W. Private 1351 Bolton Corps Medal Clasps: CC.
Medal Roll Reference: WO100/225/157 Orderly 13 General Hospital. To England expired contract 27 January 1901.
ASHMAN, A. Private 45 Metropolitan Corps Medal Clasps: CC OFS.
Medal Roll Reference: WO100/225/114 Orderly 3 General Hospital. Transferred to Base Detail RAMC.
ASHWORTH, C. S. 1st Class Sergeant 187 Blackpool Division Medal Clasps: CC OFS.
Medal Roll Reference: WO100/225/176 Supply Officer 5 Stationary Hospital. Sent to Base for England for discharge.
ASHWORTH, T. Private 1451 Accrington Corps Medal Clasps: No Clasps.
Medal Roll Reference: WO100/225/118 Orderly 4 General Hospital. Sent to England time expired 28 November 1900.
ASHWORTH, W. Private 1296 Blackpool Division Medal Clasps: CC TVL.
Medal Roll Reference: WO100/224/172 Sergeant Rhodesian Field Force Hospital.
ASHWORTH, W. Private 1419 Hebden Bridge Corps Medal Clasps: No Clasps.
Medal Roll Reference: WO100/225/58 Orderly 14 General Hospital. To HS *Simla* for duty 14 November 1900.
ASPDEN, J. Private 1445 Accrington Corps Medal Clasps: No Clasps.
Medal Roll Reference: WO100/225/118 Orderly 4 General Hospital Sent to England time expired 28 November 1900.
ASPDEN, W. Private 1259 Rishton Division Medal Clasps: CC OFS.
Medal Roll Reference: WO100/225/154 Orderly 10 General Hospital. To Base 10 October 1900.
ASPIN, D. C. Private 1568 Accrington Corps Medal Clasps: CC.
Medal Roll Reference: WO100/225/107+157 Orderly 13 General Hospital. To 1 General Hospital Base Hospital Wynberg 1 August 1900.
ASPINALL, E. Private 1058 Bolton Corps Medal Clasps: NAT.
Medal Roll Reference: WO100/225/180 Orderly 14 Stationary Hospital.
ASTON, G. H. Private 965 Dudley Corps Medal Clasps: NAT.
Medal Roll Reference: WO100/225/161 Orderly 15 General Hospital Invalided to England 26 August 1900.
ATKINS, A. Private 397 Wellingborough Corps Medal Clasps: NAT.
Medal Roll Reference: WO100/225/130 Orderly 7 General Hospital. To England time expired.
ATKINSON, W. H. Private 1689 Halifax Division Medal Clasps: CC OFS TVL.
Medal Roll Reference: WO100/225/187 Orderly 18 Brigade Field Hospital. Joined 20 March 1901. Left 30 May 1901 for discharge.
AUSTIN, E. Private 1398 St John Ambulance Brigade Medal Clasps: CC OFS TVL SA01 SA02 KSA01 KSA02.

Medal Roll Reference: WO100/225/58 WO100/271/66+168 WO100/366/23 Orderly 14 General Hospital. To SS *Manhattan* for duty 28 November 1900 South African Constabulary A Division Trooper 517. Served St John Ambulance Brigade 7 November 1899 to 9 March 1901 and South African Constabulary from 9 March 1901 to 26 May 1903.

AUTON, A. H. Private 1707 Bradford Corps Medal Clasps: CC OFS TVL.
Medal Roll Reference: WO100/225/50+201 Orderly 9 Bearer Company 4 Brigade. Earned claps while travelling from Base Depot RAMC to join this unit. Transferred to England for discharge.

AYTO, T. Private 154 Worksop Division Medal Clasps: CC OFS TVL.
Medal Roll Reference: WO100/225/61+70 Orderly Base Hospital Wynberg. 3 Hospital Train. To Base Detail RAMC Cape Town for England.

BAGLEY, W. Private 908 Derby Division Medal Clasps: NAT.
Medal Roll Reference: WO100/225/161 Orderly 15 General Hospital. Transferred to HS *Nubia* 29 December 1900.

BAGSHAW, Samuel Sergeant 1264 Whaley Bridge Division Medal Clasps: CC OFS TVL.
Medal Roll Reference: WO100/225/125 Supernumerary Officer 6 General Hospital. To Base on expiration of contract 22 October 1900.

BAKER, Cecil W. Sergeant Major 555 Metropolitan Corps Medal Clasps: CC OFS TVL.
Medal Roll Reference: WO100/225/113+230 Supply Officer 2 General Hospital. Langman Hospital. From England 18 December 1899. To Cape Town for England 15 October 1900.

BAKER, E. Private 1233 Colne Division Medal Clasps: CC.
Medal Roll Reference: WO100/225/122 Orderly 5 General Hospital.

BAKER, F. W. S. 1st Class Sergeant 135 Preston Corps Medal Clasps: CC SA01.
Medal Roll Reference: WO100/225/107 Supply Officer 1 General Hospital.

BAKER, J. L. Private 388 Birmingham Corps Medal Clasps: CC.
Medal Roll Reference: WO100/130/218 Private Imperial Yeomanry Hospital Deelfontein.

BAKER, S. H. Private 893 Metropolitan Corps Medal Clasps: NAT.
Medal Roll Reference: WO100/225/161 Orderly 15 General Hospital Invalided to England 26 August 1900.

BALDWIN, E. Private 588 Colne Division Medal Clasps: CC.
Medal Roll Reference: WO100/225/9+122 Orderly 5 General Hospital.

BALDWIN, Edward Henry Private 225 Barnoldswick Division Medal Clasps: CC.
Medal Roll Reference: WO100/225/125 Private 6 General Hospital. To Base on expiration of contract 18 June 1900.

BALDWIN, J. W. Private 332 Barnoldswick Division Medal Clasps: CC.
Medal Roll Reference: WO100/130/218 Private Imperial Yeomanry Hospital Deelfontein.

BALDWIN, P. Private 1673 Birmingham Corps (Birmingham City Division) Medal Clasps: CC OFS TVL SA01.
Medal Roll Reference: WO100/225/89+170 Orderly 20 General Hospital Joined from Base Detail. Time expired 3 July 1901. To England for discharge.

BALL, H. Private 1617 Ironbridge Corps Medal Clasps: CC.
Medal Roll Reference: WO100/225/157 Orderly 13 General Hospital. To England expired contract 10 April 1901.

BALSHAW, E. Private 1367 1701 Preston Corps Medal Clasps: CC OFS TVL SA01 KSA01 KSA02.
Medal Roll Reference: WO100/225/54+61+83+94+157+170+WO100/352/15 Orderly 13 General Hospital. To 11 General Hospital Kimberley 29 August 1900. To England on termination of engagement. Base Hospital Wynberg. Joined from Base Detail. 20 General Hospital. To England for discharge.

BANCROFT, C. W. Private 528 Blackpool Division Medal Clasps: No Clasps.
Medal Roll Reference: WO100/225/9 Orderly.

BANKS, Bertram Bede Private 335 Kendal Division Medal Clasps: CC OFS TVL NAT KSA01 KSA02.
Medal Roll Reference: WO100/225/128 WO100/273/13+200 WO100/366/148 Orderly 7 General Hospital. To England time expired. South African Constabulary E Division 1st Trooper E2927. Service in St John Ambulance Brigade from 13 March 1900 to 8 January 1901. Service in South African Constabulary 4 May 1901 to 30 May 1902. Discharged by purchase.
BANKS, G. Private 723 Dover Division Medal Clasps: CC WITT.
Medal Roll Reference: WO100/225/203 Orderly 21 Bearer Company. Sent home for discharge August 1900.
BANNISTER, A. Private 840 Preston Corps Medal Clasps: CC.
Medal Roll Reference: WO100/225/168+178 Orderly 16 General Hospital. Transferred to 7 Stationary Hospital 4 June 1900 Sent to England September 1900.
BANTING, F. J. Private 1208 Metropolitan Corps Medal Clasps: CC OFS.
Medal Roll Reference: WO100/225/138 Orderly 9 General Hospital. To Cape Town 15 April 1901.
BARFORD, F. Private 1859 Leeds Corps Medal Clasps: CC OFS SA01.
Medal Roll Reference: WO100/225/86+114 Orderly 3 General Hospital. Transferred to Base Detail Home 21 June 1901.
BARLOW, J. Private 1598 Oldham Corps Medal Clasps: CC.
Medal Roll Reference: WO100/225/107+173 Orderly 1 General Hospital 21 General Hospital.
BARLOW, J. Private 1599 Oldham Corps Medal Clasps: CC.
Medal Roll Reference: WO100/225/107+173 Orderly 1 General Hospital 21 General Hospital.
BARNES, A. H. 1st Class Sergeant 612 Accrington Corps Medal Clasps: CC OFS.
Medal Roll Reference: WO100/225/138 Supply Officer 9 General Hospital. To Concentration Camp Naauwpoort 9 May 1900.
BARNES, E. Private 682 1588 Bury Division Medal Clasps: CC WITT.
Medal Roll Reference: WO100/225/72+195 Orderly. From Stationary Hospital Burgersdorp to 24 Stationary Hospital. Transferred to Base Detail 3 April 1901. 23 Field Hospital. Discharged Time expired.
BARNES, T. Private 510 Shipley Corps Medal Clasps: NAT.
Medal Roll Reference: WO100/225/65 Orderly 13 Stationary Hospital. Invalided to England 3 August 1900.
BARNETT, E. Private 1811 Handsworth & Smethwick Corps Medal Clasps: CC OFS SA01.
Medal Roll Reference: WO100/225/86+114 WO100/224/192 Orderly 3 General Hospital. Transferred to Base Detail RAMC Home 21 June 1901.
BARNETT, S. Private 428 Metropolitan Corps Medal Clasps: CC OFS.
Medal Roll Reference: WO100/225/133 Orderly 8 General Hospital. To England 20 July 1900.
BARNETT, W. Private 859 Hebden Bridge Corps Medal Clasps: CC OFS.
Medal Roll Reference: WO100/225/133 Orderly 8 General Hospital. To Norval's Pont 21 August 1900.
BARON, J. Private 1054 Bolton Corps Medal Clasps: NAT.
Medal Roll Reference: WO100/225/65 Orderly 13 Stationary Hospital. To SS *Montrose* 8 September 1900.
BARRATT, W. Private 1196 Oldham Corps Medal Clasps: CC.
Medal Roll Reference: WO100/225/107 Orderly 1 General Hospital.
BARRETT, J. Private 995 Rishton Division Medal Clasps: NAT.
Medal Roll Reference: WO100/225/161 Orderly 15 General Hospital. Transferred to England 26 August 1900.
BARRETT, J. Sergeant 1145 Dewsbury Corps Medal Clasps: CC OFS TVL.
Medal Roll Reference: WO100/225/125 Supernumerary Officer 6 General Hospital. To Base on expiration of contract 22 October 1900.

BARRETT, J. W. L. Private 288 Metropolitan Corps Medal Clasps: CC.
Medal Roll Reference: WO100/130/218 Private 15 General Hospital Imperial Yeomanry Hospital.
Died of typhoid Deelfontein 6 September 1900.
BARRIER, J. Private 1820 Birmingham Corps (Birmingham City Division) Medal Clasps: CC
OFS SA01.
Medal Roll Reference: WO100/225/86+89+114 Orderly 3 General Hospital. 21 June 1901
transferred to Base Detail RAMC. Time expired 10 August 1901.
BARRINGER, G. Private 535 Preston Corps Medal Clasps: CC OFS TVL.
Medal Roll Reference: WO100/225/230 Private Langman Hospital.
BARROW, H. T. Private 1371 Preston Corps Medal Clasps: CC.
Medal Roll Reference: WO100/225/157 Orderly 13 General Hospital. To England contract expired
27 January 1901.
BARROW, J. Private 1266 Whaley Bridge Division Medal Clasps: CC OFS.
Medal Roll Reference: WO100/225/138 Orderly 9 General Hospital. To Base Detail 12 October
1900.
BARROWCLOUGH, F. Private 985 Oystermouth Division Medal Clasps: NAT.
Medal Roll Reference: WO100/225/161 Orderly 15 General Hospital. Transferred to England 26
August 1900.
BARTER, G. A. Private 1515 Isle of Wight Corps Medal Clasps: CC OFS TVL.
Medal Roll Reference: WO100/225/161+183 Orderly 15 General Hospital. Transferred to Pretoria
29 August 1900. 17 Stationary Hospital. To Base 24 November 1900.
BARTLAM, T. W. Private 371 Ironbridge Corps Medal Clasps: CC OFS.
Medal Roll Reference: WO100/225/133 Orderly 8 General Hospital. To England 23 January 1901.
BARTON, F. Private 1527 Oldham Corps Medal Clasps: CC OFS TVL NAT.
Medal Roll Reference: WO100/225/107+128 Orderly 1 General Hospital. Transferred to 7
General Hospital. To England time expired.
BARTON, George E. Sergeant 673 Bolton Corps Medal Clasps: CC OFS TVL SA01.
Medal Roll Reference: WO100/225/54+83 WO100/272/2 Orderly 11 General Hospital. To
England on termination of engagement. South African Constabulary B Division Medical Corporal
217.
BARTON, W. Private 633 1653 Hull Corps Medal Clasps: CC OFS TVL.
Medal Roll Reference: WO100/225/154+170 Orderly 10 General Hospital. To Base 7 August 1900
20 General Hospital Joined from Base Detail. To England for discharge.
BASON, J. M. Private 623 North Staffs Corps Medal Clasps: CC WITT.
Medal Roll Reference: WO100/225/195 Orderly 23 Field Hospital. Discharged time expired.
BASTOW, H. S. Private 1787 Keighley Corps Medal Clasps: CC OFS SA01.
Medal Roll Reference: WO100/225/86+114 Orderly 3 General Hospital. Transferred to Base
Detail RAMC. Home 21 June 1901
BATEMAN, W. Private 1047 Nelson Corps Medal Clasps: NAT.
Medal Roll Reference: WO100/225/180 Orderly 14 Stationary Hospital.
BATES, E. Private 1697 Leicester Corps Medal Clasps: CC OFS TVL.
Medal Roll Reference: WO100/225/170 Orderly 20 General Hospital Joined from Base Detail. To
England for discharge.
BATTY, W. Private 1213 1890 Leeds Corps Medal Clasps: CC OFS.
Medal Roll Reference: WO100/225/133+173 Orderly 8 General Hospital. To England 21 July
1900. 21 General Hospital.
BAXIENDALE, F. Private 1655 Accrington Corps Medal Clasps: SA01.
Medal Roll Reference: WO100/225/88 Orderly.
BAXTER, L. Private 180 Wellingborough Corps Medal Clasps: CC.
Medal Roll Reference: WO100/225/69 Orderly 8 Stationary Hospital.

BAYLISS, C. F. Private 1754 Padiham Division Medal Clasps: CC OFS SA01.
Medal Roll Reference: WO100/225/86+114 Orderly 3 General Hospital. Transferred to Base Detail RAMC. Home 21 June 1901.
BEALE, J. W. Sergeant 980 Denaby Cadeby Main Division Medal Clasps: NAT.
Medal Roll Reference: WO100/225/161 Supply Officer 15 General Hospital. Transferred to Pretoria 29 August 1900.
BEARD, S. T. 1st Class Sergeant 506 Brynmawr Division Medal Clasps: CC.
Medal Roll Reference: WO100/225/122 Supply Officer 5 General Hospital.
BEARDSLEY, E. Private 341 Ilkeston Corps Medal Clasps: CC OFS.
Medal Roll Reference: WO100/225/133 Orderly 8 General Hospital. To England 23 January 1901.
BEARDSMORE, E. A. Private 207 Wellingborough Corps Medal Clasps: CC.
Medal Roll Reference: WO100/225/125 Supernumerary Officer 6 General Hospital. To Base on expiration of contract 18 June 1900.
BEARDWOOD, W. D. Private 1370 Preston Corps Medal Clasps: CC TVL.
Medal Roll Reference: WO100/225/79 Private 18 Field Hospital Original unit 3 General Hospital after 9 Brigade Field Hospital Sent sick. To Mafeking 29 August 1900. 13 General Hospital. Time expired
BEAVAN, T. Private 707 Metropolitan Corps Medal Clasps: CC SA01.
Medal Roll Reference: WO100/225/54+83 Orderly 11 General Hospital. To England on termination of engagement.
BECCONSALL, J. Private 455 Preston Corps Medal Clasps: NAT.
Medal Roll Reference: WO100/225/128 Orderly 7 General Hospital. To England time expired.
BEDDOWS, J. A. Private 1431 Bolton Corps Medal Clasps: CC OFS TVL SA01 SA02.
Medal Roll Reference: WO100/225/128 Orderly 7 General Hospital. To England time expired.
BEEBY, Samuel Private 130 Kettering Corps Medal Clasps: No Clasps. China Medal.
Medal Roll Reference: WO100/225/8 Orderly HS *Maine*. On medal roll for HS *Maine* for China WO100/96/38+39.
BEECHEY, R. R. Private 1589 Birmingham Corps Medal Clasps: CC.
Medal Roll Reference: WO100/225/107+122 Orderly 1 General Hospital. 5 General Hospital.
BEECROFT, H. Private 419 Leeds Corps Medal Clasps: OFS TVL NAT SA01.
Medal Roll Reference: WO100/225/128 Orderly 7 General Hospital Invalided. 13 General Hospital. To England expired contract 10 April 1901.
BEESLEY, R. J. Private 44 Metropolitan Corps Medal Clasps: CC OFS.
Medal Roll Reference: WO100/225/114 Orderly 3 General Hospital Transferred to Base Detail RAMC.
BENISTON, S. Private 751 Ilkeston Corps Medal Clasps: CC SA01.
Medal Roll Reference: WO100/225/54+83 Orderly 11 General Hospital. To England on termination of engagement.
BENNETT, A. Private 1080 Preston Corps Medal Clasps: NAT.
Medal Roll Reference: WO100/225/161 Orderly 15 General Hospital. Transferred to England 14 September 1900.
BENSON, R. Private 1550 Bolton Corps Medal Clasps: CC OFS.
Medal Roll Reference: WO100/225/138 Orderly 9 General Hospital. To Base Detail 30 January 1901.
BENTLEY, S. Private 1541 Oldham Corps Medal Clasps: CC.
Medal Roll Reference: WO100/225/72+122 Orderly 24 Stationary Hospital. Transferred to Base Detail 31 March 1901 5 General Hospital.
BERNASCONI, W. J. Private 143 Metropolitan Corps Medal Clasps: CC.
Medal Roll Reference: WO100/225/107+128 Orderly 1 General Hospital. Transferred to 7 General Hospital. To England time expired.

BERRY, C. Private 931 Colne Division Medal Clasps: NAT SA01 SA02.
Medal Roll Reference: WO100/225/161 Orderly 15 General Hospital. Transferred to England 26 August 1900.
BERRY, John William Private 591 Colne Division Medal Clasps: CC.
Medal Roll Reference: WO100/225/73 Orderly 6 Stationary Hospital.
BEST, J. Private 939 New Farnley Division Medal Clasps: NAT.
Medal Roll Reference: WO100/225/161 Orderly 15 General Hospital. Transferred to England 26 August 1900.
BESWICK, D. Private 1528 Oldham Corps Medal Clasps: CC.
Medal Roll Reference: WO100/225/107 Orderly 1 General Hospital.
BESWICK, W. Private 1722 Oldham Corps Medal Clasps: OFS TVL.
Medal Roll Reference: WO100/225/203 Orderly 21 Bearer Company. Joined from 20 General Hospital Elandsfontein February 1901 and sent home for discharge June 1901.
BETTLES, Charles R. Private 454 Wellingborough Corps Medal Clasps: CC OFS.
Medal Roll Reference: WO100/225/133 Orderly 8 General Hospital. Died of disease Bloemfontein 29 June 1900.
BETTS, C. T. E. Private 845 Northampton Corps Medal Clasps: CC.
Medal Roll Reference: WO100/225/125 Private 6 General Hospital. To Base Invalided 7 July 1900.
BILLING, G. Private 1253 Padiham Division Medal Clasps: CC OFS TVL.
Medal Roll Reference: WO100/225/125 Private 6 General Hospital. To Base on expiration of contract 22 October 1900.
BILLINGSLEY, E. Private 964 Dudley Corps Medal Clasps: NAT.
Medal Roll Reference: WO100/225/161 Orderly 15 General Hospital. Transferred to HS *Nubia* 29 December 1900.
BIRCHALL, W. Private 173 Oldham Corps Medal Clasps: CC.
Medal Roll Reference: WO100/225/107 Orderly 1 General Hospital.
BIRCHENALL, J. H. Private 1195 Oldham Corps Medal Clasps: CC.
Medal Roll Reference: WO100/225/107 Orderly 1 General Hospital.
BIRD, J. Private 787 Bacup Division Medal Clasps: OFS TVL.
Medal Roll Reference: WO100/225/185 Orderly Attached to 3rd Highland Brigade Field Hospital. Transferred from 2 General Hospital 5 May 1900. To England 16 October 1900.
BIRD, Robert Henry Private 805 Metropolitan Corps Medal Clasps: CC OFS TVL.
Medal Roll Reference: WO100/225/125 Private 6 General Hospital. To Base on expiration of contract 3 September 1900.
BIRTWISTLE, Samuel H. Private 584 Bolton Corps Medal Clasps: CC.
Medal Roll Reference: WO100/225/122 Orderly 5 General Hospital. Died of disease Cape Town 9 July 1900.
BLACK, F. Private 366 North Staffs Corps Medal Clasps: CC OFS TVL SA01.
Medal Roll Reference: WO100/130/230+252 Orderly Imperial Yeomanry Hospital Pretoria. W. BLACK on Imperial Yeomanry Medal Roll.
BLACK, J. J. Private 271 Metropolitan Corps Medal Clasps: NAT.
Medal Roll Reference: WO100/225/75 Orderly Princess Christian Hospital Train.
BLACKBURN, G. S. Private 1297 Southport Division Medal Clasps: CC TVL.
Medal Roll Reference: WO100/224/172 Sergeant Rhodesian Field Force Hospital.
BLACKBURN, J. E. Private 448 Bacup Division Medal Clasps: NAT.
Medal Roll Reference: WO100/225/128 Orderly 7 General Hospital. To England time expired.
BLACKBURN, J. W. Private 22 Dewsbury Corps Medal Clasps: CC OFS TVL.
Medal Roll Reference: WO100/225/170+241 Orderly HS *Princess of Wales*. Attached RAMC 20 General Hospital. Joined from Base Detail. To England for discharge

BLACKGROVE, James Private 1066 Metropolitan Corps Medal Clasps: NAT SA01.
Medal Roll Reference: WO100/225/67 Orderly 18 General Hospital. To England 28 December
1900.
BLAKE, A. Private 1809 Birmingham Corps Medal Clasps: CC OFS TVL.
Medal Roll Reference: WO100/225/169 Orderly 17 General Hospital. Transferred to Base Detail
Cape Town 13 July 1901.
BLAKE, A. J. W. Private 1391 Leicester Corps Medal Clasps: No Clasps.
Medal Roll Reference: WO100/225/58 Orderly 14 General Hospital. To HS *Simla* for duty 14
November 1900.
BLAKEY, W. Private 746 Heanor Division Medal Clasps: CC WITT.
Medal Roll Reference: WO100/225/195 Orderly 23 Field Hospital. Discharged time expired.
BLANSHARD, G. Private 1410 1839 Dewsbury Corps Medal Clasps: CC OFS SA01.
Medal Roll Reference: WO100/225/58+86+114 Orderly 14 General Hospital. To HS *Simla* for
duty 14 November 1900. 3 General Hospital. Transferred to Base Detail RAMC. Home 21 June
1901.
BLANSHARD, R. W. Sergeant 1144 Barnoldswick Division Medal Clasps: CC OFS TVL.
Medal Roll Reference: WO100/225/113 Supply Officer 2 General Hospital. From England 28
April 1900. To Cape Town for England 18 August 1900. 9 General Hospital. To Pretoria 4 October
1900.
BLEASDALE, Robert Private 101 Bolton Corps Medal Clasps: CC OFS.
Medal Roll Reference: WO100/225/235 Private Portland Hospital. To England contract expired.
BOALER, J. Private 443 Welbeck Division Medal Clasps: CC OFS.
Medal Roll Reference: WO100/225/133 Orderly 8 General Hospital. To England 23 January 1901.
BOANS, A. Private 1198 Lincoln Adult School Division Medal Clasps: CC.
Medal Roll Reference: WO100/225/122 Orderly 5 General Hospital.
BOFFEY, R. Private 1690 Abram Colliery Division Medal Clasps: OFS TVL.
Medal Roll Reference: WO100/225/203 Orderly 21 Bearer Company. Joined from 20 General
Hospital Elandsfontein February 1901 and sent home for discharge June 1901.
BOLSTER (JUNIOR), G. Private 1400 St John Ambulance Brigade Medal Clasps: No Clasps.
Medal Roll Reference: WO100/225/58 Orderly 14 General Hospital. To HS *Simla* for duty 14
November 1900.
BOLTON, J. J. Private 1305 Preston Corps Medal Clasps: CC TVL.
Medal Roll Reference: WO100/224/172 Private Rhodesian Field Force Hospital.
BOLTON, T. Private 837 Preston Corps Medal Clasps: CC.
Medal Roll Reference: WO100/225/125 Private 6 General Hospital. To Base Invalided 16 June
1900.
BOND, B. C. Private 712 Metropolitan Corps Medal Clasps: CC SA01.
Medal Roll Reference: WO100/225/54+61+83 Orderly 11 General Hospital. To England on
termination of engagement.
BONHAM, J. Private 1522 Wellingborough Corps Medal Clasps: CC TVL SA01.
Medal Roll Reference: WO100/225/169 Orderly 17 General Hospital. Transferred to
Pietermaritzburg 30 November 1900.
BONYNGE, C. A. Private 1399 St John Ambulance Brigade Medal Clasps: No Clasps.
Medal Roll Reference: WO100/225/58 Orderly 14 General Hospital. To HS *Simla* for duty 14
November 1900.
BOOKER, Leonard A. G. Private 308 St John Ambulance Brigade (NFB Bognor) Medal Clasps:
CC. NFBUAD Medal.
Medal Roll Reference: WO100/130/218 Private Imperial Yeomanry Hospital Deelfontein.
BORER, Henry James Private 97 Caterham Division Medal Clasps: No Clasps.
Medal Roll Reference: WO100/225/235 Private Portland Hospital. Died from typhoid
Bloemfontein 12 June 1900.

BOSWORTH, E. Private 9 1658 Wellingborough Corps Medal Clasps: CC OFS TVL.
Medal Roll Reference: WO100/225/170+241 Orderly HS *Princess of Wales*. Attached RAMC. 20 General Hospital. Joined from Base Detail. To England for discharge
BOTT, G. A. Private 490 Leicester Corps Medal Clasps: CC OFS.
Medal Roll Reference: WO100/225/138 Orderly 9 General Hospital. To Base Detail 5 July 1900.
BOTTERILL, J. T. Private 1585 Wellingborough Corps Medal Clasps: CC OFS TVL.
Medal Roll Reference: WO100/225/157 Orderly 13 General Hospital. To England expired contract 10 April 1901.
BOTTERILL, Thomas Private 99 Kettering Corps Medal Clasps: CC OFS.
Medal Roll Reference: WO100/225/235 Private Portland Hospital. To England contract expired.
BOULTBEE, C. Private 1154 Birchwood Corps Medal Clasps: CC OFS.
Medal Roll Reference: WO100/225/138 Orderly 9 General Hospital. To Base Detail 12 October 1900.
BOURNE, A. G. Private 710 Metropolitan Corps Medal Clasps: CC TVL SA01.
Medal Roll Reference: WO100/225/54+83 Orderly 11 General Hospital Temporary Hospital Christiana.
BOWCOCK, William Henry Private 1130 Bolton Corps Medal Clasps: CC. China Medal.
Medal Roll Reference: WO100/225/53+248 Orderly HS *Maine*. On medal roll for HS *Maine* for China WO100/96/38+39.
BOWDEN, H. Private 1094 Metropolitan Corps Medal Clasps: NAT.
Medal Roll Reference: WO100/225/161 Orderly 15 General Hospital. Transferred to HS *Nubia* 29 December 1900.
BOWDLER, W. H. Sergeant 392 Sheffield Corps Medal Clasps: CC OFS.
Medal Roll Reference: WO100/225/133 Supply Officer 8 General Hospital. To England 23 January 1901.
BOWEN, C. T. M. Private 1377 Mill Bay Division Medal Clasps: No Clasps.
Medal Roll Reference: WO100/225/58 Orderly 14 General Hospital. To HS *Simla* for duty 14 November 1900.
BOWLES, J. H. Private 644 Bradford Corps Medal Clasps: CC SA01.
Medal Roll Reference: WO100/225/54+83 Orderly 11 General Hospital. To England on termination of engagement.
BOWRON, G. Private 1386 Mill Bay Division Medal Clasps: No Clasps.
Medal Roll Reference: WO100/225/58 Orderly 14 General Hospital. To SS *Manhattan* for duty 28 November 1900.
BOYDELL, G. Private 567 Bolton Corps Medal Clasps: CC TVL.
Medal Roll Reference: WO100/225/196 Orderly 24 Field Hospital. To Base expiration of contract 6 January 1901.
BRACEWELL, T. Private 1498 Burnley Division Medal Clasps: TVL NAT.
Medal Roll Reference: WO100/225/128 Orderly 7 General Hospital. To England time expired.
BRADLEY, J. Private 172 Edenfield Division Medal Clasps: CC.
Medal Roll Reference: WO100/225/107 Orderly 1 General Hospital.
BRADSHAW, A. Private 1479 Derby Division Medal Clasps: CC OFS TVL.
Medal Roll Reference: WO100/225/107+161+183 Orderly 1 General Hospital 15 General Hospital. Transferred to Pretoria 29 August 1900 17 Stationary Hospital. To Base 24 November 1900.
BRADSHAW, A. Private 1791 Derby Corps Medal Clasps: No Clasps.
Medal Roll Reference: No Record Found.
BRADSHAW, E. G. Private 527 Blackpool Division Medal Clasps: NAT.
Medal Roll Reference: WO100/225/95 Private.

BRAMHAM, A. Private 200 Oldham Corps Medal Clasps: CC OFS.
Medal Roll Reference: WO100/225/176 Orderly 5 Stationary Hospital Sent to Base for England for discharge.
BRAMLEY, W. Private 678 Edenfield Division Medal Clasps: CC OFS.
Medal Roll Reference: WO100/225/154 Orderly 10 General Hospital. To Base 29 June 1900.
BRANKIN, J. Private 1720 Oldham Corps Medal Clasps: CC OFS TVL.
Medal Roll Reference: WO100/225/170 Orderly 20 General Hospital. Joined from Base Detail. To England for discharge.
BRAWN, E. Private 1584 Wellingborough Corps Medal Clasps: CC.
Medal Roll Reference: WO100/225/107+157 Orderly 13 General Hospital. To 1 General hospital Base Hospital Wynberg 1 August 1900.
BREAKELL, J. Private 1076 Preston Corps Medal Clasps: NAT.
Medal Roll Reference: WO100/225/65 Orderly 13 Stationary Hospital. To HS *Dunera* 18 December 1900.
BRERETON, C. T. Private 34 Ipswich Corps Medal Clasps: CC OFS TVL.
Medal Roll Reference: WO100/225/113 Orderly 2 General Hospital. From England 18 December 1899. To Cape Town for England 15 October 1900.
BRETT, G. Private 1556 Isle of Wight Corps Medal Clasps: CC.
Medal Roll Reference: WO100/225/107 Orderly 1 General Hospital.
BREWER, J. J. Private 573 Oldham Corps Medal Clasps: CC OFS TVL.
Medal Roll Reference: WO100/225/196 Orderly 24 Field Hospital. To Base expiration of contract 6 January 1901.
BRICKLEY, J. G. Private 516 Warrington Corps Medal Clasps: CC TVL.
Medal Roll Reference: WO100/225/196+197 Supply Officer 24 Field Hospital. To Base expiration of contract 6 January 1901. 9th Brigade Bearer Company 1st Division.
BRIERLEY, C. Private 1884 Oldham Corps Medal Clasps: CC OFS TVL.
Medal Roll Reference: WO100/225/169 Orderly 17 General Hospital. Transferred to Base Detail Cape Town 13 July 1901.
BRIERLY, F. Private 1728 Oldham Corps Medal Clasps: CC OFS TVL.
Medal Roll Reference: WO100/225/170 Orderly 20 General Hospital. Joined from Base Detail. To England for discharge.
BRIERLY, L. Private 1029 Oldham Corps Medal Clasps: NAT.
Medal Roll Reference: WO100/225/65 Orderly 13 Stationary Hospital. To HS *Dunera* 18 December 1900.
BRIGGS, J. W. 1st Class Sergeant 136 Morecombe Division Medal Clasps: CC.
Medal Roll Reference: WO100/225/175 Supply Officer 3 Stationary Hospital. To Cape Town 18 May 1901.
BRIGHTWELL, H. Private 1523 Wellingborough Corps Medal Clasps: CC OFS TVL.
Medal Roll Reference: WO100/225/169 Orderly 17 General Hospital. Transferred to Pietermaritzburg 30 November 1900.
BRINDLE, H. Private 175 Adlington Division Medal Clasps: CC OFS TVL.
Medal Roll Reference: WO100/225/61+70 Orderly Base Hospital Wynberg. 3 Hospital Train. To Base Detail RAMC Cape Town for England.
BRITLAND, W. Private 404 Accrington Corps Medal Clasps: NAT.
Medal Roll Reference: WO100/225/128 Orderly 7 General Hospital. To England time expired.
BRITT, W. H. Private 1079 Preston Corps Medal Clasps: NAT.
Medal Roll Reference: WO100/225/161 Orderly 15 General Hospital. Transferred to England 14 September 1900.
BROADBENT, H. Private 1814 Bolton Corps Medal Clasps: SA01.
Medal Roll Reference: WO100/225/86 Orderly 3 General Hospital. Home 21 June 1901.

BROADHEAD, T. Private 1867 Leeds Corps Medal Clasps: CC OFS TVL.
Medal Roll Reference: WO100/225/169 Orderly 17 General Hospital Transferred to Base Detail Cape Town 13 July 1901.
BROADLEY, J. Private 1624 Haslingden Division Medal Clasps: CC.
Medal Roll Reference: WO100/225/107 Orderly 1 General Hospital.
BROCK, John T. Private 1290 Metropolitan Corps Medal Clasps: CC OFS TVL.
Medal Roll Reference: WO100/225/125 Private 6 General Hospital. Died of disease Johannesburg 3 August 1900.
BROCKBANK, A. S. Private 1885 Sheffield Corps Medal Clasps: CC OFS SA01.
Medal Roll Reference: WO100/225/86+114 Orderly 3 General Hospital. Transferred to Base Detail RAMC. Home 21 June 1901.
BROOK, F. Private 1857 Bradford Corps Medal Clasps: CC OFS SA01.
Medal Roll Reference: WO100/225/86+114 Orderly 3 General Hospital. Transferred to Base Detail RAMC 6 July 1901.
BROOKBANK, G. W. Private 15 Metropolitan Corps Medal Clasps: CC.
Medal Roll Reference: WO100/225/241 Private HS *Princess of Wales*. Attached RAMC.
BROOKES, B. Private 912 Derby Division Medal Clasps: NAT.
Medal Roll Reference: WO100/225/161 Orderly 15 General Hospital. Transferred to England 14 September 1900.
BROOKS, H. Private 1181 1591 Oldham Corps Medal Clasps: CC.
Medal Roll Reference: WO100/225/107+189 Orderly 1 General Hospital. 1 Guards Field Hospital. Possible service with South African Constabulary.
BROOKS, John William Private 1693 Hull Corps Medal Clasps: OFS TVL.
Medal Roll Reference: WO100/225/203 Orderly 21 Bearer Company. Joined from 20 General Hospital Elandsfontein February 1901 and sent home for discharge June 1901.
BROOKSBANK, B. L. Private 1779 Shipley Corps Medal Clasps: CC.
Medal Roll Reference: WO100/225/173 Orderly 21 General Hospital.
BROOMHALL, T. Private 1740 Warrington Corps Medal Clasps: CC OFS TVL SA01 SA02.
Medal Roll Reference: WO100/225/86+114+202 Orderly Attached 20 Bearer Company Served with 3 General Hospital. To General Elliott's Division 20 June 1901. Transferred to Base Detail RAMC
BROWBRIDGE, E. Private 252 Rochdale Corps Medal Clasps: CC OFS.
Medal Roll Reference: WO100/225/176 Orderly 5 Stationary Hospital. Sent to Base for England for discharge.
BROWN, A. H. Sergeant 938 Nelson Corps Medal Clasps: NAT.
Medal Roll Reference: WO100/225/162 Supply Officer 15 General Hospital. Transferred to Stationary Hospital Ladysmith 30 June 1900.
BROWN, E. T. Private 386 Birmingham Corps Medal Clasps: CC.
Medal Roll Reference: WO100/130/218 Private Imperial Yeomanry Hospital Deelfontein.
BROWN, J. F. Private 1565 Accrington Corps Medal Clasps: CC.
Medal Roll Reference: WO100/225/122 Orderly 5 General Hospital.
BROWN, J. T. Private 802 1751 Barnoldswick Division Medal Clasps: CC OFS.
Medal Roll Reference: WO100/225/133+173 Orderly 8 General Hospital. To Cape Town 7 August 1900. 21 General Hospital.
BROWN, J. W. Private 229 1838 Dewsbury Corps Medal Clasps: CC OFS SA01.
Medal Roll Reference: WO100/225/86+114+125 Orderly 3 General Hospital. Transferred to Base Detail RAMC on expiration of contract 18 June 1900. 6 General Hospital. To Base 6 July 1901.
BROWN, J. W. Private 1518 Bradford Corps Medal Clasps: No Clasps.
Medal Roll Reference: WO100/225/161 Orderly 15 General Hospital. Transferred to England 26 November 1900.

BROWN, Joseph T. Private 607 Belper Division Medal Clasps: CC OFS.
Medal Roll Reference: WO100/225/138 Orderly 9 General Hospital. Died of disease Bloemfontein 6 June 1900.
BROWN, T. Private 1447 Accrington Corps Medal Clasps: CC OFS TVL.
Medal Roll Reference: WO100/225/180+183 Orderly 14 Stationary Hospital. 17 Stationary Hospital. To Base 24 November 1900.
BROWN, W. Private 488 Leicester Corps Medal Clasps: CC OFS.
Medal Roll Reference: WO100/225/61+138 Orderly Base Hospital Wynberg. 9 General Hospital. To Base Detail 31 January 1901.
BROWN, W. A. Private 390 Sheffield Corps Medal Clasps: OFS TVL NAT SA01.
Medal Roll Reference: WO100/225/128 Orderly 7 General Hospital. To England time expired.
BROWN, Wilfred Harry Private 327 St John Ambulance Brigade (NFB Sandown) Medal Clasps: CC. NFBUAD Medal.
Medal Roll Reference: WO100/130/218 Private Imperial Yeomanry Hospital Deelfontein.
BUCK, Percy Private 602 Sheffield Corps Medal Clasps: CC OFS.
Medal Roll Reference: WO100/225/138 Orderly 9 General Hospital. Died of disease Bloemfontein 4 June 1900.
BUCKNALL, T. H. Private 278 Metropolitan Corps Medal Clasps: CC OFS TVL.
Medal Roll Reference: WO100/225/125 Private 6 General Hospital. To Base on expiration of contract 17 December 1900.
BUDD, D. B. Private 775 Metropolitan Corps Medal Clasps: CC OFS.
Medal Roll Reference: WO100/225/138 Orderly 9 General Hospital. To Base Detail 5 July 1900.
BULLIMORE, T. Private 1849 Leicester Corps Medal Clasps: CC OFS TVL.
Medal Roll Reference: WO100/225/75 Orderly No 4 Hospital Train.
BULLOCK, Walter Henry 1st Class Sergeant 472 Accrington Corps Medal Clasps: CC OFS.
Medal Roll Reference: WO100/225/133 Supply Officer 8 General Hospital. To England 20 July 1900.
BURDEKIN, J. Private 1146 Dewsbury Corps Medal Clasps: CC.
Medal Roll Reference: WO100/225/72+154 Orderly 10 General Hospital. To Base 10 October 1900. From Base Detail to 24 Stationary Hospital. Transferred to 5 General Hospital (sick) 25 March 1901.
BURDELL, W. Sergeant 988 Blackpool Division Medal Clasps: NAT.
Medal Roll Reference: WO100/225/161 Supply Officer 15 General Hospital. Transferred to England 26 August 1900.
BURDETT, C. R. Private 150 Northampton Corps Medal Clasps: No Clasps.
Medal Roll Reference: WO100/225/8 Orderly.
BURDETT, G. H. Private 257 Leicester Corps Medal Clasps: CC OFS.
Medal Roll Reference: WO100/225/176 Orderly 5 Stationary Hospital Sent to Base for England for discharge.
BURGESS, A. Private 286 Metropolitan Corps Medal Clasps: CC.
Medal Roll Reference: WO100/130/218 Private Imperial Yeomanry Hospital Deelfontein.
BURGESS, J. Private 622 North Staffs Corps Medal Clasps: CC SA01 WITT.
Medal Roll Reference: WO100/225/192 Orderly Attached 21 Field Hospital. Discharged.
BURGESS, L. H. Private 1287 Metropolitan Corps Medal Clasps: CC TVL.
Medal Roll Reference: WO100/224/172 Private Rhodesian Field Force Hospital.
BURGIN, G. Private 1011 Sheffield Corps Medal Clasps: NAT.
Medal Roll Reference: WO100/225/162 Orderly 15 General Hospital. Transferred to England 26 August 1900.
BURGOYNE, S. Private 747 Ilkeston Corps Medal Clasps: CC SA01.
Medal Roll Reference: WO100/225/54+83 Orderly 11 General Hospital. To England on termination of engagement.

BURKE, W. Private 1373 Preston Corps Medal Clasps: CC OFS TVL SA01 SA02.
Medal Roll Reference: WO100/225/73+157+197+WO100/352/16 Orderly 13 General Hospital.
To Mafeking 29 August 1900. 6 Stationary Hospital Green Point. To 9th Brigade Bearer Company
1st Division 8 September 1900. To Cape Town. KSA roll entry deleted.
BURNE, F. R. Private 1395 St John Ambulance Brigade Medal Clasps: No Clasps.
Medal Roll Reference: WO100/225/58 Orderly 14 General Hospital. To HS *Simla* for duty 14
November 1900.
BURNMAN, G. W. Private 949 Metropolitan Corps Medal Clasps: OFS NAT KSA01 KSA02.
Medal Roll Reference: WO100/225/162 WO100/273/373 WO100/366/209 Orderly 15 General
Hospital. Transferred to HS *Nubia* 29 December 1900. South African Constabulary E Division
Medical Corporal E3036. Service in St John Ambulance Brigade 3 April 1900 to 28 January 1901.
Service in South African Constabulary 14 May 1901 to 31 May 1902.
BURRELL, L. N. Private 1684 Metropolitan Corps Medal Clasps: CC OFS TVL.
Medal Roll Reference: WO100/225/58 Orderly 20 General Hospital.
BURROWS, A. Private 1632 Rochdale Corps Medal Clasps: No Clasps.
Medal Roll Reference: WO100/225/1411 Orderly.
BURTON, M. Private 918 Morecombe Division Medal Clasps: NAT.
Medal Roll Reference: WO100/225/162 Orderly 15 General Hospital. Transferred to England 26
August 1900.
BURTON, T. S. Private 1353 Bolton Corps Medal Clasps: CC OFS SA01.
Medal Roll Reference: WO100/225/54+61+83 Orderly 13 General Hospital. To Kimberley 29
August 1900. Temporary Hospital Boshof. 11 General Hospital.
BURY, C. E. Private 1771 Haslingden Division Medal Clasps: CC OFS TVL.
Medal Roll Reference: WO100/225/169 Orderly 17 General Hospital. Transferred to Base Detail
Cape Town 13 July 1901.
BUSH, W. H. Private 1682 Wellingborough Corps Medal Clasps: CC OFS TVL.
Medal Roll Reference: WO100/225/170 Orderly 20 General Hospital Joined from Base Detail. To
England for discharge.
BUTCHER, H. W. Sergeant 530 Blackpool Division Medal Clasps: NAT.
Medal Roll Reference: WO100/225/65 Supply Officer 13 Stationary Hospital. To HS *Orcana* 17 July
1900.
BUTCHER, J. E. Private 128 Metropolitan Corps Medal Clasps: CC OFS TVL SA01.
Medal Roll Reference: WO100/225/96 Orderly.
BUTTERFIELD, F. Private 826 Bradford Corps Medal Clasps: CC OFS TVL.
Medal Roll Reference: WO100/225/113 Orderly 2 General Hospital. From England 18 April 1900.
To Cape Town for England 18 August 1900.
BUTTERWORTH, T. E. Private 890 Rochdale Corps Medal Clasps: NAT.
Medal Roll Reference: WO100/225/162 Orderly 15 General Hospital. Transferred to England 26
August 1900.
BUTTERWORTH, T. E. Private 1018 Rochdale Corps Medal Clasps: NAT.
Medal Roll Reference: WO100/225/162 Orderly 15 General Hospital. Transferred to England 14
September 1900.
BUTTON, L. Private 319 St John Ambulance Brigade (NFB Haywards Heath) Medal Clasps: CC
KSA01KSA02. NFBUAD Medal.
Medal Roll Reference: WO100/130/217+WO100/356/173 Acting Sergeant Major (Conductor)
Imperial Yeomanry Hospital Deelfontein. Remaining in South Africa.
BYETT, H. E. Private 291 Metropolitan Corps Medal Clasps: CC.
Medal Roll Reference: WO100/130/217 Sergeant Imperial Yeomanry Hospital Deelfontein.
BYFORD, W. Private 115 Metropolitan Corps Medal Clasps: CC OFS.
Medal Roll Reference: WO100/225/154 Orderly 10 General Hospital. To Base 10 October 1900.

CABORN, E. A. Private 844 Oundle Division Medal Clasps: CC.
Medal Roll Reference: WO100/225/125 Private 6 General Hospital. To Base Invalided 7 July 1900.
CANA, C. C. Private 1627 Withernsea Division Medal Clasps: CC OFS TVL.
Medal Roll Reference: WO100/225/187 Orderly 18 Brigade Field Hospital Joined 20 March 1901.
Left 22 April 1901 for discharge.
CANDLER, Thomas William Private 429 Metropolitan Corps Medal Clasps: CC OFS.
Medal Roll Reference: WO100/225/133 Orderly 8 General Hospital. To England 23 January 1901.
CARCILL, W. D. Private 53 Weston-Super-Mare Division Medal Clasps: CC OFS.
Medal Roll Reference: WO100/225/114 Orderly 3 General Hospital. Transferred to Base Detail
RAMC.
CARDWELL, E. Private 521 Blackpool Division Medal Clasps: CC.
Medal Roll Reference: WO100/225/122 Orderly 5 General Hospital.
CAREY, William Private 1418 Hebden Bridge Corps Medal Clasps: No Clasps.
Medal Roll Reference: WO100/225/58 Orderly 14 General Hospital. To HS *Simla* for duty 14
November 1900.
CARMICHAEL, F. W. Private 738 1888 Hull Corps Medal Clasps: CC OFS TVL SA01.
Medal Roll Reference: WO100/225/54+83+169 Orderly 11 General Hospital. To England on
termination of engagement. 17 General Hospital. Transferred to Base Detail Cape Town 13 July
1901.
CARTER, A. C. Private 634 Hull Corps Medal Clasps: CC OFS.
Medal Roll Reference: WO100/225/13 Orderly. Number 630 on QSA medal roll.
CARTER, H. A. Private 1511 Metropolitan Corps Medal Clasps: No Clasps.
Medal Roll Reference: WO100/225/67 Orderly 18 General Hospital. To England 31 August 1900.
CARTLEDGE, T. Private 1539 Oldham Corps Medal Clasps: CC.
Medal Roll Reference: WO100/225/73 Orderly 6 Stationary Hospital.
CARTMELL, E. Private 1581 Whalley Division Medal Clasps: CC.
Medal Roll Reference: WO100/225/122 Orderly 5 General Hospital.
CASS, J. H. Sergeant 230 Leeds Corps Medal Clasps: CC.
Medal Roll Reference: WO100/225/125 Supernumerary Officer 6 General Hospital. To Base on
expiration of contract 23 June 1900.
CASSON, W. Private 777 Edenfield Division Medal Clasps: CC OFS TVL.
Medal Roll Reference: WO100/225/125 Private 6 General Hospital. To Base on expiration of
contract 3 September 1900.
CHALLINOR, L. Private 934 Oldham Corps Medal Clasps: NAT.
Medal Roll Reference: WO100/225/162 Orderly 15 General Hospital. Transferred to HS *Nubia* 29
December 1900.
CHAPMAN, J. Private 913 Derby Division Medal Clasps: NAT.
Medal Roll Reference: WO100/225/162 Orderly 15 General Hospital. Transferred to England 26
August 1900.
CHAPMAN, W. Private 1473 Blackpool Division Medal Clasps: CC OFS TVL.
Medal Roll Reference: WO100/225/169 Orderly 17 General Hospital. Transferred to
Pietermaritzburg 30 November 1900.
CHARNLEY, W. Sergeant 836 Preston Corps Medal Clasps: CC OFS SA01.
Medal Roll Reference: WO100/225/86+114 Supply Officer 3 General Hospital. Transferred to
Base Detail RAMC. Home 7 February 1901.
CHESTER, J. H. C. Private 1110 Wellingborough Corps Medal Clasps: NAT.
Medal Roll Reference: WO100/225/118 Orderly 4 General Hospital Sent to England time expired
19 December 1900.
CHILDS, W. Private 1675 Birmingham Corps (Birmingham City Division) Medal Clasps: CC OFS
TVL SA01.

Medal Roll Reference: WO100/225/67+89 Orderly 18 General Hospital. To England 27 May 1900 Time expired 8 July 1901.

CHILTON, H. Private 361 North Staffs Corps Medal Clasps: CC OFS.
Medal Roll Reference: WO100/225/133 Orderly 8 General Hospital. To England 20 July 1900.

CHILTON, T. M. Private 1107 Birmingham Corps (Birmingham City Division) Medal Clasps: TVL NAT SA01.
Medal Roll Reference: WO100/225/67 Orderly 18 General Hospital. To England 28 December 1900. Time expired 28 January 1901.

CHOWN, T. Private 395 Wellingborough Corps Medal Clasps: CC OFS.
Medal Roll Reference: WO100/225/133 Orderly 8 General Hospital. To England 20 July 1900.

CHRISTIAN, C. W. Private 1338 Leicester Corps Medal Clasps: CC OFS TVL.
Medal Roll Reference: WO100/225/157 Orderly 13 General Hospital. To England expired contract 1 June 1901.

CHRISTIAN, George Private 592 Colne Division Medal Clasps: CC OFS TVL.
Medal Roll Reference: WO100/225/113+122 Orderly 2 General Hospital. From England 18 April 1900. To Cape Town for England 18 August 1900. 5 General Hospital.

CHRISTIAN, H. Private 1339 Leicester Corps Medal Clasps: CC OFS TVL.
Medal Roll Reference: WO100/225/157 Orderly 13 General Hospital. To England expired contract 5 May 1901.

CLARK, E. W. Private 879 Hull Corps Medal Clasps: CC OFS TVL.
Medal Roll Reference: WO100/225/125 Private 6 General Hospital. To Base on expiration of contract 3 September 1900.

CLARK, G. A. Private 1597 Oldham Corps Medal Clasps: CC.
Medal Roll Reference: WO100/225/77+107 Orderly 10 Stationary Hospital. 1 General Hospital.

CLARK, J. Private 548 Metropolitan Corps Medal Clasps: CC OFS.
Medal Roll Reference: WO100/225/138 Orderly 9 General Hospital. To Base Detail 7 August 1900.

CLARK, Thomas Bryan Private 1136 Nelson Corps Medal Clasps: CC. China Medal.
Medal Roll Reference: WO100/225/53+248 Orderly HS *Maine*. On medal roll for HS *Maine* for China WO100/96/38+39.

CLARKE, W. Private 1342 Gateshead Fell Division Medal Clasps: CC OFS SA01.
Medal Roll Reference: WO100/225/54+83+157 Orderly 11 General Hospital. To Kimberley 29 August 1900. 13 General Hospital. Discharged locally on termination of engagement.

CLARKSON, S. H. T. Private 119 Dudley Corps Medal Clasps: No Clasps.
Medal Roll Reference: WO100/225/12 Private. Died of Disease Orange River Station 14 May 1900.

CLAXTON, C. R. Private 471 Metropolitan Corps Medal Clasps: CC OFS.
Medal Roll Reference: WO100/225/133 Orderly 8 General Hospital. To England 20 July 1900.

CLAY, H. Private 1152 Bradford Corps Medal Clasps: CC OFS.
Medal Roll Reference: WO100/225/154 Orderly 10 General Hospital. To Base 10 October 1900.

CLAY, W. Private 1411 Hebden Bridge Corps Medal Clasps: No Clasps.
Medal Roll Reference: WO100/225/58 Orderly 14 General Hospital. To HS *Simla* for duty 14 November 1900.

CLAYTON, A. T. Sergeant 861 Burnley Division Medal Clasps: CC OFS.
Medal Roll Reference: WO100/225/114 Orderly 3 General Hospital. Transferred to Base Detail RAMC.

CLAYTON, C. Private 1865 Leeds Corps Medal Clasps: CC OFS SA01.
Medal Roll Reference: WO100/225/86+114 Orderly 3 General Hospital. Transferred to Base Detail RAMC. Home 21 June 1901.

CLAYTON, T. Private 248 Preston Corps Medal Clasps: CC OFS TVL.
Medal Roll Reference: WO100/225/61+125 Orderly Base Hospital Wynberg 6 General Hospital.
To Base on expiration of contract 17 December 1900.
CLAYWORTH, F. Private 339 Gainsborough Division Medal Clasps: CC OFS.
Medal Roll Reference: WO100/225/133 Orderly 8 General Hospital. To England 20 July 1900.
CLEGG, W. L. 1st Class Sergeant 698 Heywood Division Medal Clasps: CC SA01.
Medal Roll Reference: WO100/225/54+83 Supply Officer 11 General Hospital. To England on
termination of engagement.
CLEMENTS, W. H. Private 1785 Metropolitan Corps Medal Clasps: CC OFS SA01.
Medal Roll Reference: WO100/225/86+114 Orderly 3 General Hospital. Transferred to Base
Detail RAMC. Home 21 June 1901.
CLEMENTS, William Private 457 Metropolitan Corps (Tottenham and Hampstead Junction
Division) Medal Clasps: CC OFS.
Medal Roll Reference: WO100/225/138 Orderly 9 General Hospital. Died of Disease
Bloemfontein 24 May 1900.
CLEWS, W. G. Private 1106 Birmingham Corps (Birmingham City Division) Medal Clasps: NAT
SA01.
Medal Roll Reference: WO100/225/67+89 Orderly 18 General Hospital. To England 28 December
1900. Time expired 28 January 1901.
COATES, D. Private 968 Dudley Corps Medal Clasps: NAT.
Medal Roll Reference: WO100/225/162 Orderly 15 General Hospital. Invalided to England 3 July
1900.
COCHRANE, N. Private 416 Oldham Corps Medal Clasps: NAT.
Medal Roll Reference: WO100/225/76+128 Orderly 7 General Hospital. To England time expired.
War Office Issue.
COCKSHOTT, T. E. Private 213 Bradford Corps Medal Clasps: CC.
Medal Roll Reference: WO100/225/125 Private 6 General Hospital. To Base on expiration of
contract 18 June 1900.
COGGAN, M. Private 1320 Sheffield Corps Medal Clasps: CC OFS TVL.
Medal Roll Reference: WO100/225/125 Private 6 General Hospital. To Base on expiration of
contract 22 October 1900.
COGGAN, W. Private 904 Derby Division Medal Clasps: NAT.
Medal Roll Reference: WO100/225/162 Orderly 15 General Hospital. Transferred to England 26
August 1900.
COGGS, J. H. Private 974 Metropolitan Corps (No 11 Wembley and Harlesden Ambulance Divi-
sion) Medal Clasps: NAT.
Medal Roll Reference: WO100/225/162 Orderly 15 General Hospital. Transferred to HS *Nubia* 29
December 1900.
COLDWELL, F. Private 1841 Dewsbury Corps Medal Clasps: CC OFS SA01.
Medal Roll Reference: WO100/225/86+115 Orderly 3 General Hospital. Transferred to Base
Detail RAMC. Home 21 June 1901.
COLEMAN, G. B. Sergeant 192 Metropolitan Corps Medal Clasps: CC OFS TVL SA01 SA02
RHOD KSA01 KSA02.
Medal Roll Reference: WO100/225/97+125+WO100/352/17 WO100/168/275
WO100/268/19+119 Supernumerary Officer 6 General Hospital Attached to RAMC. Discharged
locally on expiration of contract 20 January 1901. 1st Scottish Horse Squadron Sergeant Major 37.
Discharged 24 July 1901 Johannesburg. 2nd Lieutenant 3rd Battalion Royal Lancaster Regiment.
QSA issued 28 November 1901 3 Colony Clasps issued 23 April 1903.
COLENUTT, H. C. Private 163 Isle of Wight Corps Medal Clasps: CC OFS TVL.
Medal Roll Reference: WO100/225/61+70 Orderly Base Hospital Wynberg. 3 Hospital Train. To
Base Detail RAMC Cape Town for England.

COLLIER, R. S. Private 1067 Metropolitan Corps Medal Clasps: NAT.
Medal Roll Reference: WO100/225/67 Orderly 18 General Hospital. To England 28 December 1900.
COLLINGE, C. E. Private 1688 Hebden Bridge Corps Medal Clasps: No Clasps.
Medal Roll Reference: WO100/225/67 Orderly 18 General Hospital. To England 27 May 1900.
COLLINGE, G. Sergeant 451 Hebden Bridge Corps Medal Clasps: NAT.
Medal Roll Reference: WO100/225/128 Orderly 7 General Hospital. To England time expired.
COLLINS, G. R. N. Private 185 Metropolitan Corps Medal Clasps: CC OFS.
Medal Roll Reference: WO100/225/235 Private Portland Hospital. Servant to Lord William Bentinck. To England contract expired.
COLLINS, Henry Thomas Private 93 Metropolitan Corps Medal Clasps: CC OFS.
Medal Roll Reference: WO100/225/235 Private Portland Hospital. To England contract expired.
COLTMAN, F. Private 657 Derby Division Medal Clasps: CC SA01.
Medal Roll Reference: WO100/225/54+83 Orderly 11 General Hospital. To England on termination of engagement.
COMPSTON, Frederick Private 100 Crawshawbooth Division Medal Clasps: CC OFS.
Medal Roll Reference: WO100/225/235 Private Portland Hospital. To England contract expired.
CONNOR, R. Private 1700 Preston Corps Medal Clasps: CC OFS TVL.
Medal Roll Reference: WO100/225/170 Orderly 20 General Hospital Joined from Base Detail. To England for discharge.
COOKE, H. H. Private 337 Bedford Division (NFB Bedford) Medal Clasps: CC. NFBUAD Medal.
Medal Roll Reference: WO100/130/218 Sergeant Imperial Yeomanry Hospital Deelfontein.
COOKSEY, R. Private 770 Dudley Corps Medal Clasps: CC WITT.
Medal Roll Reference: WO100/225/195 Orderly 23 Field Hospital. Discharged time expired.
COOPER, C. Private 1623 Leicester Corps Medal Clasps: CC OFS TVL.
Medal Roll Reference: WO100/225/157 Orderly 13 General Hospital. To England expired contract 10 April 1901.
COOPER, F. R. Private 35 Preston Corps Medal Clasps: CC OFS TVL.
Medal Roll Reference: WO100/225/12+113 Orderly 2 General Hospital. From England 18 April 1900. To Cape Town for England 18 August 1900.
COOPER, F. R. Sergeant 1364 Preston Corps Medal Clasps: CC SA01.
Medal Roll Reference: WO100/225/54+83+107 Supply Officer 11 General Hospital. 1 General Hospital Wynberg. To England on termination of engagement 13 General Hospital. COOPER, T. R. on SJAB Bronze.
COOPER, Francis H. Private 348 Leicester Corps Medal Clasps: CC OFS.
Medal Roll Reference: WO100/225/133 Orderly 8 General Hospital. Died of disease Bloemfontein 3 July 1900.
COOPER, J. H. Sergeant 28 Ipswich Corps Medal Clasps: CC OFS.
Medal Roll Reference: WO100/225/115 Orderly 3 General Hospital. Transferred to Base Detail RAMC.
COOPER, John W. Private 65 Walton-le-Dale Division Medal Clasps: CC.
Medal Roll Reference: WO100/225/113 Orderly 2 General Hospital. From England 18 December 1899. To Cape Town for England 1 May 1900.
CORNALL, J. J. Private 1085 Walton-le-Dale Division Medal Clasps: NAT.
Medal Roll Reference: WO100/225/180 Orderly 14 Stationary Hospital.
COTTAM, G. Private 1566 Accrington Corps Medal Clasps: CC.
Medal Roll Reference: WO100/225/108+157 Orderly 13 General Hospital. To 1 General Hospital Wynberg 1 March 1901.
COTTAM, T. W. Private 406 Accrington Corps Medal Clasps: CC OFS.
Medal Roll Reference: WO100/225/134 Orderly 8 General Hospital. To England 20 July 1900.

COULTHERST, W. H. Private 1005 Dalton-in-Furness Division Medal Clasps: NAT.
Medal Roll Reference: WO100/225/162 Orderly 15 General Hospital. Transferred to England 26 August 1900.
COULTHURST, H. Private 1086 Walton-le-Dale Division Medal Clasps: NAT.
Medal Roll Reference: WO100/225/67 Orderly 18 General Hospital. To England 28 December 1900.
COULTON, G. Private 743 Heanor Division Medal Clasps: CC SA01.
Medal Roll Reference: WO100/225/54+83 Orderly 11 General Hospital. To England on termination of engagement.
COULTON, Samuel Private 1519 Haslingden Corps Medal Clasps: No Clasps.
Medal Roll Reference: WO100/225/67 Orderly 18 General Hospital. To England 30 May 1900.
COWEN, J. H. Private 624 Penrith Division Medal Clasps: CC SA01.
Medal Roll Reference: WO100/225/54+83 Orderly 11 General Hospital. To England on termination of engagement.
COWIN, Leonard B. 1st Class Sergeant 2 Metropolitan Corps Medal Clasps: CC OFS TVL SA01.
Medal Roll Reference: WO100/225/241 WO100/273/42+371 Supernumerary Officer HS *Princess of Wales*. Attached RAMC. South African Constabulary E Division 1 Sergeant E3034. "Medal and clasps issued 22 June 1905. Medal and clasps CC and OFS returned as medal and clasps Natal and CC already received from RAMC".
COWLEY, J. W. Private 632 Hull Corps Medal Clasps: CC OFS.
Medal Roll Reference: WO100/225/154 Orderly 10 General Hospital. To Base 14 July 1900.
COWLEY, T. E. Private 1382 Wellingborough Corps Medal Clasps: No Clasps.
Medal Roll Reference: WO100/225/58 Orderly 14 General Hospital. To HS *Simla* for duty 14 November 1900.
COWPER, P. Private 1824 Bolton Corps Medal Clasps: SA01.
Medal Roll Reference: WO100/225/86 Orderly 3 General Hospital Home 9 July 1901.
COX, A. Private 619 Oxford Division Medal Clasps: CC OFS TVL.
Medal Roll Reference: WO100/130/264 Private Imperial Yeomanry Field Hospital and Bearer Company A. J. COX on Imperial Yeomanry Bearer Corps Medal Roll.
COX, G. Private 745 Heanor Division Medal Clasps: CC SA01.
Medal Roll Reference: WO100/225/54+83 Orderly 11 General Hospital. To England on termination of engagement.
COX, G. W. Sergeant 328 Reading Division Medal Clasps: CC.
Medal Roll Reference: WO100/130/218 Staff Sergeant Imperial Yeomanry Hospital Deelfontein.
COX, H. F. 1st Class Sergeant 1 1659 Metropolitan Corps Medal Clasps: CC OFS TVL.
Medal Roll Reference: WO100/225/170+241 Supply Officer. HS *Princess of Wales*. Attached RAMC. 20 General Hospital joined from Base Detail. To England for discharge
COX, W. Private 732 Leicester Corps Medal Clasps: CC OFS TVL.
Medal Roll Reference: WO100/130/267 Private Imperial Yeomanry Field Hospital and Bearer Company. Joined Duke of Edinburgh's Volunteer Rifles at Cape Town September 1900 F. W. COX on Imperial Yeomanry Bearer Corps Medal Roll.
COX, W. Private 1103 Birmingham Corps Medal Clasps: NAT.
Medal Roll Reference: WO100/225/65 Orderly 13 Stationary Hospital. To HS *Dunera* 18 December 1900.
COX, W. Private 1274 Bury Division Medal Clasps: CC OFS.
Medal Roll Reference: WO100/225/134 Orderly 8 General Hospital. To England 10 October 1900.
COX, William Private 1883 Oldham Corps Medal Clasps: CC OFS TVL.
Medal Roll Reference: WO100/225/169 Orderly 17 General Hospital. Died of disease Standerton 23 May 1901.

CRAIG, R. J. C. K. Private 1392 St John Ambulance Brigade Medal Clasps: No Clasps.
Medal Roll Reference: WO100/225/58 Orderly 14 General Hospital. To HS *Simla* for duty 14 November 1900.

CRAMPHORN, W. Private 1509 Nuneaton Division Medal Clasps: CC TVL NAT.
Medal Roll Reference: WO100/225/61+128 Orderly Base Hospital Wynberg 7 General Hospital. To England time expired.

CRANE, F. W. Private 75 Oxford Division Medal Clasps: CC OFS.
Medal Roll Reference: WO100/225/115 Orderly 3 General Hospital. Transferred to Base Detail RAMC.

CRAVEN, E. Sergeant 29 Metropolitan Corps Medal Clasps: CC.
Medal Roll Reference: WO100/225/113 Orderly 2 General Hospital. From England 18 December 1899. To Cape Town for England 1 May 1900.

CRAWSHAW, J. Private 232 Dewsbury Corps Medal Clasps: CC JOH DIA WITT.
Medal Roll Reference: WO100/225/202 Orderly 20 Bearer Company. Discharged time expired 1 August 1900.

CRAWSHAW, J. W. Private 243 Rawtenstall Corps Medal Clasps: CC OFS.
Medal Roll Reference: WO100/225/191 Private Attached 20 Field Hospital. Left for duty at Heilbron Orange River Colony 23 June 1900.

CREED, B. R. Private 1890 Preston Corps Medal Clasps: CC OFS SA01.
Medal Roll Reference: WO100/225/86+115 Orderly 3 General Hospital. Transferred to Base Detail RAMC. Home 21 June 1901.

CREES, H. Private 270 1602 Metropolitan Corps Medal Clasps: CC.
Medal Roll Reference: WO100/225/61+72+125 Orderly 6 General Hospital. Base Hospital Wynberg invalided 9 June 1900. 24 Stationary Hospital. From Stationary Hospital Burgersdorp. Transferred to Base Detail 3 April 1901.

CRERAR, Alfred Private 1284 Haslingden Corps Medal Clasps: CC OFS.
Medal Roll Reference: WO100/225/154 Orderly 10 General Hospital. To Base 10 October 1900.

CREW, J. W. Private 1666 Royton Division Medal Clasps: OFS TVL.
Medal Roll Reference: WO100/225/180 Orderly 14 Stationary Hospital. 7 Ambulance Train.

CRISPIN, W. A. Private 739 Redruth Division Medal Clasps: CC SA01.
Medal Roll Reference: WO100/225/54+83 Orderly 11 General Hospital. To England on termination of engagement.

CRITCHFIELD, E. W. W Private 144 Metropolitan Corps Medal Clasps: CC OFS.
Medal Roll Reference: WO100/225/108+134 Orderly 1 General Hospital. 8 General Hospital. Discharged to Cape Town 15 June 1900.

CROFT, C. Private 1388 Weston-Super-Mare Division Medal Clasps: No Clasps.
Medal Roll Reference: WO100/225/58 Orderly 14 General Hospital. To HS *Simla* for duty 14 November 1900.

CROFTS, William Private 601 Sheffield Corps Medal Clasps: CC OFS.
Medal Roll Reference: WO100/225/138 Orderly 9 General Hospital.

CROOK, J. Private 199 Blackpool Division Medal Clasps: CC OFS.
Medal Roll Reference: WO100/225/176 Orderly 5 Stationary Hospital Sent to Base for England for discharge.

CROOKALL, C. F. Private 520 Blackpool Division Medal Clasps: NAT.
Medal Roll Reference: WO100/225/98 Orderly.

CROSS, J. Private 1056 Bolton Corps Medal Clasps: NAT.
Medal Roll Reference: WO100/225/65 Orderly 13 Stationary Hospital. To HS *Dunera* 18 December 1900.

CROSSE, R. H. Private 1148 Dewsbury Corps Medal Clasps: No Clasps.
Medal Roll Reference: WO100/225/14 Orderly.

CROSSLEY, F. Private 806 Oldham Corps Medal Clasps: CC OFS TVL.
Medal Roll Reference: WO100/225/113 Orderly 2 General Hospital. From England 28 April 1900.
To Cape Town for England 18 August 1900.
CROSSLEY, J. Private 898 Bolton Corps Medal Clasps: NAT.
Medal Roll Reference: WO100/225/162 Orderly 15 General Hospital. Transferred to HS *Nubia* 29
December 1900.
CROSTON, John Owen Private 197 Accrington Corps Medal Clasps: CC OFS.
Medal Roll Reference: WO100/225/176 Orderly 5 Stationary Hospital. Sent to Base for England
for discharge.
CROWTHER, J. Private 1124 Sheffield Corps Medal Clasps: NAT.
Medal Roll Reference: WO100/225/162 Orderly 15 General Hospital. Transferred to England 14
September 1900.
CROXFORD, Louis J. Private 713 Metropolitan Corps Medal Clasps: CC TVL SA01 KSA01
KSA02.
Medal Roll Reference: WO100/225/54+61+83 WO100/253/110+186 WO100/363/137 Orderly
11 General Hospital. To England on termination of engagement. Served Johannesburg Mounted
Rifles Trooper 1179 (TVL clasp) 4 April 1901 to 1 December 1901 Natal Volunteer Composite
Regiment 425.
CULLEN, A. Private 652 Derby Division Medal Clasps: CC SA01.
Medal Roll Reference: WO100/225/55+83 Orderly 11 General Hospital. To England on
termination of engagement.
CUNLIFFE, H. Private 1227 Nelson Corps Medal Clasps: CC OFS.
Medal Roll Reference: WO100/225/154 Orderly 10 General Hospital. To Base 10 October 1900.
CUNLIFFE, S. Private 1449 Accrington Corps Medal Clasps: No Clasps.
Medal Roll Reference: WO100/225/118 Orderly 4 General Hospital Sent to England time expired
28 November 1900.
CUNLIFFE, W. Private 1331 Bolton Corps Medal Clasps: CC.
Medal Roll Reference: WO100/225/158 Orderly 13 General Hospital. To England expired contract
27 January 1901.
CURRY, M. Private 1542 Oldham Corps Medal Clasps: CC.
Medal Roll Reference: WO100/225/108 Orderly 1 General Hospital.
CURZON, F. Private 833 Winsford Division Medal Clasps: OFS TVL.
Medal Roll Reference: WO100/225/185 Orderly Attached to 3rd Highland Brigade Field Hospital.
Transferred from 2 General Hospital 5 May 1900. To England 8 October 1900.
CUSHINGS, A. Private 1619 Metropolitan Corps Medal Clasps: CC OFS TVL.
Medal Roll Reference: WO100/225/122+187 Orderly 5 General Hospital. 18 Brigade Field
Hospital Joined 20 March 1901 Left 22 April 1901 for discharge.
DALE, F. Private 1819 Bolton Corps Medal Clasps: CC OFS SA01.
Medal Roll Reference: WO100/225/86+115 Orderly 3 General Hospital. Transferred to Base
Detail RAMC. Home 21 June 1901.
DALE, G. Private 1797 Birmingham Corps (Birmingham City Division) Medal Clasps: CC SA01.
Medal Roll Reference: WO100/225/55+84+89 Orderly 11 General Hospital. To England on
termination of engagement. Time expired 2 August 1901.
DALTON, E. E. Sergeant 882 Leeds Corps Medal Clasps: CC OFS SA01.
Medal Roll Reference: WO100/225/113+176+WO100/224/197 Supply Officer Attached RAMC
2 General Hospital 5 Stationary Hospital. Sent to Base for England for discharge.
DALTON, J. Private 1595 Oldham Corps Medal Clasps: CC.
Medal Roll Reference: WO100/225/76+107 Orderly 1 General Hospital. War Office Issue.
DANCE, H. G. Private 140 Metropolitan Corps Medal Clasps: CC.
Medal Roll Reference: WO100/225/108 Orderly 1 General Hospital.

DANN, John Private 1089 Haslingden Corps Medal Clasps: NAT.
Medal Roll Reference: WO100/225/162 Orderly 15 General Hospital. Transferred to England 14 September 1900.
DANN, T. Private 1773 Haslingden Corps Medal Clasps: CC.
Medal Roll Reference: WO100/225/173 Orderly 21 General Hospital.
DARBY, T. Private 920 Whaley Bridge Division Medal Clasps: NAT.
Medal Roll Reference: WO100/225/162 Orderly 15 General Hospital. Transferred to England 26 August 1900.
DARLING, G. A. Sergeant 597 Rochdale Corps Medal Clasps: CC OFS.
Medal Roll Reference: WO100/225/138 Supply Officer 9 General Hospital. To Base Detail 5 February 1901.
DASH, R. J. 1st Class Sergeant 25 Metropolitan Corps Medal Clasps: CC OFS.
Medal Roll Reference: WO100/225/115 Supply Officer 3 General Hospital. Transferred to Base Detail RAMC.
DAUGHTRY, H. Private 991 Dewsbury Corps Medal Clasps: NAT.
Medal Roll Reference: WO100/225/162 Orderly 15 General Hospital. Transferred to England 26 August 1900.
DAVIE, H. Private 1390 Leicester Corps Medal Clasps: No Clasps.
Medal Roll Reference: WO100/225/58+118 Orderly 14 General Hospital. To 4 General Hospital Mooi River. Joined from 14 General Hospital Newcastle on 9 September 1900. Sent to England time expired 28 November 1900.
DAVIES, E. G. 1st Class Sergeant 24 Metropolitan Corps Medal Clasps: CC.
Medal Roll Reference: WO100/225/2+113 Supply Officer 6 General Hospital. 2 General Hospital.
DAVIES, G. Private 162 Dowlais Division Medal Clasps: CC OFS.
Medal Roll Reference: WO100/225/62+70 Orderly Base Hospital Wynberg. 3 Hospital Train. To Base Detail RAMC Cape Town for England.
DAVIES, J. Private 1821 Bolton Corps Medal Clasps: CC OFS SA01.
Medal Roll Reference: WO100/225/86+115 Orderly 3 General Hospital. Transferred to Base Detail RAMC. Home 21 June 1901.
DAVIES, T. J. Private 182 Brynmawr Division Medal Clasps: CC.
Medal Roll Reference: WO100/225/69 Orderly 8 Stationary Hospital.
DAVIS, J. C. Private 465 Metropolitan Corps Medal Clasps: CC KSA01KSA02.
Medal Roll Reference: WO100/130/219+WO100/356/173 Sergeant Imperial Yeomanry Hospital Deelfontein. DAVIES on QSA Medal roll.
DAVIS, W. J. Private 1319 Sheffield Corps Medal Clasps: CC OFS TVL.
Medal Roll Reference: WO100/225/125+169 Private 6 General Hospital. To Base on expiration of contract 22 October 1900. 17 General Hospital. Transferred to Base Detail Cape Town 13 July 1901.
DAVISON, H. A. Private 884 Leeds Corps Medal Clasps: No Clasps.
Medal Roll Reference: WO100/225/113 Orderly 2 General Hospital.
DAWE, H. C. Sergeant 399 Metropolitan Corps Medal Clasps: CC OFS.
Medal Roll Reference: WO100/225/134 Supply Officer 8 General Hospital. To England 20 July 1900.
DAWSON, C. Private 1848 Leicester Corps Medal Clasps: CC OFS SA01.
Medal Roll Reference: WO100/225/86+115 Orderly 3 General Hospital. Transferred to Base Detail RAMC. Home 21 June 1901.
DAWSON, J. H. Private 1231 Burnley Division Medal Clasps: CC OFS.
Medal Roll Reference: WO100/225/138 Orderly 9 General Hospital. To Base Detail 12 October 1900.
DAWSON, J. H. Private 1868 Leeds Corps Medal Clasps: CC.
Medal Roll Reference: WO100/225/62 Orderly Base Hospital Wynberg.

DAWSON, T. Private 1008 Sheffield Corps Medal Clasps: NAT.
Medal Roll Reference: WO100/225/162 Orderly 15 General Hospital. Transferred to England 26 August 1900.
DAY, J. T. Private 1678 Nuneaton Division Medal Clasps: CC OFS TVL.
Medal Roll Reference: WO100/225/170 Orderly 20 General Hospital. Joined from Base Detail. To England for discharge.
DAYKIN, T. H. Private 505 Keswick Division Medal Clasps: CC OFS TVL.
Medal Roll Reference: WO100/225/230 Private Langman Hospital.
DEARNLEY, W. Private 1068 Welbeck Division Medal Clasps: OFS TVL NAT.
Medal Roll Reference: WO100/225/180+192 Orderly 14 Stationary Hospital. Attached 21 Field Hospital. Discharged.
DEE, D. J. Private 686 Nelson Corps Medal Clasps: CC WITT.
Medal Roll Reference: WO100/225/192 Orderly Attached 21 Field Hospital. Discharged.
DENNISON, J. Private 925 Kendal Division Medal Clasps: NAT.
Medal Roll Reference: WO100/225/162 Orderly 15 General Hospital. Transferred to England 26 August 1900.
DEWHURST, Edmund Private 403 Accrington Corps Medal Clasps: CC OFS TVL SA01 SA02.
Medal Roll Reference: WO100/225/134 WO100/272/65 Orderly 8 General Hospital. To England 20 July 1900 South African Constabulary Medical Corporal 1093 Reserve Battalion Corporal No 589.
DIAMOND, John Private 589 Colne Division Medal Clasps: CC.
Medal Roll Reference: WO100/225/73 Orderly 6 Stationary Hospital.
DICKENS, W. T. Private 846 Northampton Corps Medal Clasps: No Clasps.
Medal Roll Reference: WO100/225/16 Orderly.
DICKENSON, J. W. Private 1489 Leeds Corps Medal Clasps: No Clasps.
Medal Roll Reference: WO100/225/67 Orderly 18 General Hospital. To England 30 May 1900.
DICKINSON, M. Private 1261 Rishton Division Medal Clasps: CC OFS.
Medal Roll Reference: WO100/225/138 Orderly 9 General Hospital.
DICKINSON, W. Private 957 Preston Corps Medal Clasps: NAT.
Medal Roll Reference: WO100/225/163 Orderly 15 General Hospital. Transferred to England 26 August 1900.
DICKSON, I. Private 886 Crewe Division Medal Clasps: CC.
Medal Roll Reference: WO100/225/168+178 Orderly 16 General Hospital. Transferred to 7 Stationary Hospital 4 June 1900 Sent to England February 1901.
DIGGLE, S. Private 1216 Heywood Division Medal Clasps: CC OFS.
Medal Roll Reference: WO100/225/139 Orderly 9 General Hospital. To Base Detail 12 October 1900.
DIMELOW, J. T. Private 478 Warrington Corps Medal Clasps: CC TVL.
Medal Roll Reference: WO100/225/196+197 Orderly 24 Field Hospital. 9th Brigade Bearer Company 1st Division. To Base expiration of contract 6 January 1901.
DIXON, F. Private 1468 Oldham Corps Medal Clasps: No Clasps.
Medal Roll Reference: WO100/225/17+118 Orderly 4 General Hospital Sent to England time expired 28 November 1900.
DIXON, R. H. Private 129 Metropolitan Corps Medal Clasps: No Clasps.
Medal Roll Reference: WO100/225/15 Orderly.
DIXON, Robinson. Private 1040 Barnoldswick Division Medal Clasps: CC NAT SA02.
Medal Roll Reference: WO100/225/67 WO100/219/151+166 WO100/224/195 Orderly 18 General Hospital. To England 30 August 1900. RAMC 16704 Private. Discharged to England.
DIXON, W. Private 1236 Preston Corps Medal Clasps: CC OFS.
Medal Roll Reference: WO100/225/154 Orderly 10 General Hospital. To Base 27 November 1900.
DIXON, William Private 989 Dewsbury Corps Medal Clasps: NAT.

Medal Roll Reference: WO100/225/163 Orderly 15 General Hospital. Transferred to England 26 August 1900.

DODD, A. Private 566 Bolton Corps Medal Clasps: CC.
Medal Roll Reference: WO100/225/122 Orderly 5 General Hospital.

DODGSON, R. J. Private 951 Nelson Corps Medal Clasps: NAT.
Medal Roll Reference: WO100/225/163 Orderly 15 General Hospital. Transferred to England 26 August 1900.

DOE, Bertie Private 973 Metropolitan Corps Medal Clasps: NAT.
Medal Roll Reference: WO100/225/163 Orderly 15 General Hospital. Died dysentery Ladysmith 22 June 1900.

DOGGETT, J. W. Private 720 Great Eastern Railway Corps Medal Clasps: CC SA01.
Medal Roll Reference: WO100/225/55+84 Orderly 11 General Hospital. To England on termination of engagement.

DONE, R. C. Sergeant 810 Manchester Post Office Division Medal Clasps: CC OFS TVL SA01.
Medal Roll Reference: WO100/225/2+168+178 Supply Officer 7 Stationary Hospital. Sent to England February 1901. 16 General Hospital. Left 8 April 1901 for passage to England.

DONNELLY, Thomas Sergeant 877 Blackpool Division Medal Clasps: CC SA01.
Medal Roll Reference: WO100/225/178+WO100/224/199 Orderly Attached RAMC 7 Stationary Hospital. Sent to England February 1901.

DORLEY, H. Private 718 Great Eastern Railway Corps Medal Clasps: CC SA01.
Medal Roll Reference: WO100/225/55+84 Orderly 11 General Hospital. To England on termination of engagement.

DOWDALL, J. W. Private 1394 St John Ambulance Brigade Medal Clasps: No Clasps.
Medal Roll Reference: WO100/225/58 Orderly 14 General Hospital. To Johannesburg to join Johannesburg Police 21 November 1900.

DOWN, J. F. Private 316 St John Ambulance Brigade (NFB Exeter) Medal Clasps: CC SA01. NFBUAD Medal.
Medal Roll Reference: WO100/130/219 Private Imperial Yeomanry Hospital Deelfontein.

DOYLE, Patrick Private 1806 Birmingham Corps (Birmingham City Division) Medal Clasps: CC SA01.
Medal Roll Reference: WO100/225/62+89 Orderly Base Hospital Wynberg. Time expired 15 August 1901.

DRAGE, W. J. Private 396 Wellingborough Corps Medal Clasps: CC OFS.
Medal Roll Reference: WO100/225/134 Orderly 8 General Hospital Sick. To Cape Town 5 July 1900.

DRAIN, H. F. Private 1920 Metropolitan Corps Medal Clasps: CC OFS TVL SA01 SA02.
Medal Roll Reference: WO100/272/165+281 Private South African Constabulary C Division Medical Corporal C2116.

DRAKE, H. Private 1010 Sheffield Corps Medal Clasps: NAT.
Medal Roll Reference: WO100/225/163 Orderly 15 General Hospital. Invalided to England 3 July 1900.

DREW, D. H. Private 768 Northampton Corps Medal Clasps: CC SA01.
Medal Roll Reference: WO100/225/55+84 Orderly 11 General Hospital. To England on termination of engagement.

DREWERY, J. Private 930 Colne Division Medal Clasps: NAT.
Medal Roll Reference: WO100/225/163 Orderly 15 General Hospital. Transferred to England 26 August 1900.

DRIVER, R. Private 661 Medbourne Division Medal Clasps: CC OFS TVL.
Medal Roll Reference: WO100/225/194 Orderly 22 Field Hospital.

DRIVER, Thomas Private 692 Clitheroe Division Medal Clasps: CC OFS.
Medal Roll Reference: WO100/225/154 Orderly 10 General Hospital. To Base 7 August 1900.

DUERDEN, C. Private 929 Colne Division Medal Clasps: NAT.
Medal Roll Reference: WO100/225/163 Orderly 15 General Hospital. Transferred to England 26 August 1900.
DUGDALE, J. Private 1580 Whalley Division Medal Clasps: CC.
Medal Roll Reference: WO100/225/108 Orderly 1 General Hospital.
DUGDALE, Thomas Eastham Private 942 Clitheroe Division Medal Clasps: NAT.
Medal Roll Reference: WO100/225/163 Orderly 15 General Hospital. Transferred to England 26 August 1900.
DUNHAM, T. J. W. Private 1396 St John Ambulance Brigade Medal Clasps: No Clasps.
Medal Roll Reference: WO100/225/58 Orderly 14 General Hospital Invalided to England 2 December 1900 on HS *Avoca*.
DUNKLEY, W. Private 767 Northampton Corps Medal Clasps: CC WITT.
Medal Roll Reference: WO100/225/192 Orderly Attached 21 Field Hospital. Discharged.
DUNN, C. Private 1022 Oldham Corps Medal Clasps: NAT.
Medal Roll Reference: WO100/225/65 Orderly 13 Stationary Hospital. Locally discharged 23 October 1900.
DUNWELL, W. Private 1096 New Farnley Division Medal Clasps: OFS NAT.
Medal Roll Reference: WO100/225/180 Orderly 14 Stationary Hospital. 21 Bearer Company.
DUXBURY, A. E. Private 312 St John Ambulance Brigade (NFB Darwen) Medal Clasps: CC. NFBUAD Medal.
Medal Roll Reference: WO100/130/219 Private Imperial Yeomanry Hospital Deelfontein. W. I. DUXBURY on QSA Medal Roll.
EARL, T. Private 604 Sheffield Corps Medal Clasps: CC OFS.
Medal Roll Reference: WO100/225/139 Orderly 9 General Hospital. To Base Detail 7 August 1900.
EASTBURN, E. Private 1167 Leeds Corps Medal Clasps: CC OFS.
Medal Roll Reference: WO100/225/134 Orderly 8 General Hospital. To England 10 October 1900.
EASTHAM, Frederick A. Private 977 Accrington Corps Medal Clasps: NAT.
Medal Roll Reference: WO100/225/163 Orderly 15 General Hospital. Transferred to England 26 August 1900.
EASTHAM, J. P. Private 1084 Walton-le-Dale Division Medal Clasps: NAT.
Medal Roll Reference: WO100/225/67 Orderly 18 General Hospital. To England 30 August 1900.
EASTHAM, W. H. Private 1372 Preston Corps Medal Clasps: CC OFS TVL KSA01 KSA02.
Medal Roll Reference: WO100/225/158+186+WO100/352/16 Orderly 13 General Hospital. To Pretoria 18 December 1900. Attached to 8th Divisional 12th Brigade Field Hospital. Transferred to Base Detail Cape Town. H. W. EASTHAM in QSA Medal Roll.
EATON, G. Private 1605 Welbeck Division Medal Clasps: CC OFS TVL SA01.
Medal Roll Reference: WO100/225/74+84+108+122 Orderly 1 General Hospital Attached to 5 General Hospital. 11 General Hospital. 23 Bearer Company.
ECCLES, C. Sergeant 1075 Preston Corps Medal Clasps: NAT.
Medal Roll Reference: WO100/225/67 Supply Officer 18 General Hospital. To England 28 December 1900.
EDGCOMB, W. H. Private 43 Metropolitan Corps Medal Clasps: CC OFS TVL.
Medal Roll Reference: WO100/225/17+113 Orderly 6 General Hospital. 2 General Hospital.
EDMONDSON, Thomas Private 1224 Preston Corps Medal Clasps: CC OFS.
Medal Roll Reference: WO100/225/139 Orderly 9 General Hospital. To Base Detail 12 October 1900 (Mercantile Marine medal WW1).
EDWARDS, Charlie J. Private 317 St John Ambulance Brigade (NFB Haywards Heath) Medal Clasps: CC. NFBUAD Medal.
Medal Roll Reference: WO100/130/219 Private Imperial Yeomanry Hospital Deelfontein.
EDWARDS, George Private 1832 Ironbridge Corps Medal Clasps: CC SA01 SA02.

Medal Roll Reference: WO100/225/173 WO100/219/151 Orderly 21 General Hospital. RAMC 16632 Private Mafeking. Discharged. Bronze Medal duplicated on RAMC Medal Roll.

EKINS, F. Sergeant 4 1761 Northampton Corps Medal Clasps: CC OFS SA01.
Medal Roll Reference: WO100/225/87+115+241 Supply Officer HS *Princess of Wales*. Attached RAMC. 3 General Hospital. Transferred to Base Detail RAMC. Home 21 June 1901.

ELCOMBE, A. E. Private 1115 Kettering Corps Medal Clasps: NAT.
Medal Roll Reference: WO100/225/163 Orderly 15 General Hospital. Transferred to England 14 September 1900.

ELLIS, A. E. R. Sergeant 640 1844 Leicester Corps Medal Clasps: CC OFS TVL.
Medal Roll Reference: WO100/225/99+141 WO100/130/267 Supply Officer Portland Hospital. Sent home 3 September 1900. Returned to South Africa. Subsequently Imperial Yeomanry Bearer Corps.

ELLIS, Arthur Private 863 Wellingborough Corps Medal Clasps: CC OFS TVL.
Medal Roll Reference: WO100/225/125 Private 6 General Hospital. Died of disease Johannesburg 22 August 1900.

ELLIS, C. W. P. Sergeant 111 Faversham Division Medal Clasps: NAT.
Medal Roll Reference: WO100/225/75 Supply Officer Princess Christian Hospital Train.

ELLIS, E. Private 1269 Radcliffe Division Medal Clasps: CC.
Medal Roll Reference: WO100/225/122 Orderly 5 General Hospital.

ELLIS, Francis John Private 91 Metropolitan Corps Medal Clasps: CC OFS.
Medal Roll Reference: WO100/225/235 Private Portland Hospital. To England contract expired.

ELLIS, G. W. Private 1156 Birchwood Corps Medal Clasps: CC OFS.
Medal Roll Reference: WO100/225/139 Orderly 9 General Hospital. To Base Detail 12 October 1900.

ELLIS, J. E. Private 1407 Bradford Corps Medal Clasps: No Clasps.
Medal Roll Reference: WO100/225/59 Orderly 14 General Hospital. To HS *Simla* for duty 14 November 1900.

ELLIS, W. J. Private 283 Herne Bay Division Medal Clasps: NAT.
Medal Roll Reference: WO100/225/75 Orderly Princess Christian Hospital Train.

ELWELL, R. W. Private 287 Metropolitan Corps Medal Clasps: CC.
Medal Roll Reference: WO100/130/219 Sergeant Imperial Yeomanry Hospital Deelfontein.

EMERY, J. Private 1792 Derby Corps Medal Clasps: CC.
Medal Roll Reference: WO100/225/173 Orderly 21 General Hospital.

ENGLAND, A. Private 484 Tibshelf Corps Medal Clasps: NAT.
Medal Roll Reference: WO100/225/65 Orderly 13 Stationary Hospital. To SS *Formosa* 6 December 1900.

ENGLAND, H. Private 1552 Oldham Corps Medal Clasps: CC OFS.
Medal Roll Reference: WO100/225/139 Orderly 9 General Hospital. To Base Detail 30 January 1901.

ENSER, S. Private 975 Bury Division Medal Clasps: NAT.
Medal Roll Reference: WO100/225/163 Orderly 15 General Hospital. Transferred to England 26 August 1900.

ENTWISTLE, J. Private 1033 Tottington Division Medal Clasps: NAT.
Medal Roll Reference: WO100/225/163 Orderly 15 General Hospital. Transferred to HS *Nubia* 29 December 1900.

ENTWISTLE, R. Private 1345 Bolton Corps Medal Clasps: CC.
Medal Roll Reference: WO100/225/158 Orderly 13 General Hospital. To England expired contract 27 November 1900.

ENTWISTLE, W. Private 924 Radcliffe Division Medal Clasps: NAT.
Medal Roll Reference: WO100/225/163 Orderly 15 General Hospital. Transferred to England 26 August 1900.

ERRINGTON, John Private 1504 Morecombe Division Medal Clasps: TVL.
Medal Roll Reference: WO100/225/169 Orderly 17 General Hospital. Transferred to
Pietermaritzburg 30 November 1900. Died from typhoid Pietermaritzburg Fort Napier 19
December 1900.
EVANS, A. Private 1206 Metropolitan Corps Medal Clasps: CC TVL.
Medal Roll Reference: WO100/224/172 Private Rhodesian Field Force Hospital.
EVANS, A. E. Private 378 Handsworth & Smethwick Corps Medal Clasps: CC OFS.
Medal Roll Reference: WO100/225/134 Orderly 8 General Hospital. Sick to Cape Town 14 July
1900.
EVANS, Fredrick Robert 1st Class Sergeant 79 1733 Herne Bay Division Medal Clasps: CC OFS
TVL.
Medal Roll Reference: WO100/225/170+235 Staff Sergeant Supply officer Portland Hospital. To
England contract expired. 20 General Hospital.
EVANS, T. Private 605 Sheffield Corps Medal Clasps: CC OFS SA01 SA02.
Medal Roll Reference: WO100/225/139 WO100/219/205 Orderly 9 General Hospital. To Base
Detail 7 August 1900. RAMC Private No 15974. 4 January 1910 "Duplicate medal irrecoverable
Lost by Evans".
EVANS, W. Private 821 Welbeck Division Medal Clasps: CC OFS.
Medal Roll Reference: WO100/225/134 Orderly 8 General Hospital. To England 20 July 1900.
EYRE, W. Private 820 Welbeck Division Medal Clasps: CC OFS.
Medal Roll Reference: WO100/225/139 Orderly 9 General Hospital. To Base Detail 31 August
1900.
FACER, W. A. Private 1280 Brierfield Division Medal Clasps: CC OFS.
Medal Roll Reference: WO100/225/154 Orderly 10 General Hospital. To Base 10 October 1900.
FACER, W. E. Private 1277 Brierfield Division Medal Clasps: CC OFS.
Medal Roll Reference: WO100/225/154 Orderly 10 General Hospital. To Base 22 October 1900.
FAIRHURST, J. J. Private 1248 Preston Corps Medal Clasps: CC OFS.
Medal Roll Reference: WO100/225/134 Orderly 8 General Hospital. To England 10 October 1900.
FALLOWS, W. E. Private 1328 Bolton Corps Medal Clasps: CC.
Medal Roll Reference: WO100/225/158 Orderly 13 General Hospital. To England expired contract
27 November 1900.
FALSHAW, C. A. S. Private 670 Manchester Post Office Division Medal Clasps: CC SA01.
Medal Roll Reference: WO100/225/55+84 Orderly 11 General Hospital. To England on
termination of engagement.
FARNWORTH, A. Private 1362 Bolton Corps Medal Clasps: CC.
Medal Roll Reference: WO100/225/158 Orderly 13 General Hospital. To England expired contract
27 November 1900.
FARROW, Albert Private 1762 Northampton Corps Medal Clasps: CC SA01.
Medal Roll Reference: WO100/225/55+84 Orderly 11 General Hospital. To England on
termination of engagement. Died on HMT *Pinemore* from pneumonia 17 July 1901.
FAULKNER, J. E. P. Private 1383 Wellingborough Corps Medal Clasps: No Clasps.
Medal Roll Reference: WO100/225/59 Orderly 14 General Hospital. To HS *Simla* for duty 14
November 1900.
FAULKNER, J. W. Private 1384 Wellingborough Corps Medal Clasps: No Clasps.
Medal Roll Reference: WO100/225/59 Orderly 14 General Hospital. To HS *Simla* for duty 14
November 1900.
FAZACKERLEY, T. Private 196 Preston Corps Medal Clasps: CC OFS.
Medal Roll Reference: WO100/225/176 Orderly 5 Stationary Hospital Sent to Base for England
for discharge.
FEASBY, W. Private 1202 Leeds Corps Medal Clasps: CC OFS.

Medal Roll Reference: WO100/225/139 Orderly 9 General Hospital. To Base Detail 12 October 1900.

FELLOWS, E. E. Private 967 Dudley Corps Medal Clasps: NAT.
Medal Roll Reference: WO100/225/163 Orderly 15 General Hospital. Transferred to HS *Nubia* 29 December 1900.

FELSTEAD, L. W. Sergeant 1337 Leicester Corps Medal Clasps: CC.
Medal Roll Reference: WO100/225/158 Supply Officer 13 General Hospital. To England expired contract 27 November 1900. (noted as H H L FELSTEAD by William INDER).

FELTHAM, H. Private 1557 Isle of Wight Corps Medal Clasps: CC OFS TVL NAT.
Medal Roll Reference: WO100/225/108+128 Orderly 1 General Hospital. Transferred to 7 General Hospital. To England time expired.

FERGUSON, Albert Edward Private 116 Metropolitan Corps Medal Clasps: CC SA01.
Medal Roll Reference: WO100/225/55+84 Orderly 11 General Hospital. To England on termination of engagement.

FERGUSON, Alfred Private 309 St John Ambulance Brigade (NFB Haywards Heath) Medal Clasps: CC.
Medal Roll Reference: WO100/130/219 Private Imperial Yeomanry Hospital Deelfontein.

FERMINGER, C. Private 46 Metropolitan Corps Medal Clasps: CC OFS.
Medal Roll Reference: WO100/225/115 Orderly 3 General Hospital. Transferred to Base Detail RAMC.

FERRIS, T. Private 1172 Leeds Corps Medal Clasps: CC OFS.
Medal Roll Reference: WO100/225/62 Orderly Base Hospital Wynberg. 10 General Hospital. To Base 10 October 1900.

FIELD, F. Private 17 1664 Dewsbury Cor P. Medal Clasps: CC OFS TVL.
Medal Roll Reference: WO100/225/170+241 Orderly HS *Princess of Wales*. Attached RAMC. 20 General Hospital Joined from Base Detail. To England for discharge.

FIELD, J. W. Private 297 Metropolitan Corps Medal Clasps: CC.
Medal Roll Reference: WO100/130/219 Private Imperial Yeomanry Hospital Deelfontein.

FIELDING, R. H. Private 1416 Hebden Bridge Corps Medal Clasps: No Clasps.
Medal Roll Reference: WO100/225/59 Orderly 14 General Hospital. To HS *Simla* for duty 14 November 1900.

FINCH, B. H. Private 475 Metropolitan Corps Medal Clasps: CC OFS.
Medal Roll Reference: WO100/225/139 Orderly 9 General Hospital. To Base Detail 7 August 1900.

FINCH, T. H. Private 1654 Accrington Corps Medal Clasps: SA01.
Medal Roll Reference: WO100/225/88 Orderly.

FINDING, George Private 557 Birmingham Corps Medal Clasps: CC OFS.
Medal Roll Reference: WO100/225/139 Orderly 9 General Hospital. To Base Detail 7 August 1900.

FINIKIN, T. Private 496 North Staffs Corps Medal Clasps: CC OFS.
Medal Roll Reference: WO100/225/139 Orderly 9 General Hospital. To Base Detail 7 August 1900.

FISH, R. Private 1360 Bolton Corps Medal Clasps: CC.
Medal Roll Reference: WO100/225/158 Orderly 13 General Hospital. Invalided to England 13 November 1900.

FISH, W. T. Sergeant 198 1703 Blackpool Division Medal Clasps: CC OFS TVL SA01 SA02.
Medal Roll Reference: WO100/225/93+170+176 Supply Officer 20 General Hospital. 3 and 5 Stationary Hospitals. Sent to Base for England for discharge.

FISHER, A. F. Private 1757 Metropolitan Corps Medal Clasps: CC OFS SA01.
Medal Roll Reference: WO100/225/87+115 Orderly 3 General Hospital. Transferred to Base Detail RAMC. Home 9 July 1901.

FISHER, T. H. Private 1567 Accrington Corps Medal Clasps: CC OFS TVL.
Medal Roll Reference: WO100/225/158 Orderly 13 General Hospital. To England expired contract 10 April 1901.
FITCH, G. H. Private 1784 Metropolitan Corps Medal Clasps: CC OFS SA01.
Medal Roll Reference: WO100/225/87+115 Orderly 3 General Hospital. Transferred to Base Detail RAMC. Home 6 July 1901.
FITTON, G. Private 1462 Oldham Corps Medal Clasps: CC OFS TVL NAT.
Medal Roll Reference: WO100/225/163+183 Orderly 15 General Hospital. 17 Stationary Hospital. Transferred to Pretoria 29 August 1900. To Base 24 November 1900.
FLEETWOOD, E. Private 526 Blackpool Division Medal Clasps: NAT.
Medal Roll Reference: WO100/225/100 Orderly.
FLEMING, W. H. Corporal 1315 Bradford Corps Medal Clasps: CC.
Medal Roll Reference: WO100/224/172 Corporal Rhodesian Field Force Hospital.
FLETCHER, C. Private 1810 Handsworth & Smethwick Corps Medal Clasps: CC OFS SA01 SA02.
Medal Roll Reference: WO100/225/72 WO100/224/196 WO100/273/176+249 Orderly 24 Stationary Hospital. From Base Detail 15 April 1901 Attached RAMC. South African Constabulary E Division 1st Sergeant E3604.
FLETCHER, W. Sergeant 813 Bolton Corps Medal Clasps: CC OFS TVL.
Medal Roll Reference: WO100/225/125 Supernumerary Officer 6 General Hospital. Locally discharged on expiration of contract 20 February 1901.
FLOWER, G. Private 659 Northampton Corps Medal Clasps: CC WITT.
Medal Roll Reference: WO100/225/192 Orderly Attached 21 Field Hospital. Discharged.
FOLEY, H. G. Private 152 Herne Bay Division Medal Clasps: No Clasps.
Medal Roll Reference: WO100/225/18 Orderly.
FOLWELL, L. Private 735 Leicester Corps Medal Clasps: CC SA01.
Medal Roll Reference: WO100/225/55+84 Orderly 11 General Hospital. To England on termination of engagement.
FORD, J. Private 711 Metropolitan Corps Medal Clasps: CC SA01.
Medal Roll Reference: WO100/225/55+62+84 Orderly 11 General Hospital. To England on termination of engagement.
FOREMAN, A. Private 64 Leicester Corps Medal Clasps: No Clasps.
Medal Roll Reference: WO100/225/113 Orderly 2 General Hospital.
FORREST, John Shepherd Private 572 Oldham Corps Medal Clasps: CC SA01.
Medal Roll Reference: WO100/225/76+122 Supply Officer 5 General Hospital. War Office Issue
FORSTER, H. G. Private 1759 Metropolitan Corps Medal Clasps: CC OFS SA01.
Medal Roll Reference: WO100/225/87+115 Orderly 3 General Hospital. Transferred to Base Detail RAMC. Home 21 June 1901.
FORTUNE, C. W. Private 827 Bradford Corps Medal Clasps: CC OFS.
Medal Roll Reference: WO100/225/115 Orderly 3 General Hospital. Transferred to Base Detail RAMC.
FOSTER, A. Private 531 Preston Corps Medal Clasps: CC OFS TVL.
Medal Roll Reference: WO100/225/231 Private Langman Hospital.
FOSTER, A. T. Private 706 Metropolitan Corps Medal Clasps: CC TVL SA01.
Medal Roll Reference: WO100/225/55+84 Orderly 11 General Hospital. Temporary Hospital Christiana.
FOSTER, George Private 165 Tibshelf Corps Medal Clasps: CC.
Medal Roll Reference: WO100/225/62+70+175 Orderly Base Hospital Wynberg. 3 Stationary Hospital. 3 Hospital Train. Sick to 5 General Hospital Cape Town. Invalided 31 July 1901.
FOSTER, J. Private 70 Tibshelf Corps Medal Clasps: CC OFS.

Medal Roll Reference: WO100/225/115 Orderly 3 General Hospital. Transferred to Base Detail RAMC.

FOSTER, Walter James Private 529 Preston Corps Medal Clasps: CC OFS TVL.
Medal Roll Reference: WO100/225/231 Private Langman Hospital.

FOSTER, William Sergeant 193 Oldham Corps Medal Clasps: CC OFS.
Medal Roll Reference: WO100/225/176 Orderly 5 Stationary Hospital Sent to Base for England for discharge.

FOULDS, J. Private 780 1564 Morecombe Division Medal Clasps: CC OFS TVL.
Medal Roll Reference: WO100/225/75+185 Orderly No 4 Hospital Train. Attached to 3rd Highland Brigade Field Hospital. Transferred from 2 General Hospital 5 May 1900. Left sick at Kroonstad 16 August 1900.

FOULKES, W. 1st Class Sergeant 138 Redruth Division Medal Clasps: CC.
Medal Roll Reference: WO100/225/69 Supply Officer 8 Stationary Hospital.

FOX, B. G. Private 480 Metropolitan Corps Medal Clasps: CC TVL.
Medal Roll Reference: WO100/225/196+197 Orderly 24 Field Hospital. To Base expiration of contract 6 January 1901. 9th Brigade Bearer Company 1st Division.

FOX, C. H. Sergeant 519 1825 Blackpool Division Medal Clasps: OFS NAT.
Medal Roll Reference: WO100/225/18+65+139 Orderly 13 Stationary Hospital from 27 March 1900. To Base Detail 7 August 1900. To HS *Simla* 16 August 1900. Supply Officer 9 General Hospital. To Base Detail 15 July 1901.

FOX, R. Private 992 Dewsbury Corps Medal Clasps: NAT.
Medal Roll Reference: WO100/225/67 Orderly 18 General Hospital. To England 30 August 1900.

FRANCE, R. G. Corporal 1298 Blackpool Division Medal Clasps: CC TVL.
Medal Roll Reference: WO100/224/172 Corporal Rhodesian Field Force Hospital.

FRANCIS, C. W. Private 610 Belper Division Medal Clasps: CC OFS.
Medal Roll Reference: WO100/225/139 Orderly 9 General Hospital. To Base Detail 7 August 1900.

FRANCIS, W. Private 33 Wellingborough Corps Medal Clasps: No Clasps.
Medal Roll Reference: WO100/225/113 Orderly 2 General Hospital.

FRANKEL, J. Sergeant 611 Metropolitan Corps Medal Clasps: CC OFS.
Medal Roll Reference: WO100/225/139 Supply Officer 9 General Hospital. To Base Detail 7 August 1900.

FRANKLIN, H. T. Private 1401 1760 St John Ambulance Brigade Medal Clasps: CC OFS SA01.
Medal Roll Reference: WO100/225/59+115 Orderly 14 General Hospital. To HS *Simla* for duty 14 November 1900 3 General Hospital. Transferred to Base Detail RAMC. Home 21 June 1901.

FRECKNALL, W. Private 649 Worksop Division Medal Clasps: CC WITT.
Medal Roll Reference: WO100/225/203 Orderly 21 Bearer Company. Sent home for discharge August 1900.

FREEBORN, W. J. Private 142 Metropolitan Corps Medal Clasps: CC.
Medal Roll Reference: WO100/225/108 Orderly 1 General Hospital.

FREEMAN, G. Private 625 Edenfield Division Medal Clasps: CC OFS.
Medal Roll Reference: WO100/225/154 Orderly 10 General Hospital. To Base 17 July 1900.

FREEMAN, Henry Francis Private 92 Northampton Corps Medal Clasps: CC OFS.
Medal Roll Reference: WO100/225/235 Private Portland Hospital. To England contract expired.

FREEMAN, T. Private 907 Derby Division Medal Clasps: NAT.
Medal Roll Reference: WO100/225/163 Orderly 15 General Hospital. Transferred to HS *Nubia* 29 December 1900.

FRISKEN, W. Private 249 Radcliffe Division Medal Clasps: CC JOH WITT.
Medal Roll Reference: WO100/225/191 Private Attached 20 Field Hospital. Transferred to Base 4 January 1901.

FRITH, F. E. Private 676 Bolton Corps Medal Clasps: CC SA01.
Medal Roll Reference: WO100/225/55+84 Orderly 11 General Hospital. To England on termination of engagement.
FURRELL, F. Sergeant 1007 Sheffield Corps Medal Clasps: OFS NAT SA01 SA02.
Medal Roll Reference: WO100/225/132+195 Supply Officer 7 General Hospital. Transferred to Harrismith 23 Field Hospital. Discharged time expired.
GADSBY, W. H. Private 865 Wellingborough Corps Medal Clasps: CC OFS TVL SA02 KSA01 KSA02.
Medal Roll Reference: WO100/225/62+125 WO100/272/109 WO100/366/77 Orderly Base Hospital Wynberg. 6 General Hospital. To Base on expiration of contract 20 February 1901. Cape Medical Staff J Company Corporal 25390. South African Constabulary Northern Transvaal 3rd Class Trooper B1700.
GAINHAM, H. Private 1112 Madeley Division Medal Clasps: NAT.
Medal Roll Reference: WO100/225/118 Orderly 4 General Hospital Sent to England time expired 9 September 1900.
GALE, H. Private 769 Derby Division Medal Clasps: CC WITT.
Medal Roll Reference: WO100/225/195 Orderly 23 Field Hospital. Discharged time expired.
GALE, W. H. Private 518 Southport Division Medal Clasps: CC OFS.
Medal Roll Reference: WO100/225/139 Orderly 9 General Hospital. To Base Detail 7 August 1900.
GALLIER, C. Private 1831 Ironbridge Corps Medal Clasps: CC.
Medal Roll Reference: WO100/225/108 Orderly 1 General Hospital.
GALLOWAY, H. Private 1741 Warrington Corps Medal Clasps: CC OFS SA01.
Medal Roll Reference: WO100/225/87+115 Orderly 3 General Hospital. Transferred to Base Detail RAMC. Home 21 June 1901.
GARDENER, H. Private 49 Metropolitan Corps Medal Clasps: CC OFS.
Medal Roll Reference: WO100/225/115 Orderly 3 General Hospital. Transferred to Base Detail RAMC.
GARDINER, T. Private 1215 Leeds Corps Medal Clasps: CC OFS.
Medal Roll Reference: WO100/225/154 Orderly 10 General Hospital. To Base 10 October 1900.
GARDNER, Fred W. Sergeant 1102 Birmingham Corps Medal Clasps: OFS TVL NAT KSA01 KSA02.
Medal Roll Reference: WO100/225/65 WO100/366/35 Supply Officer 13 Stationary Hospital. To HS *Dunera* 18 December 1900. South African Constabulary A Division Medical Corporal A1866. Service in St John Ambulance Brigade April 1900 to January 1901. Service in South African Constabulary 5 March 1901 to 4 May 1901.
GARNER, H. Private 1099 Leicester Corps Medal Clasps: NAT.
Medal Roll Reference: WO100/225/118 Orderly 4 General Hospital Sent to England time expired 19 December 1900.
GARNER, T. H. Private 279 Metropolitan Corps Medal Clasps: CC.
Medal Roll Reference: WO100/225/125 Private 6 General Hospital. To Base on expiration of contract 18 June 1900.
GAVAN, J. Private 665 Manchester Post Office Division Medal Clasps: CC TVL SA01.
Medal Roll Reference: WO100/225/55+84 Orderly 11 General Hospital. Discharged locally on termination of engagement.
GEE, Ernest Private 501 Sheffield Corps Medal Clasps: NAT.
Medal Roll Reference: WO100/225/65 Orderly 13 Stationary Hospital Locally. Discharged 22 December 1900.
GEE, R. E. Private 1240 Preston Corps Medal Clasps: CC OFS.
Medal Roll Reference: WO100/225/134 Orderly 8 General Hospital. To England 10 October 1900.
GEE, W. F. Sergeant 765 Northampton Corps Medal Clasps: CC OFS TVL.

Medal Roll Reference: WO100/225/194 Supernumerary Officer 22 Field Hospital.

GELLING, J. C. Private 1255 Padiham Division Medal Clasps: CC.
Medal Roll Reference: WO100/225/125 Private 6 General Hospital. Invalided 21 October 1900.

GENT, T. M. Private 228 Babbington Corps Medal Clasps: CC.
Medal Roll Reference: WO100/225/125 Private 6 General Hospital. To Base on expiration of contract 5 June 1900.

GEORGE, William R. Private 1769 Bury Division Medal Clasps: CC OFS.
Medal Roll Reference: WO100/225/139 Orderly 9 General Hospital. To Base Detail 23 July 1901.

GETHEN, R. B. Private 1713 Denaby Cadeby Main Division Medal Clasps: CC OFS TVL.
Medal Roll Reference: WO100/225/122+168 Orderly 5 General Hospital. 16 General Hospital. Left 14 May 1901 for passage to England.

GIBBS, A. J. Private 620 Oxford Division Medal Clasps: CC SA01.
Medal Roll Reference: WO100/225/55+84 Orderly 11 General Hospital. To England on termination of engagement.

GIBBS, G. Private 553 Bristol Corps Medal Clasps: CC.
Medal Roll Reference: WO100/225/62+72+122 Orderly 5 General Hospital Wynberg. From Base Detail to 24 Stationary Hospital. Transferred to Base Detail 24 February 1901.

GIDDENS, Charles Sergeant 41 1794 Metropolitan Corps Medal Clasps: CC OFS TVL SA01.
Medal Roll Reference: WO100/225/19+87+113 Supply Officer 6 General Hospital. 3 General Hospital. Died of disease Kroonstad 5 May 1901.

GILMAN, H. Private 1815 Bolton Corps Medal Clasps: CC.
Medal Roll Reference: WO100/225/173 Orderly 21 General Hospital.

GLASIER, C. H. Private 432 Metropolitan Corps Medal Clasps: OFS TVL NAT SA01.
Medal Roll Reference: WO100/225/91 Orderly Attached to RAMC 7 General Hospital. To England time expired.

GLOVER, J. Private 1045 Nelson Corps Medal Clasps: NAT.
Medal Roll Reference: WO100/225/180 Orderly 14 Stationary Hospital.

GOACHER, W. Private 1826 Welbeck Division Medal Clasps: CC OFS SA01.
Medal Roll Reference: WO100/225/87+116 Orderly 3 General Hospital. Transferred to Base Detail RAMC. Home 21 June 1901.

GODDARD, T. Private 874 Leicester Corps Medal Clasps: CC OFS JOH DIA BELF.
Medal Roll Reference: WO100/225/198 Orderly 18th Brigade Bearer Company. Joined 6 May 1900. Left company on completion of engagement 20 November 1900.

GOLDING, C. Private 1648 Bury Division Medal Clasps: No Clasps.
Medal Roll Reference: WO100/225/143 Orderly.

GOLDSWORTHY, L. Private 125 Metropolitan Corps Medal Clasps: No Clasps.
Medal Roll Reference: WO100/225/19 Orderly.

GOODENOUGH, E. Private 788 Bacup Division Medal Clasps: CC OFS.
Medal Roll Reference: WO100/225/116 Orderly 3 General Hospital. Transferred to Base Detail RAMC.

GOODWIN, A. Private 638 Ipswich Corps Medal Clasps: CC OFS.
Medal Roll Reference: WO100/225/154 Orderly 10 General Hospital. To Base 7 August 1900.

GOODWIN, C. E. Private 515 Metropolitan Corps Medal Clasps: CC NAT.
Medal Roll Reference: WO100/225/196 Orderly 24 Field Hospital. To Base demobilised 10 August 1900.

GOODWIN, G. W. Private 1712 Denaby Cadeby Main Division Medal Clasps: CC OFS TVL.
Medal Roll Reference: WO100/225/170 Orderly 20 General Hospital. Joined from Base Detail. To England for discharge.

GOODWIN, John H. Private 639 Ipswich Corps Medal Clasps: CC OFS.
Medal Roll Reference: WO100/225/154 Orderly 10 General Hospital. Died of disease Bloemfontein 17 June 1900.

GORHAM, A. S. Private 226 Ramsgate Corps Medal Clasps: NAT.
Medal Roll Reference: WO100/225/75 Orderly Princess Christian Hospital Train.
GORNALL, A. Private 1579 Whalley Division Medal Clasps: CC.
Medal Roll Reference: WO100/225/122 Orderly 5 General Hospital.
GORST, J. W. Sergeant 194 1587 Walton-le-Dale Division Medal Clasps: CC OFS.
Medal Roll Reference: WO100/225/139+176 Orderly 5 Stationary Hospital. Supply Officer 9 General Hospital. To Base Detail 6 July 1901. Sent to Base for England for discharge.
GORTON, L. Private 1250 Morecombe Division Medal Clasps: CC OFS.
Medal Roll Reference: WO100/225/139 Orderly 9 General Hospital. To Base Detail 12 October 1900.
GOUDGE, H. E. Private 1739 Metropolitan Corps Medal Clasps: CC.
Medal Roll Reference: WO100/225/69 Orderly 8 Stationary Hospital.
GOULD, F. Private 1866 Leeds Corps Medal Clasps: CC.
Medal Roll Reference: WO100/225/108 Orderly 1 General Hospital.
GRACE, Richard Private 1408 Dewsbury Corps Medal Clasps: No Clasps.
Medal Roll Reference: WO100/225/59 Orderly 14 General Hospital. Died of disease Newcastle 19 January 1901.
GRADNAR, J. Private 330 Ebbw Vale Division Medal Clasps: CC.
Medal Roll Reference: WO100/130/219 Corporal Probably Imperial Yeomanry Hospital Deelfontein as G. GARDENER on Imperial Yeomanry Hospital Staff QSA Medal Roll.
GRAHAM, Edward 1st Class Sergeant 621 Haslingden Corps Medal Clasps: CC WITT.
Medal Roll Reference: WO100/225/192 Supply Officer Attached 21 Field Hospital. Discharged.
GRAHAM, L. Private 945 Metropolitan Corps Medal Clasps: OFS TVL NAT.
Medal Roll Reference: WO100/225/180+192 Orderly 14 Stationary Hospital. Attached 21 Field Hospital. Discharged.
GRAHAM, R. Private 815 Padiham Division Medal Clasps: CC.
Medal Roll Reference: WO100/225/168+178 Orderly 16 General Hospital. Transferred to 7 Stationary Hospital 4 June 1900. Sent to England September 1900.
GRAHAM, W. Private 417 Padiham Division Medal Clasps: CC OFS.
Medal Roll Reference: WO100/225/238 1st Grade Orderly Van Alen American Field Hospital.
GREATOREX, J. Private 608 Belper Division Medal Clasps: CC OFS.
Medal Roll Reference: WO100/225/139 Orderly 9 General Hospital. To Concentration Camp Naauwpoort 22 May 1900.
GREEN, Frederick William Private 1101 Leicester Corps Medal Clasps: OFS TVL NAT SA01 SA02 KSA01 KSA02.
Medal Roll Reference: WO100/225/180 WO100/273/393 WO100/366/35 Orderly 14 Stationary Hospital. South African Constabulary A Division Medical Corporal A1869. Service in St John Ambulance Brigade May 1900 to January 1901. Service in South African Constabulary from 5 March 1901 to 4 May 1901. Discharged 3 May 1904.
GREEN, Frederick William Private 132 1482 Wellingborough Corps Medal Clasps: No Clasps. China Medal.
Medal Roll Reference: WO100/225/19 Orderly HS *Maine*. On medal roll for HS *Maine* for China WO100/96/38+39.
GREEN, George Sergeant 764 Barnoldswick Division Medal Clasps: CC OFS.
Medal Roll Reference: WO100/225/204 Supply Officer 22 Bearer Company. Died of disease Dewetsdorp 1 May 1900.
GREEN, J. Private 911 Derby Division Medal Clasps: NAT.
Medal Roll Reference: WO100/225/163 Orderly 15 General Hospital. Transferred to England 26 August 1900.
GREEN, J. Private 1781 Bury Division Medal Clasps: No Clasps.
Medal Roll Reference: WO100/225/143 Orderly.

GREEN, J. Private 1786 Keighley Corps Medal Clasps: CC.
Medal Roll Reference: WO100/225/69+108 Orderly 8 Stationary Hospital. 1 General Hospital.

GREENAWAY, J. Private 1679 Oxford Division Medal Clasps: OFS TVL SA01.
Medal Roll Reference: WO100/225/88+203 Orderly 20 General Hospital. Joined 21 Bearer Company from February 1901 and sent home from Ficksburg 1 July 1901.

GREENFIELD, A. Private 1015 Sheffield Corps Medal Clasps: NAT.
Medal Roll Reference: WO100/225/163 Orderly 15 General Hospital. Transferred to HS *Nubia* 29 December 1900.

GREENFIELD, A. H. Private 1138 Barnoldswick Division Medal Clasps: CC OFS SA01 KSA01 KSA02.
Medal Roll Reference: WO100/225/55+84+154 WO100/352/148 Orderly 11 General Hospital. To England on termination of engagement. 10 General Hospital. To Base 10 October 1900. RAMC Private 15792. Discharged on termination of engagement Served 11 months with St John Ambulance Brigade which added to his service with RAMC makes him eligible for the King's South Africa Medal.

GREENHALGH, J. Private 1578 Bolton Corps Medal Clasps: CC.
Medal Roll Reference: WO100/225/108 Orderly 1 General Hospital.

GREENWOOD, D. A. Sergeant 469 Blackpool Division Medal Clasps: CC OFS.
Medal Roll Reference: WO100/225/134 Supply Officer 8 General Hospital. Sick to Cape Town 9 July 1900.

GREENWOOD, Ernest Private 702 Hebden Bridge Corps Medal Clasps: CC OFS TVL SA01 SA02.
Medal Roll Reference: WO100/225/55+84 WO100/272/177+293 Orderly 11 11 General Hospital. To England on termination of engagement. South African Constabulary C Division Corporal C2114.

GREENWOOD, G. H. Private 1908 Handsworth & Smethwick Corps Medal Clasps: No definite QSA Medal roll entry identified.
Medal Roll Reference: No definite QSA Medal roll entry identified. (Possibly WO100/170/245 Lance Corporal 8469 Warwickshire Regiment. WO100/168/319+365 Private 6351 4 Royal Lancaster Regiment. Medal Clasps CC OFS SA01).

GREENWOOD, Herbert H. 1st Class Sergeant 188 Dewsbury Corps Medal Clasps: CC SA01 SA02 JOH DIA WITT KSA01 KSA02.
Medal Roll Reference: WO100/225/202 WO100/273/72+260 WO100/366/166 Supply Officer 20 Bearer Company. Transferred to South African Constabulary 9 February 1901 E Division 1st Sergeant E646. Discharged time expired 21 February 1902. Service in St John Ambulance Brigade for 13 months. Service in South African Constabulary from 11 February 1901 to 21 February 1902.

GREENWOOD, J. Private 1477 Keighley Corps Medal Clasps: CC OFS TVL NAT.
Medal Roll Reference: WO100/225/80+163+183 Orderly 15 General Hospital Howick. Transferred to Pretoria 29 August 1900. 17 Stationary Hospital Middleburg September to November 1900. To Base 24 November 1900.

GREENWOOD, J. S. Private 1424 Hebden Bridge Corps Medal Clasps: No Clasps.
Medal Roll Reference: WO100/225/80 Orderly 15 General Hospital Howick. 20 Stationary and 17 Stationary Hospital Middleburg. Departure 10 November 1900.

GREENWOOD, W. Private 1417 Hebden Bridge Corps Medal Clasps: No Clasps.
Medal Roll Reference: WO100/225/59 Orderly 14 General Hospital. To HS *Simla* for duty 14 November 1900.

GREENWOOD, William Private 1714 Tibshelf Corps Medal Clasps: OFS TVL.
Medal Roll Reference: WO100/225/203 Orderly 20 General Hospital. Joined 21 Bearer Company from February 1901 and sent home for discharge June 1901.

GREETS, J. A. Private 234 Metropolitan Corps Medal Clasps: CC OFS TVL.
Medal Roll Reference: WO100/225/202 Orderly 20 Bearer Company. Discharged time expired 1 August 1900.
GREGSON, J. Private 517 Southport Division Medal Clasps: CC OFS.
Medal Roll Reference: WO100/225/139 Orderly 9 General Hospital. To Base Detail 7 August 1900.
GREGSON, T. Private 523 Blackpool Division Medal Clasps: NAT.
Medal Roll Reference: WO100/225/101 Orderly.
GREGSON, W. Sergeant 1220 Preston Corps Medal Clasps: CC OFS.
Medal Roll Reference: WO100/225/139 Supply Officer 9 General Hospital. To Base Detail 12 October 1900.
GREIG, F. Private 997 Rishton Division Medal Clasps: NAT.
Medal Roll Reference: WO100/225/164 Orderly 15 General Hospital. Invalided to SS *Trojan* 13 August 1900.
GREWCOCK, W. Private 653 Derby Division Medal Clasps: CC SA01.
Medal Roll Reference: WO100/225/55+84 Orderly 11 General Hospital. To England on termination of engagement.
GRIFFITHS, R. W. Private 1478 Derby Division Medal Clasps: CC OFS TVL.
Medal Roll Reference: WO100/225/164+183 Orderly 15 General Hospital. Transferred to Pretoria 29 August 1900. 17 Stationary Hospital. To Base 24 November 1900.
GRIFFITHS, W. E. Private 966 Dudley Corps Medal Clasps: NAT.
Medal Roll Reference: WO100/225/164 Orderly 15 General Hospital. Transferred to HS *Nubia* 29 December 1900.
GRIMSHAW, John Private 67 Accrington Corps Medal Clasps: CC.
Medal Roll Reference: WO100/225/19+113 Orderly 6 General Hospital. 2 General Hospital.
GRINDLEY, A. W. Private 362 North Staffs Corps Medal Clasps: NAT.
Medal Roll Reference: WO100/225/128 Orderly 7 General Hospital. To England time expired.
GRINDROD, John Private 174 Tottington Division Medal Clasps: CC OFS TVL SA01 SA02 KSA01 KSA02.
Medal Roll Reference: WO100/225/73 WO100/271/13+44 WO100/366/223 Orderly 6 Stationary Hospital St John Ambulance service: Embarked for South Africa 29 December 1899. Disembarked England 29 December 1900. South African Constabulary Headquarters Corporal HQ33. Medical Corporal B1459. Transferred to Reserve Division Trooper RD585 Service in South African Constabulary for 13 Months.
GROGAN, James Private 463 Clitheroe Division Medal Clasps: CC OFS NAT SA01 SA02.
Medal Roll Reference: WO100/225/128 WO100/273/73 Orderly 7 General Hospital. To England Time expired. South African Constabulary E Division Medical Corporal E3035. Discharged by purchase.
GROVE, W. J. Private 987 Oystermouth Division Medal Clasps: NAT.
Medal Roll Reference: WO100/225/164 Orderly 15 General Hospital. Transferred to England 26 August 1900.
GROVES, S. F. Private 353 Dowlais Division Medal Clasps: CC.
Medal Roll Reference: WO100/130/219 Lance Corporal Imperial Yeomanry Hospital Deelfontein. E. GROVES in St John Ambulance Brigade Bronze medal register.
GRUNDY, W. T. Private 1329 Bolton Corps Medal Clasps: CC SA01.
Medal Roll Reference: WO100/225/55+84 Orderly 11 General Hospital. To Kimberley 29 August 1900. Transferred to 13 General Hospital. To England on termination of engagement
GUFFOG, George Private 681 Tottington Division Medal Clasps: CC OFS TVL SA01 WITT.
Medal Roll Reference: WO100/225/204 WO100/271/14+44 Orderly Attached to 22 Bearer Company RAMC. South African Constabulary Headquarters Trooper RD584. Discharged 23 August 1901.

GUTTERIDGE, C. W. Sergeant 190 Market Harborough Division Medal Clasps: CC OFS.
Medal Roll Reference: WO100/225/62+176 Supply Officer Base Hospital Wynberg 5 Stationary
Hospital. Sent to Base for England for discharge.
GUY, F. J. V. Sergeant 466 Metropolitan Corps Medal Clasps: CC OFS.
Medal Roll Reference: WO100/225/238 Compounder Van Alen American Field Hospital.
HACKETT, J. Private 151 Nuneaton Division Medal Clasps: CC OFS TVL.
Medal Roll Reference: WO100/225/62+70 Orderly Base Hospital Wynberg. 3 Ambulance Train.
To Base Detail RAMC Cape Town for England.
HACKING, A. Private 1263 Rishton Division Medal Clasps: CC OFS.
Medal Roll Reference: WO100/225/134 Orderly 8 General Hospital. To England 10 October 1900.
HADFIELD, F. W. Private 1055 Bolton Corps Medal Clasps: NAT.
Medal Roll Reference: WO100/225/164 Orderly 15 General Hospital. Transferred to HS *Nubia* 29
December 1900.
HADLEY, J. Private 909 Derby Division Medal Clasps: NAT.
Medal Roll Reference: WO100/225/164 Orderly 15 General Hospital. Transferred to England 18
October 1900.
HAGGAR, William Thomas Private 436 Metropolitan Corps Medal Clasps: CC OFS KSA01
KSA02.
Medal Roll Reference: WO100/225/134 WO100/352/149 Orderly 8 General Hospital. To England
23 January 1901. Entitled KSA as RAMC Private 16368.
HAGUE, F. Private 1465 Oldham Corps Medal Clasps: CC OFS TVL.
Medal Roll Reference: WO100/225/180+183 Orderly 14 Stationary Hospital 17 Stationary
Hospital. To Base 24 November 1900.
HAIGH, H. Private 753 Hebden Bridge Corps Medal Clasps: CC OFS.
Medal Roll Reference: WO100/225/203 Orderly 21 Bearer Company. Sent home for discharge
August 1900.
HALES, A. Private 502 Sheffield Corps Medal Clasps: CC OFS TVL.
Medal Roll Reference: WO100/225/231 Private Langman Hospital.
HALFYARD, F. Private 1529 Oldham Corps Medal Clasps: CC OFS TVL NAT.
Medal Roll Reference: WO100/225/108+126 Orderly 1 General Hospital. Transferred to 7
General Hospital. To England time expired.
HALL, H. Private 1175 Oldham Corps Medal Clasps: CC.
Medal Roll Reference: WO100/225/108 Orderly 1 General Hospital.
HALL, H. S. Private 1474 Blackpool Division Medal Clasps: TVL.
Medal Roll Reference: WO100/225/169 Orderly 17 General Hospital. Transferred to
Pietermaritzburg 30 November 1900.
HALL, J. F. Private 1880 Oldham Corps Medal Clasps: CC OFS.
Medal Roll Reference: WO100/225/148 Orderly 9 General Hospital From 16 Field Hospital 1 May
1901.
HALL, J. H. Private 599 Dewsbury Corps Medal Clasps: CC OFS.
Medal Roll Reference: WO100/225/69+70+148 Orderly 8 Stationary Hospital. 9 General Hospital.
3 Hospital train. To Base Detail RAMC Cape Town 7 August 1900
for England.
HALL, J. H. Private 1226 1765 Nelson Corps Medal Clasps: CC OFS TVL.
Medal Roll Reference: WO100/225/62+148 Orderly Base Hospital Wynberg. 3 Ambulance Train. 9
General Hospital. To Base Detail 12 October 1900. G. H. HALL on QSA Medal Roll.
HALL, S. C. Private 1830 Nuneaton Division Medal Clasps: CC OFS SA01.
Medal Roll Reference: WO100/225/87+116 Orderly 3 General Hospital. Transferred to Base
Detail RAMC. Home 21 June 1901.

HALLAS, Benton Private 1467 Oldham Corps Medal Clasps: CC OFS TVL SA01.
Medal Roll Reference: WO100/225/180+183 WO100/271/215 Orderly 14 Stationary Hospital. 17 Stationary Hospital. To Base 24 November 1900. South African Constabulary A Division Trooper A1870. Discharged 3 November 1901.
HALLETT, E. Private 1535 Oldham Corps Medal Clasps: CC.
Medal Roll Reference: WO100/225/122 Orderly 5 General Hospital.
HALLIDAY, J. Private 561 Birmingham Corps Medal Clasps: CC OFS.
Medal Roll Reference: WO100/225/148 Orderly 9 General Hospital. To Base Detail 7 August 1900.
HALLIWELL, J. W. Private 575 Oldham Corps Medal Clasps: CC OFS.
Medal Roll Reference: WO100/225/122 Orderly 5 General Hospital. 10 General Hospital. To Base 29 January 1901.
HALLOWELL, G. H. Private 854 Hebden Bridge Corps Medal Clasps: CC.
Medal Roll Reference: WO100/225/69 Orderly 8 Stationary Hospital.
HALSTEAD, E. Private 700 Hebden Bridge Corps Medal Clasps: CC WITT.
Medal Roll Reference: WO100/225/204 Orderly Attached 22 Bearer Company. Discharged.
HAMER, J. Private 1161 Leeds Corps Medal Clasps: CC OFS.
Medal Roll Reference: WO100/225/148 Supply Officer 9 General Hospital. To Pretoria 4 October 1900.
HAMER, T. C. Sergeant 1570 Bolton Corps Medal Clasps: CC OFS TVL.
Medal Roll Reference: WO100/225/128 Supply Officer 7 General Hospital. From Cape Town. To England time expired.
HAMMON, C. A. Private 946 Padiham Division Medal Clasps: NAT.
Medal Roll Reference: WO100/225/164 Orderly 15 General Hospital. Transferred to HS *Nubia* 29 December 1900. A. C. HAMMON on QDA Medal Roll.
HAMPSON, J. Private 1239 Preston Corps Medal Clasps: CC OFS.
Medal Roll Reference: WO100/225/134 Orderly 8 General Hospital. To England 10 October 1900.
HANBURY, A. E. Private 321 St John Ambulance Brigade (NFB Woodstock) Medal Clasps: No definite QSA Medal roll entry identified. NFBUAD Medal.
Medal Roll Reference: No definite QSA Medal roll entry identified. (Probably WO100/125/168 Private 31647 62nd Company Imperial Yeomanry. Medal Clasps SA01 SA02).
HANCOCK, John E. 1st Class Sergeant 446 North Staffs Corps Medal Clasps: CC OFS TVL SA01 SA02.
Medal Roll Reference: WO100/225/238 WO100/272/178+303 Wardmaster Van Alen American Field Hospital. Transferred to South African Constabulary C Division 1st Sergeant C2110. Discharged 5 April 1902.
HANDLEY, W. A. Private 789 Radcliffe Division Medal Clasps: No Clasps.
Medal Roll Reference: WO100/225/22 Orderly.
HANKINSON, G. W. Sergeant 963 Preston Corps Medal Clasps: NAT.
Medal Roll Reference: WO100/225/164 Supply Officer 15 General Hospital. Transferred to HS *Nubia* 29 December 1900.
HANMER, J. S. Private 811 Manchester Post Office Division Medal Clasps: CC OFS.
Medal Roll Reference: WO100/225/148 Orderly 9 General Hospital. To Base Detail 7 September 1900.
HANSON, B. Private 998 Newchurch Division Medal Clasps: NAT.
Medal Roll Reference: WO100/225/164 Orderly 15 General Hospital. Transferred to England 26 August 1900.
HARDING, E. Private 1514 1777 Isle of Wight Corps Medal Clasps: CC SA01.
Medal Roll Reference: WO100/225/67+173+WO100/224/193 Orderly 18 General Hospital. To England 30 May 1900. 21 General Hospital. Attached RAMC.
HARDING, W. Private 486 Tibshelf Corps Medal Clasps: CC OFS.

Medal Roll Reference: WO100/225/148 Orderly 9 General Hospital. To Base Detail 7 August 1900.

HARDING, W. N. Private 1336 Rawtenstall Corps Medal Clasps: CC.
Medal Roll Reference: WO100/225/158 Orderly 13 General Hospital. To England expired contract 27 November 1900.

HARGREAVES, A. Private 1228 Nelson Corps Medal Clasps: CC OFS.
Medal Roll Reference: WO100/225/155 Orderly 10 General Hospital. To Base 10 October 1900.

HARGREAVES, J. A. Private 1281 Brierfield Division Medal Clasps: CC OFS.
Medal Roll Reference: WO100/225/148 Orderly 9 General Hospital. To Base Detail 12 October 1900.

HARGREAVES, J. H. Private 797 Foulridge Division Medal Clasps: CC OFS.
Medal Roll Reference: WO100/225/134 Orderly 8 General Hospital. To England 31 August 1900.

HARGREAVES, J. J. Private 1639 Hapton Division Medal Clasps: OFS TVL.
Medal Roll Reference: WO100/225/180 Orderly 14 Stationary Hospital. 7 Ambulance Train.

HARKNESS, R. Private 593 Colne Division Medal Clasps: CC.
Medal Roll Reference: WO100/225/122 Orderly 5 General Hospital.

HARLOCK, G. W. Private 1326 Metropolitan Corps Medal Clasps: CC.
Medal Roll Reference: WO100/225/158 Orderly 13 General Hospital. To England expired contract 27 November 1900.

HARNESS, C. H. Private 1379 Hull Corps Medal Clasps: No Clasps.
Medal Roll Reference: WO100/225/59 Orderly 14 General Hospital. To HS *Simla* for duty 14 November 1900.

HARNESS, John William Private 87 Hull Corps Medal Clasps: CC OFS.
Medal Roll Reference: WO100/225/235 Private Portland Hospital. To England contract expired.

HARPER, William James Private 88 North Staffs Corps Medal Clasps: CC OFS SA01 SA02 KSA01 KSA02.
Medal Roll Reference: WO100/225/235 WO100/272/303 WO100/366/116 Private Portland Hospital 2 January to 1 August 1900. To England contract expired. South African Constabulary C Division Heidelberg Corporal C2118 4 May 1901 to 31 May 1902.

HARRIMAN, C. Private 872 1622 Leicester Corps Medal Clasps: CC.
Medal Roll Reference: WO100/225/62+134 Orderly Base Hospital Wynberg. 8 General Hospital. To England 31 August 1900.

HARRINGTON, F. Private 1028 1729 Oldham Corps Medal Clasps: CC OFS TVL NAT.
Medal Roll Reference: WO100/225/170+180+192 Orderly 20 General Hospital Joined from Base Detail. To England for discharge. 14 Stationary Hospital. Attached 21 Field Hospital. Discharged.

HARRIS, A. Private 269 Metropolitan Corps Medal Clasps: CC.
Medal Roll Reference: WO100/225/125 Private 6 General Hospital. To Base on expiration of contract 5 June 1900.

HARRIS, Edgar John Frederick Private 98 Redruth Division Medal Clasps: CC OFS.
Medal Roll Reference: WO100/225/235 Private Portland Hospital. To England contract expired.

HARRIS, H. Private 1109 Birmingham Corps Medal Clasps: NAT.
Medal Roll Reference: WO100/225/67 Orderly 18 General Hospital. To England 28 December 1900.

HARRIS, J. Private 272 Metropolitan Corps Medal Clasps: NAT.
Medal Roll Reference: WO100/225/75 Orderly Princess Christian Hospital Train.

HARRIS, Thomas Private 1095 Metropolitan Corps Medal Clasps: No Clasps.
Medal Roll Reference: WO100/225/23 Orderly. Died at Sea from heatstroke 19 July 1900.

HARRISON, C. Sergeant 666 Manchester Post Office Division Medal Clasps: CC SA01.
Medal Roll Reference: WO100/225/55+84 Supply Officer 11 General Hospital. To England on termination of engagement.

HARRISON, C. Private 1025 Oldham Corps Medal Clasps: NAT.
Medal Roll Reference: WO100/225/67 Orderly 18 General Hospital. To England 28 December 1900.
HARRISON, T. Private 1803 Bolton Corps Medal Clasps: CC.
Medal Roll Reference: WO100/225/173 Orderly 21 General Hospital.
HARROP, W. T. Private 857 Rochdale Corps Medal Clasps: NAT.
Medal Roll Reference: WO100/225/164 Orderly 15 General Hospital. Transferred to England 26 August 1900.
HART, J. Private 40 Metropolitan Corps Medal Clasps: CC.
Medal Roll Reference: WO100/225/21+113 Orderly 6 General Hospital. 2 General Hospital.
HART, J. Private 260 Kettering Corps Medal Clasps: CC OFS.
Medal Roll Reference: WO100/225/176 Orderly 5 Stationary Hospital Sent to Base for England for discharge.
HARTLEY, A. Private 1687 Hebden Bridge Corps Medal Clasps: No Clasps.
Medal Roll Reference: WO100/225/67 Orderly 18 General Hospital. To England 27 May1900.
HARTLEY, G. H. Private 1036 1749 Barnoldswick Division Medal Clasps: NAT.
Medal Roll Reference: WO100/225/173+180 Orderly 21 General Hospital. 14 Stationary Hospital.
HARTLEY, H. Private 251 Nelson Corps Medal Clasps: CC OFS JOH DIA.
Medal Roll Reference: WO100/225/191 Private Attached 20 Field Hospital. Left for duty at Heilbron 13 July 1900.
HARTLEY, J. E. Private 1766 Nelson Corps Medal Clasps: CC.
Medal Roll Reference: WO100/225/173 Orderly 21 General Hospital.
HARTLEY, T. Sergeant 464 Clitheroe Division Medal Clasps: CC OFS.
Medal Roll Reference: WO100/225/134 Orderly 8 General Hospital. To England 29 June1900.
HARTSHORN, J. R. Private 1484 Sheffield Corps Medal Clasps: CC OFS TVL.
Medal Roll Reference: WO100/225/62+183 Orderly Base Hospital Wynberg. 14 Stationary Hospital. 17 Stationary Hospital. To Base 24 November 1900.
HARWOOD, W. Private 1414 Hebden Bridge Corps Medal Clasps: No Clasps.
Medal Roll Reference: WO100/225/59 Orderly 14 General Hospital. Invalided to England on HS *Simla* 14 November 1900.
HASELDEN, Gerald Sergeant 1363 1788 Bolton Corps Medal Clasps: CC OFS.
Medal Roll Reference: WO100/225/148 Orderly Base Hospital Wynberg 26 November 1900. To England expired contract 27 November 1900. Supply Officer 9 General Hospital. To Base.
HASKETH, H. M. Private 522 Blackpool Division Medal Clasps: CC OFS TVL.
Medal Roll Reference: WO100/225/22+123 Orderly 5 General Hospital OFS TVL issued off Driscoll's Scouts.
HASLAM, J. Private 1352 Bolton Corps Medal Clasps: CC.
Medal Roll Reference: WO100/225/158 Orderly 13 General Hospital. To England expired contract 27 November 1900.
HASSALL, F. Private 1532 Oldham Corps Medal Clasps: CC.
Medal Roll Reference: WO100/225/108 Orderly 1 General Hospital.
HASSELMAN, C. A. Private 280 Metropolitan Corps Medal Clasps: CC OFS TVL.
Medal Roll Reference: WO100/225/125 Private 6 General Hospital. To Base on expiration of contract 13 December 1900.
HATCH, B. or J. Private 958 Walton-le-Dale Division Medal Clasps: NAT.
Medal Roll Reference: WO100/225/164 Orderly 15 General Hospital. Transferred to Stationary Hospital Ladysmith 30 June 1900.
HATCH, G. Private 996 Rishton Division Medal Clasps: NAT.
Medal Roll Reference: WO100/225/164 Orderly 15 General Hospital. Transferred to England 26 August 1900.
HATHERLEY, P. W. Private 1607 Birmingham Corps Medal Clasps: CC OFS TVL.

Medal Roll Reference: WO100/225/123+168 Orderly 5 General Hospital. 16 General Hospital. Left 5 April 1901 for passage to England.

HAWKE, Thomas S. Private 981 Hallaton Division Medal Clasps: OFS NAT SA01 SA02. Medal Roll Reference: WO100/225/164 WO100/273/77+266 WO100/356/169 Orderly 15 General Hospital. Transferred to England 26 August 1900. South African Constabulary E Division Hospital Corporal E3040. Service in St John Ambulance Brigade 2 May 1900 to 11 September 1900. Service in South African Constabulary 4 May 1901 to 31 May 1902. Not entitled to King's South Africa Medal.

HAWKINS, Ernest A. Private 430 Metropolitan Corps Medal Clasps: TVL NAT. Medal Roll Reference: WO100/225/129 Private 7 General Hospital. Died of disease Pretoria 8 January 1901. On death register as A. E. HAWKINS.

HAWLEY, T. Private 344 Ilkeston Corps Medal Clasps: CC OFS. Medal Roll Reference: WO100/225/134 Orderly 8 General Hospital. To England 20 July 1900.

HAWORTH, J. Private 944 Accrington Corps Medal Clasps: NAT. Medal Roll Reference: WO100/225/164 Orderly 15 General Hospital. Transferred to England 26 August 1900.

HAWORTH, J. Private 1656 Accrington Corps Medal Clasps: SA01. Medal Roll Reference: WO100/225/88 Orderly.

HAWORTH, Thomas H. Private 979 Edenfield Division Medal Clasps: NAT. Medal Roll Reference: WO100/225/165 Orderly 15 General Hospital. Died typhoid Pietermaritzburg Fort Napier 31 July 1900.

HAY, J. Private 1245 Preston Corps Medal Clasps: No Clasps. Medal Roll Reference: WO100/225/24 Orderly.

HAYES, H. Private 1190 Oldham Corps Medal Clasps: CC. Medal Roll Reference: WO100/225/108 Orderly 1 General Hospital.

HAYES, T. J. Private 235 Nuneaton Division Medal Clasps: CC. Medal Roll Reference: WO100/225/125 Private 6 General Hospital. To Base on expiration of contract 18 June 1900.

HAYGARTH, A. Private 594 Colne Division Medal Clasps: CC. Medal Roll Reference: WO100/225/123 Orderly 5 General Hospital.

HAYHURST, W. H. Private 1304 Preston Corps Medal Clasps: CC TVL. Medal Roll Reference: WO100/224/172 Private Rhodesian Field Force Hospital.

HAYNES, C. Private 1829 Welbeck Division Medal Clasps: CC. Medal Roll Reference: WO100/225/173 Orderly 21 General Hospital.

HAYNES, W. Private 1073 Welbeck Division Medal Clasps: NAT. Medal Roll Reference: WO100/225/118 Orderly 4 General Hospital Sent to England time expired 19 December 1900.

HAYTHORNTHWAITE, George Private 440 1549 Barrowford Division Medal Clasps: CC OFS TVL SA01 SA02 KSA02. Medal Roll Reference: WO100/225/21+56+63+84 WO100/268/42 WO100/364/256 Orderly Base Hospital Wynberg 11 General Hospital. To England on termination of engagement. To England 20 July 1900. Served for two periods with St John Ambulance Brigade for 122days and 134 days. 1st Scottish Horse 30726 and 42012 Two periodsof service 15 February 1901 to 13 March 1902 and 24 April to 31 May 1902. Discharged 26 June 1902. KSA medal and KSA02 clasp issued on 1st Scottish Horse roll.

HEALY, T. Sergeant 346 Lincoln Adult School Division Medal Clasps: OFS TVL NAT SA01. Medal Roll Reference: WO100/225/129 Supply Officer 7 General Hospital. To England time expired.

HEANE, C. J. Private 648 Worksop Division Medal Clasps: CC SA01. Medal Roll Reference: WO100/225/56+84 Orderly 11 General Hospital. To England on termination of engagement.

HEAP, A. Private 1460 Oldham Corps Medal Clasps: NAT.
Medal Roll Reference: WO100/225/180 Orderly 14 Stationary Hospital.
HEAP, J. Sergeant 1429 Bolton Corps Medal Clasps: No Clasps.
Medal Roll Reference: WO100/225/118 Supply Officer 4 General Hospital Sent to England time expired 28 November 1900.
HEAP, W. Private 799 Colne Division Medal Clasps: CC.
Medal Roll Reference: WO100/225/168+178 Orderly 16 General Hospital. Transferred to 7 Stationary Hospital 4 June 1900. Sent to England September 1900.
HEATON, J. Private 1596 Oldham Corps Medal Clasps: CC OFS TVL.
Medal Roll Reference: WO100/225/158 Orderly 13 General Hospital. To England expired contract 10 April 1901.
HEAVINGHAM, W. J. Private 181 Metropolitan Corps Medal Clasps: CC OFS TVL.
Medal Roll Reference: WO100/225/69 Orderly 8 Stationary Hospital.
HEBRON, G. Private 1546 Bury Division Medal Clasps: CC OFS.
Medal Roll Reference: WO100/225/148 Orderly 9 General Hospital. To Base Detail 30 January 1901.
HELLIWELL, J. H. Private 1415 Hebden Bridge Corps Medal Clasps: No Clasps.
Medal Roll Reference: WO100/225/59 Orderly 14 General Hospital. To HS *Simla* for duty 14 November 1900.
HELM, T. Private 1369 Preston Corps Medal Clasps: CC.
Medal Roll Reference: WO100/225/56+158 Orderly 11 General Hospital. To Kimberley 29 August 1900. 13 General Hospital. To England on termination of engagement
HELME, H. Private 1495 Bolton Corps Medal Clasps: TVL NAT.
Medal Roll Reference: WO100/225/129 Orderly 7 General Hospital. To England time expired.
HEMINGWAY, J. Private 1205 Leeds Corps Medal Clasps: CC OFS.
Medal Roll Reference: WO100/225/69 Orderly 8 Stationary Hospital. 9 General Hospital. To Base Detail 12 October 1900.
HERN, Harold Edmund Private 326 St John Ambulance Brigade (NFB Exeter) Medal Clasps: CC. NFBUAD Medal.
Medal Roll Reference: WO100/130/219 Lance Corporal Imperial Yeomanry Hospital Deelfontein. Died Exeter in 1907 aged 29.
HESFORD, J. H. Private 1061 Bolton Corps Medal Clasps: NAT.
Medal Roll Reference: WO100/225/118 Orderly 4 General Hospital Sent to England time expired 9 September 1900.
HETT, F. Private 1072 Welbeck Division Medal Clasps: NAT.
Medal Roll Reference: WO100/225/67 Orderly 18 General Hospital. To England 28 December 1900.
HEUGH, T. H. Private 1177 Oldham Corps Medal Clasps: CC.
Medal Roll Reference: WO100/225/108 Orderly 1 General Hospital.
HEWITT, A. S. Private 481 Metropolitan Corps Medal Clasps: CC.
Medal Roll Reference: WO100/225/123 Orderly 5 General Hospital.
HEYWOOD, J. Private 816 Padiham Division Medal Clasps: NAT.
Medal Roll Reference: WO100/225/164 Orderly 15 General Hospital. Transferred to England 26 August 1900.
HEYWOOD, Joseph Private 340 Oxford Division Medal Clasps: NAT.
Medal Roll Reference: WO100/225/129 Orderly 7 General Hospital. Died brain abscess Estcourt 25 August 1900.
HICKLING, J. H. Private 166 Heanor Division Medal Clasps: CC.
Medal Roll Reference: WO100/225/108 Orderly 1 General Hospital.
HIGGINSON, H. Private 1256 Walton-le-Dale Division Medal Clasps: CC OFS.

Medal Roll Reference: WO100/225/148 Orderly 9 General Hospital. To Base Detail 12 October 1900.

HIGGINSON, T. James Private 1307 Walton-le-Dale Division Medal Clasps: CC TVL SA01. Medal Roll Reference: WO100/224/172 Private Rhodesian Field Force Hospital. Graaf Reinet DMT.

HIGINBOTHAM, E. Private 1217 Hazelgrove Division Medal Clasps: CC OFS. Medal Roll Reference: WO100/225/148 Orderly 9 General Hospital. To Base Detail 12 October 1900.

HILL, A. Private 439 Barrowford Division Medal Clasps: CC NAT. Medal Roll Reference: WO100/225/73+129 Orderly 6 Stationary Hospital. 7 General Hospital. To England time expired.

HILL, Edward Sergeant 157 1790 Derby Corps Medal Clasps: CC OFS SA01 SA02 KSA01 KSA02. Medal Roll Reference: WO100/225/69+135 WO100/273/177+269 WO100/366/170 Supply Officer 8 Stationary Hospital. 8 General Hospital. South African Constabulary E Division Medical Corporal E3474. Service in St John Ambulance Brigade from 19 January to 6 December 1900 and 26 February to 8 August 1901. Service in South African Constabulary 9 August 1901 to 31 May 1902. Discharged time expired 13 August 1902. Also member Derby Regiment 528 but no service with Derby Regiment in South Africa.

HILL, G. H. Private 1182 Oldham Corps Medal Clasps: CC. Medal Roll Reference: WO100/225/108 Orderly 1 General Hospital.

HILL, J. A. Private 645 Bradford Corps Medal Clasps: CC. Medal Roll Reference: WO100/225/56+69 Orderly 11 General Hospital. 8 Stationary Hospital. To England on termination of engagement.

HILL, Peter B. Private 1265 Whaley Bridge Division Medal Clasps: CC OFS. Medal Roll Reference: WO100/225/148+179 Orderly 9 General Hospital. 11 Stationary Hospital. To Base Detail 12 October 1900

HILL, R. Private 1071 Welbeck Division Medal Clasps: OFS TVL NAT. Medal Roll Reference: WO100/225/180+192 Orderly 14 Stationary Hospital. Attached 21 Field Hospital. Discharged.

HILL, T. Private 1030 Bury Division Medal Clasps: NAT. Medal Roll Reference: WO100/225/164 Orderly 15 General Hospital. Transferred to England 14 September 1900.

HINCKLEY, W. H. Private 1645 Bolton Corps Medal Clasps: SA01. Medal Roll Reference: WO100/224/196 Private Attached RAMC.

HINDLE, H. Private 1221 Preston Corps Medal Clasps: CC OFS. Medal Roll Reference: WO100/225/148 Orderly 9 General Hospital. To Base Detail 12 October 1900.

HINKLEY, H. Private 1874 Leeds Corps Medal Clasps: No Clasps. Medal Roll Reference: WO100/225/144 Orderly.

HINKS, H. J. E. Sergeant 112 Faversham Division Medal Clasps: NAT. Medal Roll Reference: WO100/225/75 Supply Officer Princess Christian Hospital Train.

HIRONS, A. E. Private 1808 Birmingham Corps (Birmingham City Division) Medal Clasps: CC SA01. Medal Roll Reference: WO100/225/72+89 Orderly 24 Stationary Hospital. From Base Detail 15 April 1901. Time expired 31 October 1901.

HIRST, N. Private 1210 Leeds Corps Medal Clasps: CC OFS. Medal Roll Reference: WO100/225/148 Orderly 9 General Hospital. To Base Detail 12 October 1900.

HOARE, H. Private 1214 Metropolitan Corps Medal Clasps: CC TVL SA01. Medal Roll Reference: WO100/224/172 Private Rhodesian Field Force Hospital.

HOBART, J. C. Private 1012 Sheffield Corps Medal Clasps: NAT.
Medal Roll Reference: WO100/225/164 Orderly 15 General Hospital. Transferred to HS *Nubia* 29 December 1900.
HOBBS, A. G. Sergeant 266 1554 Isle of Wight Corps Medal Clasps: CC OFS.
Medal Roll Reference: WO100/225/125+148 Supply Officer 6 General Hospital. To Base on expiration of contract 18 June 1900 9 General Hospital. To Base Detail 30 January 1901. G.A. HOBBS on QSA Medal Roll.
HOBSON, C. Private 1402 Doncaster Division Medal Clasps: No Clasps.
Medal Roll Reference: WO100/225/59 Orderly 14 General Hospital. To HS *Simla* for duty 14 November 1900.
HOBSON, J. Private 691 Clitheroe Division Medal Clasps: CC OFS.
Medal Roll Reference: WO100/225/155 Orderly 10 General Hospital. To Base 7 August 1900.
HODDLE, A. Private 60 Olney Division Medal Clasps: No Clasps.
Medal Roll Reference: WO100/225/113 Orderly 2 General Hospital.
HODGSON, J. H. Private 1422 Hebden Bridge Corps Medal Clasps: No Clasps.
Medal Roll Reference: WO100/225/59 Orderly 14 General Hospital. To HS *Simla* for duty 14 November 1900.
HODGSON, R. Private 169 Barrowford Division Medal Clasps: CC.
Medal Roll Reference: WO100/225/109 Orderly 1 General Hospital.
HOE, J. Private 485 Tibshelf Corps Medal Clasps: CC OFS TVL.
Medal Roll Reference: WO100/225/148+188 Orderly 9 General Hospital. To Base Detail 31 August 1900 19 Brigade Field Hospital Joined from 9 General Hospital Bloemfontein.
HOFF, G. P. Private 1696 Blackpool Division Medal Clasps: OFS TVL.
Medal Roll Reference: WO100/225/203 Orderly 21 Bearer Company Joined from 20 General Hospital February 1901 and sent home for discharge June 1901.
HOGG, R. Private 534 Preston Corps Medal Clasps: NAT.
Medal Roll Reference: WO100/225/65 Orderly 13 Stationary Hospital. To SS *Formosa* 8 December 1900.
HOGGARTH, F. Sergeant 618 Kendal Division Medal Clasps: CC WITT.
Medal Roll Reference: WO100/225/192 Supply Officer Attached 21 Field Hospital. Discharged.
HOGGARTH, H. Sergeant 514 Hull Corps Medal Clasps: CC.
Medal Roll Reference: WO100/225/123 Supply Officer 5 General Hospital.
HOLDEN, G. Private 1775 Edenfield Division Medal Clasps: CC SA01.
Medal Roll Reference: WO100/225/56+85 Orderly 11 General Hospital. To England on termination of engagement.
HOLDEN, George E. Private 839 Preston Corps Medal Clasps: CC OFS.
Medal Roll Reference: WO100/225/135 Orderly 8 General Hospital. Died of disease Bloemfontein 12 June 1900.
HOLDEN, Gwilym Sergeant 564 Birmingham Corps Medal Clasps: CC OFS.
Medal Roll Reference: WO100/225/148 Supply Officer 9 General Hospital. To Base Detail 5 February 1901.
HOLDEN, J. Private 1077 Preston Corps Medal Clasps: NAT.
Medal Roll Reference: WO100/225/65 Orderly 13 Stationary Hospital. To SS *Montrose* 8 September 1900.
HOLDEN, N. Private 402 Accrington Corps Medal Clasps: NAT.
Medal Roll Reference: WO100/225/129 Orderly 7 General Hospital. To England time expired.
HOLDER, C. J. Private 1376 Great Eastern Railway Corps Medal Clasps: CC OFS TVL.
Medal Roll Reference: WO100/225/77+158+186 Orderly 10 Stationary Hospital. To Cape Town 13 General Hospital. To Pretoria 18 December 1900. Attached to 8th Divisional 12th Brigade Field Hospital. Transferred to Base Detail Cape Town.
HOLGATE, F. Private 960 Walton-le-Dale Division Medal Clasps: NAT.

Medal Roll Reference: WO100/225/164 Orderly 15 General Hospital. Transferred to England 26 August 1900.

HOLGATE, T. W. Private 1142 Barnoldswick Division Medal Clasps: CC OFS.
Medal Roll Reference: WO100/225/135 Orderly 8 General Hospital. To England 10 October 1900.

HOLLING, F. Private 1715 Tibshelf Corps Medal Clasps: CC OFS TVL.
Medal Roll Reference: WO100/225/170 Orderly 20 General Hospital. Joined from Base Detail. To England for discharge.

HOLLINRAKE, Walter Private 1520 Haslingden Corps Medal Clasps: CC OFS TVL SA01 SA02.
Medal Roll Reference: WO100/225/164+183 WO100/271/215 Orderly 15 General Hospital. Transferred to Pretoria 29 August 1900. 17 Stationary Hospital. To Base 24 November 1900 South African Constabulary A Division Trooper A1878. Discharged 4 November 1902.

HOLLINS, Harry Corporal 1471 Oldham Corps Medal Clasps: CC OFS SA01 SA02.
Medal Roll Reference: WO100/225/118 WO100/273/82+271 Orderly 4 General Hospital Sent to England time expired 28 November 1900. South African Constabulary Medical Corporal E3042. Service in St John Ambulance Brigade 13 August to 9 December 1900. Service in South African Constabulary 4 May 1901 to 31 May 1902. Not entitled to King's South Africa Medal.

HOLLOWAY, Harry Private 86 Warrington Corps Medal Clasps: CC OFS.
Medal Roll Reference: WO100/225/235 Private Portland Hospital. To England contract expired.

HOLMES, R. Private 437 Keswick Division Medal Clasps: CC.
Medal Roll Reference: WO100/130/220 Private Imperial Yeomanry Hospital Deelfontein.

HOLMES, William Private 10 1659 Wellingborough Corps Medal Clasps: CC OFS TVL.
Medal Roll Reference: WO100/225/170+241 Orderly HS *Princess of Wales* Attached RAMC. 20 General Hospital. Joined from Base Detail. To England for discharge (RNASBR long service medal 576 SRA).

HOLMSHAW, W. H. Private 1119 Sheffield Corps Medal Clasps: NAT.
Medal Roll Reference: WO100/225/65 Orderly 13 Stationary Hospital. To SS *Montrose* 8 September 1900.

HOLROYD, F. B. Private 1160 Leeds Corps Medal Clasps: CC OFS.
Medal Roll Reference: WO100/225/149 Orderly 9 General Hospital. To Base Detail 12 October 1900.

HOLT, H. Private 1063 Bolton Corps Medal Clasps: NAT.
Medal Roll Reference: WO100/225/165 Orderly 15 General Hospital. Transferred to England 14 September 1900.

HOLT, J. Private 1878 Oldham Corps Medal Clasps: CC OFS TVL.
Medal Roll Reference: WO100/225/170 Orderly 20 General Hospital. Joined from Base Detail. To England for discharge.

HOLT, R. Private 902 Bolton Corps Medal Clasps: NAT.
Medal Roll Reference: WO100/225/165 Orderly 15 General Hospital. Transferred to HS *Nubia* 29 December 1900.

HOLTHAM, F. A. Private 237 Nuneaton Division Medal Clasps: CC.
Medal Roll Reference: WO100/225/125 Orderly 6 General Hospital. To Base on expiration of contract 18 June 1900.

HOOK, G. Private 643 Leicester Corps Medal Clasps: CC OFS TVL.
Medal Roll Reference: WO100/130/265 Private Imperial Yeomanry Field Hospital and Bearer Company.

HOOLE, J. V. Private 1744 Whalley Division Medal Clasps: CC.
Medal Roll Reference: WO100/225/173 Orderly 21 General Hospital.

HOPKINS, R. Private 1291 Metropolitan Corps Medal Clasps: CC OFS TVL.
Medal Roll Reference: WO100/225/125 Orderly 6 General Hospital. To Base on expiration of contract 22 October 1900.

HOPKINSON, J. J. Private 476 Bury Division Medal Clasps: CC OFS.
Medal Roll Reference: WO100/225/69+149 Orderly 8 Stationary Hospital. 9 General Hospital. To Base Detail 17 August 1900.
HORNBROOK, J. Private 456 St John Ambulance Brigade (NFB Cockington) Medal Clasps: CC SA01. NFBUAD Medal.
Medal Roll Reference: WO100/130/219 Sergeant Imperial Yeomanry Hospital Deelfontein.
HORNSEY, F. Private 1621 Desborough Division Medal Clasps: CC OFS TVL.
Medal Roll Reference: WO100/225/123+168 Orderly 5 General Hospital. 16 General Hospital. Left 1 April 1901 for passage to England.
HORROCKS, J. Private 1494 Bolton Corps Medal Clasps: TVL NAT.
Medal Roll Reference: WO100/225/129 Orderly 7 General Hospital. To England time expired.
HORROCKS, J. Private 679 Edenfield Division Medal Clasps: CC OFS.
Medal Roll Reference: WO100/225/155 Orderly 10 General Hospital. To Base 7 August 1900.
HORSFALL, W. T. Private 880 Hull Corps Medal Clasps: CC OFS.
Medal Roll Reference: WO100/225/135 Orderly 8 General Hospital. To England 31 August 1900.
HORSFIELD, W. Private 804 1750 Barnoldswick Division Medal Clasps: CC OFS.
Medal Roll Reference: WO100/225/135+173 Orderly 8 General Hospital. To England 31 August 1900. 21 General Hospital.
HORSLEY, M. Private 1126 Heanor Division Medal Clasps: OFS TVL NAT.
Medal Roll Reference: WO100/225/180+192 Orderly 14 Stationary Hospital. Attached 21 Field Hospital. Discharged.
HOUGHTON, E. Private 1667 Wellingborough Corps Medal Clasps: No Clasps.
Medal Roll Reference: WO100/225/144 Orderly.
HOUGHTON, Edward Private 195 Walton-le-Dale Division Medal Clasps: CC OFS.
Medal Roll Reference: WO100/225/176 Orderly 5 Stationary Hospital. Died of disease Bloemfontein 17 June 1900.
HOUGHTON, J. B. Private 263 Northampton Corps Medal Clasps: CC.
Medal Roll Reference: WO100/225/125 Orderly 6 General Hospital. Invalided 14 May 1900.
HOWARD, A. Sergeant Major 1294 Preston Corps Medal Clasps: CC TVL.
Medal Roll Reference: WO100/224/172 1st Class Staff Sergeant Rhodesian Field Force Hospital.
HOWARD, Edwin Matthew Private 1128 Oldham Corps Medal Clasps: CC. China Medal.
Medal Roll Reference: WO100/225/53+248 Orderly HS *Maine*. On medal roll for HS *Maine* for China WO100/96/38+39.
HOWARTH, D. Private 1547 Rochdale Corps Medal Clasps: CC.
Medal Roll Reference: WO100/225/123 Orderly 5 General Hospital.
HOWARTH, F. Private 1545 Oldham Corps Medal Clasps: CC.
Medal Roll Reference: WO100/225/109 Orderly 1 General Hospital.
HOWARTH, J. W. Private 452 Heywood Division Medal Clasps: CC OFS.
Medal Roll Reference: WO100/225/135 Orderly 8 General Hospital. To England 20 July 1900.
HOWARTH, M. Private 1241 Preston Corps Medal Clasps: CC OFS.
Medal Roll Reference: WO100/225/149 Orderly 9 General Hospital. To Base Detail 12 October 1900.
HOWCROFT, T. R. Private 1064 Bolton Corps Medal Clasps: OFS TVL NAT SA01 SA01 KSA01 KSA02.
Medal Roll Reference: WO100/225/180+192 WO100/273/83+272 WO100/366/171 Orderly 14 Stationary Hospital. Attached 21 Field Hospital. Discharged. South African Constabulary E Division Trooper E2928. Service in St John Ambulance Brigade April to November 1900. In South Africa 16 May to 16 October 1900. Service in South African Constabulary 4 May 1901 to 31 May 1902.
HOWELL, J. Private 394 Sheffield Corps Medal Clasps: CC.
Medal Roll Reference: WO100/130/219 Sergeant Imperial Yeomanry Hospital Deelfontein.

HOYLE, A. Private 1020 Rochdale Corps Medal Clasps: NAT.
Medal Roll Reference: WO100/225/65 Orderly 13 Stationary Hospital. To HS *Dunera* 18 December 1900.
HOYLE, F. Private 1019 Rochdale Corps Medal Clasps: NAT.
Medal Roll Reference: WO100/225/165 Orderly 15 General Hospital. Transferred to HS *Nubia* 29 December 1900.
HOYLE, John Henry Private 19 Haslingden Corps Medal Clasps: CC.
Medal Roll Reference: WO100/225/241 Private HS *Princess of Wales*. Attached RAMC.
HOYLE, T. Private 1450 Accrington Corps Medal Clasps: No Clasps.
Medal Roll Reference: WO100/225/118 Orderly 4 General Hospital Sent to England time expired 28 November 1900.
HUBBERSTY, R. Private 1225 Preston Corps Medal Clasps: CC SA01.
Medal Roll Reference: WO100/225/56+85+149 Orderly 11 General Hospital. 9 General Hospital. To Base Detail 12 October 1900. To England on termination of engagement.
HUBY, C. G. Private 1378 Hull Corps Medal Clasps: No Clasps.
Medal Roll Reference: WO100/225/25+59 Orderly 14 General Hospital. To SS *Manhattan* for duty 28 November 1900.
HUDSON, W. H. Private 1480 Derby Division Medal Clasps: No Clasps.
Medal Roll Reference: WO100/225/67 Orderly 18 General Hospital. Discharged 30 May 1900.
HUGHES, E. Private 447 North Staffs Corps Medal Clasps: CC OFS.
Medal Roll Reference: WO100/225/135 Orderly 8 General Hospital. To England 20 July 1900.
HUGHES, W. H. Private 570 Bolton Corps Medal Clasps: CC.
Medal Roll Reference: WO100/225/123 Orderly 5 General Hospital.
HUGILL, John W. Private 1043 Nelson Corps Medal Clasps: NAT.
Medal Roll Reference: WO100/225/165 Orderly 15 General Hospital. Died typhoid Howick 1 October 1900.
HULME, H. W. Private 1524 North Staffs Corps Medal Clasps: No Clasps.
Medal Roll Reference: WO100/225/25 Orderly.
HULME, P. Private 491 North Staffs Corps Medal Clasps: NAT.
Medal Roll Reference: WO100/225/65 Orderly 13 Stationary Hospital. To SS *Formosa* 6 December 1900.
HULSE, W. John Private 1014 Sheffield Corps Medal Clasps: NAT KSA01 KSA02.
Medal Roll Reference: WO100/225/165 WO100/352/164 Orderly 15 General Hospital. Transferred to HS *Nubia* 29 December 1900. Entitled KSA as RAMC Private 15705.
HUMPHREYS, W. H. Sergeant 759 1845 Oldham Corps Medal Clasps: CC OFS TVL SA01 KSA01 KSA02.
Medal Roll Reference: WO100/225/63+87+116+195+WO100/352/21+165 Supply Officer Base Hospital Wynberg. 3 General Hospital. Transferred to Base Detail RAMC. To base Detail 28 June 1901. 23 Field Hospital. Transferred sick to Cape Town on disembarkation. Did not re-join unit.
HUMPHREYSON, A. G. Private 1576 Bolton Corps Medal Clasps: CC.
Medal Roll Reference: WO100/225/158 Orderly 13 General Hospital. To England expired contract 10 April 1901.
HUMPHRIES, W. Private 1804 Denaby Cadeby Main Division Medal Clasps: CC OFS.
Medal Roll Reference: WO100/225/72 Orderly 24 Stationary Hospital. From Base Detail 15 April 1901 Was sent on escort duty with a prisoner to Base.
HUNT, G. L. Private 16 1661 Hull Corps Medal Clasps: CC OFS TVL SA01.
Medal Roll Reference: WO100/225/171+241 Orderly HS *Princess of Wales*. Attached RAMC. 20 General Hospital. Joined from Base Detail. To England for discharge.
HUNTER, H. G. Sergeant 68 1322 Kendal Division Medal Clasps: CC OFS TVL.
Medal Roll Reference: WO100/225/113+158 Supply Officer 2 General Hospital. 13 General Hospital. To England expired contract 5 May 1901.

HUTCHINGS, A. Private 847 Northampton Corps Medal Clasps: CC OFS TVL SA02.
Medal Roll Reference: WO100/225/149 WO100/271/217 Orderly 9 General Hospital. To Base Detail 31 August 1900. South African Constabulary A Division Trooper A2279.
HUXLEY, W. Private 363 North Staffs Corps Medal Clasps: CC.
Medal Roll Reference: WO100/130/220 Private Imperial Yeomanry Hospital Deelfontein.
HYDES, F. H. E. Private 158 Derby Corps Medal Clasps: CC OFS.
Medal Roll Reference: WO100/225/109+135 Orderly 1 General Hospital. 8 General Hospital Sick to Cape Town 5 July 1900.
IBBOTSON, J. W. Private 1179 Oldham Corps Medal Clasps: CC OFS.
Medal Roll Reference: WO100/225/149 Orderly 9 General Hospital. To Base Detail 15 April 1901.
IDDON, W. Private 959 Walton-le-Dale Division Medal Clasps: NAT.
Medal Roll Reference: WO100/225/165 Orderly 15 General Hospital. Transferred to England 26 August 1900.
ILLINGSWORTH, A. Private 1881 Oldham Corps Medal Clasps: CC.
Medal Roll Reference: WO100/225/173 Orderly 21 General Hospital.
ILLINGWORTH, A. Private 1153 1857 Bradford Corps Medal Clasps: CC OFS SA01.
Medal Roll Reference: WO100/225/87+116+135 Orderly 8 General Hospital. To England 10 October 1900. 3 General Hospital. Transferred to Base Detail RAMC. Home 21 June 1901
INDER, Henry Ewart Private 1442 Kendal Division Medal Clasps: CC OFS TVL NAT SA01.
Medal Roll Reference: WO100/225/63+112B+180+183 WO100/286/44 Orderly Base Hospital Wynberg 2 General Hospital. 6 General Hospital. 17 Stationary Hospital. 14 Stationary Hospital. To Base 24 November 1900. 1st Scottish Horse Trooper 25839. Discharged Johannesburg 18 August 1901.
INDER, William Sidney Sergeant 38 1321 Kendal Division Medal Clasps: CC OFS TVL.
Medal Roll Reference: WO100/225/112B+158 Supply Officer 13 General Hospital. Discharged locally expired contract 15 June 1901. Died pneumonia Bloemfontein 7 January 1902.
INSKIP, T. Private 1425 Birchwood Corps Medal Clasps: No Clasps.
Medal Roll Reference: WO100/225/59 Orderly 14 General Hospital. To HS *Simla* for duty 14 November 1900.
ION, William W. Private 786 Kendal Division Medal Clasps: CC.
Medal Roll Reference: WO100/225/125 Orderly 6 General Hospital. To Stationary Hospital Norval's Pont 8 June 1900. Died typhoid Springfontein 13 July 1900.
IRVINE, E. Private 1310 Belfast Division Medal Clasps: CC TVL.
Medal Roll Reference: WO100/224/172 Corporal Rhodesian Field Force Hospital.
JACKSON, A. Private 1818 Bolton Corps Medal Clasps: CC.
Medal Roll Reference: WO100/225/72+112B Orderly 24 Stationary Hospital. From Base Detail Transferred to Base Detail 29 June 1901.
JACKSON, C. Private 617 Heywood Division Medal Clasps: CC OFS.
Medal Roll Reference: WO100/225/155 Orderly 10 General Hospital. To Base 7 August 1900.
JACKSON, C. Private 1674 Handsworth & Smethwick Corps Medal Clasps: CC OFS TVL.
Medal Roll Reference: WO100/225/171 Orderly 20 General Hospital. Joined from Base Detail. To England for discharge.
JACKSON, D. Private 629 Burnley Division Medal Clasps: CC OFS.
Medal Roll Reference: WO100/225/155 Orderly 10 General Hospital. To Base 7 August 1900.
JACKSON, E. G. Private 905 Derby Division Medal Clasps: NAT.
Medal Roll Reference: WO100/225/165 Orderly 15 General Hospital. Invalided to England 18 October 1900.
JACKSON, G. Private 1469 Oldham Corps Medal Clasps: No Clasps.
Medal Roll Reference: WO100/225/118 Orderly 4 General Hospital Sent to England time expired 28 November 1900.
JACKSON, George Private 1163 Leeds Corps Medal Clasps: CC OFS SA01 SA02.

Medal Roll Reference: WO100/225/26+149 WO100/219/157 Orderly 9 General Hospital. To Base Detail 15 April 1901. RAMC Private 15869 (Incorrectly shown as South African Constabulary A1875 on WO100/225/149).

JACKSON, George Private 1455 Oldham Corps Medal Clasps: CC OFS TVL SA01 SA02.
Medal Roll Reference: WO100/225/26+68 WO100/271/123+220 Orderly 18 General Hospital. To England 30 May 1900 South African Constabulary A Division Medical Corporal A1875 (Incorrectly numbered SJAB 1163 on WO100/271/123).

JACKSON, H. Sergeant 1174 Oldham Corps Medal Clasps: CC.
Medal Roll Reference: WO100/225/76+109 Supply Officer 1 General Hospital. War Office Issue

JACKSON, J. Private 558 Birmingham Corps Medal Clasps: CC OFS.
Medal Roll Reference: WO100/225/149 Orderly 9 General Hospital. To Base Detail 7 August 1900.

JACKSON, J. Private 730 Leicester Corps Medal Clasps: CC WITT.
Medal Roll Reference: WO100/225/195 Orderly 23 Field Hospital. Discharged time expired.

JACKSON, J. Private 1186 Oldham Corps Medal Clasps: CC.
Medal Roll Reference: WO100/225/109 Orderly 1 General Hospital.

JACKSON, J. Private 1187 Oldham Corps Medal Clasps: CC.
Medal Roll Reference: WO100/225/109 Orderly 1 General Hospital.

JACKSON, J. Private 1694 No Bronze Medal roll entry. Medal Clasps: No Clasps.
Medal Roll Reference: WO100/225/51 Orderly.

JACKSON, J. T. Private 246 Hazelgrove Division Medal Clasps: NAT.
Medal Roll Reference: WO100/225/75 Orderly Princess Christian Hospital Train.

JACKSON, J. W. Private 784 Kendal Division Medal Clasps: CC OFS TVL.
Medal Roll Reference: WO100/225/125 Private 6 General Hospital. To Base on expiration of contract 3 September 1900.

JACKSON, R. Private 782 Hazelgrove Division Medal Clasps: CC OFS TVL.
Medal Roll Reference: WO100/225/26 Orderly 6 General Hospital.

JACKSON, R. Private 919 Morecombe Division Medal Clasps: NAT.
Medal Roll Reference: WO100/225/165 Orderly 15 General Hospital. Discharged in South Africa 3 October 1900.

JACOB, M. Private 276 Metropolitan Corps Medal Clasps: CC.
Medal Roll Reference: WO100/225/125 Private 6 General Hospital. To Stationary Hospital Norval's Pont 5 June 1900.

JAMES, John Private 1159 1869 Leeds Corps Medal Clasps: CC OFS TVL SA01 SA02.
Medal Roll Reference: WO100/225/27+149 WO100/222/16 Orderly 9 General Hospital. To Base Detail 12 October 1900. 9 General Hospital. To Base Detail 15 July 1901. General Hospital Pretoria. To 38 Stationary Hospital 23 March 1902. RAMC 16603 on WO100/225/27. Bronze Medal duplicated on RAMC Medal Roll.

JANSON, J. Private 1149 Dewsbury Corps Medal Clasps: CC OFS.
Medal Roll Reference: WO100/225/155 Orderly 10 General Hospital. To Base 10 October 1900. J. I'ANSON on QSA Medal Roll.

JAY, W. E. Private 656 Derby Division Medal Clasps: CC WITT.
Medal Roll Reference: WO100/225/192 Orderly Attached 21 Field Hospital. Discharged.

JEFFERSON, A. Private 1817 Hull Corps Medal Clasps: CC OFS SA01.
Medal Roll Reference: WO100/225/87+115 Orderly 3 General Hospital. Transferred to Base Detail RAMC. Home 21 June 1901.

JENNESON, Herbert William Private 168 Hull Corps Medal Clasps: CC.
Medal Roll Reference: WO100/225/109 Orderly 1 General Hospital.

JERVIS, C. H. Private 936 Kettering Corps Medal Clasps: NAT.
Medal Roll Reference: WO100/225/165 Orderly 15 General Hospital. Invalided to SS *Dunera* 17 September 1900.

JODRELL, D. H. Private 783 1742 Whaley Bridge Division Medal Clasps: CC OFS TVL. Medal Roll Reference: WO100/225/126 Orderly 6 General Hospital. To Base on expiration of contract 3 September 1900. 9 General Hospital. To Base Detail 15 July 1901.

JOHNSON, A. Sergeant 1184 Oldham Corps Medal Clasps: CC OFS TVL. Medal Roll Reference: WO100/225/112B+149 Supply Officer 9 General Hospital. To Base Detail 12 October 1900.

JOHNSON, H. Private 1403 Doncaster Division Medal Clasps: No Clasps. Medal Roll Reference: WO100/225/59 Orderly 14 General Hospital. To HS *Simla* for duty 14 November 1900.

JOHNSON, J. Private 204 Nuneaton Division Medal Clasps: NAT. Medal Roll Reference: WO100/225/75 Orderly Princess Christian Hospital Train.

JOHNSON, Thomas Holmes Sergeant 121 1437 Hull Corps Medal Clasps: No Clasps. China Medal. Medal Roll Reference: WO100/225/26 Orderly HS *Maine*. On medal roll for HS *Maine* for China WO100/96/38+39.

JOHNSON, W. Private 358 Northampton Corps Medal Clasps: NAT. Medal Roll Reference: WO100/225/129 Orderly 7 General Hospital. Invalided to England.

JOHNSON, William Private 543 Warrington Corps Medal Clasps: CC OFS TVL SA01 SA02 KSA01 KSA02. Medal Roll Reference: WO100/225/196 WO100/272/77 WO100/366/224 Orderly 24 Field Hospital. Attached RAMC 16 March 1900. To Base expiration of contract 6 January 1901. South African Constabulary Medical Corporal B1460. Service with South African Constabulary 4 May 1901 to 31 May 1902.

JOHNSON, William Thomas Sergeant 94 1681 Northampton Corps Medal Clasps: CC OFS TVL. Medal Roll Reference: WO100/225/171+235 Supply Officer Portland Hospital. To England contract expired. 20 General Hospital.

JOLLY, John Private 524 Blackpool Division Medal Clasps: CC NAT KSA01 KSA02. Medal Roll Reference: WO100/225/65 WO100/352/172 Orderly 13 Stationary Hospital (Princess Christian Hospital) Entitled King's South Africa Medal as RAMC Private 15653.

JONAS, Malcolm Emmanuel 1st Class Sergeant 113 Metropolitan Corps Medal Clasps: CC OFS TVL KSA01 KSA02. Medal Roll Reference: WO100/225/56 WO100/271/48 WO100/366/39 Supply Officer 11 General Hospital. To England on termination of engagement. Served South African Constabulary Reserve Division RD196 and A Division Trooper A1986 27 March 1901 to 8 June 1902.

JONES, C. Private 1121 Sheffield Corps Medal Clasps: NAT. Medal Roll Reference: WO100/225/165 Orderly 15 General Hospital. Invalided to SS *Dunera* 17 September 1900.

JONES, C. W. Private 1387 Mill Bay Division Medal Clasps: No Clasps. Medal Roll Reference: WO100/225/59 Orderly 14 General Hospital. To SS *Manhattan* for duty 28 November 1900.

JONES, F. Private 412 Oldham Corps Medal Clasps: NAT. Medal Roll Reference: WO100/225/129 Orderly 7 General Hospital. To England time expired.

JONES, F. Private 1540 Oldham Corps Medal Clasps: OFS TVL NAT. Medal Roll Reference: WO100/225/200 Orderly 7 Bearer Company 14 Brigade 7th Division.

JONES, H. Private 1847 Leicester Corps Medal Clasps: CC OFS. Medal Roll Reference: WO100/225/149 Orderly 9 General Hospital. To Base Detail 15 July 1901.

JONES, J. Private 77 Metropolitan Corps Medal Clasps: CC OFS. Medal Roll Reference: WO100/225/116 Orderly 3 General Hospital. Transferred to Base Detail RAMC.

JONES, J. Private 628 Dowlais Division Medal Clasps: CC OFS.
Medal Roll Reference: WO100/225/155 Orderly 10 General Hospital. To Base 7 August 1900.
JONES, S. H. Private 494 North Staffs Corps Medal Clasps: NAT.
Medal Roll Reference: WO100/225/66 Orderly 13 Stationary Hospital. To SS *Formosa* 6 December 1900.
JONES, T. Private 1768 Radcliffe Division Medal Clasps: CC SA01 SA02.
Medal Roll Reference: WO100/225/173 Orderly 21 General Hospital.
JOULE, H. Private 474 Bolton Corps Medal Clasps: NAT.
Medal Roll Reference: WO100/225/66 Orderly 13 Stationary Hospital. To SS *Formosa* 6 December 1900.
JUMP, E. Private 1074 Walton-le-Dale Division Medal Clasps: OFS NAT.
Medal Roll Reference: WO100/225/180+192 Orderly 14 Stationary Hospital. Attached 21 Field Hospital. 1 Stationary Hospital. Discharged.
KAY, E. Private 1032 Edenfield Division Medal Clasps: NAT.
Medal Roll Reference: WO100/225/68 Orderly 18 General Hospital. To England 30 August 1900.
KAY, J. Private 1065 Bolton Corps Medal Clasps: NAT.
Medal Roll Reference: WO100/225/66 Orderly 13 Stationary Hospital. To HS *Dunera* 18 December 1900.
KAY, J. Private 1246 Preston Corps Medal Clasps: CC OFS TVL.
Medal Roll Reference: WO100/225/126+155 Private 6 General Hospital. 10 General Hospital. To Base on expiration of contract 22 October 1900
KAY, Thomas Private 1365 Preston Corps Medal Clasps: CC.
Medal Roll Reference: WO100/225/158 Orderly 13 General Hospital. To England expired contract 27 November 1900.
KAY, William J. Private 1090 Haslingden Corps Medal Clasps: NAT.
Medal Roll Reference: WO100/225/165 Orderly 15 General Hospital. Transferred to England 14 September 1900.
KEEFE, H. R. Private 47 Metropolitan Corps Medal Clasps: CC OFS.
Medal Roll Reference: WO100/225/116 Orderly 3 General Hospital. Transferred to Base Detail RAMC.
KEEP, F. Private 1725 Desborough Division Medal Clasps: CC OFS TVL.
Medal Roll Reference: WO100/225/201 Orderly 9 Bearer Company 4 Brigade. Earned claps while travelling from Base Depot RAMC to join this unit. Transferred to England for discharge.
KEIGHLEY, H. Private 1252 Morecombe Division Medal Clasps: CC OFS TVL.
Medal Roll Reference: WO100/225/126 Private 6 General Hospital. To Base on expiration of contract 22 October 1900.
KELLETT, C. Private 1699 Preston Corps Medal Clasps: CC OFS TVL.
Medal Roll Reference: WO100/225/171 Orderly 20 General Hospital. Joined from Base Detail. To England for discharge.
KELLY, G. Private 542 Warrington Corps Medal Clasps: CC TVL.
Medal Roll Reference: WO100/225/196 Orderly 24 Field Hospital. To Base invalided.
KENDALL, Joseph Private 1006 Rushton Division Medal Clasps: NAT SA01 SA02.
Medal Roll Reference: WO100/225/165 WO100/219/131 Orderly 15 General Hospital. Transferred to England 26 August 1900. RAMC Private 16545 30 Stationary Hospital Home 24 August 1902.
KENDALL, W. Private 1459 Oldham Corps Medal Clasps: TVL.
Medal Roll Reference: WO100/225/169 Orderly 17 General Hospital. Transferred to Pietermaritzburg 30 November 1900.
KENNEDY, M. W. Private 1251 Morecombe Division Medal Clasps: CC OFS TVL.
Medal Roll Reference: WO100/225/126 Supernumerary Officer 6 General Hospital. To Base on expiration of contract 22 October 1900.

KENNEDY, P. Private 897 Bolton Corps Medal Clasps: NAT.
Medal Roll Reference: WO100/225/165 Orderly 15 General Hospital. Discharged in South Africa 3 October 1900.

KENWARD, A. J. Private 50 1919 Metropolitan Corps Medal Clasps: CC OFS TVL SA01 SA02 KSA01 KSA02.
Medal Roll Reference: WO100/225/115 WO100/272/193+311 WO100/366/118 Orderly 3 General Hospital. Transferred to Base Detail RAMC. South African Constabulary C Division Medical Corporal C2119. Served St John Ambulance Brigade 24 November 1899 to 4 December 1900. Served South African Constabulary 11 May 1901 to 31 May 1902. Discharged 7 April 1903.

KENWORTHY, B. Private 1723 Oldham Corps Medal Clasps: No Clasps.
Medal Roll Reference: WO100/225/59 Orderly 14 General Hospital. To HS *Dunera* 11 February 1901.

KENYON, J. W. Private 421 Oldham Corps Medal Clasps: CC OFS.
Medal Roll Reference: WO100/225/238 2nd Grade Orderly Van Alen American Field Hospital.

KEW, A. Private 156 Leeds Corps Medal Clasps: CC.
Medal Roll Reference: WO100/225/69 Orderly 8 Stationary Hospital.

KILVINGTON, Henry Private 222 Bradford Corps Medal Clasps: CC OFS TVL SA01 SA02.
Medal Roll Reference: WO100/225/126 WO100/272/192+311 Private 6 General Hospital. To Base on expiration of contract 18 June 1900. South African Constabulary C Division 1st Class Sergeant C2117 Discharged 16 March 1903.

KING, B. Private 954 Nelson Corps Medal Clasps: NAT.
Medal Roll Reference: WO100/225/165 Orderly 15 General Hospital. Transferred to England 26 August 1900.

KING, C. E. Private 424 Metropolitan Corps Medal Clasps: CC TVL NAT.
Medal Roll Reference: WO100/225/27+129 Orderly 7 General Hospital. To Base for discharge. Service with 1st Brabant's Horse Sergeant 30374 CC clasp.

KING, F. Private 642 Leicester Corps Medal Clasps: CC WITT.
Medal Roll Reference: WO100/225/204 Orderly Attached 22 Bearer Company. Discharged.

KING, John Private 1423 Hebden Bridge Corps Medal Clasps: No Clasps.
Medal Roll Reference: WO100/225/59 Orderly 14 General Hospital. Died of disease Newcastle 30 October 1900.

KING, William Private 442 1652 Metropolitan Corps Medal Clasps: CC OFS TVL NAT SA01 SA02.
Medal Roll Reference: WO100/225/102+129 Orderly 7 General Hospital. Attached to RAMC. To England time expired.

KINGSTON, Samuel Sergeant 117 Northampton Corps Medal Clasps: No Clasps. China Medal.
Medal Roll Reference: WO100/225/27 Orderly HS *Maine*. On medal roll for HS *Maine* for China WO100/96/38+39.

KINGSTON, W. Private 359 Northampton Corps Medal Clasps: NAT.
Medal Roll Reference: WO100/225/129 Orderly 7 General Hospital. To England time expired.

KIRK, J. W. Private 227 Babbington Corps Medal Clasps: CC.
Medal Roll Reference: WO100/225/126 Private 6 General Hospital. To Base on expiration of contract 18 June 1900.

KIRK, Stuart Private 389 Sheffield Corps Medal Clasps: CC TVL SA01 SA02.
Medal Roll Reference: WO100/225/63+129 Orderly Base Hospital Wynberg 7 General Hospital. Service with 1st Brabant's Horse Sergeant 30375 CC clasp from 9 February 1901 to 6 January 1902.

KITCHEN, A. Private 1421 Hebden Bridge Corps Medal Clasps: No Clasps.
Medal Roll Reference: WO100/225/59 Orderly 14 General Hospital. To HS *Simla* for duty 14 November 1900.

KITCHEN, L. Private 1448 Accrington Corps Medal Clasps: CC OFS TVL.

Medal Roll Reference: WO100/225/180+183 Orderly 14 Stationary Hospital and 17 Stationary Hospital Middleburg. To Base 24 November 1900.

KITCHEN, P. Private 1165 Leeds Corps Medal Clasps: CC OFS.
Medal Roll Reference: WO100/225/149 Orderly 9 General Hospital. To Base Detail 12 October 1900.

KITCHEN, W. H. Private 1361 Bolton Corps Medal Clasps: CC.
Medal Roll Reference: WO100/225/159 Orderly 13 General Hospital. To England expired contract 27 November 1900.

KITCHEN, W. H. Private 1485 Leeds Corps Medal Clasps: No Clasps.
Medal Roll Reference: WO100/225/118 Orderly 4 General Hospital Sent to England time expired 28 November 1900.

KITCHING, H. Private 646 Bradford Corps Medal Clasps: CC.
Medal Roll Reference: WO100/225/56 Orderly 11 General Hospital. To England on termination of engagement.

KNIGHT, F. B. Private 468 Metropolitan Corps Medal Clasps: CC OFS TVL SA01 SA02.
Medal Roll Reference: WO100/130/220 WO100/271/125+222 Private Imperial Yeomanry Hospital Deelfontein. South African Constabulary A Division Medical Corporal A1874 Discharge 5 February 1902.

KNIGHT, G. Private 793 Metropolitan Corps Medal Clasps: CC OFS JOH DIA BELF.
Medal Roll Reference: WO100/225/198 Private 18th Brigade Bearer Joined Company 6 May 1900. Taken prisoner by enemy (missing in action) 24 August 1900. Rejoined. Left company on completion of engagement 20 November 1900.

KNIGHT, S. W. Private 425 Metropolitan Corps Medal Clasps: CC OFS.
Medal Roll Reference: WO100/225/135 Orderly 8 General Hospital. To England 23 January 1901.

KNIGHT, W. Sergeant 139 Wellingborough Corps Medal Clasps: CC.
Medal Roll Reference: WO100/225/123 Supply Officer 5 General Hospital.

KNIGHT, William Private 1201 Leeds Corps Medal Clasps: CC OFS.
Medal Roll Reference: WO100/225/149 Private 9 General Hospital. Died of disease Bloemfontein 27 July 1900.

KNOTT, G. F. Private 545 Rochdale Corps Medal Clasps: CC OFS TVL.
Medal Roll Reference: WO100/225/196 Orderly 24 Field Hospital. To Base expiration of contract 6 January 1901.

KNOWLES, Jonas Private 798 Colne Division Medal Clasps: CC OFS.
Medal Roll Reference: WO100/225/135 Orderly 8 General Hospital. To England 31 August 1900.

KNOWLES, S. Private 1050 Bolton Corps Medal Clasps: NAT.
Medal Roll Reference: WO100/225/181 Orderly 14 Stationary Hospital.

KNOWLES, W. Private 1368 Preston Corps Medal Clasps: CC.
Medal Roll Reference: WO100/225/159 Orderly 13 General Hospital. To England expired contract 27 November 1900.

LAMB, Thomas Private 6 1668 Hull Corps Medal Clasps: CC OFS TVL.
Medal Roll Reference: WO100/225/171+241 Orderly HS *Princess of Wales*. Attached RAMC. 20 General Hospital. Joined from Base Detail. To England for discharge

LAMBERT, W. Private 1141 Barnoldswick Division Medal Clasps: CC OFS.
Medal Roll Reference: WO100/225/155 Orderly 10 General Hospital. To Base 10 October 1900.

LANCASTER, E. Private 380 Birmingham Corps Medal Clasps: CC.
Medal Roll Reference: WO100/130/220 Corporal Imperial Yeomanry Hospital Deelfontein.

LANCASTER, J. W. Private 1443 1782 Accrington Corps Medal Clasps: CC OFS.
Medal Roll Reference: WO100/225/149+181 Orderly 9 General Hospital. To Base Detail 15 July 1901. 14 Stationary Hospital.

LANCHBERRY, William E. Private 20 Westgate-on-Sea Division Medal Clasps: CC.
Medal Roll Reference: WO100/225/241 Private HS *Princess of Wales*. Attached RAMC. Died typhoid Netley UK 15 July 1900.
LANE, Charles William Private 333 Isle of Wight Corps Medal Clasps: CC OFS.
Medal Roll Reference: WO100/225/238 2nd Grade Orderly Van Alen American Field Hospital.
LANGDOWN, W. H. Sergeant 264 Portsmouth Division Medal Clasps: CC OFS TVL.
Medal Roll Reference: WO100/225/66+126+129 Orderly 7 General Hospital. From Cape Town. 6 General Hospital. To Base Invalided 7 June 1900. To England time expired.
LANGTON, W. L. Sergeant 1308 Leicester Corps Medal Clasps: CC TVL.
Medal Roll Reference: WO100/224/172 Sergeant Rhodesian Field Force Hospital.
LANGTREE, T. Private 1446 Accrington Corps Medal Clasps: No Clasps.
Medal Roll Reference: WO100/225/118 Orderly 4 General Hospital Sent to England time expired 28 November 1900.
LARBEY, G. Private 202 Preston Corps Medal Clasps: CC OFS.
Medal Roll Reference: WO100/225/176 Orderly 5 Stationary Hospital Sent to Base for England for discharge.
LATHAM, J. J. Private 1125 Heanor Division Medal Clasps: NAT.
Medal Roll Reference: WO100/225/165 Orderly 15 General Hospital. Transferred to England 14 September 1900.
LAW, H. Private 1776 Bacup Division Medal Clasps: CC SA01.
Medal Roll Reference: WO100/225/56+85 Orderly 11 General Hospital. To England on termination of engagement.
LAWRENCE, E. Private 888 Handsworth & Smethwick Corps Medal Clasps: CC.
Medal Roll Reference: WO100/225/178 Orderly 7 Stationary Hospital Sent to England February 1901. LAWRENCE, W. E. on QSA medal roll.
LAWRENCE, W. E. Private 219 Metropolitan Corps Medal Clasps: CC.
Medal Roll Reference: WO100/225/126 Private 6 General Hospital. To Base on expiration of contract 22 July1900.
LAWRENCE, W. L. Private 292 Swindon Division Medal Clasps: CC.
Medal Roll Reference: WO100/130/220 Lance Corporal Imperial Yeomanry Hospital Deelfontein.
LAWSON, J. E. Private 1499 Burnley Division Medal Clasps: TVL.
Medal Roll Reference: WO100/225/169 Orderly 17 General Hospital. Transferred to Pietermaritzburg 30 November 1900.
LAYCOCK, G. H. Private 1046 Barrowford Division Medal Clasps: OFS NAT.
Medal Roll Reference: WO100/225/181+192 Orderly 14 Stationary Hospital. Attached 21 Field Hospital. Discharged.
LEACH, Francis Private 265 Isle of Wight Corps Medal Clasps: CC OFS SA01 SA02 RoK KSA01 KSA02.
Medal Roll Reference: WO100/225/126 WO100/271/17+49 WO100/366/96 Private 6 General Hospital. To Base on expiration of contract 16 June 1900. South African Constabulary Headquarters Trooper HQ32 Corporal. Reserve Division RD583. B Division Medical Corporal B1568.
LEADER, Frederick G. Private 721 Great Eastern Railway Corps Medal Clasps: CC OFS.
Medal Roll Reference: WO100/225/192 Orderly Attached 21 Field Hospital. Died of disease Wynberg 5 July 1900.
LEAVER, C. Private 687 Nelson Corps Medal Clasps: CC OFS.
Medal Roll Reference: WO100/225/192 Orderly Attached 21 Field Hospital. Discharged.
LEE, T. Private 895 Bolton Corps Medal Clasps: NAT.
Medal Roll Reference: WO100/225/165 Orderly 15 General Hospital. Transferred to HS *Nubia* 29 December 1900.

LEE, W. Private 1222 Preston Corps Medal Clasps: CC OFS.
Medal Roll Reference: WO100/225/149 Orderly 9 General Hospital. To Base Detail 12 October 1900.
LEECE, T. Private 896 Bolton Corps Medal Clasps: NAT.
Medal Roll Reference: WO100/225/165 Orderly 15 General Hospital. Transferred to HS *Nubia* 29 December 1900.
LEEMING, T. C. Private 1270 Radcliffe Division Medal Clasps: CC.
Medal Roll Reference: WO100/225/123 Orderly 5 General Hospital.
LEES, G. Private 809 Oldham Corps Medal Clasps: CC OFS TVL.
Medal Roll Reference: WO100/225/126 Private 6 General Hospital. To Base on expiration of contract 20 February 1901.
LEES, J. Private 1188 Oldham Corps Medal Clasps: CC.
Medal Roll Reference: WO100/225/109 Orderly 1 General Hospital.
LEES, S. Private 577 Oldham Corps Medal Clasps: CC TVL.
Medal Roll Reference: WO100/225/196 Orderly 24 Field Hospital. To Base invalided 17 November 1900.
LEES, S. Private 1879 Oldham Corps Medal Clasps: OFS.
Medal Roll Reference: WO100/225/190 Orderly Attached to 1 Corps Troops Field Hospital.
LEES, Sydney J. Private 1873 Leeds Corps Medal Clasps: CC.
Medal Roll Reference: WO100/225/173 Orderly 21 General Hospital.
LEESON, T. P. Private 445 Leicester Corps Medal Clasps: CC OFS.
Medal Roll Reference: WO100/225/135 Orderly 8 General Hospital. To England 20 July 1900.
LEESON, W. Private 737 Hull Corps Medal Clasps: CC SA01.
Medal Roll Reference: WO100/225/56+85 Orderly 11 General Hospital. To England on termination of engagement.
LEGGE, H. G. B. 1st Class Sergeant 3 Metropolitan Corps Medal Clasps: CC.
Medal Roll Reference: WO100/225/241 Supernumerary Officer HS *Princess of Wales*. Attached RAMC.
LEIGHTON, J. Private 697 Kendal Division Medal Clasps: CC SA01.
Medal Roll Reference: WO100/225/56+85 Orderly 11 General Hospital. To England on termination of engagement.
LEVICK, F. Private 1299 Welbeck Division Medal Clasps: CC TVL.
Medal Roll Reference: WO100/224/172 Private Rhodesian Field Force Hospital.
LEWIS, C. H. Private 932 Northampton Corps Medal Clasps: NAT.
Medal Roll Reference: WO100/225/165 Orderly 15 General Hospital. Transferred to England 30 August 1900.
LEWIS, E. Private 184 Brynmawr Division Medal Clasps: CC.
Medal Roll Reference: WO100/225/69 Orderly 8 Stationary Hospital.
LEWIS, E. K. Private 293 Swindon Division Medal Clasps: CC.
Medal Roll Reference: WO100/130/220 Private Imperial Yeomanry Hospital Deelfontein.
LEYLAND, J. R. Private 1571 Bolton Corps Medal Clasps: CC.
Medal Roll Reference: WO100/225/109 Orderly 1 General Hospital.
LIDDELL, T. Private 500 Sheffield Corps Medal Clasps: NAT.
Medal Roll Reference: WO100/225/66 Orderly 13 Stationary Hospital. To HS *Dunera* 18 December 1900.
LILES, J. Private 1537 Oldham Corps Medal Clasps: CC OFS.
Medal Roll Reference: WO100/225/123+155 Orderly 5 General Hospital. 10 General Hospital. To Base 10 October 1900.
LIMB, W. Private 824 Welbeck Division Medal Clasps: CC OFS.
Medal Roll Reference: WO100/225/149 Orderly 9 General Hospital. To Base Detail 8 August 1900.

LINGARD, James Private 405 Accrington Corps Medal Clasps: CC OFS.
Medal Roll Reference: WO100/225/238 1st Grade Orderly Van Alen American Field Hospital.
LINNELL, J. Private 848 Northampton Corps Medal Clasps: No Clasps.
Medal Roll Reference: WO100/225/29 Orderly.
LINTON, F. A. Private 350 Abram Colliery Division Medal Clasps: NAT.
Medal Roll Reference: WO100/225/129 Orderly 7 General Hospital. To England time expired.
LISTER, C. Private 21 1669 Leeds Corps Medal Clasps: CC OFS TVL SA01.
Medal Roll Reference: WO100/225/171+241 Orderly HS *Princess of Wales*. Attached RAMC.
20 General Hospital Joined from Base Detail. To England for discharge.
LISTER, Higson Private 511 Shipley Corps Medal Clasps: No Clasps.
Medal Roll Reference: WO100/225/28 Orderly. Died typhoid Princess Christian Hospital Pinetown 12 June 1900.
LITTLE, W. Private 218 Metropolitan Corps Medal Clasps: CC OFS SA01 SA02.
Medal Roll Reference: WO100/225/28+126 Private 6 General Hospital. To Base Invalided 30 May 1900.
LITTLER, S. Private 1035 Manchester Post Office Division Medal Clasps: NAT.
Medal Roll Reference: WO100/225/166 Orderly 15 General Hospital. Transferred to England 14 September 1900.
LIVERMORE, A. J. Private 724 Great Eastern Railway Corps Medal Clasps: CC OFS TVL.
Medal Roll Reference: WO100/130/267 Corporal Imperial Yeomanry Field Hospital and Bearer Company. Transferred to Maitland Yeomanry Hospital September 1900.
LLOYD, A. Private 32 Northampton Corps Medal Clasps: CC OFS TVL.
Medal Roll Reference: WO100/225/112B Orderly 6 General Hospital.
LLOYD, D. W. Private 708 Metropolitan Corps Medal Clasps: CC.
Medal Roll Reference: WO100/225/56 Orderly 11 General Hospital. To England on termination of engagement.
LONG, Charles E. Private 862 Wellingborough Corps Medal Clasps: CC OFS SA01 SA02.
Medal Roll Reference: WO100/225/149 WO100/273/100+289 WO100/366/176 Orderly 9 General Hospital. To Base Detail 22 July 1900. South African Constabulary Medical Corporal E2929. Service in St John Ambulance Brigade 1 April to 29 July 1900. Service in South African Constabulary 4 May 1901 to 31 May 1902. Not entitled to King's South Africa Medal.
LONG, J. Private 1147 Dewsbury Corps Medal Clasps: CC OFS.
Medal Roll Reference: WO100/225/155 Orderly 10 General Hospital. To Base 10 October 1900.
LONG, T. Private 1433 Bury Division Medal Clasps: No Clasps.
Medal Roll Reference: WO100/225/118 Orderly 4 General Hospital Sent to England time expired 28 November 1900.
LONGDEN, J. Private 1483 1843 Sheffield Corps Medal Clasps: CC OFS TVL.
Medal Roll Reference: WO100/225/166+169 Orderly 15 General Hospital. Transferred to England 26 November 1900. 17 General Hospital. Transferred to Base Detail Cape Town 13 July 1901.
LONGMORE, W. E. Private 541 Warrington Corps Medal Clasps: CC TVL.
Medal Roll Reference: WO100/225/196+197 Orderly 24 Field Hospital. To Base expiration of contract 6 January 1901 9th Brigade Bearer Company 1st Division.
LORD, C. Private 950 Nelson Corps Medal Clasps: NAT.
Medal Roll Reference: WO100/225/166 Orderly 15 General Hospital. Transferred to England 26 August 1900.
LORD, J. A. Private 1631 Rochdale Corps Medal Clasps: OFS TVL.
Medal Roll Reference: WO100/225/181 Orderly 14 Stationary Hospital. 7 Ambulance Train.
LORD, W. E. Private 357 Northampton Corps Medal Clasps: NAT.
Medal Roll Reference: WO100/225/129 Orderly 7 General Hospital. To England time expired.

LOUCH, H. G. Private 282 Portsmouth Division Medal Clasps: CC OFS TVL.
Medal Roll Reference: WO100/225/126 Private 6 General Hospital. To Base on expiration of contract 15 June 1901.
LOUP, H. Private 547 Metropolitan Corps Medal Clasps: CC OFS.
Medal Roll Reference: WO100/225/149 Orderly 9 General Hospital. To Base Detail 7 August 1900.
LOVICK, R. Private 1038 Barnoldswick Division Medal Clasps: OFS TVL NAT.
Medal Roll Reference: WO100/225/181+192 Orderly 14 Stationary Hospital. Attached 21 Field Hospital. Discharged.
LOWE, F. Private 1104 Birmingham Corps Medal Clasps: NAT.
Medal Roll Reference: WO100/225/68 Orderly 18 General Hospital. To England 28 December 1900.
LOWE, G. Private 492 North Staffs Corps Medal Clasps: No Clasps.
Medal Roll Reference: WO100/225/28 Orderly.
LOWE, J. Private 1070 Welbeck Division Medal Clasps: OFS NAT.
Medal Roll Reference: WO100/225/181+192 Orderly 14 Stationary Hospital 21. Attached 21 Field Hospital. Discharged.
LUCK, H. W. Private 275 Metropolitan Corps Medal Clasps: CC.
Medal Roll Reference: WO100/225/126 Private 6 General Hospital. To Base on expiration of contract 18 June 1900.
LUTHERS, L. Private 1311 Barnoldswick Division Medal Clasps: CC TVL.
Medal Roll Reference: WO100/224/172 Private Rhodesian Field Force Hospital.
LYON, J. Private 1493 Bolton Corps Medal Clasps: CC OFS TVL SA01.
Medal Roll Reference: WO100/225/129 Orderly 7 General Hospital. To England time expired.
LYONS, T. H. Private 322 St John Ambulance Brigade (NFB Croxley Mills) Dickinson's Fire Brigade Medal Clasps: CC. NFBUAD Medal.
Medal Roll Reference: WO100/130/220 Lance Corporal Imperial Yeomanry Hospital Deelfontein.
MABERLEY, B. E. Corporal 1111 Handsworth & Smethwick Corps Medal Clasps: OFS TVL NAT SA01 SA02 KSA01 KSA02.
Medal Roll Reference: WO100/225/118 WO100/271/141+239 WO100/366/43 Orderly 4 General Hospital. Sent to England time expired 19 December 1900. South African Constabulary A Division Medical Corporal A1868. Service in South African Constabulary from 4 May 1901. Discharged 10 February 1903.
MacKNESS, Arthur George 1st Class Sergeant 26 Northampton Corps
Medal Roll Reference: No QSA Medal roll entry identified.
MADDOCK, Joseph Private 544 Warrington Corps Medal Clasps: CC TVL.
Medal Roll Reference: WO100/225/196+197 Orderly 24 Field Hospital 9th Brigade Bearer Company 1st Division. Died of disease Mafeking 18 January 1901.
MADEN, E. Private 14 1670 Nelson Corps Medal Clasps: CC OFS TVL.
Medal Roll Reference: WO100/225/171+241 Orderly HS *Princess of Wales*. Attached RAMC. 20 General Hospital. Joined from Base Detail. To England for discharge
MAITLAND, E. A. Private 774 Metropolitan Corps Medal Clasps: CC SA01.
Medal Roll Reference: WO100/225/56+85 Orderly 11 General Hospital. To England on termination of engagement.
MAJOR, J. W. Private 1203 Leeds Corps Medal Clasps: CC OFS.
Medal Roll Reference: WO100/225/150 Orderly 9 General Hospital. To Base Detail 12 October 1900.
MAKEN, H. Sergeant 354 Worksop Division Medal Clasps: TVL NAT.
Medal Roll Reference: WO100/225/129 Supply Officer 7 General Hospital. To England time expired.

MAKIN, J. Private 1770 Bury Division Medal Clasps: CC OFS.
Medal Roll Reference: WO100/225/63+190 Orderly Base Hospital Wynberg Attached. To 1 Corps Troops Field Hospital.
MAKIN, S. Private 794 Radcliffe Division Medal Clasps: CC OFS.
Medal Roll Reference: WO100/225/3 Orderly.
MALKIN, John W. Private 148 Warrington Corps Medal Clasps: No Clasps.
Medal Roll Reference: WO100/225/30 Private 418 on Medal Roll. Died of Disease Woodstock Cape Town 19 March 1900.
MALLENDER, T. A. Private 1612 Worksop Division Medal Clasps: CC.
Medal Roll Reference: WO100/225/123 Orderly 5 General Hospital.
MALTBY, H. Private 1828 Welbeck Division Medal Clasps: CC.
Medal Roll Reference: WO100/225/173 Orderly 21 General Hospital.
MANDERVILLE, J. W. Private 856 Rishton Division Medal Clasps: CC.
Medal Roll Reference: WO100/225/69 Orderly 8 Stationary Hospital.
MANLEY, T. W. Private 217 Metropolitan Corps Medal Clasps: CC.
Medal Roll Reference: WO100/225/126 Private 6 General Hospital. To Base on expiration of contract 23 June 1900.
MANSHIP, Ernest Private 1122 Sheffield Corps Medal Clasps: NAT.
Medal Roll Reference: WO100/225/166 Orderly 15 General Hospital. Died typhoid Howick 16 September 1900.
MANSSUER, C. J. Sergeant 637 Warrington Corps Medal Clasps: CC OFS.
Medal Roll Reference: WO100/225/155 Supply Officer 10 General Hospital 4 March 1901.
MANTON, G. Private 559 1798 Birmingham Corps Medal Clasps: CC OFS SA01 SA02 KSA01 KSA02.
Medal Roll Reference: WO100/225/72+150 WO100/273/112 WO100/366/179 Orderly 9 General Hospital. To Base Detail 7 August 1900. 24 Stationary Hospital. From Base Detail 15 April 1901. South African Constabulary E Division Medical Corporal E3603. Service in St John Ambulance Brigade 1 April 1900 to 22 August 1900 and 26 February 1901 to 4 November 1901. Service in South African Constabulary 6 November 1901 to 31 May 1902.
MARCHANT, Thomas Egbert Private 106 Caterham Division Medal Clasps: CC OFS.
Medal Roll Reference: WO100/225/235 Private Portland Hospital. To England contract expired.
MARLOR, S. Private 574 Oldham Corps Medal Clasps: CC OFS TVL.
Medal Roll Reference: WO100/225/196 Orderly 24 Field Hospital. To Base invalided 8 September 1900.
MARRIOTT, E. A. Private 1668 Wellingborough Corps Medal Clasps: OFS TVL.
Medal Roll Reference: WO100/225/181 Orderly 14 Stationary Hospital. 7 Ambulance Train. 3 Ambulance Train.
MARRISON, H. Private 497 Sheffield Corps Medal Clasps: CC OFS.
Medal Roll Reference: WO100/225/231 Private Langman Hospital.
MARSDEN, Arthur Private 250 Southport Division Medal Clasps: CC OFS.
Medal Roll Reference: WO100/225/191 Private Attached 20 Field Hospital. Died of disease Drakens Hoch Bloemfontein 18 April 1900.
MARSDEN, F. T. Private 1457 Oldham Corps Medal Clasps: CC OFS TVL NAT.
Medal Roll Reference: WO100/225/166 Orderly 15 General Hospital. Transferred to Pretoria 29 August 1900.
MARSDEN, T. Private 1454 Oldham Corps Medal Clasps: No Clasps.
Medal Roll Reference: WO100/225/181+183 Orderly 14 Stationary Hospital. 17 Stationary Hospital. To Base 24 November 1900.
MARSDEN, W. Private 1178 Oldham Corps Medal Clasps: CC.
Medal Roll Reference: WO100/225/123 Orderly 5 General Hospital.
MARSHALL, G. Private 990 Dewsbury Corps Medal Clasps: CC OFS TVL NAT.

Medal Roll Reference: WO100/225/166+183 Orderly 15 General Hospital. Transferred to England 26 August 1900.

MARSHALL, W. Private 641 Leicester Corps Medal Clasps: CC WITT.
Medal Roll Reference: WO100/225/109+203 Orderly 1 General Hospital 20 General Hospital. Transferred to 21 Bearer Company. Sent home for discharge August 1901.

MARTIN, AH Private 422 Oldham Corps Medal Clasps: CC OFS TVL.
Medal Roll Reference: WO100/225/231 Private Langman Hospital.

MARTIN, W. Private 261 Leicester Corps Medal Clasps: CC.
Medal Roll Reference: WO100/225/126 Private 6 General Hospital. To Base on expiration of contract 18 June 1900.

MARTIN, W. Private 1746 Whalley Division Medal Clasps: CC OFS TVL.
Medal Roll Reference: WO100/225/169 Orderly 17 General Hospital. Transferred to Base Detail Cape Town 13 July 1901.

MARTINDALE, H. Private 926 Kendal Division Medal Clasps: NAT.
Medal Roll Reference: WO100/225/166 Orderly 15 General Hospital. Invalided to England 6 August 1900.

MARTON, J. G. Private 1262 Rishton Division Medal Clasps: CC OFS.
Medal Roll Reference: WO100/225/155 Orderly 10 General Hospital. To Base 10 October 1900 17 Stationary Hospital. To Base 24 November 1900.

MASON, A. Private 1852 Leicester Corps Medal Clasps: CC OFS SA01.
Medal Roll Reference: WO100/225/87+116 Orderly 3 General Hospital. Transferred to Base Detail RAMC. Home 21 June 1901.

MASON, Albert Private 1341 1846 Leicester Corps Medal Clasps: CC OFS SA01.
Medal Roll Reference: WO100/225/87+116+150+159 Orderly Base Hospital Wynberg 13 General Hospital. To England expired contract 27 November 1900. 3 General Hospital. Transferred to Base Detail RAMC. Home 21 June 1901. 9 General Hospital. To Base Detail 23 July 1901.

MASON, G. E. Private 1260 Rishton Division Medal Clasps: CC OFS SA01.
Medal Roll Reference: WO100/225/56+85+155 Orderly 11 General Hospital. 10 General Hospital. To Base 10 October 1900. To England on termination of engagement.

MASON, W. Private 59 Withernsea Division Medal Clasps: CC OFS TVL.
Medal Roll Reference: WO100/225/112B Orderly 6 General Hospital.

MASSEY, Richard Private 1470 Oldham Corps Medal Clasps: CC OFS TVL.
Medal Roll Reference: WO100/225/181+183 Orderly 14 Stationary Hospital. 17 Stationary Hospital. Died of disease Pretoria 2 December 1900.

MATHER, T. Private 1244 Preston Corps Medal Clasps: CC OFS.
Medal Roll Reference: WO100/225/135 Orderly 8 General Hospital. To England 10 October 1900.

MATTHEWS, Herbert Edward Private 89 Hull Corps Medal Clasps: CC OFS.
Medal Roll Reference: WO100/225/235 Private Portland Hospital. To England contract expired.

MAUDE, J. Private 881 Leeds Corps Medal Clasps: CC OFS.
Medal Roll Reference: WO100/225/150 Orderly 9 General Hospital. To Base Detail 11 June 1900.

MAY, C. E. Private 878 Withernsea Division Medal Clasps: CC OFS.
Medal Roll Reference: WO100/225/150 Orderly 9 General Hospital. To Base Detail 31 August 1900.

MAY, G. Private 744 Heanor Division Medal Clasps: CC OFS.
Medal Roll Reference: WO100/225/56 Orderly 11 General Hospital Convoy duty. To Boshof.

MAYALL, S. Private 1458 Oldham Corps Medal Clasps: No Clasps.
Medal Roll Reference: WO100/225/181 Orderly 14 Stationary Hospital.

MAYOH, J. Private 1235 Preston Corps Medal Clasps: CC OFS.
Medal Roll Reference: WO100/225/135 Orderly 8 General Hospital. To England 10 October 1900.

MAYOR, W. Private 1721 Oldham Corps Medal Clasps: No Clasps.
Medal Roll Reference: WO100/225/60 Orderly 14 General Hospital. To HS *Dunera* for duty 11 February 1901.
McALLISTER, J. C. Private 994 Dalton-in-Furness Division Medal Clasps: NAT.
Medal Roll Reference: WO100/225/119 Orderly 4 General Hospital Sent to England time expired 19 December 1900.
McBRIDE, C. Private 667 Manchester Post Office Division Medal Clasps: CC OFS TVL.
Medal Roll Reference: WO100/225/194 Orderly 22 Field Hospital.
McCRACKEN, James Arthur Private 477 Bury Division Medal Clasps: CC OFS TVL SA01 SA02.
Medal Roll Reference: WO100/225/123 WO100/271/53 WO100/272/87+128 Orderly 5 General Hospital. South African Constabulary Reserve Division Trooper RD587 Headquarters Depot HQ36 B Division B1645
McGRATH, J. Private 683 Adlington & Heath Charnock Division Medal Clasps: CC.
Medal Roll Reference: WO100/225/56 Orderly 11 General Hospital. To England on termination of engagement.
McIVOR, J. Private 560 Birmingham Corps Medal Clasps: CC OFS.
Medal Roll Reference: WO100/225/150 Orderly 9 General Hospital. To Base Detail 7 August 1900.
McKEAN, C. A. Private 970 Reading Division Medal Clasps: NAT.
Medal Roll Reference: WO100/225/119 Orderly 4 General Hospital Sent to England time expired 19 December 1900.
McKELVIE, D. H. Private 834 Winsford Division Medal Clasps: CC OFS JOH DIA BELF.
Medal Roll Reference: WO100/225/198 Orderly 18th Brigade Bearer Company. Joined 6 May 1900. Left company on completion of engagement 20 November 1900.
McNAMARA, William John 1st Class Sergeant 81 Leicester Corps Medal Clasps: CC OFS.
Medal Roll Reference: WO100/225/235 Staff Sergeant Portland Hospital. To England contract expired.
MEADON, George Fox Private 525 Blackpool Division Medal Clasps: OFS NAT SA01 SA02.
Medal Roll Reference: WO100/225/30 WO100/273/115+305 Orderly. South African Constabulary E2038 Corporal. Service in St John Ambulance Brigade 20 March 1900 to 17 July 1900. Service in South African Constabulary 4 May 1901 to 31 May 1902.
MEADOWS, J. Private 1042 Abram Colliery Division Medal Clasps: NAT.
Medal Roll Reference: WO100/225/66 Orderly 13 Stationary Hospital. To HS *Dunera* 18 December 1900.
MEAKINS, C. T. Private 325 St John Ambulance Brigade (NFB Stony Stratford) Medal Clasps: CC. NFBUAD Medal.
Medal Roll Reference: WO100/130/221 Private Imperial Yeomanry Hospital Deelfontein.
MEARS, H. Private 971 Reading Division Medal Clasps: NAT.
Medal Roll Reference: WO100/225/118+171 20 General Hospital Joined from Base Detail. To England for discharge. Orderly 4 General Hospital Invalided to England 3 August 1900.
MEASURES, W. H. Private 819 Welbeck Division Medal Clasps: CC.
Medal Roll Reference: WO100/225/168+178 Orderly 16 General Hospital. Transferred to 7 Stationary Hospital 4 June 1900 Sent to England September 1900. MEASURES, H. W. on QSA medal roll.
MEASURES, W. H. Private 984 Crewe Division Medal Clasps: NAT.
Medal Roll Reference: WO100/225/119 Orderly 4 General Hospital Sent to England time expired 19 December 1900.
MEEK, F. Private 571 Bolton Corps Medal Clasps: CC OFS TVL SA01.
Medal Roll Reference: WO100/225/92+123+155 Orderly 5 General Hospital. 10 General Hospital. To Base 29 June 1900.

MELLOR, C. Private 1686 Hebden Bridge Corps Medal Clasps: CC OFS TVL.
Medal Roll Reference: WO100/225/201 Orderly 9 Bearer Company 4 Brigade Earned claps while travelling from Base Depot RAMC to join this unit. Transferred to England for discharge.
MELLOR, F. Private 807 Oldham Corps Medal Clasps: CC OFS.
Medal Roll Reference: WO100/225/150 Orderly 9 General Hospital. To Base Detail 31 August 1900.
MELLOR, J. Private 413 Oldham Corps Medal Clasps: NAT.
Medal Roll Reference: WO100/225/129 Orderly 7 General Hospital. To England time expired.
MELLOR, J. Private 1356 Bolton Corps Medal Clasps: CC.
Medal Roll Reference: WO100/225/159 Orderly 13 General Hospital. To England expired contract 27 November 1900.
MELLOR, J. S. Private 1531 Oldham Corps Medal Clasps: CC.
Medal Roll Reference: WO100/225/72+109 Orderly 1 General Hospital. 24 Stationary Hospital. From Base Detail 15 April 1901. Transferred to 5 General Hospital sick 2 May 1901
MELLOR, J. T. Private 1268 Whaley Bridge Division Medal Clasps: CC OFS.
Medal Roll Reference: WO100/225/150 Orderly 9 General Hospital. To Base Detail 12 October 1900.
MELLOR, Samuel Private 247 Burnley Division Medal Clasps: CC OFS JOH DIA.
Medal Roll Reference: WO100/225/191 Private Attached 20 Field Hospital. Transferred sick to Heilbron 13 July 1900.
MELLOR, W. Private 917 Oldham Corps Medal Clasps: NAT KSA01 KSA02.
Medal Roll Reference: WO100/225/119 WO100/361/77 Orderly 4 General Hospital. Served in St John Ambulance Brigade from 7 April 1900 to 21 December 1900. Discharged in South Africa on 22 December 1900 and joined Imperial Hospital Corps (Transvaal) which was doing duty at 4 General Hospital. Served 22 December 1900 to 31 May 1902
METCALFE, E. Private 1272 Bury Division Medal Clasps: CC OFS.
Medal Roll Reference: WO100/225/135 Orderly 8 General Hospital. To England 10 October 1900.
METCALFE, J. Private 688 Nelson Corps Medal Clasps: CC WITT.
Medal Roll Reference: WO100/225/193 Orderly Attached 21 Field Hospital. Discharged.
MIDDLETON, Fred Private 54 Weston-Super-Mare Division Medal Clasps: CC OFS SA01 SA02 KSA01 KSA02.
Medal Roll Reference: WO100/225/116 WO100/219/158 WO100/352/183 Orderly 3 General Hospital. Transferred to Base Detail. RAMC Number 16239.
MIDDLETON, W. Private 1173 Leeds Corps Medal Clasps: CC OFS.
Medal Roll Reference: WO100/225/150 Orderly 9 General Hospital. To Base Detail 12 October 1900.
MILES, A. H. Sergeant 1288 Metropolitan Corps Medal Clasps: CC TVL.
Medal Roll Reference: WO100/224/172 Private Rhodesian Field Force Hospital.
MILLER, A. E. Private 1583 Northampton Corps Medal Clasps: CC.
Medal Roll Reference: WO100/225/123 Orderly 5 General Hospital.
MILLER, A. H. D. Private 1021 Rochdale Corps Medal Clasps: OFS TVL NAT.
Medal Roll Reference: WO100/225/181 Orderly 14 Stationary Hospital. Attached 21 Field Hospital. Discharged.
MILLER, C. Private 675 Bolton Corps Medal Clasps: CC.
Medal Roll Reference: WO100/225/56 Orderly 11 General Hospital. To England on termination of engagement.
MILLER, G. H. T. Private 1559 Ramsgate Corps Medal Clasps: CC.
Medal Roll Reference: WO100/225/56 Orderly 11 General Hospital. To England on termination of engagement.
MILLER, H. Private 1506 Morecombe Division Medal Clasps: OFS TVL NAT SA01.
Medal Roll Reference: WO100/225/129 Orderly 7 General Hospital. To England time expired.

MILLICHAMP, E. A. Private 1027 Oldham Corps Medal Clasps: NAT.
Medal Roll Reference: WO100/225/66 Orderly 13 Stationary Hospital. To HS *Dunera* 18 December 1900.
MILLIGAN, J. Private 1003 Dalton-in-Furness Division Medal Clasps: NAT.
Medal Roll Reference: WO100/225/119 Orderly 4 General Hospital Sent to England time expired 19 December 1900.
MILLINGTON, G. R. Private 483 Great Eastern Railway Corps Medal Clasps: CC OFS.
Medal Roll Reference: WO100/225/150 Orderly 9 General Hospital. To Base Detail 1 August 1900.
MILLNS, J. Private 1316 Tibshelf Corps Medal Clasps: CC TVL.
Medal Roll Reference: WO100/224/172 Private Rhodesian Field Force Hospital.
MILNES, A. H. Private 1706 Bradford Corps Medal Clasps: CC OFS TVL.
Medal Roll Reference: WO100/225/171 Orderly 20 General Hospital. Joined from Base Detail. To England for discharge.
MITCHELL, H. Private 355 Worksop Division Medal Clasps: TVL NAT.
Medal Roll Reference: WO100/225/130 Orderly 7 General Hospital. To England time expired.
MITCHELL, J. A. Private 1816 Bolton Corps Medal Clasps: CC.
Medal Roll Reference: WO100/225/72 Orderly 24 Stationary Hospital. From Base Detail Transferred to Base Detail 29 June 1901.
MITCHELL, John Private 245 Clitheroe Division Medal Clasps: CC JOH WITT.
Medal Roll Reference: WO100/225/191 Private Attached 20 Field Hospital. Transferred to Base 14 August 1900.
MITCHELL, William Private 105 Metropolitan Corps Medal Clasps: CC OFS.
Medal Roll Reference: WO100/225/235 Private Portland Hospital. To England contract expired.
MOFFATT, R. Private 1891 Preston Corps Medal Clasps: CC.
Medal Roll Reference: WO100/225/69 Orderly 8 Stationary Hospital.
MOFFITT, W. R. Private 972 Reading Division Medal Clasps: NAT.
Medal Roll Reference: WO100/225/119 Orderly 4 General Hospital Sent to England time expired 19 December 1900.
MONDY, E. Private 635 Nelson Corps Medal Clasps: CC WITT.
Medal Roll Reference: WO100/225/193 Orderly Attached 21 Field Hospital. Discharged.
MOORE, A. Private 1606 Welbeck Division Medal Clasps: CC OFS TVL.
Medal Roll Reference: WO100/225/123+187 Orderly 5 General Hospital. Joined 18 Brigade Field Hospital 20 March 1901. Left 22 April 1901 for discharge.
MOORE, A. E. Private 1238 Preston Corps Medal Clasps: CC OFS TVL.
Medal Roll Reference: WO100/225/126 Private 6 General Hospital. To Base on expiration of contract 22 October 1900.
MOORE, F. Private 215 Metropolitan Corps Medal Clasps: CC.
Medal Roll Reference: WO100/225/126 Private 6 General Hospital. To Base Invalided 9 May 1900.
MOORE, J. W. Private 444 Welbeck Division Medal Clasps: NAT.
Medal Roll Reference: WO100/225/130 Orderly 7 General Hospital. To England time expired.
MOORE, John Private 102 Welbeck Division Medal Clasps: CC OFS.
Medal Roll Reference: WO100/225/235 Private Portland Hospital. To England contract expired.
MORGAN, E. Private 183 Brynmawr Division Medal Clasps: CC.
Medal Roll Reference: WO100/225/69 Orderly 8 Stationary Hospital.
MORLEY, T. Private 614 Metropolitan Corps Medal Clasps: CC OFS.
Medal Roll Reference: WO100/225/155 Orderly 10 General Hospital. To Base 7 August 1900.
MORRIS, A. Private 352 Dowlais Division Medal Clasps: CC.
Medal Roll Reference: WO100/130/221 Lance Corporal Imperial Yeomanry Hospital Deelfontein.
MORRIS, A. J. Private 334 1553 Isle of Wight Corps Medal Clasps: CC OFS.

Medal Roll Reference: WO100/225/109+238 2nd Grade Orderly Van Alen American Field Hospital. Transferred to Plague Camp Cape Town 1 General Hospital.

MORRIS, F. J. Private 1685 Isle of Wight Corps Medal Clasps: OFS TVL.
Medal Roll Reference: WO100/225/203 Orderly 20 General Hospital Transferred to 21 Bearer Company 1 February 1901 and sent home for discharge June 1901.

MORRIS, J. E. Private 1254 Padiham Division Medal Clasps: CC OFS TVL.
Medal Roll Reference: WO100/225/126 Private 6 General Hospital. To Base on expiration of contract 22 October 1900.

MORRISH, F. Private 58 Bristol Corps Medal Clasps: CC.
Medal Roll Reference: WO100/225/112B Orderly.

MORRISON, A. Private 1191 Oldham Corps Medal Clasps: CC.
Medal Roll Reference: WO100/225/109 Orderly 1 General Hospital.

MORRISON, David Hugh Campbell Sergeant 631 Hull Corps Medal Clasps: OFS TVL.
Medal Roll Reference: WO100/225/155+203 Orderly 10 General Hospital. To Base 7 August 1900 20 General Hospital Transferred to 21 Bearer Company February 1901.

MORT, A. Private 1572 Bolton Corps Medal Clasps: CC.
Medal Roll Reference: WO100/225/123 Orderly 5 General Hospital.

MORTIMER, J. Private 1594 Oldham Corps Medal Clasps: CC OFS TVL.
Medal Roll Reference: WO100/225/76+123+187 Orderly 5 General Hospital. To 18 Brigade Field Hospital 20 March 1901. Left 22 April 1901 for discharge. War Office Issue.

MORTON, A. Private 356 Worksop Division Medal Clasps: No Clasps.
Medal Roll Reference: WO100/225/30 Orderly.

MOSLEY, F. Private 1123 Sheffield Corps Medal Clasps: NAT.
Medal Roll Reference: WO100/225/166 Orderly 15 General Hospital. Transferred to England 14 September 1900.

MOSS, J. Private 1708 Leeds Corps Medal Clasps: CC OFS TVL.
Medal Roll Reference: WO100/225/171 Orderly 20 General Hospital. Joined from Base Detail. To England for discharge.

MOTT, G. E. Private 1738 Metropolitan Corps Medal Clasps: CC OFS SA01.
Medal Roll Reference: WO100/225/87+116 Orderly 3 General Hospital. Transferred to Base Detail RAMC. Home 21 June 1901.

MOULDS, C. E. Private 928 Radcliffe Division Medal Clasps: NAT.
Medal Roll Reference: WO100/225/119 Orderly 4 General Hospital. Sent to England time expired 9 September 1900. MOULD, C. E. on QSA medal roll.

MOULDS, W. E. Private 393 Sheffield Corps Medal Clasps: CC.
Medal Roll Reference: WO100/130/221 Private Imperial Yeomanry Hospital Deelfontein.

MOWLE, G. H. Private 1745 Whalley Division Medal Clasps: CC OFS SA01.
Medal Roll Reference: WO100/225/87+116 Orderly 3 General Hospital. Transferred to Base Detail RAMC. Home 21 June 1901.

MULLINS, A. H. Private 123 Hull Corps Medal Clasps: No Clasps.
Medal Roll Reference: WO100/225/30 Orderly.

MULLOWNEY, J. Private 536 Preston Corps Medal Clasps: CC OFS TVL.
Medal Roll Reference: WO100/225/231 Private Langman Hospital.

MUNDAY, L. Private 178 Wellingborough Corps Medal Clasps: CC.
Medal Roll Reference: WO100/225/69 Orderly 8 Stationary Hospital.

MURPHY, J. Private 1355 Bolton Corps Medal Clasps: CC.
Medal Roll Reference: WO100/225/159 Orderly 13 General Hospital. To England expired contract 27 November 1900.

MURRAY, G. Private 1677 Handsworth & Smethwick Corps Medal Clasps: OFS TVL.
Medal Roll Reference: WO100/225/203 Orderly 20 General Hospital Elandsfontein Transferred to 21 Bearer Company February 1901 and sent home for discharge June 1901.
MURRAY, N. R. Private 290 Metropolitan Corps Medal Clasps: CC.
Medal Roll Reference: WO100/130/220 Sergeant Imperial Yeomanry Hospital Deelfontein.
MURRAY, W. H. Private 785 Kendal Division Medal Clasps: CC OFS TVL.
Medal Roll Reference: WO100/225/112B Orderly.
MUSSON, W. J. Private 731 Leicester Corps Medal Clasps: CC.
Medal Roll Reference: WO100/225/56 Orderly 11 General Hospital. To England on termination of engagement.
MYERS, J. Private 36 Preston Corps Medal Clasps: CC OFS TVL KSA01 KSA02.
Medal Roll Reference: WO100/225/112B+WO100/352/16 Orderly 6 General Hospital.
NEALE, W. Private 1212 Leeds Corps Medal Clasps: CC OFS.
Medal Roll Reference: WO100/225/135 Orderly 8 General Hospital. To England 10 October 1900.
NEEDHAM, W. J. Private 1405 Welbeck Division Medal Clasps: No Clasps.
Medal Roll Reference: WO100/225/60 Orderly 14 General Hospital. To HS *Simla* for duty 14 November 1900.
NEVE, B. Private 296 Metropolitan Corps Medal Clasps: CC.
Medal Roll Reference: WO100/130/221 Private Imperial Yeomanry Hospital Deelfontein.
NEWELL, A. Private 864 Wellingborough Corps Medal Clasps: CC OFS TVL.
Medal Roll Reference: WO100/225/126 Private 6 General Hospital. To Base on expiration of contract 15 September 1900. A NEVILLE in QSA Medal Roll.
NEWELL, S. Private 1942 Wellingborough Corps Medal Clasps: CC OFS TVL SA01 SA02.
Medal Roll Reference: WO100/271/144+243 Private South African Constabulary A Division A1876 Medical Corporal.
NEWMAN, Frank Bertram Private 338 Bedford Division (NFB Bedford) Medal Clasps: CC. NFBUAD Medal.
Medal Roll Reference: WO100/130/221 Lance Corporal Imperial Yeomanry Hospital Deelfontein.
NEWNES, John Edward Private 85 Warrington Corps Medal Clasps: CC OFS.
Medal Roll Reference: WO100/225/235 Private Portland Hospital. To England contract expired.
NEWPORT, Herbert H. Private 311 St John Ambulance Brigade (NFB Frome) Medal Clasps: CC SA01. NFBUAD Medal.
Medal Roll Reference: WO100/130/221 Private Imperial Yeomanry Hospital Deelfontein.
NEWSOME, Frank Private 1876 Leeds Corps Medal Clasps: CC OFS.
Medal Roll Reference: WO100/225/150 Orderly 9 General Hospital. To Base Detail 23 July 1901.
NEWSOME, G. F. Private 1357 Bolton Corps Medal Clasps: CC.
Medal Roll Reference: WO100/225/56+159 Orderly 11 General Hospital. To England on termination of engagement 13 General Hospital. To Kimberly 27 August 1900.
NEWSOME, Sam Private 1875 Leeds Corps Medal Clasps: CC OFS.
Medal Roll Reference: WO100/225/150 Orderly 9 General Hospital. To Base Detail 23 July 1901.
NEWSON, G. Private 1000 Mill Bay Division Medal Clasps: NAT.
Medal Roll Reference: WO100/225/119 Orderly 4 General Hospital Sent to England time expired 19 December 1900.
NEWTON, A. W. Sergeant 423 Metropolitan Corps Medal Clasps: OFS TVL NAT SA01.
Medal Roll Reference: WO100/225/130 Supply Officer 7 General Hospital. To England time expired.
NEWTON, F. Private 1309 Welbeck Division Medal Clasps: CC TVL.
Medal Roll Reference: WO100/224/173 Private Rhodesian Field Force Hospital.
NEWTON, F. Private 1323 Newtown Division Medal Clasps: CC.
Medal Roll Reference: WO100/225/159 Orderly 13 General Hospital. To England expired contract 27 November 1900.

NICHOLAS, John Thomas Private 843 Haslingden Corps Medal Clasps: CC OFS TVL.
Medal Roll Reference: WO100/225/126 Private 6 General Hospital. To Base on expiration of contract 16 September1900.

NICHOLL, R. M. Private 1724 Oldham Corps Medal Clasps: OFS TVL.
Medal Roll Reference: W100/225/203 Orderly 20 General Hospital Elandsfontein. Joined 21 Bearer Company February 1901 and sent home for discharge June 1901.

NICHOLLS, E. Private 1653 Accrington Corps Medal Clasps: SA01.
Medal Roll Reference: WO100/225/88 Orderly.

NICHOLS, H. T. P. Private 1601 Metropolitan Corps Medal Clasps: CC.
Medal Roll Reference: WO100/225/109+159 Orderly 13 General Hospital. To 1 General Hospital Base Hospital Wynberg 1 February 1901.

NICHOLSON, R. Private 1346 Bolton Corps Medal Clasps: CC.
Medal Roll Reference: WO100/225/159 Orderly 13 General Hospital. To England expired contract 27 November 1900.

NICHOLSON, R. H. Private 1204 Leeds Corps Medal Clasps: CC OFS.
Medal Roll Reference: WO100/225/69+150 Orderly 8 Stationary Hospital. 9 General Hospital. To Base Detail 12 October 1900.

NIGHTINGALE, H. G. Private 655 Derby Division Medal Clasps: CC OFS.
Medal Roll Reference: WO100/225/155 Orderly 10 General Hospital. To Base 15 July 1900.

NORFOLK, James 1st Class Sergeant 315 No 2 District Staff Medal Clasps: NAT.
Medal Roll Reference: WO100/225/166 Supply Officer 15 General Hospital. Transferred to England 26 August 1900.

NORTHCOTE, J. Private 1292 Metropolitan Corps Medal Clasps: CC TVL SA01.
Medal Roll Reference: WO100/224/173 Private Rhodesian Field Force Hospital.

NORTON, J. A. Private 1730 Oldham Corps Medal Clasps: CC OFS TVL SA01.
Medal Roll Reference: WO100/225/60+88 Orderly 14 General Hospital. To HS *Dunera* for duty 11 February 1901.

NOWELL, W. Private 1060 Bolton Corps Medal Clasps: NAT.
Medal Roll Reference: WO100/225/119 Orderly 4 General Hospital Sent to England time expired 9 September 1900.

NOWELL, W. Private 755 Hebden Bridge Corps Medal Clasps: CC.
Medal Roll Reference: WO100/225/57 Orderly 11 General Hospital. To England on termination of engagement.

NUNN, R. Private 1385 Haverhill Division Medal Clasps: No Clasps.
Medal Roll Reference: WO100/225/60 Orderly 14 General Hospital. To HS *Simla* for duty 14 November 1900.

NUTTALL, A. R. Sergeant 1432 Bolton Corps Medal Clasps: TVL.
Medal Roll Reference: WO100/225/168+181 Supply Officer 16 General Hospital (2 Stationary Hospital). 14 Stationary Hospital. Discharged in South Africa 5 June 1900.

NUTTALL, Harold Private 956 Haslingden Corps Medal Clasps: NAT.
Medal Roll Reference: WO100/225/119 Orderly 4 General Hospital Sent to England time expired 9 September 1900.

NUTTALL, J. Private 546 Rochdale Corps Medal Clasps: CC OFS.
Medal Roll Reference: WO100/225/150 Orderly 9 General Hospital. To Base Detail 7 August 1900.

NUTTALL, John Howard Private 587 Bolton Corps Medal Clasps: CC OFS TVL SA01.
Medal Roll Reference: WO100/225/92+123+155 Orderly 5 General Hospital. 10 General Hospital. To Base 29 January 1901.

NUTTER, James Private 1135 Blackpool Division Medal Clasps: CC. China Medal.
Medal Roll Reference: WO100/225/53+248 Orderly HS *Maine*. On medal roll for HS *Maine* for China WO100/96/38+39.

O'SHEA, J. T. Private 871 Leicester Corps Medal Clasps: CC OFS TVL.
Medal Roll Reference: WO100/225/126 Private 6 General Hospital. To Base on expiration of contract 20 February 1901.
OATES, G. E. Private 941 Denaby Main Division Medal Clasps: NAT.
Medal Roll Reference: WO100/225/119 Orderly 4 General Hospital Sent to England time expired 9 September 1900.
OGDEN, C. H. Private 1753 Padiham Division Medal Clasps: CC OFS SA01.
Medal Roll Reference: WO100/225/87+116+202 Orderly 3 General Hospital. Transferred to Base Detail RAMC. 20 Bearer Company. To General Elliott's Division 20 June 1901.
OGDEN, D. Private 762 Heywood Division Medal Clasps: CC WITT.
Medal Roll Reference: WO100/225/193 Orderly Attached 21 Field Hospital. Discharged.
OGDEN, G. L. Private 776 Edenfield Division Medal Clasps: CC OFS TVL.
Medal Roll Reference: WO100/225/126 Private 6 General Hospital. To Base on expiration of contract 3 September 1900.
OGDEN, J. Private 1877 Oldham Corps Medal Clasps: CC.
Medal Roll Reference: WO100/225/109 Orderly 1 General Hospital.
OLDFIELD, John William Private 1192 Oldham Corps Medal Clasps: CC OFS TVL KSA01 KSA02.
Medal Roll Reference: WO100/225/123 WO100/271/146 WO100/366/46 Orderly 5 General Hospital. South African Constabulary A Division Medical Corporal A1873. St John Ambulance Brigade service from May to November 1900. South Africa Constabulary service from 4 May 1901.
OLDHAM, Frederick Hope 1st Class Sergeant 664 Crewe Division Medal Clasps: CC OFS TVL SA01.
Medal Roll Reference: WO100/225/57+85 Supply Officer 11 General Hospital.
OLDHAM, H. E. Private 781 Hazelgrove Division Medal Clasps: CC OFS TVL.
Medal Roll Reference: WO100/225/33+112B Orderly 6 General Hospital.
OLIVER, W. C. Private 285 Metropolitan Corps Medal Clasps: CC.
Medal Roll Reference: WO100/130/221 Sergeant Imperial Yeomanry Hospital Deelfontein.
OLLIS, Charles Private 63 Dudley Corps Medal Clasps: CC OFS TVL.
Medal Roll Reference: WO100/225/112B Orderly 6 General Hospital.
ORCHARD, C. 1st Class Sergeant 438 Metropolitan Corps Medal Clasps: CC OFS TVL.
Medal Roll Reference: WO100/130/221 Acting Sergeant Major Imperial Yeomanry Hospital Deelfontein.
ORMEROD, G. Private 680 Tottington Division Medal Clasps: CC SA01.
Medal Roll Reference: WO100/225/57+85 Orderly 11 General Hospital. To England on termination of engagement.
OSBORNE, J. W. Private 1436 Bury Division Medal Clasps: No Clasps.
Medal Roll Reference: WO100/225/119 Orderly 4 General Hospital Sent to England for discharge time expired 28 August 1900.
OULTON, T. E. Private 170 Whaley Bridge Division Medal Clasps: CC.
Medal Roll Reference: WO100/225/109 Orderly 1 General Hospital.
OVERSTALL, Ted Private 705 Haslingden Corps Medal Clasps: CC SA01.
Medal Roll Reference: WO100/225/57+85 Orderly 11 General Hospital. To England on termination of engagement.
OWEN, A. Private 1209 1871 Leeds Corps Medal Clasps: CC OFS.
Medal Roll Reference: WO100/225/135+190 Orderly 8 General Hospital. To England 10 October 1900. Attached to 1 Corps Troops Field Hospital.
OWEN, J. Private 1330 Bolton Corps Medal Clasps: CC.
Medal Roll Reference: WO100/225/159 Orderly 13 General Hospital. To England expired contract 27 November 1900.

PAGET, Charles H. Private 647 Bradford Corps Medal Clasps: CC OFS TVL SA01 SA02 KSA01 KSA02.

Medal Roll Reference: WO100/225/57 WO100/272/224+343 WO100/366/124 Orderly 11 General Hospital. South African Constabulary C Division Medical Corporal C2120. Served St John Ambulance Brigade 25 March 1900 to 5 October 1900. Served South African Constabulary 4 May to 31 May 1902.

PAINE, G. Private 323 St John Ambulance Brigade (NFB Newhaven) Medal Clasps: CC.
Medal Roll Reference: WO100/130/222 Private Imperial Yeomanry Hospital Deelfontein.

PAKES, F. Private 1380 Northampton Corps Medal Clasps: No Clasps.
Medal Roll Reference: WO100/225/60 Orderly 14 General Hospital. To HS *Simla* for duty 14 November 1900.

PALLETT, Arthur Patrick Private 90 Metropolitan Corps Medal Clasps: CC OFS.
Medal Roll Reference: WO100/225/235 Private Portland Hospital. To England contract expired.

PALLETT, W. Private 384 Birmingham Corps Medal Clasps: CC.
Medal Roll Reference: WO100/130/222 Private Imperial Yeomanry Hospital Deelfontein.

PALMER, C. Private 461 Metropolitan Corps Medal Clasps: CC.
Medal Roll Reference: WO100/130/221 Quartermaster Sergeant Imperial Yeomanry Hospital Deelfontein.

PANTER, Alfred N. Private 7 Keswick Division Medal Clasps: CC.
Medal Roll Reference: WO100/225/241 Private HS *Princess of Wales*. Attached RAMC.

PARFITT, W. Private 1805 Handsworth & Smethwick Corps Medal Clasps: CC.
Medal Roll Reference: WO100/225/173 Orderly 21 General Hospital.

PARKER, J. Private 1350 Bolton Corps Medal Clasps: CC OFS TVL.
Medal Roll Reference: WO100/225/77+159+186 Orderly 10 Stationary Hospital. To Cape Town 13 General Hospital. To Pretoria 18 December 1900. Attached. to 8th Divisional 12th Brigade Field Hospital. Transferred to Base Detail Cape Town.

PARKER, R. H. Private 1491 Leeds Corps Medal Clasps: No Clasps.
Medal Roll Reference: WO100/225/68 Orderly 18 General Hospital. Discharged 30 May 1900.

PARKER, S. Private 694 Clitheroe Division Medal Clasps: CC OFS.
Medal Roll Reference: WO100/225/155 Orderly 10 General Hospital. To Base 7 August 1900.

PARKER, S. F. K. Private 894 Metropolitan Corps Medal Clasps: NAT.
Medal Roll Reference: WO100/225/119 Orderly 4 General Hospital Sent to England for discharge time expired 19 December 1900.

PARKER, Thomas. Private 539 Walton-le-Dale Division Medal Clasps: NAT.
Medal Roll Reference: WO100/225/33 Orderly.

PARKIN, Albert Private 1508 Nuneaton Division Medal Clasps: TVL NAT.
Medal Roll Reference: WO100/225/130 Orderly 7 General Hospital. To England time expired.

PARKIN, J. A. Private 391 Sheffield Corps Medal Clasps: CC OFS.
Medal Roll Reference: WO100/225/135 Orderly 8 General Hospital. To England 20 July 1900.

PARKINSON, E. Sergeant 186 Preston Corps Medal Clasps: CC JOH DIA WITT.
Medal Roll Reference: WO100/225/191 Sergeant Attached 20 Field Hospital. Transferred to base 4 January 1901.

PARKINSON, G. Private 1242 Preston Corps Medal Clasps: CC OFS.
Medal Roll Reference: WO100/225/135 Orderly 8 General Hospital. To England 10 October 1900.

PARKINSON, Grimshaw Private 407 Accrington Corps Medal Clasps: CC OFS.
Medal Roll Reference: WO100/225/135 Orderly 8 General Hospital. Sick to Cape Town 31 July 1900.

PARKINSON, J. T. Private 1037 Barnoldswick Division Medal Clasps: NAT.
Medal Roll Reference: WO100/225/166 Orderly 15 General Hospital. Transferred to England 14 September 1900.

PARKINSON, Robert Private 955 Haslingden Corps Medal Clasps: NAT.
Medal Roll Reference: WO100/225/119 Orderly 4 General Hospital Sent to England for discharge time expired 19 December 1900.
PARNALL, J. Private 299 Metropolitan Corps Medal Clasps: CC.
Medal Roll Reference: WO100/130/222 Civilian Compounder Imperial Yeomanry Hospital Deelfontein.
PARTINGTON, E. Private 1273 Bury Division Medal Clasps: CC OFS.
Medal Roll Reference: WO100/225/155 Orderly 10 General Hospital. To Base 10 October 1900.
PATERSON, A. W. Private 23 Ramsgate Corps Medal Clasps: CC.
Medal Roll Reference: WO100/225/241 Private HS *Princess of Wales*. Attached RAMC.
PATRICK, W. Private 1695 Blackpool Division Medal Clasps: No Clasps.
Medal Roll Reference: WO100/225/146 Orderly.
PEACE, F. H. Private 503 Sheffield Corps Medal Clasps: No Clasps.
Medal Roll Reference: WO100/225/33 Orderly.
PEACOCK, A. T. Private 1812 Sheffield Corps Medal Clasps: CC OFS TVL.
Medal Roll Reference: WO100/225/171 Orderly 20 General Hospital. Joined from Base Detail. To England for discharge.
PEAKER, E. D. Private 122 Hull Corps Medal Clasps: No Clasps.
Medal Roll Reference: WO100/225/33 Orderly.
PEARCE, Charles Private 563 Birmingham Corps Medal Clasps: CC OFS.
Medal Roll Reference: WO100/225/150 Private 9 General Hospital. Died of disease Bloemfontein 29 May 1900.
PEARMAN, E. Private 1481 Derby Division Medal Clasps: CC OFS TVL.
Medal Roll Reference: WO100/225/166+183 Orderly 15 General Hospital. Transferred to Pretoria 29 August 1900 17 Stationary Hospital. To Base 24 November 1900.
PEARSON, W. A. Private 1312 Barnoldswick Division Medal Clasps: CC.
Medal Roll Reference: WO100/224/172 Private Rhodesian Field Force Hospital.
PEAT, George 1st Class Sergeant 80 Welbeck Division Medal Clasps: CC OFS.
Medal Roll Reference: WO100/225/235 Staff Sergeant Portland Hospital. To England contract expired.
PEAT, T. Private 684 Bacup Division Medal Clasps: CC OFS.
Medal Roll Reference: WO100/225/57 Orderly 11 General Hospital Convoy duty to Boshof.
PECK, H. Private 887 Handsworth & Smethwick Corps Medal Clasps: CC.
Medal Roll Reference: WO100/225/69 Orderly 8 Stationary Hospital.
PEGLEY, William 1st Class Sergeant 114 Metropolitan Corps Medal Clasps: No Clasps.
Medal Roll Reference: WO100/225/4 Sergeant 1st Class. Died in The London Hospital 25 July 1900. Cause unknown.
PEGRAM, William C. Private 818 Great Eastern Railway Corps Medal Clasps: NAT.
Medal Roll Reference: WO100/225/119 Orderly 4 General Hospital. Died of typhoid Mooi River 11 August 1900.
PEMBERTON, W. Private 1318 Tibshelf Corps Medal Clasps: CC TVL.
Medal Roll Reference: WO100/224/172 Private Rhodesian Field Force Hospital.
PENDLEBURY, W. Private 1354 Bolton Corps Medal Clasps: CC.
Medal Roll Reference: WO100/225/159 Orderly 13 General Hospital. To England expired contract 27 November 1900.
PERIGO, E. Private 1185 Oldham Corps Medal Clasps: CC OFS TVL NAT.
Medal Roll Reference: WO100/225/109+130 Orderly 1 General Hospital. To 7 General Hospital. Invalided to England.
PERRETT, J. Private 709 Metropolitan Corps Medal Clasps: CC.
Medal Roll Reference: WO100/225/57 Orderly 11 General Hospital. To England on termination of engagement.

PERRY, J. Private 551 Metropolitan Corps Medal Clasps: CC OFS.
Medal Roll Reference: WO100/225/150 Orderly 9 General Hospital. To Base Detail 7 August 1900.
PERRY, P. J. Private 1600 Metropolitan Corps Medal Clasps: CC OFS TVL.
Medal Roll Reference: WO100/225/159 Orderly 13 General Hospital. To England expired contract 10 April 1901.
PERRYMAN, T. F. Private 126 Metropolitan Corps Medal Clasps: No Clasps.
Medal Roll Reference: WO100/225/33 Orderly.
PETT, Monty W. Private 314 St John Ambulance Brigade (NFB Exeter) Medal Clasps: CC. NFBUAD Medal.
Medal Roll Reference: WO100/130/222 Private Imperial Yeomanry Hospital Deelfontein.
PEZZEY, H. Private 725 Great Eastern Railway Corps Medal Clasps: CC WITT.
Medal Roll Reference: WO100/225/193 Orderly Attached 21 Field Hospital. Discharged.
PHILIPSON, John T. Private 351 Tibshelf Corps Medal Clasps: NAT.
Medal Roll Reference: WO100/225/130 Orderly 7 General Hospital. To England time expired.
PHILLIPS, E. P. 1st Class Sergeant 1229 Metropolitan Corps Medal Clasps: CC TVL.
Medal Roll Reference: WO100/224/172 2nd Class Staff Sergeant Rhodesian Field Force Hospital. Transferred to 3 Stationary Hospital De Aar 19 February 1901.
PHILLIPS, J. H. Private 734 Leicester Corps Medal Clasps: CC OFS TVL.
Medal Roll Reference: WO100/130/265 Private Imperial Yeomanry Field Hospital and Bearer Company J. PHILLIPS on Imperial Yeomanry Bearer Corps Medal Roll.
PHILLIPS, J. R. Private 892 Rochdale Corps Medal Clasps: NAT.
Medal Roll Reference: WO100/225/119 Orderly 4 General Hospital Sent to England for discharge time expired 9 September 1900.
PHILLIPS, W. Private 1629 Royton Division Medal Clasps: No Clasps.
Medal Roll Reference: WO100/225/145 Orderly.
PICKARD, W. Private 1049 Dalton-in-Furness Division Medal Clasps: NAT.
Medal Roll Reference: WO100/225/66 Orderly 13 Stationary Hospital. To HS *Dunera* 18 December 1900.
PICKERING, G. Private 1062 Bolton Corps Medal Clasps: NAT.
Medal Roll Reference: WO100/225/166 Orderly 15 General Hospital. Transferred to England 14 September 1900.
PICKLES, George H. Private 756 Hebden Bridge Corps Medal Clasps: CC OFS.
Medal Roll Reference: WO100/225/195 Orderly 23 Field Hospital. Died of disease Naauwpoort 8 May 1900.
PICKLES, John Private 758 Hebden Bridge Corps Medal Clasps: CC WITT.
Medal Roll Reference: WO100/225/193 Orderly Attached 21 Field Hospital. Died of disease Senekal 2 July 1900.
PICKOVER, R. Private 1637 Barrowford Division Medal Clasps: No Clasps.
Medal Roll Reference: WO100/225/145 Orderly.
PICKUP, Fred Private 1091 Haslingden Corps Medal Clasps: NAT.
Medal Roll Reference: WO100/225/166 Orderly 15 General Hospital. Transferred to England 14 September 1900.
PICKUP, Thomas Private 512 Haslingden Corps Medal Clasps: CC OFS TVL.
Medal Roll Reference: WO100/225/231 Private Langman Hospital.
PILCHER, L. W. Private 159 Herne Bay Division Medal Clasps: No Clasps.
Medal Roll Reference: WO100/225/33 Orderly.
PILKINGTON, E. Private 582 Bolton Corps Medal Clasps: CC.
Medal Roll Reference: WO100/225/123 Orderly 5 General Hospital.
PILKINGTON, E. Private 1636 Barrowford Division Medal Clasps: No Clasps.
Medal Roll Reference: WO100/225/125 Orderly.

PILKINGTON, T. Private 1059 Bolton Corps Medal Clasps: NAT.
Medal Roll Reference: WO100/225/166 Orderly 15 General Hospital. Transferred to England 14 September 1900.
PILLING, A. Private 978 Edenfield Division Medal Clasps: NAT.
Medal Roll Reference: WO100/225/119 Orderly 4 General Hospital Sent to England for discharge time expired 9 September 1900.
PILLING, J. Private 947 Nelson Corps Medal Clasps: NAT.
Medal Roll Reference: WO100/225/119 Orderly 4 General Hospital. Invalided to England 11 February 1901.
PILLING, J. T. Private 1755 Padiham Division Medal Clasps: CC TVL SA01.
Medal Roll Reference: WO100/225/146 Orderly.
PINNOCK, J. Private 241 Wellingborough Corps Medal Clasps: CC JOH DIA WITT.
Medal Roll Reference: WO100/225/202 Orderly 20 Bearer Company. Discharged time expired 1 August 1900.
PINNOCK, W. H. Private 242 Wellingborough Corps Medal Clasps: CC OFS.
Medal Roll Reference: WO100/225/202 Orderly 20 Bearer Company. Invalided to England 30 June 1900.
PITCHFORD, John H. Private 1069 Welbeck Division Medal Clasps: CC OFS NAT SA01 SA02.
Medal Roll Reference: WO100/225/166 WO100/273/133+323 Orderly 15 General Hospital. Transferred to HS *Nubia* 29 December 1900. South African Constabulary E Division Hospital Corporal E3041. St John Ambulance Brigade service from 16 May 1900 to 7 January 1901. South African Constabulary service from 4 May 1901 to 28 January 1902 Discharged unsuitable.
PLAISTER, G. R. Sergeant 1200 Metropolitan Corps Medal Clasps: CC OFS.
Medal Roll Reference: WO100/225/136 Supply Officer 8 General Hospital. To England 10 October 1900.
PLATT, H. Private 1183 Oldham Corps Medal Clasps: CC.
Medal Roll Reference: WO100/225/76+109 Orderly 1 General Hospital. War Office Issue.
PLATTS, John James Private 1317 Tibshelf Corps Medal Clasps: CC TVL.
Medal Roll Reference: WO100/224/172 Private Rhodesian Field Force Hospital. Invalided to England (date unknown).
PLUMB, Percy W. Sergeant 214 1526 Metropolitan Corps Medal Clasps: CC SA01.
Medal Roll Reference: WO100/225/57+75+85 Supply Officer Princess Christian Hospital Train. 11 General Hospital. Died of disease Kimberley 13 January 1901.
POCKLINGTON, J. Private 1024 Oldham Corps Medal Clasps: NAT.
Medal Roll Reference: WO100/225/68 Orderly 18 General Hospital. To England 28 December1900.
PODMORE, E. Private 1735 North Staffs Corps Medal Clasps: OFS TVL.
Medal Roll Reference: W100/225/203 Orderly General Hospital Elandsfontein. Transferred to 21 Bearer Company 20 February 1901 and sent home for discharge June 1901.
POLLARD, H. Private 259 Kettering Corps Medal Clasps: CC OFS.
Medal Roll Reference: WO100/225/176 Orderly 5 Stationary Hospital Sent to Base for England for discharge.
POLLITT, S. Private 581 Bolton Corps Medal Clasps: CC.
Medal Roll Reference: WO100/225/124 Orderly 5 General Hospital.
POMFRET, J. Private 1502 Rishton Division Medal Clasps: TVL NAT.
Medal Roll Reference: WO100/225/130 Orderly 7 General Hospital. To England time expired.
POOLER, J. Private 1113 Madeley Division Medal Clasps: NAT.
Medal Roll Reference: WO100/225/119 Orderly 4 General Hospital. Sent to England for discharge time expired 9 September 1900.
POPE, A. B. Private 56 Newton Abbott Division Medal Clasps: CC OFS TVL.
Medal Roll Reference: WO100/225/112B Orderly 6 General Hospital.

POPE, S. 1st Class Sergeant 900 Derby Division Medal Clasps: NAT.
Medal Roll Reference: WO100/225/119 Supply Officer 4 General Hospital. Sent to England for discharge time expired 9 September 1900.
PORTER, E. Private 685 Bacup Division Medal Clasps: CC.
Medal Roll Reference: WO100/225/57 Orderly 11 General Hospital. Discharged locally on termination of engagement. T. A. E. PORTER on QSA Medal Roll.
POTTINGER, James Andrew Private 103 Welbeck Division Medal Clasps: CC OFS KSA01 KSA02.
Medal Roll Reference: WO100/225/236 WO100/356/176 Sergeant Portland Hospital. Arrived Cape Town 28 December 1899. Transferred to Imperial Yeomanry Hospital Pretoria 1 August 1900. Embarked for England at Durban 16 January 1902. Served 2 years 18 days. Entitled King's South Africa Medal.
POTTINGER, W. Private 1510 Metropolitan Corps Medal Clasps: TVL NAT.
Medal Roll Reference: WO100/225/130 Orderly 7 General Hospital. To England time expired.
POTTS, Walter Robert Private 410 Oldham Corps Medal Clasps: NAT.
Medal Roll Reference: WO100/225/130 Orderly 7 General Hospital Invalided to England.
POWELL, C. H. Private 118 Crewe Division Medal Clasps: CC OFS.
Medal Roll Reference: WO100/225/116 Orderly 3 General Hospital. Transferred to Base Detail RAMC. Died Typhoid Netley 4 January 1901.
PRESCOTT, J. Private 1300 Preston Corps Medal Clasps: CC TVL.
Medal Roll Reference: WO100/224/172 Private Rhodesian Field Force Hospital.
PRESSDEE, E. G. Private 986 Oystermouth Division Medal Clasps: NAT.
Medal Roll Reference: WO100/225/120 Orderly 4 General Hospital Sent to England for discharge time expired 9 September 1900.
PRICE, J. Private 298 Metropolitan Corps Medal Clasps: CC.
Medal Roll Reference: WO100/130/222 Corporal Imperial Yeomanry Hospital Deelfontein.
PRICE, John Private 499 Sheffield Corps Medal Clasps: NAT.
Medal Roll Reference: WO100/225/66 Orderly 13 Stationary Hospital. To SS *Formosa* 6 December 1900.
PRIDMORE, F. Private 1729 Desborough Division Medal Clasps: CC OFS TVL.
Medal Roll Reference: WO100/225/201 Orderly 9 Bearer Company 4 Brigade. Earned claps while travelling from Base Depot RAMC to join this unit. Transferred to England for discharge.
PRIESTLEY, H. Private 742 Heanor Division Medal Clasps: CC OFS.
Medal Roll Reference: WO100/225/195 Orderly 23 Field Hospital. Invalided to England.
PRIESTLY, W. Sergeant 616 New Farnley Division Medal Clasps: CC OFS.
Medal Roll Reference: WO100/225/156 Supply Officer 10 General Hospital. To Base 8 August 1900.
PRINCE, G. F. Private 30 Metropolitan Corps Medal Clasps: CC.
Medal Roll Reference: WO100/225/112B Orderly 6 General Hospital.
PROCTOR, F. Private 1783 Accrington Corps Medal Clasps: CC OFS.
Medal Roll Reference: WO100/225/150 Orderly 9 General Hospital. To Base Detail 15 July 1901.
PROCTOR, J. A. Private 1267 Whaley Bridge Division Medal Clasps: CC.
Medal Roll Reference: WO100/225/124 Orderly 5 General Hospital.
PYEWELL, C. Private 61 Wellingborough Corps Medal Clasps: CC OFS TVL.
Medal Roll Reference: WO100/225/112B Orderly 6 General Hospital.
QUINCEY, Albert S. Private 1381 1823 Wellingborough Corps Medal Clasps: CC OFS SA01 SA02.
Medal Roll Reference: WO100/225/60+150 Orderly 14 General Hospital. To HS *Simla* for duty 14 November 1900 9 General Hospital. To Base Detail 23 July 1901 Formerly 1381.
QUINCEY, Harry Roughton Private 240 Wellingborough Corps Medal Clasps: CC SA01 SA02 JOH DIA WITT KSA01 KSA02.

Medal Roll Reference: WO100/225/1+35+191 WO100/256/249 WO100/277/216
WO100/356/130 Private Attached 20 Field Hospital Also served Kitchener's Fighting Scouts 612
Provisional Transvaal Constabulary 965 24 August 1900. To 1 January 1901 118 Company 25
Battalion Imperial Yeomanry 18039.

QUINN, T. Private 1577 Bolton Corps Medal Clasps: CC.
Medal Roll Reference: WO100/225/109 Orderly 1 General Hospital.

RAINBOW, Charles John Private 1676 Handsworth & Smethwick Corps Medal Clasps: OFS
TVL.
Medal Roll Reference: WO100/225/203 Orderly 21 Bearer Company Joined from 20 General
Hospital February 1901 and sent home for discharge July 1901.

RAMSEY, C. Private 1562 Barnoldswick Division Medal Clasps: CC OFS TVL.
Medal Roll Reference: WO100/225/63+70 Orderly Base Hospital Wynberg. 3 Hospital Train. To
Base Detail RAMC Cape Town for England.

RAMSEY, F. Private 1286 Leeds Corps Medal Clasps: CC OFS TVL.
Medal Roll Reference: WO100/225/126 Private 6 General Hospital. To Base on expiration of
contract 22 October 1900.

RATCLIFFE, W. Private 1031 Bury Division Medal Clasps: NAT.
Medal Roll Reference: WO100/225/68 Orderly 18 General Hospital. To England 30 August 1900.

RAVESTEYN, W. A. Private 1560 Bath City Division Medal Clasps: CC OFS TVL NAT SA01.
Medal Roll Reference: WO100/225/109+130 Orderly 1 General Hospital 7 General Hospital.

RAWCLIFFE, George Sergeant 408 Accrington Corps Medal Clasps: NAT.
Medal Roll Reference: WO100/225/130 Supply Officer 7 General Hospital. To England time
expired.

RAWCLIFFE, T. H. Private 400 Accrington Corps Medal Clasps: NAT.
Medal Roll Reference: WO100/225/130 Orderly 7 General Hospital. To England time expired.

RAWLINSON, D. Private 1335 Radcliffe Division Medal Clasps: CC.
Medal Roll Reference: WO100/225/159 Orderly 13 General Hospital. To England expired contract
5 May 1901.

RAWSON, F. Private 630 Hebden Bridge Corps Medal Clasps: CC WITT.
Medal Roll Reference: WO100/225/195 Orderly 23 Field Hospital. Invalided to England.

RAWSTHORNE, J. Private 1536 Oldham Corps Medal Clasps: CC OFS TVL NAT.
Medal Roll Reference: WO100/225/110+130 Orderly 1 General Hospital 7 General Hospital From
1 General Hospital. To England time expired.

RAWSTRON, H. Private 999 Newchurch Division Medal Clasps: NAT.
Medal Roll Reference: WO100/225/120 Orderly 4 General Hospital Sent to England for discharge
time expired 9 September 1900.

RAWSTRON, J. Private 790 Newchurch Division Medal Clasps: No Clasps.
Medal Roll Reference: WO100/225/35 Orderly.

READ, J. W. Private 750 Ilkeston Corps Medal Clasps: CC WITT.
Medal Roll Reference: WO100/225/195 Orderly 23 Field Hospital. Discharged time expired.

RECORD, J. Private 852 Burnley Division Medal Clasps: CC OFS TVL.
Medal Roll Reference: WO100/225/126 Private 6 General Hospital. To Base on expiration of
contract 3 September 1900.

REDDAN, S. Private 42 Metropolitan Corps Medal Clasps: CC OFS TVL.
Medal Roll Reference: WO100/225/112B Orderly 6 General Hospital.

REDFERN, C. E. Private 910 Derby Division Medal Clasps: NAT.
Medal Roll Reference: WO100/225/120 Orderly 4 General Hospital Sent to England for discharge
time expired 9 September 1900.

REDHEAD, Edward Dawson Sergeant 1441 Kendal Division Medal Clasps: OFS TVL KSA01
KSA02.

Medal Roll Reference: WO100/225/68 WO100/271/114 WO100/366/48 Supply Officer 18 General Hospital. To England 30 August 1900 South African Constabulary A Division Quarter Master Sergeant A1865 4 May 1901. To 26 February 1902. Died typhoid Potchefstroom 26 February 1902.

RENSHAW, W. Private 1118 Sheffield Corps Medal Clasps: NAT.
Medal Roll Reference: WO100/225/166 Orderly 15 General Hospital. Transferred to England 14 September 1900.

REYNOLDS, A. Private 1098 Derby Division Medal Clasps: NAT.
Medal Roll Reference: WO100/225/68 Orderly 18 General Hospital. To England 28 December 1900.

RHODES, A. Private 1780 Shipley Corps Medal Clasps: CC.
Medal Roll Reference: WO100/225/174 Orderly 21 General Hospital.

RHODES, H. Sergeant 1127 1586 Oldham Corps Medal Clasps: CC OFS.
Medal Roll Reference: WO100/225/53+136+248 Orderly HS *Maine* 8 General Hospital Sick. To Cape Town 8 March 1901.

RHODES, J. Private 1497 Bolton Corps Medal Clasps: CC OFS TVL SA01.
Medal Roll Reference: WO100/225/130 Orderly 7 General Hospital. To England time expired.

RHODES, R. Private 1306 Preston Corps Medal Clasps: CC TVL.
Medal Roll Reference: WO100/224/172 Private Rhodesian Field Force Hospital.

RHODES, William Private 1534 Oldham Corps Medal Clasps: CC OFS.
Medal Roll Reference: WO100/225/150 Orderly 9 General Hospital.

RICE, A. H. Private 508 Northampton Corps Medal Clasps: CC OFS.
Medal Roll Reference: WO100/225/232 Private Langman Hospital Invalided home Since Lieutenant 3/VSC Northants regiment.

RICE, H. J. Private 1683 Wellingborough Corps Medal Clasps: CC OFS TVL.
Medal Roll Reference: WO100/225/171 Orderly 20 General Hospital Joined from Base Detail. To England for discharge.

RICH, W. J. Private 716 Mill Bay Division Medal Clasps: CC WITT.
Medal Roll Reference: WO100/225/193 Orderly Attached 21 Field Hospital. Discharged.

RICHARDS, J. Private 1397 St John Ambulance Brigade Medal Clasps: No Clasps.
Medal Roll Reference: WO100/225/60 Orderly 14 General Hospital. To HS *Simla* for duty 14 November 1900.

RICHARDSON, C. R. S. Private 1207 Metropolitan Corps Medal Clasps: CC.
Medal Roll Reference: WO100/224/172 Private Rhodesian Field Force Hospital.

RICHARDSON, F. W. Private 669 Manchester Post Office Division Medal Clasps: CC WITT.
Medal Roll Reference: WO100/225/204 Orderly Attached 22 Bearer Company. Discharged.

RICHARDSON, Wallace Robert Private 51 Metropolitan Corps Medal Clasps: CC.
Medal Roll Reference: WO100/225/112B Orderly 6 General Hospital. Died of disease 2 General Hospital Wynberg 30 March 1900.

RICHMOND, A. Private 1155 Birchwood Corps Medal Clasps: CC SA01.
Medal Roll Reference: WO100/225/57+85+150 Orderly 11 General Hospital. To England on termination of engagement 9 General Hospital. To Base Detail 12 October 1900.

RICHMOND, S. Private 689 Nelson Corps Medal Clasps: CC WITT.
Medal Roll Reference: WO100/225/193 Orderly Attached 21 Field Hospital. Discharged.

RIDGEON, E. A. Private 760 Great Eastern Railway Corps Medal Clasps: CC WITT.
Medal Roll Reference: WO100/225/204 Orderly Attached 22 Bearer Company. Discharged.

RIDGWAY, A. Private 1034 Manchester Post Office Division Medal Clasps: NAT.
Medal Roll Reference: WO100/225/181 Orderly 14 Stationary Hospital.

RIDING, J. T. Private 244 Clitheroe Division Medal Clasps: CC OFS JOH DIA WITT.
Medal Roll Reference: WO100/225/191 Private Attached 20 Field Hospital. Transferred sick. To Pretoria 6 June 1900. OFS clasp recovered.

RIDLEY, A. Private 704 Haslingden Corps Medal Clasps: CC.
Medal Roll Reference: WO100/225/57 Orderly 11 General Hospital. To England on termination of engagement.
RIDOUT, W. W. Private 238 Herne Bay Division Medal Clasps: NAT.
Medal Roll Reference: WO100/225/75 Orderly Princess Christian Hospital Train.
RIGBY, A. Sergeant 1017 Preston Corps Medal Clasps: NAT.
Medal Roll Reference: WO100/225/130 Supply Officer 7 General Hospital. To England time expired.
RIGBY, J. Private 1544 Oldham Corps Medal Clasps: CC OFS.
Medal Roll Reference: WO100/225/124+156 Orderly 5 General Hospital Orderly 10 General Hospital. To Base 10 October 1900.
RILEY, J. Private 1347 Bolton Corps Medal Clasps: CC TVL.
Medal Roll Reference: WO100/225/79+159+WO100/224/197 Orderly Original Unit 3 General Hospital after 9th Brigade Field Hospital Sent back. To Mafeking time expired13 General Hospital. To Mafeking 29 August 1900 9th Brigade Field Hospital Attached RAMC.
RINGROSE, J. Private 273 Bradford Corps Medal Clasps: CC.
Medal Roll Reference: WO100/225/126 Private 6 General Hospital. To Base on expiration of contract 18 June 1900.
ROBBINS, W. Private 1758 Reading Division Medal Clasps: CC OFS TVL.
Medal Roll Reference: WO100/225/77+110 Orderly 10 Stationary Hospital 1 General Hospital. To Cape Town 1 General Hospital.
ROBERTS, A. E. Private 1053 Bolton Corps Medal Clasps: NAT.
Medal Roll Reference: WO100/225/120 Orderly 4 General Hospital Sent to England for discharge time expired 9 September 1900.
ROBERTS, E. Private 1530 Oldham Corps Medal Clasps: CC OFS TVL NAT.
Medal Roll Reference: WO100/225/110+130 Orderly 1 General Hospital 7 General Hospital From 1 General Hospital To England time expired.
ROBERTS, G. H. Private 866 Wellingborough Corps Medal Clasps: CC OFS.
Medal Roll Reference: WO100/225/116 Orderly 3 General Hospital. Transferred to Base Detail RAMC.
ROBERTSHAW, S. Private 701 Hebden Bridge Corps Medal Clasps: CC.
Medal Roll Reference: WO100/225/57 Orderly 11 General Hospital. To England on termination of engagement.
ROBERTSON, Francis Private 717 Mill Bay Division GWR??? Medal Clasps: CC WITT.
Medal Roll Reference: WO100/225/193 Orderly Attached 21 Field Hospital. Died of disease Senekal 17 July 1900.
ROBINSON, A. A. Private 903 1732 Derby Division Medal Clasps: OFS TVL NAT SA01 SA02.
Medal Roll Reference: WO100/225/36+93+120+171 Orderly 4 General Hospital. Invalided to England 21 August 1900. 20 General Hospital Joined from Base Detail. To England for discharge.
ROBINSON, F. Private 1171 Leeds Corps Medal Clasps: CC OFS.
Medal Roll Reference: WO100/225/136 Orderly 8 General Hospital. To England 10 October 1900.
ROBINSON, F. Private 1444 Accrington Corps Medal Clasps: CC OFS TVL.
Medal Roll Reference: WO100/225/181+183 Orderly 14 Stationary Hospital and Middleburg 17 Stationary Hospital. To Base 24 November 1900.
ROBINSON, H. C. Private 660 Market Harborough Division Medal Clasps: CC WITT.
Medal Roll Reference: WO100/225/203 Orderly 21 Bearer Company. Home for discharge August 1901.
ROBINSON, H. F. Private 376 Handsworth & Smethwick Corps Medal Clasps: CC OFS.
Medal Roll Reference: WO100/225/136 Orderly 8 General Hospital. To England 20 July 1900.
ROBINSON, John Corporal 1132 1899 Bolton Corps Medal Clasps: CC OFS TVL SA01 SA02.

Medal Roll Reference: WO100/225/53+248 WO100/271/114+253 Orderly HS *Maine*. South African Constabulary A Division Medical Corporal A1867.

ROBINSON, John W. Private 850 Northampton Corps Medal Clasps: CC OFS. China Medal. Medal Roll Reference: WO100/225/136 Orderly 8 General Hospital. To England 20 July 1900 8 General Hospital. To England 31 August 1900. On medal roll for HS *Maine* for China WO100/96/38+39.

ROBINSON, S. Private 1543 Oldham Corps Medal Clasps: CC. Medal Roll Reference: WO100/225/110 Orderly 1 General Hospital.

ROBSON, William Sergeant 189 Bradford Corps Medal Clasps: CC OFS TVL SA01 SA02. Medal Roll Reference: WO100/225/126 WO100/272/228+352 Supernumerary Officer 6 General Hospital. To Base on expiration of contract 18 June 1900. South African Constabulary C Division 1st Class Sergeant C2112 Discharged 29 October 1902.

RODD, C. H. Private 565 Redruth Division Medal Clasps: CC OFS. Medal Roll Reference: WO100/225/124+156 Orderly 5 General Hospital. 10 General Hospital. To Base 13 April 1901.

RODGERS, J. Private 1117 Sheffield Corps Medal Clasps: OFS NAT. Medal Roll Reference: WO100/225/181+193 Orderly 14 Stationary Hospital. Attached 21 Field Hospital. Discharged.

RODGERS, W. Private 609 Belper Division Medal Clasps: CC OFS. Medal Roll Reference: WO100/225/151 Orderly 9 General Hospital. To Base Detail 7 September 1900.

ROGERS, C. Private 1521 Handsworth & Smethwick Corps Medal Clasps: No Clasps. Medal Roll Reference: WO100/225/120 Orderly 4 General Hospital Sent to England for discharge time expired 28 November 1900.

ROGERS, C. H. Private 906 Derby Division Medal Clasps: NAT. Medal Roll Reference: WO100/225/120 Orderly 4 General Hospital Sent to England for discharge time expired 19 December 1900.

ROGERS, F. E. Private 52 Metropolitan Corps Medal Clasps: CC OFS. Medal Roll Reference: WO100/225/116 Orderly 3 General Hospital. Transferred to Base Detail RAMC.

ROGERS, J. Private 374 Ironbridge Corps Medal Clasps: CC OFS. Medal Roll Reference: WO100/225/136 Orderly 8 General Hospital. To England 23 January 1901.

ROGERS, W. H. Private 822 Welbeck Division Medal Clasps: CC OFS. Medal Roll Reference: WO100/225/116 Orderly 3 General Hospital. Transferred to Base Detail RAMC.

ROGERSON, W. Private 533 Preston Corps Medal Clasps: NAT. Medal Roll Reference: WO100/225/66 Supply Officer 13 Stationary Hospital. To SS *Formosa* 6 December 1900.

ROLFE, J. F. W. Private 922 Dover Division Medal Clasps: OFS NAT. Medal Roll Reference: WO100/225/130 Orderly 7 General Hospital. Transferred to Harrismith.

ROSCOW, J. Private 1344 Bolton Corps Medal Clasps: CC. Medal Roll Reference: WO100/225/159 Orderly 13 General Hospital. To England expired contract 27 November 1900.

ROSE, A. H. Private 216 Metropolitan Corps Medal Clasps: CC OFS TVL SA01. Medal Roll Reference: WO100/225/126 Private 6 General Hospital. To Base on expiration of contract 17 December 1900.

ROSE, Harry T. N. Private 268 Ramsgate Corps Medal Clasps: CC. Medal Roll Reference: WO100/225/126 Private 6 General Hospital. To Base on expiration of contract 18 June1900 (RNASBR Long Service Medal 37 SBS 2Cl).

ROSE, J. Private 1078 Preston Corps Medal Clasps: NAT.
Medal Roll Reference: WO100/225/120 Orderly 4 General Hospital Sent to England for discharge time expired 9 September 1900.
ROSEVEARE, Edwin 1st Class Sergeant 191 Newton Abbott Division Medal Clasps: CC JOH WITT.
Medal Roll Reference: WO100/225/191 Private Attached 20 Field Hospital. Transferred to Base 14 August 1900.
ROSS, Charles G. Private 55 Westgate-on-Sea Division Medal Clasps: CC OFS SA01 SA02.
Medal Roll Reference: WO100/225/112B WO100/273/140+332 WO100/366/189 Orderly 6 General Hospital. South African Constabulary Medical Corporal E2930. St John Ambulance Brigade service 18 December 1899 to 2 May 1900. South African Constabulary service 4 May 1901 to 31 May 1902. Transferred to South African Constabulary Reserve. Not entitled to King's South Africa Medal.
ROSTRON, George William Private 923 Tottington Division Medal Clasps: CC OFS TVL NAT SA01.
Medal Roll Reference: WO100/225/120 WO100/271/22+56 Orderly 4 General Hospital. Sent to England for discharge time expired 19 December 1900. South African Constabulary Headquarters Depot Trooper HQ204 Reserve Division RD588 Discharged 17 November 1901.
ROTHWELL, J. J. Private 1501 Radcliffe Division Medal Clasps: TVL.
Medal Roll Reference: WO100/225/169 Orderly 17 General Hospital. Transferred to Pietermaritzburg 30 November 1900.
ROWEN, T. H. Private 1289 Metropolitan Corps Medal Clasps: CC OFS TVL.
Medal Roll Reference: WO100/225/126 Private 6 General Hospital. To Base on expiration of contract 22 October 1900.
ROWLAND, A. Private 343 Ilkeston Corps Medal Clasps: CC.
Medal Roll Reference: WO100/130/222 Private Imperial Yeomanry Hospital Deelfontein.
ROWLAND, C. A. Private 749 Ilkeston Corps Medal Clasps: CC WITT.
Medal Roll Reference: WO100/225/195 Orderly 23 Field Hospital. Discharged time expired.
ROWLAND, S. Private 748 Ilkeston Corps Medal Clasps: CC WITT.
Medal Roll Reference: WO100/225/195 Orderly 23 Field Hospital. Discharged time expired.
ROY, J. E. Private 1324 1922 Metropolitan Corps Medal Clasps: CC OFS TVL SA01.
Medal Roll Reference: WO100/225/159 WO100/271/114+253 Orderly 13 General Hospital. To England expired contract 27 November 1900. South African Constabulary
A Division Corporal A1872. Discharged 22 November 1901.
ROYDS, I. Private 1194 Oldham Corps Medal Clasps: CC.
Medal Roll Reference: WO100/225/110 Orderly 1 General Hospital.
RUDLAND, L. G. Private 431 Metropolitan Corps Medal Clasps: CC OFS.
Medal Roll Reference: WO100/225/136 Orderly 8 General Hospital. To England 20 July 1900.
RUSHBY, Harold Private 875 Leicester Corps Medal Clasps: CC OFS TVL.
Medal Roll Reference: WO100/225/126 Private 6 General Hospital. To Base on expiration of contract 3 September 1900.
RUSHTON, A. Private 1651 Bacup Division Medal Clasps: OFS TVL.
Medal Roll Reference: WO100/225/146+181 Orderly 14 Stationary Hospital. 7 Ambulance Train. 3 Ambulance Train.
RUSHTON, A. R. Private 851 Rochdale Corps Medal Clasps: CC OFS.
Medal Roll Reference: WO100/225/116 Orderly 3 General Hospital. Transferred to Base Detail.
RUSHTON, R. F. Private 1283 Barrowford Division Medal Clasps: CC OFS.
Medal Roll Reference: WO100/225/151 Orderly 9 General Hospital. To Base Detail 26 September 1900.
RUSSELL, Charles Orton Private 1856 Bradford Corps Medal Clasps: CC SA02.

Medal Roll Reference: WO100/225/110 WO100/240/129+189 Orderly 1 General Hospital. Private 165 CCF Company Cape Medical Staff Corps 7 February to 27 August 1902.

RYALL, Harry B. Private 5 Metropolitan Corps Medal Clasps: CC.
Medal Roll Reference: WO100/225/241 Private HS *Princess of Wales*. Attached RAMC.

RYAN, J. Sergeant 1507 Nuneaton Division Medal Clasps: CC.
Medal Roll Reference: WO100/225/63 Supply Officer Base Hospital Wynberg. 7 General Hospital. To England time expired.

RYLES, D. Private 1051 Bolton Corps Medal Clasps: OFS TVL NAT.
Medal Roll Reference: WO100/225/181+193 Orderly 14 Stationary Hospital. Attached 21 Field Hospital. Discharged.

SABIN, H. J. Private 1796 Birmingham Corps (Birmingham City Division) Medal Clasps: CC SA01.
Medal Roll Reference: WO100/225/89+174 Orderly 21 General Hospital. Time expired 10 August 1901

SANDERS, H. Private 364 North Staffs Corps Medal Clasps: NAT.
Medal Roll Reference: WO100/225/130 Orderly 7 General Hospital. To England time expired.

SANDERS, M. Sergeant 1257 Padiham Division Medal Clasps: CC OFS.
Medal Roll Reference: WO100/225/156 Supply Officer 10 General Hospital. To Base 18 October 1900.

SANDERSON, G. Private 57 Isle of Wight Corps Medal Clasps: CC OFS TVL.
Medal Roll Reference: WO100/225/112B Orderly 6 General Hospital.

SANKEY, T. A. Sergeant 1218 Blackpool Division Medal Clasps: CC OFS.
Medal Roll Reference: WO100/225/151 Supply Officer 9 General Hospital. To Base Detail 12 October 1900.

SANTEN, B. Private 329 Metropolitan Corps Medal Clasps: CC kSA01KSA02.
Medal Roll Reference: WO100/130/222+WO100/356/173 Sergeant Imperial Yeomanry Hospital Deelfontein.

SARGINSON, T. C. Private 927 Kendal Division Medal Clasps: No Clasps.
Medal Roll Reference: WO100/225/39 Orderly. T. W. SARGINSON on QSA Medal Roll.

SAUNDERS, A. E. Private 11 1660 Metropolitan Corps Medal Clasps: CC OFS TVL.
Medal Roll Reference: WO100/225/171+241 Orderly HS *Princess of Wales*. Attached RAMC. 20 General Hospital Joined from Base Detail. To England for discharge.

SAVAGE, F. Private 1634 Nelson Corps Medal Clasps: OFS TVL.
Medal Roll Reference: WO100/225/181 Orderly 14 Stationary Hospital. 7 Ambulance Train.

SAWFORD, James S. Private 320 St John Ambulance Brigade (NFB Aylesbury) Medal Clasps: CC. NFBUAD Medal.
Medal Roll Reference: WO100/130/223 Private Imperial Yeomanry Hospital Deelfontein.

SAWFORD, John W. Private 133 Wellingborough Corps Medal Clasps: No Clasps.
Medal Roll Reference: WO100/225/37 Orderly. Died of disease Orange River Station 30 April 1900.

SAXON, E. Private 1533 Oldham Corps Medal Clasps: CC OFS TVL NAT.
Medal Roll Reference: WO100/225/110+131 Orderly 1 General Hospital. 7 General Hospital. To England time expired.

SAYER, James H. 1st Class Sergeant 82 Metropolitan Corps Medal Clasps: CC OFS.
Medal Roll Reference: WO100/225/236 Staff Sergeant Portland Hospital. To England contract expired.

SCAIFE, C. Private 613 Colne Division Medal Clasps: CC OFS.
Medal Roll Reference: WO100/225/151 Supply Officer 9 General Hospital. To Base Detail 9 May 1901.

SCATTERGOOD, W. E. Private 1009 Sheffield Corps Medal Clasps: NAT.
Medal Roll Reference: WO100/225/131 Orderly 7 General Hospital. Invalided to England.

SCHOFIELD, C. Private 415 Oldham Corps Medal Clasps: NAT.
Medal Roll Reference: WO100/225/131 Orderly 7 General Hospital. To England time expired.
SCHOFIELD, H. Private 203 Oldham Corps Medal Clasps: CC.
Medal Roll Reference: WO100/225/126 Private 6 General Hospital. To Base on expiration of contract 18 June 1900.
SCHOFIELD, Thomas Private 1285 Haslingden Corps Medal Clasps: CC OFS TVL.
Medal Roll Reference: WO100/225/126 Private 6 General Hospital. To Base on expiration of contract 22 October 1900.
SCHOLES, F. Private 1333 Royton Division Medal Clasps: CC.
Medal Roll Reference: WO100/225/159 Orderly 13 General Hospital. To England expired contract 27 November 1900.
SCOTSON, Robert Private 668 Manchester Post Office Division Medal Clasps: CC OFS TVL.
Medal Roll Reference: WO100/130/263 Corporal Imperial Yeomanry Field Hospital and Bearer Company.
SCOTT, G. Private 674 Bolton Corps Medal Clasps: CC WITT.
Medal Roll Reference: WO100/225/195 Orderly 23 Field Hospital. Discharged time expired.
SCOTT, J. E. Private 1093 Tibshelf Corps Medal Clasps: NAT.
Medal Roll Reference: WO100/225/68 Orderly 18 General Hospital. To England 28 December 1900.
SEARCY, T. Private 662 Medbourne Division Medal Clasps: CC.
Medal Roll Reference: WO100/225/57 Orderly 11 General Hospital. To England on termination of engagement.
SEDDON, J. Private 1630 Royton Division Medal Clasps: OFS TVL SA01 SA02.
Medal Roll Reference: WO100/225/181 Orderly 14 Stationary Hospital. 7 Ambulance Train.
SEDGWICK, F. Private 426 Lincoln Adult School Division Medal Clasps: CC OFS.
Medal Roll Reference: WO100/225/136 Orderly 8 General Hospital. To England 23 July 1900.
SELBY, J. F. Private 650 1613 Worksop Division Medal Clasps: CC OFS TVL.
Medal Roll Reference: WO100/225/57+159 Orderly 11 General Hospital. 13 General Hospital. To England on termination of engagement.
SELLARS, H. R. Private 1406 1855 Bradford Corps Medal Clasps: CC.
Medal Roll Reference: WO100/225/60+72 Orderly 14 General Hospital. To HS *Simla* for duty 14 November 1900. 24 Stationary Hospital. From Base Detail. Transferred to Base Detail 18 April 1901.
SETTLE, E. Private 1150 Bradford Corps Medal Clasps: CC OFS.
Medal Roll Reference: WO100/225/136 Orderly 8 General Hospital. To England 10 October 1900.
SETTLE, J. T. Private 1237 Preston Corps Medal Clasps: CC OFS TVL.
Medal Roll Reference: WO100/225/126 Private 6 General Hospital. To Base on expiration of contract 22 October 1900.
SEVERS, F. Private 1271 Radcliffe Division Medal Clasps: CC.
Medal Roll Reference: WO100/225/124 Orderly 5 General Hospital.
SEWELL, H. Private 1496 Bolton Corps Medal Clasps: OFS TVL NAT SA01.
Medal Roll Reference: WO100/225/131 Orderly 7 General Hospital. To England time expired.
SEWELL, P. E. Private 1430 Bolton Corps Medal Clasps: TVL NAT.
Medal Roll Reference: WO100/225/131 Orderly 7 General Hospital. To England time expired.
SEYMOUR, C. R. Private 733 Leicester Corps Medal Clasps: CC WITT.
Medal Roll Reference: WO100/225/204 Orderly Attached 22 Bearer Company. Discharged.
SHACKLETON, J. J. Private 411 Oldham Corps Medal Clasps: TVL NAT SA01.
Medal Roll Reference: WO100/225/76 Orderly 7 General Hospital. To England time expired. War Office Issue.
SHACKLETON, R. Private 915 Padiham Division Medal Clasps: NAT.
Medal Roll Reference: WO100/225/131 Orderly 7 General Hospital. Invalided to England.

SHARP, W. Private 1488 Leeds Corps Medal Clasps: No Clasps.
Medal Roll Reference: WO100/225/120 Orderly 4 General Hospital. Sent to England for discharge time expired 28 November 1900.
SHARPLES, S. Private 916 Oldham Corps Medal Clasps: NAT.
Medal Roll Reference: WO100/225/76+131 Orderly 7 General Hospital. To England time expired. War Office Issue.
SHARPLES, W. Private 538 Walton-le-Dale Division Medal Clasps: NAT.
Medal Roll Reference: WO100/225/66 Orderly 13 Stationary Hospital. To SS *Formosa* 6 December 1900.
SHARPLES, W. Private 855 Rishton Division Medal Clasps: CC.
Medal Roll Reference: WO100/225/69 Orderly 8 Stationary Hospital.
SHATWELL, C. T. Private 1625 Haslingden Division Medal Clasps: CC.
Medal Roll Reference: WO100/225/110+174 Orderly 1 General Hospital. 21 General Hospital.
SHAW, A. Private 274 Bradford Corps Medal Clasps: CC.
Medal Roll Reference: WO100/225/126 Private 6 General Hospital. To Base Invalided 9 June 1900.
SHAW, Charles Frederick Private 1057 Bolton Corps Medal Clasps: CC OFS TVL NAT SA01 SA02.
Medal Roll Reference: WO100/225/181+193 WO100/271/23+57 WO100/272/134 Orderly 14 Stationary Hospital. Attached 21 Field Hospital. Discharged. South African Constabulary Reserve Division Trooper RD590 Headquarters Depot HQ34 Transferred to B Division 1 February 1902 Medical Corporal B1644.
SHAW, C. H. Private 1223 Preston Corps Medal Clasps: CC OFS.
Medal Roll Reference: WO100/225/152 Orderly 9 General Hospital. To Base Detail 12 October 1900.
SHAW, E. E. Private 921 Hazelgrove Division Medal Clasps: NAT.
Medal Roll Reference: WO100/225/131 Orderly 7 General Hospital. Transferred to Harrismith.
SHAW, George. Private 651 Worksop Division Medal Clasps: CC OFS TVL SA01 SA02.
Medal Roll Reference: WO100/225/194 WO100/272/235+364 Orderly 22 Field Hospital. South African Constabulary C Division Trooper C2115. Discharged 21 December 1902.
SHAW, H. Private 658 Northampton Corps Medal Clasps: CC OFS TVL SA01.
Medal Roll Reference: WO100/130/234+251+266 Orderly Imperial Yeomanry Hospital Pretoria. Imperial Yeomanry Field Hospital and Bearer Company.
SHAW, H. Sergeant 870 Hallaton Division Medal Clasps: CC OFS.
Medal Roll Reference: WO100/225/126+156 WO100/366/191 Supply Officer 6 General Hospital. To Stationary Hospital Norval's Pont 8 June 1900. 10 General Hospital. South African Constabulary E Division Trooper E4185. Discharged by purchase. Not entitled to King's South Africa Medal.
SHAW, W. Private 171 Padiham Division Medal Clasps: CC.
Medal Roll Reference: WO100/225/110 Orderly 1 General Hospital.
SHEARD, J. T. B. Private 66 Blackpool Division Medal Clasps: CC.
Medal Roll Reference: WO100/225/112B Orderly 6 General Hospital.
SHELDON, H. Private 626 Manchester Post Office Division Medal Clasps: CC OFS.
Medal Roll Reference: WO100/225/156 Orderly 10 General Hospital. To Base 7 August 1900.
SHENTON, J. W. Private 233 Leeds Corps Medal Clasps: CC.
Medal Roll Reference: WO100/225/127 Private 6 General Hospital. To Base on expiration of contract 23 June 1900.
SHEPHERD, J. Private 1642 Keighley Corps Medal Clasps: No Clasps.
Medal Roll Reference: WO100/225/146 Orderly.
SHIPLEY, G. W. Private 289 Metropolitan Corps Medal Clasps: CC.
Medal Roll Reference: WO100/130/223 Private Imperial Yeomanry Hospital Deelfontein.

SHIPTON, J. Private 1108 Birmingham Corps Medal Clasps: NAT.
Medal Roll Reference: WO100/225/181 Orderly 14 Stationary Hospital.
SHRUBSOLE, W. L. Private 462 Metropolitan Corps Medal Clasps: NAT.
Medal Roll Reference: WO100/225/131 Orderly 7 General Hospital. To England time expired.
SHUFFLEBOTTOM, C. Private 962 Preston Corps Medal Clasps: CC.
Medal Roll Reference: WO100/225/178 Orderly 7 Stationary Hospital. Sent to England September 1900.
SIDDALL, A. Private 1569 Bolton Corps Medal Clasps: CC.
Medal Roll Reference: WO100/225/110+159 Orderly 13 General Hospital. To 1 General Hospital Base Hospital Wynberg 1 February 1901.
SIDDLE, Fred Private 1505 Morecombe Division Medal Clasps: TVL.
Medal Roll Reference: WO100/225/169 Orderly 17 General Hospital. Died of disease Standerton 21 November 1900.
SILVER, T. Private 1301 Preston Corps Medal Clasps: CC TVL.
Medal Roll Reference: WO100/224/172 Private Rhodesian Field Force Hospital.
SIM, J. Private 1211 Leeds Corps Medal Clasps: CC OFS.
Medal Roll Reference: WO100/225/151 Orderly 9 General Hospital. To Base Detail 15 April 1901.
SIMM, J. Private 1052 Bolton Corps Medal Clasps: NAT.
Medal Roll Reference: WO100/225/120 Orderly 4 General Hospital. Sent to England for discharge time expired 9 September 1900.
SIMMONS, G. H. Private 1850 Leicester Corps Medal Clasps: CC OFS.
Medal Roll Reference: WO100/225/151 Orderly 9 General Hospital. To Base Detail 15 July 1901.
SIMS, J. A. Private 1097 Derby Division Medal Clasps: NAT.
Medal Roll Reference: WO100/225/66 Orderly 13 Stationary Hospital. To HS *Dunera* 18 December 1900.
SINFIELD, F. T. Private 223 Ilkeston Corps Medal Clasps: CC.
Medal Roll Reference: WO100/225/127 Private 6 General Hospital. To Base Invalided 1 July 1900.
SINGLETON, William James Private 1476 Haslingden Corps Medal Clasps: No Clasps.
Medal Roll Reference: WO100/225/120 Orderly 4 General Hospital. Sent to England for discharge time expired 28 November 1900.
SINNISTER, J. Private 414 Oldham Corps Medal Clasps: NAT.
Medal Roll Reference: WO100/225/131 Orderly 7 General Hospital. To England time expired.
SLANEY, T. J. Private 1278 Brierfield Division Medal Clasps: CC OFS.
Medal Roll Reference: WO100/225/151 Orderly 9 General Hospital. To Base Detail 12 October 1900.
SLATER, A. W. Sergeant 318 St John Ambulance Brigade (NFB Barnes/Mortlake) Medal Clasps: CC. NFBUAD Medal.
Medal Roll Reference: WO100/130/222 Sergeant Imperial Yeomanry Hospital Deelfontein.
SLATER, H. E. Private 1139 Barnoldswick Division Medal Clasps: CC OFS.
Medal Roll Reference: WO100/225/156 Orderly 10 General Hospital. To Base 10 October 1900.
SLATER, W. Private 8 Nelson Corps Medal Clasps: CC.
Medal Roll Reference: WO100/225/241 Private HS *Princess of Wales*. Attached RAMC.
SLEE, F. W. Private 876 Leicester Corps Medal Clasps: CC OFS.
Medal Roll Reference: WO100/225/116 Orderly 3 General Hospital. Transferred to Base Detail RAMC.
SLEIGHT, G. H. B. Private 145 Withernsea Division Medal Clasps: CC.
Medal Roll Reference: WO100/225/73 Orderly 6 Stationary Hospital.
SLEIGHT, W. E. Private 73 Hull Corps Medal Clasps: CC OFS.
Medal Roll Reference: WO100/225/117 Orderly 3 General Hospital. Transferred to Base Detail RAMC.

SMALLWOOD, C. W. Private 210 Withernsea Division Medal Clasps: CC.
Medal Roll Reference: WO100/225/127 Private 6 General Hospital. To Base on expiration of contract 23 June 1900.
SMITH, A. C. Private 869 Hull Corps Medal Clasps: CC OFS.
Medal Roll Reference: WO100/225/151 Orderly 9 General Hospital. To Base Detail 31 August 1900.
SMITH, C. Private 1193 Oldham Corps Medal Clasps: CC.
Medal Roll Reference: WO100/225/110 Orderly 1 General Hospital.
SMITH, C. A. Sergeant 952 Nelson Corps Medal Clasps: TVL NAT.
Medal Roll Reference: WO100/225/131 Supply Officer 7 General Hospital. To England time expired.
SMITH, C. H. Private 208 Ironbridge Corps Medal Clasps: CC.
Medal Roll Reference: WO100/225/127 Private 6 General Hospital. To Base on expiration of contract 18 June 1900.
SMITH, C. T. Private 1736 Metropolitan Corps Medal Clasps: No Clasps.
Medal Roll Reference: WO100/225/146 Orderly.
SMITH, C. W. R. Private 255 Market Harborough Division Medal Clasps: CC OFS.
Medal Roll Reference: WO100/225/176 Orderly 5 Stationary Hospital Sent to Base for England for discharge.
SMITH, E. Private 549 Metropolitan Corps Medal Clasps: CC OFS.
Medal Roll Reference: WO100/225/151 Orderly 9 General Hospital. To Base Detail 7 August 1900.
SMITH, E. S. Private 603 Sheffield Corps Medal Clasps: CC OFS.
Medal Roll Reference: WO100/225/151 Orderly 9 General Hospital. To Base Detail 23 June 1900.
SMITH, F. Private 1461 Oldham Corps Medal Clasps: CC OFS TVL SA01 SA02.
Medal Roll Reference: WO100/225/181+183 WO100/273/147+341 Orderly 14 Stationary Hospital and 17 Stationary Hospital Middleburg. To Base 24 November 1900. South African Constabulary E Division Corporal E2931. Service in St John Ambulance Brigade 13 August 1900 to 6 December 1900. Service in South African Constabulary from 4 May 1901. Died of disease Vet River 5 March 1902.
SMITH, F. Private 1940 Metropolitan Corps
Medal Roll Reference: No QSA identified.
SMITH, G. Private 1170 Leeds Corps Medal Clasps: CC OFS.
Medal Roll Reference: WO100/225/151 Orderly 9 General Hospital. To Base Detail 12 October 1900.
SMITH, G. H. Private 552 1833 Metropolitan Corps Medal Clasps: CC OFS TVL SA01.
Medal Roll Reference: WO100/225/74+85+110+151 Orderly 1 General Hospital. 9 General Hospital. To Base Detail 12 October 1900. 11 General Hospital. 23 Bearer Company.
SMITH, H. Private 382 Birmingham Corps Medal Clasps: CC.
Medal Roll Reference: WO100/130/223 Private Imperial Yeomanry Hospital Deelfontein.
SMITH, H. J. Private 305 St John Ambulance Brigade (NFB Marlow) Medal Clasps: CC. NFBUAD Medal.
Medal Roll Reference: WO100/130/223 Corporal Imperial Yeomanry Hospital Deelfontein.
SMITH, J. P. Private 1016 Sheffield Corps Medal Clasps: CC OFS.
Medal Roll Reference: WO100/225/131+195 Orderly 7 General Hospital. Transferred to 23 Field Hospital Harrismith. Discharged time expired.
SMITH, J. T. Private 441 Foulridge Division Medal Clasps: NAT.
Medal Roll Reference: WO100/225/131 Orderly 7 General Hospital. To England time expired.
SMITH, J. W. Private 306 St John Ambulance Brigade (NFB Barnes/Mortlake) Medal Clasps: CC. NFBUAD Medal.
Medal Roll Reference: WO100/130/222 Sergeant Imperial Yeomanry Hospital Deelfontein.

SMITH, M. Private 1151 1840 Dewsbury Corps Medal Clasps: CC OFS.
Medal Roll Reference: WO100/225/151+174 Orderly 9 General Hospital. 21 General Hospital. To Base Detail 12 October 1900.
SMITH, R. C. Private 62 Market Harborough Division Medal Clasps: CC OFS TVL.
Medal Roll Reference: WO100/225/112A Orderly.
SMITH, R. J. Private 1393 St John Ambulance Brigade Medal Clasps: No Clasps.
Medal Roll Reference: WO100/225/60 Orderly 14 General Hospital. To HS *Simla* for duty 14 November 1900.
SMITH, S. J. Private 141 Metropolitan Corps Medal Clasps: CC.
Medal Roll Reference: WO100/225/110 Orderly 1 General Hospital.
SMITH, S. J. Private 467 Metropolitan Corps Medal Clasps: CC OFS.
Medal Roll Reference: WO100/225/136 Orderly 8 General Hospital. Sick to Cape Town 7 September 1900.
SMITH, Stafford S. Private 1219 1857 Blackpool Division Medal Clasps: CC OFS.
Medal Roll Reference: WO100/225/151 Orderly 9 General Hospital. To Base.
SMITH, Stanley Private 761 Metropolitan Corps Medal Clasps: CC
Medal Roll Reference: WO100/225/57 Orderly 11 General Hospital. Died typhoid Kimberley 13 July 1900.
SMITH, T. Private 1243 Preston Corps Medal Clasps: CC OFS TVL.
Medal Roll Reference: WO100/225/127 Private 6 General Hospital. To Base on expiration of contract 22 November 1900.
SMITH, T. F. Sergeant 1358 Bolton Corps Medal Clasps: CC OFS.
Medal Roll Reference: WO100/225/160+176 Supply Officer 13 General Hospital. To England expired contract 27 November 1900 5 Stationary Hospital Sent to Base for England for discharge.
SMITH, W. Private 220 Metropolitan Corps Medal Clasps: CC.
Medal Roll Reference: WO100/225/127 Private 6 General Hospital. To Base on expiration of contract 23 June 1900.
SMITH, W. Private 1105 Birmingham Corps Medal Clasps: NAT.
Medal Roll Reference: WO100/225/120 Orderly 4 General Hospital. Sent to England for discharge time expired 28 November 1900.
SMITH, W. Private 1157 Birchwood Corps Medal Clasps: CC OFS.
Medal Roll Reference: WO100/225/151 Orderly 9 General Hospital. To Base Detail 15 April 1901.
SMITH, W. R. Private 808 Oldham Corps Medal Clasps: CC OFS.
Medal Roll Reference: WO100/225/117 Orderly 3 General Hospital. Transferred to Base Detail RAMC.
SNAPE, G. Private 1516 Preston Corps Medal Clasps: TVL.
Medal Roll Reference: WO100/225/169 Orderly 17 General Hospital. Transferred to Pietermaritzburg 30 November 1900.
SNOWDEN, E. Private 1166 Leeds Corps Medal Clasps: CC OFS.
Medal Roll Reference: WO100/225/156 Orderly 10 General Hospital. To Base 10 October 1900.
SNOWDEN, G. F. Private 1164 1892 Leeds Corps Medal Clasps: CC OFS SA01.
Medal Roll Reference: WO100/225/87+117+136 Orderly 8 General Hospital. To England 31 August 1900. 3 General Hospital. Transferred to Base Detail RAMC. Home 21 June 1901.
SOARS, G. F. Private 487 Leicester Corps Medal Clasps: CC OFS.
Medal Roll Reference: WO100/225/151 Orderly 9 General Hospital. To Base Detail 7 August 1900.
SOLLY, H. Private 729 Leicester Corps Medal Clasps: CC WITT.
Medal Roll Reference: WO100/225/195 Orderly 23 Field Hospital. Discharged time expired.
SONLEY, F. Private 993 Hull Corps Medal Clasps: TVL NAT.
Medal Roll Reference: WO100/225/131 Orderly 7 General Hospital. To England time expired.

SONNENFIELD, M. W. Private 310 St John Ambulance Brigade (NFB) Medal Clasps: CC. NFBUAD Medal.
Medal Roll Reference: WO100/130/222 Corporal Imperial Yeomanry Hospital Deelfontein.
SOUTHWOOD, C. Private 284 Metropolitan Corps Medal Clasps: CC.
Medal Roll Reference: WO100/130/222 Sergeant Imperial Yeomanry Hospital Deelfontein.
SPEECHLEY, Walter Robert Private 370 Kettering Corps Medal Clasps: CC OFS.
Medal Roll Reference: WO100/225/73+136 Orderly 6 Stationary Hospital. 8 General Hospital. To England 20 July 1900.
SPEERS, W. N. Private 1800 Birmingham Corps (Birmingham City Division) Medal Clasps: CC SA01.
Medal Roll Reference: WO100/225/64+89 Orderly Base Hospital Wynberg. Time expired 15 August 1901.
SPENDLOVE, H. C. Private 387 Birmingham Corps Medal Clasps: CC.
Medal Roll Reference: WO100/130/223 Private Imperial Yeomanry Hospital Deelfontein.
SPICER, J. F. Private 935 Northampton Corps Medal Clasps: OFS TVL NAT SA01.
Medal Roll Reference: WO100/225/39+103+131+195 Orderly 7 General Hospital. Transferred to 23 Field Hospital Harrismith. Discharged time expired.
SPOTSWOOD, J. G. Sergeant 1558 St John Ambulance Brigade Medal Clasps: CC OFS TVL SA01 SA02.
Medal Roll Reference: WO100/225/64 WO100/271/193+261 Orderly Base Hospital Wynberg. South African Constabulary A Division Medical Sergeant A1944. Discharged 17 April 1902.
SPOWAGE, Seymour Private 513 Haslingden Corps Medal Clasps: CC OFS.
Medal Roll Reference: WO100/225/151 Orderly 9 General Hospital. To Base Detail 7 August 1900.
SQUIRES, David Private 95 Christchurch Division Medal Clasps: CC OFS.
Medal Roll Reference: WO100/225/236 Private Portland Hospital. To England contract expired.
STAFFORD, A. Private 562 Birmingham Corps Medal Clasps: CC OFS.
Medal Roll Reference: WO100/225/151 Orderly 9 General Hospital. To Base Detail 7 August 1900.
STANLEY, H. R. Private 39 Metropolitan Corps Medal Clasps: CC OFS TVL.
Medal Roll Reference: WO100/225/112A Orderly 6 General Hospital.
STANLEY, P. Private 342 Ilkeston Corps Medal Clasps: CC.
Medal Roll Reference: WO100/130/223 Private Imperial Yeomanry Hospital Deelfontein.
STANSFIELD, J. Private 1332 Royton Division Medal Clasps: CC.
Medal Roll Reference: WO100/225/57+160 Orderly 11 General Hospital. To Kimberley 29 August 1900. 13 General Hospital. To England on termination of engagement
STANSFIELD, J. W. Private 1409 Dewsbury Corps Medal Clasps: No Clasps.
Medal Roll Reference: WO100/225/60 Orderly 14 General Hospital. To HS *Simla* for duty 14 November 1900.
STANTON, G. E. Private 1807 Welbeck Division Medal Clasps: CC.
Medal Roll Reference: WO100/225/81+110 Private 26 Stationary Hospital. 1 General Hospital.
STANTON, John William Private 1827 Welbeck Division Medal Clasps: CC.
Medal Roll Reference: WO100/225/81+110 Private 26 Stationary Hospital. 1 General Hospital.
STARKEY, W. B. Private 800 1561 Barnoldswick Division Medal Clasps: CC OFS TVL.
Medal Roll Reference: WO100/225/127 Private 6 General Hospital. To Base on expiration of contract 3 September 1900.
STARKIE, A. Private 801 Barnoldswick Division Medal Clasps: CC.
Medal Roll Reference: WO100/225/127 Private 6 General Hospital Invalided 5 September 1900.
STARKIE, J. Private 842 Preston Corps Medal Clasps: CC OFS TVL.
Medal Roll Reference: WO100/225/127 Private 6 General Hospital. To Base on expiration of contract 22 November 1900. J. STARKEY on QSA Medal Roll.

STATHAM, A. L. Private 832 Penrith Division Medal Clasps: CC OFS.
Medal Roll Reference: WO100/225/117 Orderly 3 General Hospital. Transferred to Base Detail RAMC.

STAYLEY, A. Private 763 Abram Colliery Division Medal Clasps: CC OFS TVL.
Medal Roll Reference: WO100/225/194 Orderly 22 Field Hospital.

STEAD, P. Private 1709 Leeds Corps Medal Clasps: CC OFS TVL SA01.
Medal Roll Reference: WO100/225/68 Orderly 18 General Hospital. To England 27 May 1900.

STEELE, W. Private 1023 Oldham Corps Medal Clasps: OFS NAT.
Medal Roll Reference: WO100/225/181+193 Orderly 14 Stationary Hospital. Attached 21 Field Hospital. Discharged.

STEPHENSON, John Private 595 Colne Division Medal Clasps: CC.
Medal Roll Reference: WO100/225/124 Orderly 5 General Hospital (RNASBR Long Service Medal 633 Res Wardmaster).

STEVENS, F. T. Private 1822 Hull Corps Medal Clasps: CC OFS SA01.
Medal Roll Reference: WO100/225/87+117 Orderly 3 General Hospital. Transferred to Base Detail RAMC. Home 21 June 1901.

STEVENS, Thomas Private 304 St John Ambulance Brigade (NFB Cockington) Medal Clasps: CC SA01. NFBUAD Medal.
Medal Roll Reference: WO100/130/223 Private Imperial Yeomanry Hospital Deelfontein.

STEVENSON, John W. Private 373 Ironbridge Corps Medal Clasps: CC OFS SA01.
Medal Roll Reference: WO100/130/223 WO100/273/151+347 Private Imperial Yeomanry Hospital Deelfontein. South African Constabulary E Division Trooper E3037. Service in South African Constabulary 4 May to 30 November 1901. Discharged inefficiency 31December 1901.

STEWART, B. Y. Private 433 Metropolitan Corps Medal Clasps: OFS TVL NAT SA01.
Medal Roll Reference: WO100/225/91+131 Orderly Attached. To RAMC 7 General Hospital. To England time expired.

STOCKS, W. T. Private 1737 Metropolitan Corps Medal Clasps: No Clasps.
Medal Roll Reference: WO100/225/146. Orderly.

STODD, P. Sergeant 372 Ironbridge Corps Medal Clasps: OFS TVL NAT.
Medal Roll Reference: WO100/225/131 Supply Officer 7 General Hospital. To England time expired.

STONE, J. Private 615 Metropolitan Corps Medal Clasps: CC OFS.
Medal Roll Reference: WO100/225/156 Orderly 10 General Hospital. To Base 13 June 1901.

STONE, William Henry Private 127 1439 Metropolitan Corps Medal Clasps: No Clasps. China Medal.
Medal Roll Reference: WO100/225/37 Orderly HS *Maine*. On medal roll for HS *Maine* for China WO100/96/38+39.

STONIER, Thomas Private 367 North Staffs Corps Medal Clasps: CC OFS TVL.
Medal Roll Reference: WO100/225/238 Private Van Alen American Field Hospital. Died typhoid Johannesburg 14 July 1900.

STOPFORD, S. Private 1082 Preston Corps Medal Clasps: OFS NAT.
Medal Roll Reference: WO100/225/182+193 Orderly 14 Stationary Hospital. Attached 21 Field Hospital. Discharged.

STOTT, E. Private 1644 Newchurch Division Medal Clasps: No Clasps.
Medal Roll Reference: WO100/225/146 Orderly.

STOTT, J. Private 1466 Oldham Corps Medal Clasps: No Clasps.
Medal Roll Reference: WO100/225/182 Orderly 14 Stationary Hospital and Middleburg.

STRATFORD, Samuel Private 96 Withernsea Division Medal Clasps: CC OFS.
Medal Roll Reference: WO100/225/236 Private Portland Hospital. To England contract expired.

STRONG, H. Private 795 Barrowford Division Medal Clasps: No Clasps.
Medal Roll Reference: WO100/225/38 Orderly.

STROUD, G. H. R. Private 281 Ebbw Vale Division Medal Clasps: CC OFS TVL.
Medal Roll Reference: WO100/225/127 Private 6 General Hospital. To Base Invalided 22 July 1900.

STUBBS, J. A. Private 48 Metropolitan Corps Medal Clasps: CC OFS.
Medal Roll Reference: WO100/225/117 Orderly 3 General Hospital. Transferred to Base Detail RAMC.

STURGESS, W. Private 1680 Northampton Corps Medal Clasps: CC OFS SA01.
Medal Roll Reference: WO100/225/136 Orderly 8 General Hospital. To England 1 June 1900.

STUTTARD, W. Private 1234 Colne Division Medal Clasps: CC.
Medal Roll Reference: WO100/225/124 Orderly 5 General Hospital.

SUGDEN, B. Private 1517 Bradford Corps Medal Clasps: No Clasps.
Medal Roll Reference: WO100/225/120 Orderly 4 General Hospital. Sent to England for discharge time expired 28 November 1900.

SUMMERSCALES, T. E. Private 71 Dewsbury Corps Medal Clasps: CC OFS.
Medal Roll Reference: WO100/225/117 Orderly 3 General Hospital. Transferred to Base Detail RAMC.

SUMNER, E. Private 1343 Bolton Corps Medal Clasps: CC.
Medal Roll Reference: WO100/225/160 Orderly 13 General Hospital. To England expired contract 27 November 1900.

SUMNER, W. T. R. Private 728 Great Eastern Railway Corps Medal Clasps: CC WITT.
Medal Roll Reference: WO100/225/195 Orderly 23 Field Hospital. Discharged time expired.

SUTCLIFFE, H. Private 803 Barnoldswick Division Medal Clasps: CC OFS.
Medal Roll Reference: WO100/225/151 Orderly 9 General Hospital. To Base Detail 6 March 1901.

SUTHERLAND, A. Sergeant 1487 1861 Leeds Corps Medal Clasps: CC OFS TVL NAT.
Medal Roll Reference: WO100/225/68 Supply Officer 18 General Hospital. To England 30 August 1900. 17 General Hospital. Transferred to Base Detail Cape Town 13 July 1901.

SUTTON, George Thomas Private 1131 Bolton Corps Medal Clasps: CC. China Medal.
Medal Roll Reference: WO100/225/53+248 Orderly HS *Maine*. On medal roll for HS *Maine* for China WO100/96/38+39.

SWARBRICK, R. Private 532 Preston Corps Medal Clasps: CC OFS TVL.
Medal Roll Reference: WO100/225/232 Private Langman Hospital.

SWETTENHAM, J. A. Private 671 Manchester Post Office Division Medal Clasps: CC OFS TVL SA01.
Medal Roll Reference: WO100/130/259+263 Corporal Imperial Yeomanry Field Hospital and Bearer Company.

SWINDALL, Harold B. A. Private 1513 Wellingborough Corps Medal Clasps: CC OFS TVL SA01.
Medal Roll Reference: WO100/225/182+183 WO100/271/154 Orderly 14 Stationary Hospital and 17 Stationary Hospital Middleburg. To Base 24 November 1900. South African Constabulary A Division Trooper A 1877. Discharged 27 August 1901.

SYKES, F. Private 1638 Barrowford Division Medal Clasps: No Clasps.
Medal Roll Reference: WO100/225/146 Orderly.

SYKES, H. Private 1456 Oldham Corps Medal Clasps: CC OFS TVL.
Medal Roll Reference: WO100/225/166+184 Orderly 15 General Hospital. Transferred to Pretoria 29 August 1900. 17 Stationary Hospital. To Base 24 November 1900.

SYKES, L. Private 69 Leeds Corps Medal Clasps: CC OFS.
Medal Roll Reference: WO100/225/117 Orderly 3 General Hospital. Transferred to Base Detail RAMC.

SYSON, J. Private 224 Ilkeston Corps Medal Clasps: CC JOH DIA WITT.
Medal Roll Reference: WO100/225/202 Orderly 20 Bearer Company. Discharged time expired 1 August 1900.

TABOR, W. Private 161 Isle of Wight Corps Medal Clasps: CC.
Medal Roll Reference: WO100/225/64+70 Orderly Base Hospital Wynberg. Transferred sick to 5 General Hospital Cape Town.

TADMAN, J. L. Private 773 Great Eastern Railway Corps Medal Clasps: CC.
Medal Roll Reference: WO100/225/57 Orderly 11 General Hospital. To England on termination of engagement.

TAPPER, H. D. Private 948 Metropolitan Corps Medal Clasps: CC OFS.
Medal Roll Reference: WO100/225/131+195 Orderly 7 General Hospital. Transferred to Harrismith 23 Field Hospital. Discharged time expired.

TARBOX, A. M. Private 792 Metropolitan Corps Medal Clasps: CC OFS TVL.
Medal Roll Reference: WO100/225/127 Private 6 General Hospital. To Base on expiration of contract 3 September 1900.

TARLTON, Luther Private 153 Birchwood Corps Medal Clasps: CC OFS TVL.
Medal Roll Reference: WO100/225/64+70 Orderly Base Hospital Wynberg 3 Hospital Train. To Base Detail RAMC Cape Town for England.

TASSELL, F. Private 868 Wellingborough Corps Medal Clasps: CC OFS TVL.
Medal Roll Reference: WO100/225/41+112A Orderly 6 General Hospital.

TATTERSALL, A. Private 1044 Nelson Corps Medal Clasps: NAT.
Medal Roll Reference: WO100/225/166 Orderly 15 General Hospital. Transferred to England 14 September 1900.

TATTERSALL, W. Private 585 Bolton Corps Medal Clasps: CC SA01.
Medal Roll Reference: WO100/225/124 Orderly 5 General Hospital.

TAYLOR, A. Private 1799 Birmingham Corps Medal Clasps: CC.
Medal Roll Reference: WO100/225/64 Orderly Base Hospital Wynberg.

TAYLOR, A. F. Private 453 Wellingborough Corps Medal Clasps: CC OFS.
Medal Roll Reference: WO100/225/136 Orderly 8 General Hospital. To England 20 July 1900.

TAYLOR, C. R. Private 1719 Oldham Corps Medal Clasps: CC OFS TVL.
Medal Roll Reference: WO100/225/171 Orderly 20 General Hospital Joined from Base Detail. To England for discharge.

TAYLOR, D. Private 933 Oldham Corps Medal Clasps: NAT.
Medal Roll Reference: WO100/225/131 Orderly 7 General Hospital. Invalided to England.

TAYLOR, Edwin Sergeant 703 Haslingden Corps Medal Clasps: CC WITT.
Medal Roll Reference: WO100/225/195 Supernumerary Officer 23 Field Hospital. Discharged time expired.

TAYLOR, F. Private 120 Nuneaton Division Medal Clasps: No Clasps.
Medal Roll Reference: WO100/225/40 Orderly.

TAYLOR, F. Private 754 Hebden Bridge Corps Medal Clasps: CC OFS.
Medal Roll Reference: WO100/225/204 Orderly Attached 22 Bearer Company.

TAYLOR, G. Private 576 Oldham Corps Medal Clasps: CC.
Medal Roll Reference: WO100/225/73 Orderly 6 Stationary Hospital.

TAYLOR, G. Private 817 Padiham Division Medal Clasps: CC.
Medal Roll Reference: WO100/225/168+178 Orderly 16 General Hospital. Transferred to 7 Stationary Hospital 4 June 1900. Sent to England September 1900.

TAYLOR, H. Private 1633 Nelson Corps Medal Clasps: OFS TVL.
Medal Roll Reference: WO100/225/182 Orderly 14 Stationary Hospital. 7 Ambulance Train. 3 Ambulance Train.

TAYLOR, J. Private 236 Ironbridge Corps Medal Clasps: CC TVL SA01 SA02.
Medal Roll Reference: WO100/225/41+127 Private 6 General Hospital. To Base on expiration of contract 23 June 1900.

TAYLOR, J. Private 401 Accrington Corps Medal Clasps: NAT.
Medal Roll Reference: WO100/225/132 Orderly 7 General Hospital. To England time expired.

TAYLOR, J. Private 507 Hebden Bridge Corps Medal Clasps: CC OFS.
Medal Roll Reference: WO100/225/151 Orderly 9 General Hospital. To Base Detail 8 August 1900.
TAYLOR, J. Private 1197 Oldham Corps Medal Clasps: CC.
Medal Roll Reference: WO100/225/110 Orderly 1 General Hospital.
TAYLOR, R. Private 695 Clitheroe Division Medal Clasps: CC OFS.
Medal Roll Reference: WO100/225/156 Orderly 10 General Hospital. To Base 7 August 1900.
TAYLOR, R. Private 1647 Edenfield Division Medal Clasps: No Clasps.
Medal Roll Reference: WO100/225/147 Orderly.
TAYLOR, R. W. Private 1426 Birchwood Corps Medal Clasps: No Clasps.
Medal Roll Reference: WO100/225/60 Orderly 14 General Hospital. To HS *Simla* for duty 14 November 1900.
TAYLOR, S. Private 654 Derby Division Medal Clasps: CC OFS TVL.
Medal Roll Reference: WO100/130/267 Private Imperial Yeomanry Field Hospital and Bearer Company Transferred to Maitland Yeomanry Hospital 3 September 1900.
TAYLOR, S. Private 1087 Haverhill Division Medal Clasps: NAT.
Medal Roll Reference: WO100/225/66 Orderly 13 Stationary Hospital. To HS *Dunera* 18 December 1900.
TAYLOR, W. Private 1452 Accrington Corps Medal Clasps: NAT.
Medal Roll Reference: WO100/225/166+184 Orderly 15 General Hospital. Transferred to Pretoria 29 August 1900. 17 Stationary Hospital. To Base 24 November 1900.
TAYLOR, W. G. Private 550 Metropolitan Corps Medal Clasps: CC OFS.
Medal Roll Reference: WO100/225/152 Orderly 9 General Hospital. To Base Detail 23 June 1900.
TAYLOR, W. H. Private 1500 1767 Radcliffe Division Medal Clasps: CC.
Medal Roll Reference: WO100/225/120+174 Orderly 4 General Hospital Sent to England for discharge time expired 28 November 1900. 21 General Hospital.
TAYLOR, William Private 1538 Oldham Corps Medal Clasps: CC OFS TVL.
Medal Roll Reference: WO100/225/124+169 Orderly 5 General Hospital 10 General Hospital. To Base 29 January 1901 17 General Hospital. Died of Disease Standerton 15 May 1901.
TEALE, C. E. Private 78 Metropolitan Corps Medal Clasps: CC OFS.
Medal Roll Reference: WO100/225/117 Orderly 3 General Hospital. Transferred to Base Detail RAMC.
TEALE, G. H. Private 76 Metropolitan Corps Medal Clasps: CC OFS.
Medal Roll Reference: WO100/225/117 Orderly 3 General Hospital. Transferred to Base Detail RAMC.
TEAR, A. Private 1763 Northampton Corps Medal Clasps: CC SA01.
Medal Roll Reference: WO100/225/57+85 Orderly 11 General Hospital. To England on termination of engagement.
TEMPEST, E. Private 1486 Leeds Corps Medal Clasps: No Clasps.
Medal Roll Reference: WO100/225/120 Orderly 4 General Hospital Sent to England for discharge time expired 28 November 1900.
TERRY, William Henry Private 231 Dewsbury Corps Medal Clasps: CC JOH DIA WITT.
Medal Roll Reference: WO100/225/202 Orderly 20 Bearer Company. Discharged time expired 1 August 1900 (MSM RAMC Sgt Mjr 28834 LG 22 February 1919).
THIRTLE, W. Private 727 Great Eastern Railway Corps Medal Clasps: CC WITT.
Medal Roll Reference: WO100/225/193 Orderly Attached 21 Field Hospital. Discharged.
THOMAS, E. Private 1004 Blackpool Division Medal Clasps: NAT.
Medal Roll Reference: WO100/225/132 Orderly 7 General Hospital. To England time expired.
THOMAS, F. Private 368 North Staffs Corps Medal Clasps: CC OFS.
Medal Roll Reference: WO100/225/132 Orderly 7 General Hospital. To England time expired.

THOMAS, F. Private 556 Birmingham Corps Medal Clasps: CC OFS.
Medal Roll Reference: WO100/225/152 Orderly 9 General Hospital. To Base Detail 7 August 1900.
THOMAS, G. Private 331 Ebbw Vale Division Medal Clasps: CC.
Medal Roll Reference: WO100/130/223 Private Imperial Yeomanry Hospital Deelfontein.
THOMPSON, G. Private 1872 Leeds Corps Medal Clasps: CC.
Medal Roll Reference: WO100/225/110 Orderly 1 General Hospital.
THOMPSON, W. Private 677 Radcliffe Division Medal Clasps: CC.
Medal Roll Reference: WO100/225/57 Orderly 11 General Hospital. To England on termination of engagement.
THOMPSON, W. A. Private 239 Wellingborough Corps Medal Clasps: CC OFS.
Medal Roll Reference: WO100/225/202 Orderly 20 Bearer Company. Invalided to England 30 June 1900.
THORNBER, William H. Private 450 Burnley Division Medal Clasps: CC OFS.
Medal Roll Reference: WO100/225/136 Private 8 General Hospital. Died of disease Bloemfontein 3 June 1900.
THORNEYCROFT, E. Private 434 Metropolitan Corps Medal Clasps: CC OFS.
Medal Roll Reference: WO100/225/136 Orderly 8 General Hospital. To England 20 July 1900.
THORNHILL, J. Private 1711 Leeds Corps Medal Clasps: CC OFS TVL.
Medal Roll Reference: WO100/225/171 Orderly 20 General Hospital. Joined from Base Detail. To England for discharge.
THORNLEY, Oliver Private 1334 Royton Division Medal Clasps: CC.
Medal Roll Reference: WO100/225/160 Orderly 13 General Hospital. Died of disease Wynberg Base Hospital Cape Town 8 September 1900.
THORNLEY, T. Private 1573 Bolton Corps Medal Clasps: CC.
Medal Roll Reference: WO100/225/110+174 Orderly 1 General Hospital. 21 General Hospital.
THORNTON, J. D. Private 1313 Keighley Corps Medal Clasps: CC TVL.
Medal Roll Reference: WO100/224/172 Private Rhodesian Field Force Hospital.
THORNTON, William Private 1702 Crewe Division Medal Clasps: CC OFS TVL.
Medal Roll Reference: WO100/225/171 Orderly 20 General Hospital. Died of disease Elandsfontein 1 March 1901.
THORPE, D. Private 752 Hebden Bridge Corps Medal Clasps: CC OFS TVL.
Medal Roll Reference: WO100/225/194 Orderly 22 Field Hospital.
TILDESLEY, W. Private 493 North Staffs Corps Medal Clasps: NAT.
Medal Roll Reference: WO100/225/66 Supply Officer 13 Stationary Hospital. To HS *Dunera* 18 December 1900.
TINCOMB, A. H. Private 715 Mill Bay Division Medal Clasps: CC WITT.
Medal Roll Reference: WO100/225/193 Orderly Attached 21 Field Hospital. Discharged.
TINKER, Arthur Private 1801 Welbeck Division Medal Clasps: CC.
Medal Roll Reference: WO100/225/174 Orderly 21 General Hospital.
TITCHINER, A. T. Private 479 Metropolitan Corps Medal Clasps: CC SA01.
Medal Roll Reference: WO100/225/124 Orderly 5 General Hospital.
TITE, J. R. Private 349 Leicester Corps Medal Clasps: CC OFS.
Medal Roll Reference: WO100/225/136 Orderly 8 General Hospital. To England 23 January 1901.
TITHERINGTON, B. Private 146 Colne Division Medal Clasps: CC OFS TVL.
Medal Roll Reference: WO100/225/64+70 Orderly Base Hospital Wynberg. 3 Hospital Train. To Base Detail RAMC Cape Town for England.
TITHERINGTON, James Private 1232 Colne Division Medal Clasps: CC.
Medal Roll Reference: WO100/225/124 Orderly 5 General Hospital (RNASBR Long service medal and bar 127 SBS2 Cl). TITTERINGTON, J. on QSA medal roll.
TODD, J. Private 1716 Tibshelf Corps Medal Clasps: CC OFS TVL.

Medal Roll Reference: WO100/225/171 Orderly 20 General Hospital Joined from Base Detail. To England for discharge.

TOLLAFIELD, J. Private 74 Metropolitan Corps Medal Clasps: CC OFS.
Medal Roll Reference: WO100/225/117 Orderly 3 General Hospital. Transferred to Base Detail RAMC.

TOLSON, C. H. Private 828 Dewsbury Corps Medal Clasps: No Clasps.
Medal Roll Reference: WO100/225/41 Orderly.

TOLTON, Albert Edward Private 600 Dewsbury Corps Medal Clasps: CC OFS.
Medal Roll Reference: WO100/225/152 Orderly 9 General Hospital. To Base Detail 23 July 1901.

TOMPKINS, J. Private 867 Wellingborough Corps Medal Clasps: OFS.
Medal Roll Reference: WO100/225/185 Orderly 2 General Hospital Attached to 3rd Highland Brigade Field Hospital from 5 May 1900. Transferred sick to Kroonstad 1 June 1900.

TOWERS, T. Sergeant 1083 1705 Preston Corps Medal Clasps: OFS TVL NAT.
Medal Roll Reference: WO100/225/120 Orderly 4 General Hospital Sent to England for discharge time expired 9 September 1900. 20 General Hospital. Joined from Base Detail. To England for discharge.

TOWLER, J. B. Private 1349 Bolton Corps Medal Clasps: CC.
Medal Roll Reference: WO100/225/160 Orderly 13 General Hospital. To England expired contract 27 November 1900.

TOWNLEY, G. Private 1453 Oldham Corps Medal Clasps: CC OFS TVL.
Medal Roll Reference: WO100/225/182+184 Orderly 14 Stationary Hospital. 17 Stationary Hospital. To Base 24 November 1900.

TRANT, B. P. Private 277 Metropolitan Corps Medal Clasps: CC SA01.
Medal Roll Reference: WO100/225/110+127+WO100/224/195 Orderly 1 General Hospital. 6 General Hospital. To Base Invalided 1 May 1900.

TRANTER, T. Private 209 Ironbridge Corps Medal Clasps: CC.
Medal Roll Reference: WO100/225/127 Private 6 General Hospital. To Base on expiration of contract 23 June 1900.

TRANTRUM, R. Private 427 Metropolitan Corps Medal Clasps: CC OFS.
Medal Roll Reference: WO100/225/136 Orderly 8 General Hospital. To England 20 July 1900.

TRESCOWTHICK, John Charles Private 1134 Blackpool Division Medal Clasps: CC. China Medal.
Medal Roll Reference: WO100/225/53+248 Orderly HS *Maine*. On medal roll for HS *Maine* for China WO100/96/38+39.

TRIMMER, Alfred John Sergeant Major 302 Metropolitan Corps (NFB Bedford) Medal Clasps: CC. NFBUAD Medal.
Medal Roll Reference: WO100/130/223 Acting Sergeant Major Imperial Yeomanry Hospital Deelfontein.

TROTT, C. Private 1574 Bolton Corps Medal Clasps: CC.
Medal Roll Reference: WO100/225/110 Orderly 1 General Hospital.

TRUSLOVE, F. W. Private 377 Handsworth & Smethwick Corps Medal Clasps: CC OFS.
Medal Roll Reference: WO100/225/136 Orderly 8 General Hospital. To England 20 July 1900.

TUNSTALL, George H. Private 1475 Haslingden Corps Medal Clasps: NAT.
Medal Roll Reference: WO100/225/167 Orderly 15 General Hospital. Transferred to England 26 November 1900.

TURNER, J. H. Sergeant 504 1793 Kendal Division Medal Clasps: OFS NAT KSA01 KSA02.
Medal Roll Reference: WO100/225/66+111+152+WO100/352/19 Supply Officer 13 Stationary Hospital (Princess Christian Hospital Pinetown Natal) 30 March 1900 to 18 December 1900. To HS *Dunera* 18 December 1900. 1 General Hospital. 9 General Hospital.

TWEEDALE, W. Private 253 Rochdale Corps Medal Clasps: NAT.
Medal Roll Reference: WO100/225/75 Orderly Princess Christian Hospital Train.

TYLER, C. W. Private 940 New Farnley Division Medal Clasps: NAT.
Medal Roll Reference: WO100/225/132 Orderly 7 General Hospital. To England time expired.
TYMMS, P. Sergeant 418 Handsworth & Smethwick Corps Medal Clasps: CC.
Medal Roll Reference: WO100/130/223 Sergeant Imperial Yeomanry Hospital Deelfontein.
UNDERDOWN, William Henry Private 164 Ramsgate Corps Medal Clasps: CC.
Medal Roll Reference: WO100/225/42 Orderly.
UNSWORTH, R. Private 1247 Preston Corps Medal Clasps: CC OFS.
Medal Roll Reference: WO100/225/136 Orderly 8 General Hospital. To England 10 October 1900.
UTTLEY, W. S. Private 699 Hebden Bridge Corps Medal Clasps: CC.
Medal Roll Reference: WO100/225/57 Orderly 11 General Hospital. To England on termination of engagement.
UZZELL, William John Private 295 Great Western Railway Medal Clasps: CC OFS TVL SA01 SA02.
Medal Roll Reference: WO100/130/224 WO100/272/252+371 Private Imperial Yeomanry Hospital Deelfontein SAC C Division Trooper C2111 Discharged 26 October 1902.
VARLEY, H. Private 1158 Birchwood Corps Medal Clasps: CC OFS TVL.
Medal Roll Reference: WO100/225/64+70 Orderly Base Hospital Wynberg. 3 Hospital Train. Sick to 5 General Hospital Cape Town.
VARLY, W. H. Private 1279 Brierfield Division Medal Clasps: CC OFS.
Medal Roll Reference: WO100/225/156 Orderly 10 General Hospital. To Base 10 October 1900.
VAUGHAN, Frederick Henry Sergeant 1795 Hull Corps Medal Clasps: CC.
Medal Roll Reference: WO100/225/174 Supply Officer 21 General Hospital.
VAUGHAN, W. H. Private 825 North Staffs Corps Medal Clasps: CC OFS TVL.
Medal Roll Reference: WO100/225/127 Private 6 General Hospital. Locally discharged on expiration of contract 31 March 1901.
VENN, Charles H. Private 473 Bolton Corps Medal Clasps: NAT.
Medal Roll Reference: WO100/225/66 Orderly 13 Stationary Hospital. To SS *Formosa* 6 December 1900.
VICKERS, F. Private 1348 Bolton Corps Medal Clasps: CC.
Medal Roll Reference: WO100/225/160 Orderly 13 General Hospital. To England expired contract 27 November 1900.
VICKERS, R. Private 1048 Dalton-in-Furness Division Medal Clasps: NAT.
Medal Roll Reference: WO100/225/167 Orderly 15 General Hospital. Invalided to England 17 September 1900.
VICKERY, J. A. Private 736 Redruth Division Medal Clasps: CC OFS TVL.
Medal Roll Reference: WO100/130/266 Private Imperial Yeomanry Field Hospital and Bearer Company.
VINTER, A. Private 347 Lincoln Adult School Division Medal Clasps: CC.
Medal Roll Reference: WO100/130/224 Corporal Imperial Yeomanry Hospital Deelfontein.
WADDINGTON, W. Private 853 Hebden Bridge Corps Medal Clasps: CC.
Medal Roll Reference: WO100/225/178 Orderly 7 Stationary Hospital. Sent to England September 1900.
WADE, R. E. J. Private 1698 Leicester Corps Medal Clasps: CC OFS TVL SA01.
Medal Roll Reference: WO100/225/85+187 Orderly 18 Brigade Field Hospital. Joined 20 March 1901. Left 30 May 1901 for discharge.
WADSWORTH, J. W. Private 1413 Hebden Bridge Corps Medal Clasps: No Clasps.
Medal Roll Reference: WO100/225/60 Orderly 14 General Hospital. To SS *Manhattan* for duty 28 November 1900.
WAINSCOTT, H. Private 1120 Sheffield Corps Medal Clasps: NAT.
Medal Roll Reference: WO100/225/66 Orderly 13 Stationary Hospital. To HS *Dunera* 18 December 1900.

WAINWRIGHT, A. P. Corporal 1168 Leeds Corps Medal Clasps: CC TVL.
Medal Roll Reference: WO100/224/172 Corporal Rhodesian Field Force Hospital.
WAINWRIGHT, J. Sergeant 177 1862 Leeds Corps Medal Clasps: CC.
Medal Roll Reference: WO100/225/73+175 Orderly 6 Stationary Hospital. 3 Stationary Hospital
De Aar.
WAKEFORD, E. Private 579 Oldham Corps Medal Clasps: CC TVL.
Medal Roll Reference: WO100/225/196 Orderly 24 Field Hospital. To Base expiration of contract
6 January 1901.
WALDERGRAVE, F. J. Private 267 Portsmouth Division Medal Clasps: CC OFS TVL.
Medal Roll Reference: WO100/225/64 Orderly Base Hospital Wynberg. 6 General Hospital. To
Base on expiration of contract 17 December1900.
WALDRON, C. Private 583 Bolton Corps Medal Clasps: CC.
Medal Roll Reference: WO100/225/124 Orderly 5 General Hospital.
WALDRON, F. Private 586 Bolton Corps Medal Clasps: CC.
Medal Roll Reference: WO100/225/124 Orderly 5 General Hospital.
WALKDEN, S. 1st Class Sergeant 137 Bolton Corps Medal Clasps: No Clasps.
Medal Roll Reference: WO100/225/5 Orderly.
WALKER, A. Private 829 Dewsbury Corps Medal Clasps: No Clasps.
Medal Roll Reference: WO100/225/45 Orderly.
WALKER, F. J. Private 294 Swindon Division Medal Clasps: CC.
Medal Roll Reference: WO100/130/224 Private Imperial Yeomanry Hospital Deelfontein.
WALKER, George Frederick William Private 969 Dudley Corps Medal Clasps: OFS NAT.
Medal Roll Reference: WO100/225/132 Orderly 7 General Hospital. Transferred to Harrismith.
WALKER, J. Private 943 Clitheroe Division Medal Clasps: NAT.
Medal Roll Reference: WO100/225/66 Orderly 13 Stationary Hospital. To SS *Montrose* 8 September
1900.
WALKER, T. Private 937 Hapton Division Medal Clasps: NAT.
Medal Roll Reference: WO100/225/132 Orderly 7 General Hospital. To England time expired.
WALKER, T. 1st Class Sergeant 690 Nelson Corps Medal Clasps: CC WITT.
Medal Roll Reference: WO100/225/195 Supernumerary Officer 23 Field Hospital. Discharged time
expired.
WALKER, W. Private 1428 Derby Division Medal Clasps: No Clasps.
Medal Roll Reference: WO100/225/60 Orderly 14 General Hospital. Invalided to England on HS
Simla 14 November 1900.
WALLBANK, T. Private 537 Preston Corps Medal Clasps: NAT.
Medal Roll Reference: WO100/225/66 Orderly 13 Stationary Hospital. To HS *Simla* 16 August
1900.
WALLBANK, W. H. Sergeant 1133 1492 Bolton Corps Medal Clasps: CC OFS TVL.
Medal Roll Reference: WO100/225/53+167+184+248 Supply Officer HS *Maine* 15 General
Hospital. Transferred to Pretoria 29 August 1900. 17 Stationary Hospital. To Base 24 November
1900.
WALMSLEY, A. Private 1366 Preston Corps Medal Clasps: CC.
Medal Roll Reference: WO100/225/71+160 Orderly 13 General Hospital. 11 General Hospital. To
Kimberley 29 August 1900. To England on termination of engagement
WALMSLEY, G. Private 580 Bolton Corps Medal Clasps: CC.
Medal Roll Reference: WO100/225/124 Orderly 5 General Hospital.
WALMSLEY, W. Private 568 Bolton Corps Medal Clasps: CC.
Medal Roll Reference: WO100/225/73 Orderly 6 General Hospital.
WALSH, P. Private 627 Dowlais Division Medal Clasps: CC OFS.
Medal Roll Reference: WO100/225/156 Orderly 10 General Hospital. To Base 22 June 1900.

WALSH, W. H. Private 1325 Metropolitan Corps Medal Clasps: CC.
Medal Roll Reference: WO100/225/71+160 Orderly 13 General Hospital. To Kimberley 29 August 1900. 11 General Hospital. To England on termination of engagement
WALTERS, T. Private 381 Birmingham Corps Medal Clasps: CC.
Medal Roll Reference: WO100/130/224 Private Imperial Yeomanry Hospital Deelfontein.
WALTON, W. Sergeant 953 Nelson Corps Medal Clasps: TVL NAT.
Medal Roll Reference: WO100/225/132 Supply Officer 7 General Hospital. Invalided to England. E. WALTON on QSA Medal Roll.
WALTON, F. L. A. Private 1864 Leeds Corps Medal Clasps: CC.
Medal Roll Reference: WO100/225/72 Orderly 24 Stationary Hospital. From Base Detail. Transferred to Base Detail 29 June 1901.
WALTON, W. H. Private 482 Great Eastern Railway Corps Medal Clasps: CC OFS.
Medal Roll Reference: WO100/225/152 Orderly 9 General Hospital. To Base Detail 7 August 1900.
WANT, W. H. Private 383 Birmingham Corps Medal Clasps: CC.
Medal Roll Reference: WO100/130/224 Private Imperial Yeomanry Hospital Deelfontein.
WARD, A. E. Private 258 Leicester Corps Medal Clasps: CC OFS.
Medal Roll Reference: WO100/225/176 Orderly 5 Stationary Hospital. Sent to Base for England for discharge.
WARD, C. A. Private 726 Northampton Corps Medal Clasps: CC WITT.
Medal Roll Reference: WO100/225/204 Orderly Attached 22 Bearer Company. Discharged.
WARD, Ernest Private 1092 Tibshelf Corps Medal Clasps: NAT.
Medal Roll Reference: WO100/225/66 Orderly 13 Stationary Hospital. To SS *Montrose* 8 September 1900.
WARD, W. H. Private 554 Birmingham Corps Medal Clasps: CC OFS.
Medal Roll Reference: WO100/225/152 Orderly 9 General Hospital. To Base Detail 7 August 1900.
WARDALE, A. Private 823 Welbeck Division Medal Clasps: CC OFS TVL.
Medal Roll Reference: WO100/225/127 Private 6 General Hospital. To Base on expiration of contract 3 September 1900.
WARDLEY, Thomas Cowlishaw Private 155 Worksop Division Medal Clasps: CC OFS TVL KSA01 KSA02.
Medal Roll Reference: WO100/225/64+69 WO100/359/97 Orderly Base Hospital Wynberg Private Cape Medical Staff Corps 25355.
WARE, W. 1st Class Sergeant 901 Derby Division Medal Clasps: NAT.
Medal Roll Reference: WO100/225/120 Orderly 4 General Hospital. Sent to England for discharge time expired 9 September 1900.
WARN, A. E. Private 307 St John Ambulance Brigade (NFB Croxley Mills Dickinson's Fire Brigade) Medal Clasps: CC. NFBUAD Medal.
Medal Roll Reference: WO100/130/224 Private Imperial Yeomanry Hospital Deelfontein.
WARNER, W. J. Private 262 Wellingborough Corps Medal Clasps: CC.
Medal Roll Reference: WO100/225/127 Private 6 General Hospital. To Base on expiration of contract 23 June 1900.
WARREN, S. Private 1434 Bury Division Medal Clasps: No Clasps.
Medal Roll Reference: WO100/225/120 Orderly 4 General Hospital. Sent to England for discharge time expired 28 November 1900.
WARREN, W. S. Private 1389 Weston-Super-Mare Division Medal Clasps: No Clasps.
Medal Roll Reference: WO100/225/60 Orderly 14 General Hospital. To HS *Simla* for duty 14 November 1900.
WASS, A. T. Private 1162 Leeds Corps Medal Clasps: CC SA01.

Medal Roll Reference: WO100/225/71+85+152 Orderly 9 General Hospital. To Base Detail 12 October 1900. 11 General Hospital. To England on termination of engagement.

WATERWORTH, S. Private 1039 Barnoldswick Division Medal Clasps: NAT.
Medal Roll Reference: WO100/225/111 Orderly 1 General Hospital.

WATKIN, J. Private 1340 Leicester Corps Medal Clasps: CC OFS TVL.
Medal Roll Reference: WO100/225/160 Orderly 13 General Hospital. To England expired contract 5 May 1901.

WATKINS, F. H. Private 12 Metropolitan Corps Medal Clasps: CC.
Medal Roll Reference: WO100/225/242 Private HS *Princess of Wales*. Attached RAMC.

WATKINS, H. R. Private 1013 Sheffield Corps Medal Clasps: TVL NAT.
Medal Roll Reference: WO100/225/132 Orderly 7 General Hospital. To England time expired.

WATSON, J. Private 449 Hapton Division Medal Clasps: NAT.
Medal Roll Reference: WO100/225/132 Orderly 7 General Hospital. To England time expired.

WATSON, J. Private 778 Newchurch Division Medal Clasps: CC OFS.
Medal Roll Reference: WO100/225/117 Orderly 3 General Hospital. Transferred to Base Detail RAMC.

WATSON, E. Private 606 Belper Division Medal Clasps: CC OFS.
Medal Roll Reference: WO100/225/152 Orderly 9 General Hospital. To Base Detail 23 June 1900.

WATSON, J. Private 1756 Gateshead Fell Division Medal Clasps: CC OFS TVL SA01.
Medal Roll Reference: WO100/225/80 Orderly 20 Stationary Hospital. Woodstock February 1901 to April 1901. Then to Waterval Onder.

WATSON, W. Private 37 Preston Corps Medal Clasps: CC OFS TVL.
Medal Roll Reference: WO100/225/42+112A Orderly 6 General Hospital.

WATSON, W. Private 254 Nelson Corps Medal Clasps: CC OFS.
Medal Roll Reference: WO100/225/176 Orderly 5 Stationary Hospital. Sent to Base for England for discharge.

WATSON, W. Private 766 Northampton Corps Medal Clasps: CC WITT.
Medal Roll Reference: WO100/225/195 Orderly 23 Field Hospital. Discharged time expired.

WEBB, H. C. Private 1088 Haverhill Division Medal Clasps: NAT.
Medal Roll Reference: WO100/225/120 Orderly 4 General Hospital. Sent to England for discharge time expired 19 December 1900.

WEBBER, R. Private 324 St John Ambulance Brigade (NFB Exeter) Medal Clasps: CC SA01. NFBUAD Medal.
Medal Roll Reference: WO100/130/224 Private Imperial Yeomanry Hospital Deelfontein.

WEBSTER, H. Private 1592 Oldham Corps Medal Clasps: CC.
Medal Roll Reference: WO100/225/124 Orderly 5 General Hospital.

WELLARD, R. E. Private 13 Reading Division Medal Clasps: CC.
Medal Roll Reference: WO100/225/242 Private HS *Princess of Wales*. Attached RAMC.

WELLS, A. W. Private 873 Leicester Corps Medal Clasps: CC OFS TVL.
Medal Roll Reference: WO100/225/45+112A Orderly 6 General Hospital.

WELLS, J. Private 1525 1836 Dewsbury Corps Medal Clasps: CC OFS SA01.
Medal Roll Reference: WO100/225/87+117+121 Orderly 4 General Hospital Sent to England for discharge time expired 28 November 1900. 3 General Hospital. Transferred to Base Detail RAMC. Home 21 June 1901.

WELLS, W. S. T. Private 779 Metropolitan Corps Medal Clasps: CC OFS TVL.
Medal Roll Reference: WO100/225/127 Private 6 General Hospital. Invalided to Base 5 August 1900.

WESLEY, G. Private 360 Northampton Corps Medal Clasps: CC OFS.
Medal Roll Reference: WO100/225/137 Orderly 8 General Hospital Sick. To Cape Town 20 July 1900.

WESLEY, W. Corporal 722 Great Eastern Railway Corps Medal Clasps: CC OFS TVL.
Medal Roll Reference: WO100/130/263 Sergeant Imperial Yeomanry Field Hospital and Bearer Company.
WEST-SYMES, E. B. Private 885 1582 Leeds Corps Medal Clasps: CC OFS.
Medal Roll Reference: WO100/225/64+117 Orderly 3 General Hospital. Transferred to Base Detail RAMC. Base Hospital Wynberg. Died of disease Cape Town 28 April 1901.
WEST, H. Private 982 Preston Corps Medal Clasps: NAT.
Medal Roll Reference: WO100/225/132 Orderly 7 General Hospital. Transferred to Harrismith.
WESTON, S. B. Private 301 Metropolitan Corps Medal Clasps: CC.
Medal Roll Reference: WO100/130/224 Private Imperial Yeomanry Hospital Deelfontein.
WETH, F. J. Private 149 Colne Division Medal Clasps: CC OFS TVL.
Medal Roll Reference: WO100/225/104 Orderly.
WETHERALL, D. H. Private 345 1672 Reading Division Medal Clasps: CC OFS TVL SA01.
Medal Roll Reference: WO100/225/172+232 Orderly Langman Hospital Invalided Home To England for discharge. 20 General Hospital Joined from Base Detail.
WHALLEY, S. Private 147 Morecombe Division Medal Clasps: CC.
Medal Roll Reference: WO100/225/124 Orderly 5 General Hospital.
WHALLEY, W. Private 176 North Staffs Corps Medal Clasps: CC.
Medal Roll Reference: WO100/225/73 Orderly 6 Stationary Hospital.
WHEELHOUSE, G. Private 1420 Hebden Bridge Corps Medal Clasps: No Clasps.
Medal Roll Reference: WO100/225/60 Orderly 14 General Hospital. To SS *Manhattan* for duty 28 November 1900.
WHEWAY, J. Sergeant 124 1837 Nuneaton Division Medal Clasps: CC OFS SA01.
Medal Roll Reference: WO100/225/87+117+156 Supply Officer 10 General Hospital. To Base 10 October 1900. 3 General Hospital. Transferred to Base Detail RAMC. Home 21 June 1901.
WHIPP, L. T. Private 201 Accrington Corps Medal Clasps: CC OFS.
Medal Roll Reference: WO100/225/177 Orderly 5 Stationary Hospital Sent to Base for England for discharge.
WHITAKER, F. W. Sergeant 1490 1863 Leeds Corps Medal Clasps: CC.
Medal Roll Reference: WO100/225/64+68+77 Supply Officer Base Hospital Wynberg 10 Stationary Hospital. To Cape Town 18 General Hospital. To England 30 August 1900.
WHITAKER, J. W. Private 590 Colne Division Medal Clasps: CC.
Medal Roll Reference: WO100/225/73 Orderly 6 Stationary Hospital.
WHITAKER, W. Private 375 Metropolitan Corps Medal Clasps: CC OFS.
Medal Roll Reference: WO100/225/137 Orderly 8 General Hospital. To England 20 October 1900.
WHITE, A. Private 860 1860 Kettering Corps Medal Clasps: CC OFS KSA01 KSA02.
Medal Roll Reference: WO100/225/69+111+WO100/352/22+215 Orderly 8 Stationary Hospital. 1 General Hospital.
WHITE, T. W. Private 891 Rochdale Corps Medal Clasps: OFS NAT.
Medal Roll Reference: WO100/225/132+195 Orderly 7 General Hospital. Transferred to Harrismith 23 Field Hospital. Discharged time expired.
WHITE, W. H. Private 1604 Welbeck Division Medal Clasps: CC.
Medal Roll Reference: WO100/225/124 Orderly 5 General Hospital.
WHITEHEAD, J. A. Private 1752 Padiham Division Medal Clasps: CC.
Medal Roll Reference: WO100/225/111 Orderly 1 General Hospital.
WHITELEY, J. H. Private 1140 Barnoldswick Division Medal Clasps: CC OFS.
Medal Roll Reference: WO100/225/137 Orderly 8 General Hospital. To England 20 October 1900.
WHITELEY, W. Private 1180 Oldham Corps Medal Clasps: CC.
Medal Roll Reference: WO100/225/111 Orderly 1 General Hospital.
WHITFIELD, F. H. Sergeant 889 Rochdale Corps Medal Clasps: NAT.
Medal Roll Reference: WO100/225/182 Supply Officer 14 Stationary Hospital and Middleburg.

WHITHAM, J. Seymour Sergeant 1295 Burnley Division Medal Clasps: CC TVL.
Medal Roll Reference: WO100/224/172 2nd Class Staff Sergeant Rhodesian Field Force Hospital.
WHITLING, A. E. R. Private 598 Dewsbury Corps Medal Clasps: CC OFS SA02
Medal Roll Reference: WO100/225/64 WO100/239/223 Orderly Base Hospital Wynberg. 9
General Hospital. To Base Detail 8 June 1900. Trooper "O" Squadron Cape Colonial Forces.
WHITLOCK, H. Private 849 Northampton Corps Medal Clasps: No Clasps.
Medal Roll Reference: WO100/225/45 Orderly.
WHITTAKER, Charles F. M. Private 336 Kendal Division Medal Clasps: TVL NAT.
Medal Roll Reference: WO100/225/44+132 Orderly 7 General Hospital. To England time expired.
WHITTAKER, H. Private 976 Bury Division Medal Clasps: NAT.
Medal Roll Reference: WO100/225/132 Orderly 7 General Hospital. To England time expired.
WHITTINGTON, Ambrose Private 1555 Isle of Wight Corps Medal Clasps: CC OFS TVL
SA01 SA02.
Medal Roll Reference: WO100/225/111 WO100/271/163+272 Orderly 1 General Hospital Served
South African Constabulary A Division Medical Corporal A1871. Discharged 30 June 1902.
WHITTLE, B. Private 961 Walton-le-Dale Division Medal Clasps: OFS TVL NAT.
Medal Roll Reference: WO100/225/182+193 Orderly 14 Stationary Hospital. Attached 21 Field
Hospital. Discharged.
WHITTLE, F. Private 899 Bolton Corps Medal Clasps: NAT.
Medal Roll Reference: WO100/225/132 Orderly 7 General Hospital. Transferred to Harrismith.
WHITWORTH, J. Private 1435 Bury Division Medal Clasps: No Clasps.
Medal Roll Reference: WO100/225/121 Orderly 4 General Hospital. Sent to England for discharge
time expired 28 November 1900.
WIDDUP, R. Private 796 Barrowford Division Medal Clasps: No Clasps.
Medal Roll Reference: WO100/225/45 Orderly.
WIGGINS, J. H. Private 569 Bolton Corps Medal Clasps: CC.
Medal Roll Reference: WO100/225/124 Orderly 5 General Hospital.
WIGNALL, E. Private 256 Leicester Corps Medal Clasps: CC OFS.
Medal Roll Reference: WO100/225/177 Orderly 5 Stationary Hospital. Sent to Base for England
for discharge.
WILD, R. Private 1593 Oldham Corps Medal Clasps: CC.
Medal Roll Reference: WO100/225/124 Orderly 5 General Hospital.
WILDING, C. Sergeant 835 Walton-le-Dale Division Medal Clasps: CC OFS.
Medal Roll Reference: WO100/225/117 Supply Officer 3 General Hospital. Transferred to Base
Detail RAMC.
WILDMAN, H. Private 1041 Foulridge Division Medal Clasps: NAT.
Medal Roll Reference: WO100/225/182 Orderly 14 Stationary Hospital.
WILKINS, A. G. Private 1503 1834 Bury Division Medal Clasps: CC SA01 SA02.
Medal Roll Reference: WO100/225/111+167 WO100/219/148 Orderly 15 General Hospital.
Transferred to England 26 November 1900. 1 General Hospital. Private RAMC 16487.
WILKINSON, A. Private 757 Hebden Bridge Corps Medal Clasps: CC.
Medal Roll Reference: WO100/225/71 Orderly 11 General Hospital. To England on termination
of engagement.
WILKINSON, H. Private 1282 Barrowford Division Medal Clasps: No Clasps.
Medal Roll Reference: WO100/225/46 Orderly.
WILKINSON, Walter Private 696 Clitheroe Division Medal Clasps: CC.
Medal Roll Reference: WO100/225/71 Orderly 11 General Hospital. To England on termination
of engagement.
WILLAN, J. W. Private 858 Accrington Corps Medal Clasps: CC OFS TVL.
Medal Roll Reference: WO100/225/127 Private 6 General Hospital. To Base on expiration of
contract 3 September 1900.

WILLIAMS, A. Private 1143 Leeds Corps Medal Clasps: CC SA01.
Medal Roll Reference: WO100/225/71+85+152 Orderly 11 General Hospital. To England on termination of engagement. 9 General Hospital. To Base Detail 12 October 1900.
WILLIAMS, G. Private 596 Metropolitan Corps Medal Clasps: CC OFS.
Medal Roll Reference: WO100/225/152 Orderly 9 General Hospital. To Base Detail 1 August 1900.
WILLIAMS, G. H. Private 1189 Oldham Corps Medal Clasps: CC.
Medal Roll Reference: WO100/225/111 Orderly 1 General Hospital.
WILLIAMS, H. T. 1st Class Sergeant 636 Warrington Corps Medal Clasps: CC OFS.
Medal Roll Reference: WO100/225/156 Supply Officer 10 General Hospital. To Base 7 August 1900.
WILLIAMS, J. E. Sergeant 740 Bradford Corps Medal Clasps: CC WITT.
Medal Roll Reference: WO100/225/203 Orderly 21 Bearer Company. Home for discharge August 1901.
WILLIAMS, J. J. Private 1802 Handsworth & Smethwick Corps Medal Clasps: CC SA01 SA02.
Medal Roll Reference: WO100/225/174 Orderly 21 General Hospital.
WILLIAMSON, J. Private 714 Metropolitan Corps Medal Clasps: CC.
Medal Roll Reference: WO100/225/71 Orderly 11 General Hospital. To England on termination of engagement.
WILLIAMSON, J. W. Sergeant 540 Preston Corps Medal Clasps: CC.
Medal Roll Reference: WO100/225/124 Supply Officer 5 General Hospital.
WILLIAMSON, W. Private 838 Preston Corps Medal Clasps: CC OFS TVL.
Medal Roll Reference: WO100/225/127 Private 6 General Hospital. To Base on expiration of contract 3 September 1900. WILLIAMSON, J. on QSA medal roll.
WILLIMGHAM, E. Private 18 Hull Corps Medal Clasps: CC.
Medal Roll Reference: WO100/225/241 Private HS *Princess of Wales*. Attached RAMC.
WILLIS, W. Private 495 North Staffs Corps Medal Clasps: NAT.
Medal Roll Reference: WO100/225/66 Orderly 13 Stationary Hospital. Locally discharged 28 August 1900.
WILLMORE, Charles E. Private 303 St John Ambulance Brigade (NFB Hythe) Medal Clasps: CC. NFBUAD Medal.
Medal Roll Reference: WO100/130/224 Sergeant Imperial Yeomanry Hospital Deelfontein Died pneumonia Deelfontein 2 January 1901.
WILLS, B. E. Private 134 Kettering Corps Medal Clasps: No Clasps.
Medal Roll Reference: WO100/225/42 Orderly.
WILSON, Ernest L. Private 104 Gateshead Fell Division Medal Clasps: CC OFS.
Medal Roll Reference: WO100/225/236 Private Portland Hospital. To England contract expired.
WILSON, F. L. Private 1563 Morecombe Division Medal Clasps: CC OFS TVL.
Medal Roll Reference: WO100/225/105 Supply Officer Imperial Yeomanry Hospital Pretoria. To England contract expired 7 April 1901.
WILSON, J. Private 831 Penrith Division Medal Clasps: CC OFS TVL.
Medal Roll Reference: WO100/225/112A Orderly 6 General Hospital.
WILSON, J. Private 1665 Accrington Corps Medal Clasps: SA01.
Medal Roll Reference: WO100/225/88 Orderly.
WILSON, John Herbert Private 1129 Oldham Corps Medal Clasps: CC. China Medal.
Medal Roll Reference: WO100/225/53+248 Orderly HS *Maine*. On medal roll for HS *Maine* for China WO100/96/38+39.
WILSON, T. H. Private 883 Leeds Corps Medal Clasps: No Clasps.
Medal Roll Reference: WO100/225/45 Orderly.

WINDLE, Thomas Private 693 Clitheroe Division Medal Clasps: CC OFS.
Medal Roll Reference: WO100/225/156 Orderly 10 General Hospital. Died of disease
Bloemfontein 15 July 1900.
WINFIELD, E. Private 1275 Bury Division Medal Clasps: No Clasps.
Medal Roll Reference: WO100/225/46 Orderly.
WINGFIELD, L. F. Private 458 Metropolitan Corps Medal Clasps: CC OFS.
Medal Roll Reference: WO100/225/137 Orderly 8 General Hospital. To England 23 January 1901.
WINPENNY, J. R. Private 167 Hull Corps Medal Clasps: CC.
Medal Roll Reference: WO100/225/111 Orderly 1 General Hospital.
WINSBOROUGH, W. Private 1249 Preston Corps Medal Clasps: No Clasps.
Medal Roll Reference: WO100/225/46 Orderly.
WINTERBOTTOM, W. Private 1551 Whaley Bridge Division Medal Clasps: No Clasps.
Medal Roll Reference: WO100/225/47 Orderly.
WINTERBOURNE, James Private 160 Reading Division Medal Clasps: CC OFS TVL.
Medal Roll Reference: WO100/225/64+70 Private Base Hospital Wynberg. 3 Hospital Train. To
Base Detail RAMC Cape Town for England.
WINYARD, E. H. G. Private 498 Sheffield Corps Medal Clasps: CC OFS TVL.
Medal Roll Reference: WO/100/225/232 Private Langman Hospital.
WOAN, J. Private 1081 Preston Corps Medal Clasps: NAT.
Medal Roll Reference: WO100/225/68 Orderly 18 General Hospital. To England 30 August 1900.
WOOD, A. E. Private 1375 Preston Corps Medal Clasps: CC.
Medal Roll Reference: WO100/225/160 Orderly 13 General Hospital. To England expired contract
27 November 1900. E WOOD in QSA Medal Roll.
WOOD, C. E. Sergeant 1114 Leeds Corps Medal Clasps: NAT.
Medal Roll Reference: WO100/225/121 Orderly 4 General Hospital. Sent to England for discharge
time expired 19 December 1900.
WOOD, E. Private 1176 Oldham Corps Medal Clasps: CC.
Medal Roll Reference: WO100/225/111 Orderly 1 General Hospital.
WOOD, F. H. Private 385 Birmingham Corps Medal Clasps: CC.
Medal Roll Reference: WO100/130/224 Private Imperial Yeomanry Hospital Deelfontein.
WOOD, G. Private 1842 Dewsbury Corps Medal Clasps: CC.
Medal Roll Reference: WO100/225/111 Orderly 1 General Hospital.
WOOD, G. Private 1889 Hull Corps Medal Clasps: CC OFS TVL.
Medal Roll Reference: WO100/225/169 Orderly 17 General Hospital. Transferred to Base Detail
Cape Town 13 July 1901.
WOOD, H. Private 211 Bradford Corps Medal Clasps: CC.
Medal Roll Reference: WO100/225/127 Private 6 General Hospital. To Base Invalided 1 July 1900.
WOOD, H. Private 1464 Oldham Corps Medal Clasps: No Clasps.
Medal Roll Reference: WO100/225/182 Orderly 14 Stationary Hospital.
WOOD, J. Private 1359 Bolton Corps Medal Clasps: CC.
Medal Roll Reference: WO100/225/160 Orderly 13 General Hospital. To England expired contract
27 November 1900.
WOOD, J. E. Private 812 Bolton Corps Medal Clasps: CC OFS TVL.
Medal Roll Reference: WO100/225/106 Orderly.
WOOD, J. R. Private 1643 Whaley Bridge Division Medal Clasps: No Clasps.
Medal Roll Reference: WO100/225/146 Orderly.
WOOD, John Private 1137 Nelson Corps Medal Clasps: CC. China Medal.
Medal Roll Reference: WO100/225/53+248 Orderly HS *Maine*. On medal roll for HS *Maine* for
China WO100/96/38+39.

WOOD, L. 212 1704 No Bronze Medal roll entry. Medal Clasps: CC OFS TVL.
Medal Roll Reference: WO100/225/64+127+172 Orderly Base Hospital Wynberg. 6 General Hospital. To Base on expiration of contract 18 June 1900. 20 General Hospital Joined from Base Detail. To England for discharge.

WOOD, Mark Private 365 North Staffs Corps Medal Clasps: CC OFS SA01 SA02.
Medal Roll Reference: WO100/225/137 WO100/272/383 Orderly 8 General Hospital. Sick to Cape Town 9 July 1900. South African Constabulary C Division C2122. Discharged 19 September 1902.

WOOD, R. Private 1646 Bolton Corps Medal Clasps: SA01.
Medal Roll Reference: WO100/225/147 Orderly.

WOOD, R. H. Private 1772 Edenfield Division Medal Clasps: CC.
Medal Roll Reference: WO100/225/174 Orderly 21 General Hospital.

WOOD, T. Private 1463 1882 Oldham Corps Medal Clasps: CC OFS TVL.
Medal Roll Reference: WO100/225/174+182+184 Orderly 21 General Hospital. 14 Stationary Hospital and 17 Stationary Hospital Middleburg. To Base 24 November 1900.

WOOD, W. Private 1472 Oldham Corps Medal Clasps: No Clasps.
Medal Roll Reference: WO100/225/182 Orderly 14 Stationary Hospital.

WOODBRIDGE, T. Private 772 Metropolitan Corps Medal Clasps: CC.
Medal Roll Reference: WO100/225/71 Orderly 11 General Hospital. To England on termination of engagement.

WOODBURN, M. J. Private 1002 Dalton-in-Furness Division Medal Clasps: NAT.
Medal Roll Reference: WO100/225/132 Orderly 7 General Hospital. To England time expired.

WOODCOCK, J. R. Private 409 Accrington Corps Medal Clasps: NAT.
Medal Roll Reference: WO100/225/132 Orderly 7 General Hospital. To England time expired.

WOODHAM, Albert Private 131 Wellingborough Corps Medal Clasps: No Clasps.
Medal Roll Reference: WO100/225/42 Orderly. Died of disease Orange River Station 24 March 1900.

WOODHEAD, T. Private 1710 Worksop Division Medal Clasps: CC OFS TVL.
Medal Roll Reference: WO100/225/172 Orderly 20 General Hospital. Joined from Base Detail. To England for discharge.

WOODING, J. Private 221 Wellingborough Corps Medal Clasps: CC.
Medal Roll Reference: WO100/225/127 Private 6 General Hospital. To Base on expiration of contract 23 June 1900.

WOODS, John Thomas 1st Class Sergeant 27 Northampton Corps Medal Clasps: CC.
Medal Roll Reference: WO100/225/5 Supplementary Officer.

WOODS, R. A. Private 1199 Metropolitan Corps Medal Clasps: CC TVL.
Medal Roll Reference: WO100/224/172 Private Rhodesian Field Force Hospital.

WOOLLAN, T. Private 1293 Metropolitan Corps Medal Clasps: CC TVL.
Medal Roll Reference: WO100/224/172 Private Rhodesian Field Force Hospital.

WOOLLARD, J. Private 1314 Keighley Corps Medal Clasps: CC TVL.
Medal Roll Reference: WO100/224/172 Private Rhodesian Field Force Hospital. Invalided to England (date unknown).

WOOLNER, R. H. Private 914 Derby Division Medal Clasps: NAT.
Medal Roll Reference: WO100/225/132 Orderly 7 General Hospital. To England time expired.

WORSLEY, S. Private 1575 Bolton Corps Medal Clasps: CC OFS TVL.
Medal Roll Reference: WO100/225/124+187 Orderly 5 General Hospital. 18 Brigade Field Hospital Joined 20 March 1901. Left 22 April 1901 for discharge.

WORTHINGTON, W. Private 1303 Preston Corps Medal Clasps: CC TVL.
Medal Roll Reference: WO100/224/172 Private Rhodesian Field Force Hospital.

WOTTON, A. Private 1858 Bradford Corps Medal Clasps: No Clasps.
Medal Roll Reference: WO100/224/147 Orderly.

WRATHALL, L. Private 1230 Burnley Division Medal Clasps: CC OFS TVL KSA01 KSA02. Medal Roll Reference: WO100/225/64+70+WO100/352/20 Orderly Base Hospital Wynberg. (see E. C. roll CCF Coy CMSC). 3 Hospital Train. Sick to 5 General Hospital.

WREN, George William Private 31 Reading Division Medal Clasps: CC. Medal Roll Reference: WO100/225/42+112A Orderly 6 General Hospital.

WRIGHT, A. G. Sergeant 1789 Derby Corps Medal Clasps: CC OFS SA01 SA02 KSA01 KSA02. Medal Roll Reference: WO100/225/176 WO100/273/168+185+369 WO100/366/201 Orderly 5 Stationary Hospital. South African Constabulary E Division Sergeant E3473. Discharged 18 August 1902. Service with St John Ambulance Brigade 26 February 1901 to 9 August 1901. Service with South African Constabulary 9 August 1901 to 31 May 1902. Discharged time expired. Also served 2nd Derby Regiment.

WRIGHT, J. W. Private 398 Nelson Corps Medal Clasps: TVL NAT. Medal Roll Reference: WO100/225/132 Orderly 7 General Hospital. To England time expired.

WRIGHT, James Cuthbert Private 206 Wellingborough Corps Medal Clasps: CC. Medal Roll Reference: WO100/225/127 Orderly 6 General Hospital. To Base Invalided 18 May 1900.

WRIGHT, Joseph 1st Class Sergeant 771 Kendal Division Medal Clasps: CC OFS SA01. Medal Roll Reference: WO100/225/71+85 Supply Officer 11 General Hospital. Temporary Hospital Boshof.

WRIGHT, W. Private 1100 Leicester Corps Medal Clasps: OFS TVL NAT. Medal Roll Reference: WO100/225/182+193 Orderly 14 Stationary Hospital. Attached 21 Field Hospital. Discharged.

WYATT, T. Private 435 Metropolitan Corps Medal Clasps: CC OFS. Medal Roll Reference: WO100/225/137 Orderly 8 General Hospital. To England 20 July 1900.

WYLLIE, John Alexander 1st Class Sergeant 470 Accrington Corps Medal Clasps: CC OFS. Medal Roll Reference: WO100/225/137 Supply Officer 8 General Hospital. To England 20 July 1900.

YARDLEY, A. Private 1427 Derby Division Medal Clasps: No Clasps. Medal Roll Reference: WO100/225/60 Orderly 14 General Hospital. Invalided to England 29 August 1900.

YARNALL, W. H. Sergeant 672 Bolton Corps Medal Clasps: CC. Medal Roll Reference: WO100/225/71 Supply Officer 11 General Hospital. To England on termination of engagement.

YEATES, J. S. Private 830 Penrith Division Medal Clasps: CC OFS TVL. Medal Roll Reference: WO100/225/6 Supplementary Officer 6 General Hospital.

YEATES, W. Private 841 Preston Corps Medal Clasps: CC OFS TVL. Medal Roll Reference: WO100/225/127 Private 6 General Hospital. To Base on expiration of contract 3 September 1900.

YORK, F. Private 1512 Wellingborough Corps Medal Clasps: No Clasps. Medal Roll Reference: WO100/225/167 Orderly 15 General Hospital.

YOUREN, L. Private 1169 Leeds Corps Medal Clasps: CC OFS. Medal Roll Reference: WO100/225/152 Orderly 9 General Hospital. To Base Detail 12 October 1900.

YOXALL, A. Private 1276 Brierfield Division Medal Clasps: CC OFS. Medal Roll Reference: WO100/225/152 Orderly 9 General Hospital. To Base Detail 12 October 1900.

Appendix II

Royal Army Medical Corps Medal Roll

In total 83 men are listed on the St John Ambulance Brigade Bronze Medal roll as having been directly recruited to the Royal Army Medical Corps. 81 of these are unique names to this roll while, as previously mentioned, two of the men are duplicated in the main volunteer medal roll. Private G. EDWARDS 16632 is also present on the main volunteer roll with St John Ambulance Brigade number 1832 and Private J. JAMES 16603 is present on the main volunteer roll as St John Ambulance Brigade number 1159 and subsequently 1869. All 83 men present on the roll are listed below together with their Queen's South Africa Medal entitlement where this is known.

ALLEN, H. Private 15827 Whaley Bridge Section Medal Clasps: CC OFS SA01 SA02. Medal Roll Reference: WO100/224/14 RAMC.

BAKER, W. Private 15867 Leeds Corps Medal Clasps: CC SA01 SA02. Medal Roll Reference: WO100/224/189 RAMC.

BENNETT, Horace Private 16715 Ironbridge Corps Medal Clasps: CC SA01 SA02. Medal Roll Reference: WO100/219/165 RAMC to England.

BERRY, Ralph Private 16585 Preston Corps Medal Clasps: SA02. Medal Roll Reference: WO100/219/190 RAMC. 13 Stationary Hospital Pinetown. Date embarkation 15 March 1902.

BIDWELL, George Private 16778 Newton Abbott Division Medal Clasps: SA02. Medal Roll Reference: WO100/224/197 RAMC.

BLACKHAM, Ernest Private 15872 Leeds Corps Medal Clasps: CC SA01 SA02. Medal Roll Reference: WO100/220/30 RAMC.

BOLTON, T. Private 16586 Preston Corps Medal Clasps: CC SA02. Medal Roll Reference: WO100/219/190 RAMC. Base Detail Wynberg/ Date embarkation 22 December 1901.

BOWLING, George Higgins Private 16587 Preston Corps Medal Clasps: CC SA02. Medal Roll Reference: WO100/219/190 RAMC. Base Detail Wynberg. Date embarkation 24 December 1901.

BRADBURY, Randolph Handel Private 16588 Preston Corps Medal Clasps: CC SA02. Medal Roll Reference: WO100/219/190 RAMC. Base Detail Wynberg. Date embarkation 20 December 1901.

BRIERLY, J. Private 15875 Barnoldswick Division Medal Clasps: CC SA01 SA02. Medal Roll Reference: WO100/219/144 RAMC. No Number on Bronze Medal Roll. BRIERLY, A. on St John Bronze Medal Roll.

BROMLEY, Frederick Private 17238 Accrington Corps Medal Clasps: SA02. Medal Roll Reference: WO100/220/37 RAMC. Discharged at own request 2 September 1902

BROUGHTON, J.D. Private 15893 Barnoldswick Division Medal Clasps: SA01 SA02. Medal Roll Reference: WO100/224/17 RAMC. Number 15875 incorrectly noted on St John Bronze Medal Roll.

BROWN, David Private 16908 Leeds Corps Medal Clasps: OFS SA02. Medal Roll Reference: WO100/220/38 RAMC.

BURTON, John James Private 16542 Withernsea Division Medal Clasps: CC SA02. Medal Roll Reference: WO100/219/150 RAMC.

CARTER, Robert Private 15876 Preston Corps Medal Clasps: SA01 SA02. Medal Roll Reference: WO100/220/53 RAMC.

CLARKE, Richard Private 16590 Preston Corps Medal Clasps: CC SA02. Medal Roll Reference: WO100/219/165 RAMC to England.

CLARKSON, F. Private 15870 Leeds Corps Medal Clasps: CC SA01 SA02.

Medal Roll Reference: WO100/219/136+178 RAMC. To base Detail.
COBERN, George Henry Private 16684 Ironbridge Corps Medal Clasps: CC SA01 SA02.
Medal Roll Reference: WO100/219/166 RAMC to England.
COMMANDER, W. Private 16605 Derby Division Medal Clasps: CC SA01 SA02.
Medal Roll Reference: WO100/219/106 WO100/220/63 RAMC.
COSTER, Charles Private 16680 Metropolitan Corps Medal Clasps: CC SA01 SA02.
Medal Roll Reference: WO100/219/165 RAMC to England.
CRAVEN, Harry Private 16964 Leeds Corps
Medal Roll Reference: NO QSA identified
CREWE, R. Private 16591 Preston Corps Medal Clasps: CC SA02.
Medal Roll Reference: WO100/219/166 RAMC to England.
De VALADARES, John Edward Private 16606 Worksop Division Medal Clasps: SA02.
Medal Roll Reference: WO/100/224/195 RAMC.
DEWHURST, W.H. Private 15877 Barnoldswick Division Medal Clasps: CC SA01 SA02.
Medal Roll Reference: WO100/219/212 RAMC.
DIXON, F. Private 17617 Bedford Division Medal Clasps: CC SA02.
Medal Roll Reference: WO100/219/138 RAMC.
DOCKRAY, John Private 15868 Leeds Corps Medal Clasps: CC SA01 SA02.
Medal Roll Reference: WO100/220/86 RAMC.
DUGDALE, Harold Private 15856 Clitheroe Division Medal Clasps: CC SA01 SA02.
Medal Roll Reference: WO100/219/219 RAMC.
ECCLES, James Private 16592 Preston Corps Medal Clasps: CC SA02.
Medal Roll Reference: WO100/219/166 RAMC to England.
EDWARDS, George Private 16632 Ironbridge Corps Medal Clasps: CC SA01 SA02.
Medal Roll Reference: WO100/225/173 WO100/219/151 21 General Hospital RAMC. 16632
Private Mafeking Discharged. (St John Ambulance Brigade number 1832).
FEARNS, Dennis Private 15926 Bolton Corps Medal Clasps: CC OFS SA01 SA02.
Medal Roll Reference: WO100/220/99 RAMC.
FORSTER, Charles Private 16056 Warrington Corps Medal Clasps: CC OFS TVL SA01 SA02.
Medal Roll Reference: WO100/219/151 RAMC. Mafeking. To Field Hospital Lord Methuen's
Column.
FOX, Fred Hanson Private 16602 Metropolitan Corps Medal Clasps: CC SA01 SA02.
Medal Roll Reference: WO100/219/166 WO100/224/221 WO100/236/90 Attached to RAMC.
Thomas H Fox Employed as Chef at 12 General Hospital Springfontein during months of June
July August and September 1901. (Possibly also Bethune's Mounted Infantry Trooper 1176.
Enlisted 5 September 1900 OFS TVL Imperial Hospital Corps.)
GIBSON, Thomas Private 16528 Crewe Division Medal Clasps: TVL SA02.
Medal Roll Reference: WO100/224/196 RAMC.
GORDON, Samuel Private 16593 Preston Corps Medal Clasps: TVL SA02.
Medal Roll Reference: WO100/219/190 RAMC. Base 16 General Hospital Elandsfontein. Date
embarkation 22 December 1901.
GRAHAM, Thomas Henry Private 16633 Gateshead Fell Division Medal Clasps: CC OFS SA02.
Medal Roll Reference: WO100/219/184 RAMC.
GREEN, Arthur Private 15822 Warrington Corps Medal Clasps: TVL SA01 SA02.
Medal Roll Reference: WO100/224/189 RAMC.
HALLIWELL, Arthur Private 17143 Burnley Division Medal Clasps: CC.
Medal Roll Reference: WO100/219/160 RAMC. 1 General Hospital.
HARRISON, Arthur Private 15889 Heckmondwike & Liversedge Division Medal Clasps: CC
SA01 SA02.
Medal Roll Reference: WO100/224/186 RAMC.

HAYDOCK, Robert Private 15928 Accrington Corps Medal Clasps: CC SA01 SA02.
Medal Roll Reference: WO100/219/144 RAMC.
HESELDEN, William Henry Private 15890 Heckmondwike & Liversedge Division
Medal Roll Reference: No QSA identified. Died of disease Norval's Pont 6 March 1902.
HIGGINSON, Edward Private 16510 Walton-le-Dale Division
Medal Roll Reference: No QSA identified.
HIGHAM, Walter Private 15823 Warrington Corps Medal Clasps: CC OFS TVL SA01 SA02.
Medal Roll Reference: WO100/224/33 WO100/219/152 RAMC. To Field Hospital Lord
Methuen's Column.
HILLSDON, Walter Private 15866 Boughton Division
Medal Roll Reference: No QSA identified
HOLDEN, William Henry Private 16594 Preston Corps Medal Clasps: CC SA02.
Medal Roll Reference: WO100/219/190 RAMC. Base Detail Wynberg. Date embarkation 24
December 1901.
HOLLINGSWORTH, Thomas Private 16971 Warrington Corps Medal Clasps: CC OFS TVL
SA02.
Medal Roll Reference: WO100/224/201 RAMC.
HUGHES, William Private 16488 Metropolitan Corps Medal Clasps: CC OFS TVL SA02.
Medal Roll Reference: WO100/219/144 RAMC.
IRONS, John Edward Richard Private 17194 Bedford Division Medal Clasps: CC SA02.
Medal Roll Reference: WO100/219/147 RAMC.
JAMES, John Private 16603 Hull Corps Medal Clasps: CC OFS TVL SA01 SA02.
Medal Roll Reference: WO100/225/27+149 WO100/222/16 RAMC. 9 General Hospital. To Base
Detail 12 October 1900. To Base Detail 15 July 1901. General Hospital Pretoria. To 38 Stationary
Hospital 23 March 1902. (St John Ambulance Brigade number 1159 Hull Corps and subsequently
1869 Leeds Corps).
JODRELL, Richard Henry Private 15831 Whaley Bridge Section Medal Clasps: CC SA01 SA02.
Medal Roll Reference: WO100/219/152 WO100/222/165 RAMC. 21 General Hospital
Discharged.
KIRKHAM, Peter Private 15824 Warrington Corps Medal Clasps: OFS TVL SA01 SA02.
Medal Roll Reference: WO100/222/17 RAMC. The General Hospital Pretoria. To 6 Field Hospital
14 September 1901.
KIRKHAM, W.T. Private 15884 Blackpool Division Medal Clasps: SA01 SA02.
Medal Roll Reference: WO100/220/183 RAMC.
KNAPTON, T. Private 16607 Leeds Corps Medal Clasps: CC OFS TVL SA02.
Medal Roll Reference: WO100/222/19 RAMC. General Hospital Pretoria To Pietermaritzburg 19
August 1902.
LEEK, James Frederick Private 17296 Millom Ironworks Division Medal Clasps: SA02.
Medal Roll Reference: WO100/221/7 RAMC.
LEEK, Jesse Private 17297 Millom Ironworks Division Medal Clasps: SA02.
Medal Roll Reference: WO100/221/7 RAMC.
MAY, Ernest Private 16807 Reading Division Medal Clasps: OFS SA02.
Medal Roll Reference: WO/100/221/37 RAMC. 16607 on St John Bronze Medal Roll.
MELLOR, Arthur Private 15832 Whaley Bridge Section Medal Clasps: CC OFS TVL SA01 SA02.
Medal Roll Reference: WO/100/224/14 RAMC. 15833 ON QSA Medal Roll.
MELLOR, Gilbert Private 15833 Whaley Bridge Section Medal Clasps: CC OFS TVL SA01
SA02.
Medal Roll Reference: WO/100/224/14 RAMC. 15832 ON QSA Medal Roll.
MILLICHIP, Thomas Private 15932 Ironbridge Corps Medal Clasps: CC OFS TVL SA01 SA02.
Medal Roll Reference: WO100/221/43 RAMC.

NUTTALL, Fred Private 15972 Bolton Corps Medal Clasps: TVL SA01 SA02.
Medal Roll Reference: WO100/221/61 RAMC. 17 Stationary Hospital.
PARK, Thomas Herbert Private 16595 Preston Corps Medal Clasps: TVL SA02.
Medal Roll Reference: WO100/219/190 RAMC. 31 Stationary Hospital Ermelo. Date embarkation
30 December 1901.
PARNELL, W. Private 16871 Millom Ironworks Division Medal Clasps: CC OFS SA02.
Medal Roll Reference: WO100/221/75 RAMC.
PEAKE, Benjamin Thomas Private 17065 Millom Ironworks Division Medal Clasps: TVL SA02.
Medal Roll Reference: WO100/219/229 RAMC.
PEARSON, Anthony Private 16596 Preston Corps Medal Clasps: TVL SA02.
Medal Roll Reference: WO100/219/190 RAMC. 17 General Hospital Standerton. Date
embarkation 30 December 1901.
PETTY, Arthur Private 15881 Barnoldswick Division Medal Clasps: CC OFS TVL SA01 SA02.
Medal Roll Reference: WO100/219/144 RAMC.
ROBERTS, John Private 16546 Kettering Corps Medal Clasps: CC OFS TVL SA02.
Medal Roll Reference: WO100/219/179 RAMC.
ROBINSON, Thomas Private 16598 Preston Corps Medal Clasps: TVL SA02.
Medal Roll Reference: WO100/219/190 RAMC. 17 General Hospital Standerton Date
embarkation 30 December 1901.
ROMAINE, Louis Private 16900 Metropolitan Corps Medal Clasps: CC OFS TVL SA02.
Medal Roll Reference: WO100/219/144 RAMC.
RUSSELL, George William W. Private 17140 Hull Corps Medal Clasps: TVL SA02.
Medal Roll Reference: WO100/221/104 RAMC.
SCHOFIELD, W. Private 16805 Woking Division Medal Clasps: CC SA02.
Medal Roll Reference: WO100/224/200 RAMC.
SLATER, Horace Private 15825 Warrington Corps Medal Clasps: CC SA01 SA02.
Medal Roll Reference: WO100/219/153 RAMC. Discharged
SUGDEN, Ernest Henry Private 15994 Keighley Corps Medal Clasps: TVL SA01 SA02.
Medal Roll Reference: WO100/222/19 RAMC. General Hospital Pretoria To Pietermaritzburg 19
August 1902.
TASKER, Sam Private 16872 Leeds Corps Medal Clasps: TVL SA02.
Medal Roll Reference: WO100/222/19 RAMC. General Hospital Pretoria To Cape Town 11
November 1902.
TURNER, A. Private 15936 Ironbridge Corps Medal Clasps: TVL SA01 SA02.
Medal Roll Reference: WO100/222/20 RAMC. General Hospital Pretoria To Pietermaritzburg 19
August 1902.
TURNER, Arthur Private 16599 Preston Corps Medal Clasps: TVL SA02.
Medal Roll Reference: WO100/219/190 RAMC. 17 General Hospital Standerton. Died of disease
Pretoria 9 May 1902.
TURNER, Charles Private 15887 Blackpool Division
Medal Roll Reference: No QSA identified.
VAISEY, Harold John Private 16019 Swindon Division Medal Clasps: SA01 SA02.
Medal Roll Reference: WO100/219/148 RAMC.
VICARS, J. Private 15871 Leeds Corps Medal Clasps: CC SA01 SA02.
Medal Roll Reference: WO100/219/179 RAMC.
WADDINGTON, Ernest Private 16600 Preston Corps Medal Clasps: CC OFS TVL SA02.
Medal Roll Reference: WO100/219/190 RAMC. Base Detail Wynberg. Date embarkation 24
December 1901.
WALSH, J. Private 16601 Preston Corps Medal Clasps: CC SA02.
Medal Roll Reference: WO100/219/190 RAMC. Base Detail Wynberg. Date embarkation 22
December 1901.

WARMINGTON, Arthur Private 16057 Leicester Corps Medal Clasps: SA01 SA02.
Medal Roll Reference: WO100/224/195 RAMC.
WOOD, Smith Private 15880 Barnoldswick Division Medal Clasps: SA01 SA02.
Medal Roll Reference: WO100/224/16 RAMC.
WOODBOURNE, Thomas Private 16608 Colne Division Medal Clasps: OFS SA02.
Medal Roll Reference: WO100/224/188 RAMC. WOODBURN on QSA roll.
ZEALANDER, Emmanuel Private 16901 Metropolitan Corps Medal Clasps: CC OFS SA02.
Medal Roll Reference: WO100/219/131 RAMC. Kroonstad. Also served 30 Stationary Hospital.
Home 24 August 1902.

Appendix III

Senior Trainers Medal Roll

Thirty-nine men and one woman are listed as being recipients of the Bronze St John Ambulance Brigade Medal for their services in training and preparing those who volunteered to serve in South Africa. None of the 40 actually travelled to South Africa during the conflict. In all but one case the full details of the men are recorded including their rank and the Division, Corps or District where they served. In one case however the recipient is only identified as George Thomason. However, reference to the St John Service Medal roll for the period clearly shows he was the District Chief Surgeon for No 4 District receiving his Service Medal in 1901.

Name	Rank	Ambulance Division Corps or District
ANDLAND, William E.	District Chief Surgeon	No III District
ARMITAGE, George	Chief Superintendent	Leeds Corp
BECK, H.	Chief Superintendent	Handsworth Corps
BROOMHEAD, James	Chief Surgeon	Haslington Corps
BROWN, John	Honorary Surgeon	No I District
CARVELL, John MacLean	Honorary Surgeon	No I District
CASSIDI, Francis Richard	Honorary Surgeon	Derby Division
CHAMBERS, Harry Crompton	Chief Superintendent	Sheffield Corps
COATES, Matthew	Honorary Surgeon	No I District
DUNNE, J.	Sergeant	No I District
ELAM, James	Sergeant	No I District
GOSLING, George	Superintendent	Blackpool Division
GRIFFITHS, John Samuel	Assistant Commissioner	No II District
HALLATT, Harrie John	Sergeant	No I District
HILTON, Thomas Hornsby	Chief Superintendent	Wellingborough Corps
JOHNSTON, John	Honorary Surgeon	Bolton Corps
JONES, J.S.	Chief Superintendent	Oldham Corps
KING, J.S.	Chief Superintendent	Leicester Corps
LITTLE, F.S.G.	Chief Superintendent	Preston Corps
LOMAX, Frederick	Chief Superintendent	Bolton Corps
MALKIN, Sydney William	Assistant Commissioner	No V District
MARTIN, A.	Private	No I District
MOLLOY, Leonard Greenham Star	Honorary Surgeon	Blackpool Division
NELSON, Thomas	Chief Surgeon	Birmingham Corps
OGDEN, Joseph	Chief Superintendent	Accrington Corps
OSBORN, Samuel	District Chief Surgeon	No I District
PEPPER, F.	Private	No I District
PIERS, Shute Barrington	District Superintendent of Stores	No I District
PONTIN, William James Henry	Superintendent	No I District

POPE, Frank Montague	Chief Surgeon	Leicester Corps
RAMSAY, L	Lady Superintendent	Walton-le-Dale Nursing Division
RANDLE, Ashby John Edward	Superintendent	Nuneaton Division
SELLERS, William Henry Irvin	Chief Surgeon	Preston Corps
THOMPSON, John Henry	Honorary Surgeon	Bolton Corps
THOMSON, George	District Chief Surgeon	No IV District
TRENERY, F.T.	Chief Superintendent	Kettering Corps
VILVEN, S.R.	First officer	No I District
WHITE, J.W.	Chief Superintendent	Ironbridge Corps
WILKINSON, James Bates	Chief Surgeon	Oldham Corps
WOOLSTON, Thomas Henry	Assistant Commissioner	No III District

Appendix IV

Senior Leaders Medal Roll

Fifteen of the most senior personnel in the Order of St John Ambulance Brigade received the Bronze South Africa Medal. None of the recipients appear to have travelled themselves to serve in South Africa during the conflict. All the medals were present by King Edward VII at Buckingham Palace on 31 May 1902.

Name	Rank
BARNES, Mr W. G.	Supervised despatch of Ambulance and Medical Comforts for Troops
BOWDLER, Colonel Cyril William CB	Chief Commissioner St John Ambulance Brigade
BRASIER, Mr William John Church	Brigade Chief Superintendent
EDWARDS, Mr W. R. ACA	Accountant of the Order
ELLISTON, Lieutenant Colonel George Sampson MRCS VD	Deputy Commissioner No III District
HOLBECKE, Lieutenant Colonel Richard	Supervised despatch of Ambulance and Medical Comforts for Troops
KNUTSFORD, The Viscount GCMG	Director and Chairman Ambulance Department
KNUTSFORD, The Viscountess	
MILBURN, Major Charles Henry MB	Deputy Commissioner No VI District
MORGAN, Mr William Henry	Chief Superintendent Metropolitan Corps
NINNIS, Inspector General Belgrave	Deputy Commissioner No I District
PERROTT, Colonel Herbert Charles Bt.	Secretary of the Order and Chief Secretary Ambulance Department
TRIMBLE, Lieutenant Colonel Charles Joseph LRCP VD	Deputy Commissioner No IV District
VERNON, Mr William MRCS	Deputy Commissioner No II District
WARDELL, Mr Stewart Crawford	Deputy Commissioner No V District

Appendix V

King's South Africa medals awarded to St John Ambulance Brigade Personnel

Name	SJAB No	Ambulance Division or Corps	Unit Served
AFFLECK, F.H.	1327	Metropolitan Corps	SJAB
AUSTIN, E.	1398	SJAB	SAC
BALSHAW, E.	1367	Preston Corps	SJAB
BANKS, Bertram Bede	335	Kendal Division	SAC
BURNMAN, G.W.	949	Metropolitan Corps	SAC
BUTTON, L.	319	SJAB (NFB Haywards Heath)	IYH
COLEMAN, G.B.	192	Metropolitan Corps	SJAB Attached RAMC
CROXFORD, Louis J.	713	Metropolitan Corps	Johannesburg Mounted Rifles Natal Volunteer Composite Regiment
DAVIS, J.C.	465	Metropolitan Corps	IYH
EASTHAM, W.H.	1372	Preston Corps	SJAB
GADSBY, W.H.	865	Wellingborough Corps	SAC
GARDNER, Fred W.	1102	Birmingham Corps	SAC
GAUNT, J.F.	Local		SJAB Local
GREEN, Frederick William	1101	Leicester Corps	SAC
GREENFIELD, A.H.	1138	Barnoldswick Division	RAMC
GREENWOOD, Herbert H.	188	Dewsbury Corps	SAC
GRINDROD, John	174	Tottington Division	SAC
HAGGAR, W.T.	436	Metropolitan Corps	RAMC
HARPER, William James	88	North Staffs Corps	SAC Portland Hospital
HAYTHORNTHWAITE, George	440	Barrowford Division	1st Scottish Horse
HILL, Edward	157	Derby Corps	SAC
HOWCROFT, Thomas R.	1064	Bolton Corps	SAC
HULSE, W.J.	1014	Sheffield Corps	RAMC
HUMPHREYS, W.H.	759	Oldham Corps	SJAB
JOHNSON, William	543	Warrington Corps	SAC
JOLLY, J.	524	Blackpool Division	RAMC
JONAS, Malcolm Emmanuel	113	Metropolitan Corps	SAC
KENWARD, A.J.	50	Metropolitan Corps	SAC
LEACH, Francis	265	Isle of Wight Corps	SAC
MABERLEY, B.E.	1111	Handsworth & Smethwick Corps	SAC
MANTON, G.	559	Birmingham Corps	SAC

MELLOR, W.	917	Oldham Corps	Imperial Hospital Corps
MIDDLETON, F.	54	Weston-Super-Mare Division	RAMC
MYERS, J.	36	Preston Corps	SJAB
OLDFIELD, John William	1192	Oldham Corps	SAC
PAGET, Charles H.	647	Bradford Corps	SAC
POTTINGER, James Andrew	103	Welbeck Division	IYH Portland Hospital
QUINCEY, H.R.	240	Wellingborough Corps	Kitchener's Fighting Scouts Provisional Transvaal Constabulary Imperial Yeomanry
REDHEAD, Edward Dawson	1441	Kendal Division	SAC
SANTEN, B.	329	Metropolitan Corps	IYH
TURNER, J.H.	504	Kendal Division	SJAB
WARDLEY, T.C.	155	Worksop Division	Cape Medical Staff Corps
WHITE, A.	860	Kettering Corps	SJAB
WRATHALL, L.	1230	Burnley Division	SJAB
WRIGHT, A.G.	1789	Derby Corps	SAC

Appendix VI

St John Ambulance Brigade personnel who also served in the South African Constabulary

The roll of St John Ambulance Brigade personnel who also served with the South African Constabulary.

An * by the name indicates that the man was eligible for the King's South Africa Medal.

Name	KSA	SJAB Number	SAC Number	SAC Rank
AUSTIN, E.	*	1398	A517	Trooper
BANKS, Bertram Bede[1]	*	335	E2927	Trooper
BARTON, George E[2]		673	B217	Medical Corporal
BURNMAN, G.W.	*	949	A517	Trooper
COWIN, L.B.		2	E2927	Trooper
DEWHURST, Edmund[2]		403	B217	Medical Corporal
DRAIN, H.F.		1920	E3036	Medical Corporal
FLETCHER, C.		1810	E3034	Sergeant
GADSBY, W.H.	*	865	B1093 RD589	Medical Corporal
GARDNER, Fred W.[2]	*	1102	C2116	Medical Corporal
GREEN, Frederick William[1]	*	1101	E3604	Sergeant
GREENWOOD, Ernest[3]		702	C2114	Corporal
GREENWOOD, Herbert H.[3]	*	188	B1700	Trooper
GRINDROD, John[2]	*	174	A1866	Medical Corporal
GROGAN, James[2]		463	E3035	Medical Corporal
GUFFOG, George[2]		681	RD584	Trooper
HALLAS, Benton[1]		1467	A1869	Sergeant
HANCOCK, John E.		446	E646	Sergeant
HARPER, William James[3]	*	88	B1459 HQ33 RD585	Medical Corporal
HAWKE, Thomas S.[2]		981	A1870	Trooper
HILL, Edward	*	157	C2110	Sergeant
HOLLINRAKE, Walter[1]		1520	C2118	Corporal
HOLLINS, Harry[1]		1471	E3040	Hospital Corporal
HOWCROFT, Thomas R.[2]	*	1064	E2928	Trooper
HUTCHINGS, A.		847	E3474	Medical Corporal
JACKSON, George[1]		1455	A1878	Trooper
JOHNSON, William[3]	*	543	E3042	Medical Corporal
JONAS, Malcolm Emmanuel	*	113	A2279	Trooper
KENWARD, A.J.	*	50	A1875	Medical Corporal

KILVINGON, Henry[3]		222	C2117	1st Class Sergeant
KNIGHT, F.B.		468	B1460	Medical Corporal
LEACH, Francis[2]	*	265	A1986 RD196	Trooper
LONG, Charles E.[2]		862	C2119	Medical Corporal
MABERLEY, B.E.[2]	*	1111	A1874	Medical Corporal
MANTON, G.	*	559	B1568 HQ32 RD583	Medical Corporal
McCRACKEN, James A.[2]		477	B1645 HQ36 RD587	Trooper
MEADON, George Fox[1]		525	E2929	Medical Corporal
NEWELL, S.		1942	A1868	Medical Corporal
OLDFIELD, John William[1]	*	1192	E3603	Medical Corporal
PAGET, Charles H.[3]	*	647	E2038	Corporal
PITCHFORD, John H.[3]		1069	E3041	Corporal
REDHEAD, Edward Dawson[1]	*	1441	A1876	Medical Corporal
ROBINSON, John[2]		1132	A1867	Medical Corporal
ROBSON, William[3]		189	C2112	1st Class Sergeant
ROSS, Charles G.[2]		55	A1873	Medical Corporal
ROSTRON, George W.[2]		923	HQ204 RD588	Trooper
ROY, J.E.		1324	C2120	Medical Corporal
SHAW, Charles Frederick[2]		1057	B1644 HQ34 RD590	Medical Corporal
SHAW, George[3]		651	C2115	Trooper
SHAW, H.		870	A1865	QM Sergeant
SMITH, F.		1461	E2930	Medical Corporal
SPOTSWOOD, J.G.		1558	A1872	Corporal
STEVENSON, John W.[2]		373	E3037	Trooper
SWINDALL, Harold B.A.[2]		1513	A1877	Trooper
UZZELL, William John[1]		295	C2111	Corporal
WHITTINGTON, Ambrose F.[2]		1555	E4185	Trooper
WOOD, Mark[3]		365	E2931	Corporal
WRIGHT, A.G.	*	1789	A1944	Medical Sergeant

[1] Present at 1 St John's Square Clerkenwell on 31 March 1901 census.
[2] Present at 49 St John's Square Clerkenwell on 31 March 1901 census.
[3] Present at 30 St John's Lane Clerkenwell on 31 March 1901 census.

Two other men possibly served with the South African Constabulary, 1001 Private F. ARSCOTT and 1181 Private H. BROOKS.

Appendix VII

National Fire Brigade Union Ambulance Division Medal Roll

Name	Fire Brigade	Rank	Contingent	QSA Medal roll reference	Clasps
ALEXANDER, Samuel A.	NFB Ilford SJAB 313	Sergeant	1st	WO100/130/217+252 IYH Deelfontein Died	CC SA01
AVERY, George H.	NFB Cockington	Private	2nd	WO100/130/217 IYH Deelfontein	CC
BARKER, J.R.	NFB Brierfield	Corporal	2nd	WO100/130/217 IYH Deelfontein Johannesburg Mounted Rifles 1496 34922	CC
BARTLEY, W.S.	NFB Worthing	Orderly	3rd/4th	WO100/130/230+251 IYH Pretoria	CC OFS TVL SA01
BOOKER, Leonard A.G.	NFB Bognor SJAB 308	Private	1st	WO100/130/218 IYH Deelfontein	CC
BROWN, Wilfred H.	NFB Sandown SJAB 327	Private	1st	WO100/130/218 IYH Deelfontein	CC
BUTTON, L.	NFB Haywards Heath SJAB 319	Acting Sergeant-Major	1st	WO100/130/217+WO100/356/173 IYH Deelfontein Remained in South Africa	CC KSA01 KSA02
COOKE, H.H.	NFB Bedford SJAB 337	Sergeant	1st	WO100/130/218 IYH Deelfontein	CC
CROOK, William	NFB Darwen	Private	2nd	WO100/130/218 IYH Deelfontein	CC
DOWN, J.F.	NFB Exeter SJAB 316	Private	1st	WO100/130/219 IYH Deelfontein	CC SA01
DOWNING, T.W.	NFB Conisbrough	Corporal	3rd/4th	WO100/130/231+248 IYH Pretoria	CC OFS TVL SA01
DUXBURY, W.T.	NFB Darwen SJAB 312	Private	1st	WO100/130/219 IYH Deelfontein	CC
EDGES, George	NFB Stamford	Private	3rd/4th	WO100/130/256 Imperial Yeomanry Field Hospital Died 1902	CC OFS TVL
EDWARDS, Charlie	NFB Haywards Heath SJAB 317	Private	1st	WO100/130/219 IYH Deelfontein	CC
FERGUSON, Alfred	NFB Haywards Heath SJAB 309	Private	1st	WO100/130/219 IYH Deelfontein	CC

GRAVETT, G.J.	NFB Worthing	Orderly	3rd/ 4th	WO100/130/232+251 IYH Pretoria	CC OFS TVL SA01
GREENFIELD, H.J.	NFB Newhaven		1st		
HANBURY, A. Ernest	NFB Woodstock SJAB 321	Sergeant	2nd	WO100/130/217 IYH Deelfontein	CC
HERN, Harold E.	NFB Exeter SJAB 326	Lance Corporal	1st	WO100/130/219 IYH Deelfontein	CC
HORNBROOK, J.	NFB Cockington SJAB 456	Sergeant	1st	WO100/130/219 IYH Deelfontein	CC SA01
JENKINS, B.W.	NFB Marazion	Private	2nd	WO100/130/220 IYH Deelfontein	CC
LYONS, T.	NFB Croxley Mills Dickinson's Fire Brigade SJAB 322	Lance Corporal	1st	WO100/130/220 IYH Deelfontein	CC
MEAKINS, C.D.	NFB Stony Stratford SJAB 325	Private	1st	WO100/130/221 IYH Deelfontein	CC
MELLUISH, William	NFB Exeter	Sergeant	2nd	WO100/130/220 IYH Deelfontein	CC SA01
NEWMAN, Frank B.	NFB Bedford SJAB 338	Lance Corporal	1st	WO100/130/221 IYH Deelfontein	CC
NEWPORT, Herbert H.	NFB Frome SJAB 311	Private	1st	WO100/130/221 IYH Deelfontein	CC SA01
NORFOLK, J.	No II District Staff SJAB 315	Supernumerary Officer	1st	WO100/225/166 15 General Hospital. To England 26 August 1900	NAT
PAINE, G.	NFB Newhaven SJAB 323	Private	1st	WO100/130/222 IYH Deelfontein	CC
PETT, Monty W.	NFB Exeter SJAB 314	Private	1st	WO100/130/222 IYH Deelfontein	CC
RAYMOND, George	NFB Cockington	Private	2nd	WO100/130/222 IYH Deelfontein	CC
SAUNDERS, George S.	NFB Cockington	Private	2nd	WO100/130/223 IYH Deelfontein Died	CC
SAWFORD, James S.	NFB Aylesbury SJAB 320	Private	1st	WO100/130/223 IYH Deelfontein	CC
SEMMENS George	NFB Marazion	Private	2nd	WO100/130/223 IYH Deelfontein	CC
SLATER, A.W.	NFB Barnes/Mortlake	Sergeant	1st	WO100/130/222 IYH Deelfontein	CC
SMITH, F.W.	NFB Barnes/Mortlake	Sergeant	1st	WO100/130/222 IYH Deelfontein	CC

SMITH, H.J.	NFB Marlow SJAB 305	Corporal	1st	WO100/130/223 IYH Deelfontein	CC
SONNENFIELD, M.M.	NFB SJAB 310	Corporal	1st	WO100/130/222 IYH Deelfontein	CC
SPILSBURY, E.	NFB Malvern/Malvern Wells	Orderly	3rd/ 4th	WO100/130/235+251 IYH Pretoria	CC OFS TVL SA01
STEVENS, Thomas	NFB Cockington SJAB 304	Private	1st	WO100/130/223 IYH Deelfontein	CC SA01
STONE, Thomas H.	NFB Darwen	Private	2nd	WO100/130/222 IYH Deelfontein	CC SA01
STONE, Walter	NFB Brierfield	Orderly	2nd		
TRIMMER, A.J.	NFB Bedford SJAB 302	Acting Sergeant-Major	1st	WO100/130/223 IYH Deelfontein	CC
VOSPER, Charles	NFB Exeter	Sergeant	2nd	WO100/130/224 IYH Deelfontein	CC SA01
WARN, A.E.	NFB Croxley Mills Dickinson's Fire Brigade SJAB 307	Private	1st	WO100/130/224 IYH Deelfontein	CC
WEBBER, R.	NFB Exeter SJAB 324	Private	1st	WO100/130/224 IYH Deelfontein	CC SA01
WHITE, William A.	NFB Battle	Orderly	3rd/ 4th	WO100/130/235+251 IYH Pretoria	CC OFS TVL SA01
WILLARD, Herbert	NFB New Malden	Private	2nd	WO100/130/224 IYH Deelfontein	CC
WILLMORE, Charles	NFB Hythe SJAB 303	Sergeant	1st	WO100/130/224 IYH Deelfontein Died	CC

Appendix VIII

Medal Groups

Queen's South Africa Medal and St John Ambulance Brigade Bronze Medal Imperial Yeomanry Bearer Company

Queen's South Africa 1899-1902, 3 clasps, Cape Colony, Orange Free State, Transvaal Cpl. R.R. Scotson, Imp: Yeo: Bearer Coy.

St John Medal for South Africa 1899-1902 668. Pte. R. SCOTSON. Manchester P.O. Div.

Robert R. SCOTSON was born on 7 July 1872 at Hulme in Lancashire. After leaving school, at the age of 18, he was appointed in September 1890 as a sorting clerk 307747 in the Manchester post office. Prior to his service in South Africa, he was residing at 38 Deramore Street, Moss Side, Manchester and was a member of the Manchester Post Office Ambulance Division of the St John Ambulance Brigade. Allocated number 668, he was part of the large draft of men who were sent to work with the Imperial Yeomanry but one of only 12 men who became part of the Imperial Yeomanry Bearer Company. On his return to England, he resumed his job in the post office working as a sorting Clerk and Telegraphist. He moved to live at 74 Middleton St, Moss Side. He finally retired from the post office on 7 July 1932 by which time he had accumulated 42 years and 8 months service. He died 4 years later on 24 November 1936 in the General Hospital at Altringham. At the time of his death, he was resident at Ankersholme, Moss Lane, Timperley, Cheshire.

Queen's South Africa Medal, St John Ambulance Brigade Bronze Medal and 1897 Jubilee Medal Trio.

Queen's South Africa 1899-1902, 2 clasps, Natal, Transvaal 430 Ordly: E. A. Hawkins. St. John Amb: Bde

St. John Medal for South Africa 1899-1902 430 Pte. E.A. Hawkins. Met: Corps.;

Jubilee Medal 1897, bronze Private E. A. Hawkins.

Ernest A. HAWKINS served at No 7 General Hospital initially at Estcourt in Natal and subsequently based in Pretoria when the hospital moved there in November 1900. His contract time expired but he had become ill and died in Pretoria on 8 January 1901. He was buried at Church Street West cemetery in Pretoria on 10 January 1901. The records of his death and burial list him as A.E. HAWKINS.

He is commemorated on the Metropolitan Corps, St John Ambulance Brigade memorial in St Pauls Cathedral where his name is inscribed Private A.E. HAWKINS.

Queen's South Africa Medal, St John Ambulance Brigade Bronze Medal and 1911 Coronation Medal Trio.

Queen's South Africa 1899-1902 Natal 539 Ordly: T. Parker, St. John Amb: Bde
St. John Medal for South Africa 1899-1902 539. Pte. T. Parker. Walton-le-Dale Div.
Coronation 1911, St. John Ambulance Brigade Sgt. T. Parker.

Thomas PARKER was a private in the Walton-le-Dale Ambulance Division of the St John Ambulance Brigade at the start of the South African War. He was given recruitment number 539 and served as an Orderly but the details of the precise location where he served is not included in the Queen's South Africa Medal Roll His service qualified him for the Natal Clasp which is confirmed in WO100/225/33.

After his return to England, he clearly remained an active member of the St John Ambulance Brigade and as a Sergeant was involved during the celebrations of King George V's coronation in 1911 for which he received the silver 1911 Coronation Medal with St John Ambulance Brigade reverse.

The following year his Service Medal of the Order of St John was issued on 21 May with the medal being presented to him by Viscount Knutsford the Sub Prior at St Johns Gate on 19 July. Unfortunately, this medal has become separated from his other awards.

St John Ambulance Brigade Bronze Medal and double issue of the Queen's South Africa Medal

Queen's South Africa 1899-1902, 4 clasps, CC OFS TVL SA01 25839 Tpr. H.E. Inder. Scottish Horse

Queen's South Africa 1899-1902 OFS NAT TVL 1442 Ordly. H.E. Inder St. John Amb: Bde
St. John Medal for South Africa 1899-1902 1442 Pte. H.E. Inder. Kendal Div.

Henry Ewart INDER was born at Cardington, Bedfordshire on 17 March 1881. He volunteered as a member of the Kendal Ambulance Division of the St John Ambulance Brigade to serve in South Africa being allocated the number 1442. He served during his first tour of duty as an Orderly at No 2 General Hospital Wynberg, No 14 Stationary Hospital Pietermaritzburg and No 17 Stationary Hospital Middleburg. He was sent back to the Base Hospital for discharge on 24 November 1900. He subsequently enlisted with the 1st Scottish Horse as Trooper 25839. He was finally discharged in Johannesburg on 13 August 1901.

He settled in South Africa and in 1921 he was head surveyor with the Langlaagte Gold Mining Company in the Transvaal. He died in South Africa in 1965.

His brother William Sidney INDER also served with the St John Ambulance Brigade at No 2 General Hospital and No 13 General Hospital. He was the author of *On Active Service with the S.J.A.B. South African War, 1899-1902* which was published posthumously following his death from pneumonia at Bloemfontein on 7 January 1902. The book gives an extremely comprehensive account of his experience serving with the St John Ambulance Brigade during the South African War.

Queen's South Africa Medal and St John Ambulance Brigade Bronze Medal Royal Army Medical Corps

Queen's South Africa 1899-1902, 4 clasps, Cape Colony, Orange Free State, Transvaal, South Africa 1902 16546 Pte. J. Roberts. R.A.M.C.

St. John Medal for South Africa 1899-1902 16546. Pte. R. Roberts Kettering Corps.

John Pascoe ROBERTS was born at Sithney, Elston, Cornwall on 19 June 1879. On leaving school he was employed as a gardener which was his occupation when he was recruited to the Royal Army Medical Corps. A member of the Kettering Corps, he attested on 25 November 1901 as Private 16456. He served in South Africa from 30 December 1901 to 29 August 1902 and was finally discharged being declared medically unfit for further service on 5 January 1903. He returned to work as a gardener and in 1911 was living at Wix Hill, West Horsley, Leatherhead with his wife Alice Amelia and their 3-year-old son John. He saw service during WW1 enlisting on 24 June 1916 with the Army Service Corps and was with 274 MT Coy at Plumstead. He remained in England throughout the War and was therefore not awarded any WW1 campaign medals. He was demobilised on 4 July 1919 and once again returned to his work as a gardener at Ersham Lodge, Hailsham East Sussex. By 1939 he had moved to Gardeners Lodge 75 Meadowside Twickenham. He died on 7 March 1941.

Queen's South Africa Medal and St John Ambulance Brigade Bronze Medal and World War One Medal Pair

Queen's South Africa 1899-1902, 2 clasps, Cape Colony, Orange Free State 407 Ordly: G. Parkinson. St John Amb: Bde
St John Medal for South Africa 1899-1902 407. Pte. G. Parkinson. Accrington Corps. British War and Victory Medals 32533 Pte. G. Parkinson. R. Lanc. R.
Silver War Badge B46689

Grimshaw PARKINSON was born on 21 January 1881. He grew up in Accrington at 4 Cedar Street and on leaving school was employed as a cotton weaver. He was a member of Accrington Corps and was recruited to serve in South Africa with number 407. He served as an Orderly at No 8 General Hospital but was transferred sick to Cape Town on 31 July 1900 during the typhoid epidemic at the hospital. On his return to England, he resumed work as a cotton weaver.

During the summer of 1902 he married Rose and their son George was born in 1907. In 1911 they were living at 21 Peter Street but moved to 190 Burnley Road prior to World War One. He attested for the Royal Lancaster Regiment on 10 December 1915 and served two periods in France from 17 December 1916 to 22 October 1917 and 13 June 1918 to 30 August 1918 before being discharged on 23 November 1918. During his service he sustained a gunshot wound to the chest being awarded a Silver War Badge number B46689. He subsequently volunteered for further service in Ireland from 3 April 1919 before finally being demobilised on 3 November 1919.

He returned to his work as a cotton weaver living at 21 Cross Edge Oswaldtwistle. By 1939 he had moved again to 29 Devonshire Street Accrington. He died on 18 March 1963 at which time he had been resident at 19 Scott Street Clayton-le-Moors.

Queen's South Africa Medal, King's South Africa Medal and St John Ambulance Brigade Bronze Medal Trio.

Queen's South Africa 1899-1902 Cape Colony Orange Free State Transvaal 543 Ordly W. Johnson. St. John Amb: Bde

King's South Africa 1901-02 South Africa 1901 South Africa 1902 1460 Cpl. W. Johnson. S.A.C.

St John Medal for South Africa 1899-1902 542 Pte. W. Johnson. Warrington Corps.

William JOHNSON was a private in the Warrington Corps of the St John Ambulance Brigade when he volunteered for service in South Africa. He was given the recruitment number 543 and was sent as an Orderly to 24 Field Hospital attached to the Royal Army Medical Corps on 16 March 1900. He served until his contract expired on 6 January 1901.

He was subsequently recruited into the South African Constabulary on 4 May 1901. He served as a Medical Corporal number B1460 with B Division in the Transvaal until the end of the war.

He was one of only 21 St John Ambulance Brigade men who received the King's South Africa Medal as a result of his combined service with both the South African Constabulary and the St John Ambulance Brigade.

St John Ambulance Brigade and South African Constabulary Group

India General Service 1854-95 Sikkim 1888 528 Pte. E. Hill. 2nd. Bn. Derby. R.

Queen's South Africa 1899-1902 Cape Colony Orange Free State Transvaal 1790 S. Officer E. Hill. St. John Amb: Bde

King's South Africa 1901-02 South Africa 1901, South Africa 1902 3474 Corpl: E. Hill. S.A.C

St. John Medal for South Africa 1899-1902 157. Sergt. E. Hill. Derby Corps

1914-15 Star 206 Sjt. E. Hill. Notts: & Derby: R.

British War and Victory Medals 206 Sjt. E. Hill. Notts. & Derby. R.

Territorial Force Efficiency Medal GVR. 331437 Sjt: E. Hill. 5/ Notts: & Derby R.

Edward HILL was born at Friskney, Boston, Lincolnshire in 1868. After leaving school he served in the army in India qualifying for the India General Service medal with Sikkim 1888 clasp. Subsequently on his return to England he worked as a labourer. He married Annie Brindley on 7 September 1893 in Derbyshire.

He became a member of the Derby Corps of the St John Ambulance Brigade and was an early volunteer for service in South Africa as a Sergeant with the recruitment number 157. In South Africa he served as a Supply Officer with No 8 General Hospital at Bloemfontein and No 8 Stationary Hospital at Port Elizabeth. He served for two periods, initially from 19 January to 6 December 1900 and then 26 February to 8 August 1901. Subsequently he was recruited as Medical Corporal E3473 in E Division of the South African Constabulary serving during the latter part of the war from 9 August 1901 to 31 May 1902. He was finally discharged time expired on 13 August 1902.

On his return home he returned to his work as a labourer and subsequently joined the Midland Railway at the Derby locomotive department. In April 1908 he attested in the Notts and Derby Regiment as a Territorial member at the age of 40 by which time he was living at 120 Almond Street, Derby. In 1915 he was mobilised at the age of 46 and proceeded to France on 1 March but soon returned to home service on 24 April 1915. He was finally demobilised on 29 June 1917 and returned to his work in the locomotive department as a fire watchman at Derby locomotive depot. It is uncertain when he died.

Group to Chief Surgeon

The Order of St John of Jerusalem, Knight of Grace.
The Order of St John of Jerusalem, Honorary Associate's breast badge.
St John Medal for South Africa 1899-1902 Chief Surg. J.B. Wilkinson. Oldham Corps.
Jubilee Medal 1935.
Service Medal Order of St John Chief Surgeon J.B. Wilkinson, 10. July. 1908.

James Bates WILKINSON was born at Godmanchester, Huntingdonshire, on 4 July 1857. He graduated MB CM from the University of Edinburgh in 1883 and MD in 1885. He practised in London, Peterborough and Manchester before moving to Oldham in 1887. As Chief Surgeon in the Oldham Corps he was involved in preparing ambulance men for their South African War service and for this role he was awarded the Bronze St. John Ambulance Brigade Medal for South Africa along with 39 others who performed similar duties. During the South African War, Oldham Corps contributed 128 men to serve in South Africa, second only to the Metropolitan Corps. He served as School Medical Officer for Oldham from 1906 until his retirement in 1936. He was made an Honorary Associate of the Order of St. John on 25 April 1899. His St John Service Medal was issued on 30 July 1907 being presented by HRH Prince of Wales on 10 July 1908 at Marlborough House. He was advanced to Knight of Grace on 21 October 1921. He died on 22 February 1941.

Sources & Bibliography

St John Archive

First Aid Journal 1899-1903
Register of issue of Special South African Bronze Medals 1899-1902

National Archive
Queen's South Africa Medal Roll Imperial Yeomanry WO100/130
Queen's South Africa Medal Roll Royal Army Medical Corps WO100/219-224
Queen's South Africa Medal Roll St John Ambulance Brigade WO100/225
Queen's South Africa Medal Roll South African Constabulary WO100/271-3
King's South Africa Medal Roll Royal Army Medical Corps WO100/352
King's South Africa Medal Roll Imperial Yeomanry WO100/356
King's South Africa Medal Roll South African Constabulary WO100/366

Published sources
Peter Beighton NFB Union Ambulance Division in the Anglo-Boer War; A Medallic Review. *The Journal of the Orders and Medals Research Society* 2003: 256-262.
Peter Beighton St John Bronze Medal for South Africa. *The Journal of the Orders and Medals Research Society* 2003: 176-181.
R. E. Cole-Mackintosh St John Ambulance Brigade: Boer war Casualties. *The Journal of the Orders and Medals Research Society* 1978: 248-255.
Stephen Durant Men in Khaki and Firemen in Glittering Helmets (*Medal News* 2002; 6:74-75).
W. S. Inder *On Active Service with the S.J.A.B. South African War, 1899-1902* (Atkinson and Pollitt, Kendal 1903).
Medal Year Book 2024. (Token Publishing).
Alexander M. Palmer *The Boer War Casualty Roll 1899-1902* (Military Minded 1999).
Rick Thornton and Peter Beighton *The Royal Naval Reserve Long Service and Good Conduct Medal as awarded to The Royal Naval Auxiliary Sick Berth Reserve.* (Private Publication).
Charles W. Tozer *The Insignia and Medals of The Order of St John.* (J.B. Hayward & Son, 1975).
J. C. (Kay) De Villiers *Healers Helpers and Hospitals* (Protea Book House, Pretoria, 2008).

Electronic Sources
Ancestry https://www.ancestry.co.uk
Anglo Boer War https://www.angloboerwar.com
British Medal Forum https://britishmedalforum.com
First Aid Journal https://issuu.com/museumoftheorderofstjohn/docs/first_aid_journal
Order of St John Annual Reports https://issuu.com/museumoftheorderofstjohn/docs
Welcome Collection Archive https://wellcomecollection.org/collections/what-s-in-the-collections

www.ingramcontent.com/pod-product-compliance
Lightning Source LLC
Chambersburg PA
CBHW040122120426
42814CB00009B/341